Communities
in early modern England

Blackburn
College

Library
01254 292120

Politics, culture and society in early modern Britain

General editors
PROFESSOR ANN HUGHES
DR ANTHONY MILTON
PROFESSOR PETER LAKE

This important series publishes monographs that take a fresh and challenging look at the interactions between politics, culture and society in Britain between 1500 and the mid-eighteenth century. It counteracts the fragmentation of current historiography through encouraging a variety of approaches which attempt to redefine the political, social and cultural worlds, and to explore their interconnection in a flexible and creative fashion. All the volumes in the series question and transcend traditional inter-disciplinary boundaries, such as those between political history and literary studies, social history and divinity, urban history and anthropology. They contribute to a broader understanding of crucial developments in early modern Britain.

Communities in early modern England

Networks, place, rhetoric

edited by Alexandra Shepard
and Phil Withington

Manchester
University Press
Manchester and New York

While copyright in the volume as a whole is vested in Manchester
University Press, copyright in individual chapters belongs to their
respective authors, and no chapter may be reproduced in whole or in part
without the express permission in writing of both author and publisher.

Published by Manchester University Press
Oxford Road, Manchester M13 9NR, UK
and Room 400, 175 Fifth Avenue, New York, NY 10010, USA
www.manchesteruniversitypress.co.uk

Distributed exclusively in the USA by
Palgrave, 175 Fifth Avenue, New York NY 10010, USA

Distributed exclusively in Canada by
UBC Press, University of British Columbia, 2029 West Mall,
Vancouver, BC, Canada V6T 1Z2

British Library Cataloguing-in-Publication Data
A catalogue record for this book is available from the British Library

Library of Congress Cataloging-in-Publication Data
A catalog record for this book is available from the Library of Congress

ISBN-10: 0 7190 5477 X

ISBN-13: 978 0 7190 5477 8

First edition published 2000 by Manchester University Press

First digital, on-demand edition produced by Lightning Source 2007

To the memory of
Nan Withington

Contents

Contents

List of tables and illustrations

TABLE

ILLUSTRATIONS

List of contributors

IAN W. ARCHER is Fellow, Tutor and Lecturer in Modern History at Keble College, Oxford

GEOFF BALDWIN is the Lloyd Fellow at Christ's College, Cambridge

NATASHA GLAISYER is a Research Fellow at Peterhouse, Cambridge

PAUL GRIFFITHS is a Lecturer in Social and Economic History at the University of Leicester

STEVE HINDLE is a Warwick Research Fellow in the Department of History at the University of Warwick

CRAIG MULDREW is a University Lecturer and a Fellow at Queens' College, Cambridge

MARGARET PELLING is a Reader in the Social History of Medicine in the Faculty of Modern History at the University of Oxford

JASON SCOTT-WARREN is a Lecturer in English Renaissance Literature at the University of York

MARGARET SENA is a graduate student in the Department of History at Princeton University

ALEXANDRA SHEPARD is a Lecturer in History at the University of Sussex

CATHY SHRANK is a Lecturer in English at the University of Aberdeen

PHIL WITHINGTON is a Lecturer in Cultural History at the University of Aberdeen

Preface

This book began as a conversation in the Maypole in Cambridge. Its completion brings us full circle, some four years later, again in Cambridge, this time over a slightly better bottle of red wine. Without the goodwill, insight and healthy scepticism of friends and colleagues the volume would not have progressed far beyond the pub door. It has been especially rewarding to work with a group of contributors from whom we have learned so much. We hope the result suggests the importance of networks of mutual exchange within a profession increasingly threatened by a culture of competitive individualism.

We are also indebted to many others for abetting yet another book about community. A conference on this volume's theme was held at St John's College, Oxford, in November 1998, and we are grateful to the President and Fellows for allowing us to hold it there. We are also thankful to Ian Archer, Warren Boutcher and Paul Slack for chairing sessions, and to the many participants for their interest and comments - in particular Mark Jenner for his stimulating refutation of the whole project. We would not be writing this preface had Jason Reese not lent his laptop computer at the eleventh hour; nor would we be writing it in such convivial circumstances had Cathy Shrank not provided dinner. They both know this is the thin end of the wedge.

A.S.
P.J.W.

List of abbreviations

BL   British Library

DNB   *Dictionary of National Biography*

HMSO   His/Her Majesty's Stationery Office

PRO   Public Record Office

Chapter 1

Introduction: communities in early modern England

Phil Withington and Alexandra Shepard

Community – 'that difficult word', according to Raymond Williams – has suffered more than most from a problem intrinsic to historical analysis: namely the tensions between its past and current meanings.[1] Many words of conceptual importance – be they 'class', 'society', 'culture' or 'private' – have contemporary significations which bear little relation to their respective inferences in the past. These significations, rooted in contemporary theory and debate, are both important and contentious, forming the prisms through which the past is refracted and understood. However, previous meanings of words were often as diverse, contested and contingent on the complex dynamics of particular circumstance. Disputed concepts, such as 'puritan', 'party', 'custom' and 'comedy', not only frame current discussions about early modern religious, parliamentary and literary history, but at the time were unstable, conflictual and appropriable designations. Over time, the inferences, significance and usage of words change, not so much in an evolutionary fashion as in ways continually related to the contexts in which, about which, and by whom the terms are used. For example, while the word 'manners' has lost much of the moral purchase it possessed in the early modern period, the word 'nation' has developed from denoting local gatherings at medieval church councils and universities into an organising concept of political legitimacy and identity. Whereas the term 'politics' traditionally denoted sets of institutions, practices and ideas related to the running of the 'polis', in later twentieth-century culture – and so in recent social and gender historiography – it has become a synonym of 'power'. In each instance, the conceptual transformation of the word at once forms and provides insight into the dynamics of broader socio-economic and cultural change. In this way, words themselves constitute nothing less than archaeological sites: layered pits full of the debris and traces of past battles, social configurations, and dominant and subordinate meanings.

From the outset, then, it is worth bearing in mind the different ways a word like 'community' can be deployed. In the first instance, it is a contemporary concept of analysis informing both the types of question the interpreter asks and the types of evidence in which answers may be found. Second, it is a word that was actually used and contested by people in the past. Third, it is a term that, over time, has both gained and lost meanings between the period under study and the period of study. In each of these phases of usage there will be alternative definitions and contradictory connotations. Although it is ostensibly the same word, the dominant meaning of a term in one epoch may be different from the dominant meaning in another. This is especially true of the word 'community'. As Conal Condren has observed,

> the laudatory connotations of community and the diversity of its use are good indications that the word community was for most people [in the seventeenth century] one to be co-opted. Monarchs were justified in their existence for defending community; Levellers, clubmen and Cavalier poets all evoked the word community, associating it with patriotism and even civilisation itself'.[2]

The word remains an emotive and explicitly ideological term in contemporary political discourse, as well as a term with particular connotations in contemporary historiography. The main aim of this introduction is to place these connotations in context by outlining previous and alternative meanings of the word. Along with the chapters that follow, it will, hopefully, remind readers why community was both a significant concept in the past and remains an important mode of analysis in the present. This is not the same as providing a synthetic, new or consummate definition of the term. On the contrary, as the following chapters demonstrate, it is precisely through its polyvalence, appropriability and capacity for synonymy – rather than any particular set of associated values and assumptions – that the word 'community' derives its significance. Consequently, the relatively recent attempts to remove the term from the vocabulary of the early modern historian, as a result of its perceived ideological baggage, are misplaced.[3] Concepts of community should be discussed and fought over, not ignored; the archaeological site dug deeper, and more forensically, rather than simply filled in.

Raymond Williams summarises the current status of the term 'community' as 'the warmly persuasive word to describe an existing set of relationships, or the warmly persuasive word to describe an alternative set of relationships'. He notes that, 'unlike all other terms of social organization (*state, nation, society*, etc.) it seems never to be used unfavourably, and never to be given any positive or distinguishing term'.[4] Williams's comments illustrate two key aspects of the term: its conceptual vagueness, and its rhetorical warmth. Its vagueness is well known – George A. Hillery famously counted ninety-four contemporary definitions of the term, with no common feature beyond the involvement of people.[5] Its rhetorical warmth, as well as its fuzzy definition, makes it remarkably adaptable. On the one hand, 'community' has been appropriated by historians to denote sets of organic, hierarchical and consensual social relations with implicitly conservative undertones. These may be the gentry-dominated 'county communities' of English seventeenth-century revisionist historiography or the 'religious and political totality' that, according to many English and German urban historians, constituted the pre-Reformation town.[6] At the other end of the spectrum, community's 'implications of comprehensiveness and neighbourliness' have been used to encapsulate a quite contrary, radical tradition of resistance and social conflict.[7] For historians like Peter Blickle, 'the demand for communal autonomy was a precondition for positive resistance by rural classes to attempted domination by feudal-aristocratic classes, forming the basis for a German and Swiss tradition of populist, anti-feudal politics'.[8] Similarly historians like E. P. Thompson and Andy Wood have argued that the rural and industrial communities of early modern England – with their potential for autonomous association, inclusivity and self-regulation – inculcated distinctive and, on occasion, highly politicised 'plebeian cultures' which pre-dated the better documented socio-political movements of the later eighteenth century.[9]

For much of the nineteenth century, and most of the twentieth, community's eminently appropriable warmth has served as the converse and critique of modernity in general, and modern concepts of 'society' in particular. In their idealistic forms, concepts of community tend to represent either a quality of social relations that existed prior to the emergence of a commercial, capitalist and integrated society or ways of living which are an alternative to – or a qualification of – the values and practices predominant in such societies. Just as notions of an ideal corporate community informed Hegelian philosophy, and the peasant commune Marxist historiography, so from the nineteenth century 'the word [was] normally chosen for experiments in an alternative kind of group-living'.[10] Until relatively recently, the most influential deployment of community in early modern English historiography has been along these lines: namely the recurring distinction made between, on the one hand, modes of 'affective community' – characterised by regular, personal interaction and 'a common way of life' – and, on the other hand, forms of 'rational instrumental association', involving limited, often institutionally mediated relationships, predicated on contract and self-interest.[11] These ideal types were characterised most famously by Tönnies as *Gemeinschaft* and *Gesellschaft*, the rough-and-ready translations of which are 'community' and 'society'.[12] The antecedents of these dichotomous 'types' were complex and political, and included Otto von Gierke's phasal history of voluntary German association and H. S. Maine's depiction of 'progressive' historical change.[13] They entered

English historical discourse through a variety of channels, most notably in the work of Max Weber and R. H. Tawney, and have subsequently dominated how the term 'community' is both used and refuted by historians.[14]

As Richard M. Smith has shown, there is a tendency among early modern social historians to regard the period 1450 to 1750 as England's transition from one type of social organisation (*Gemeinschaft*) to the other (*Gesellschaft*). This has involved historians conflating *Gemeinschaft* with late medieval rural and urban settlements and showing how, between 1450 and 1750, these 'communities' at once unravelled and congealed into something more approximate to a stratified, commercialised, rational, and centralised society. Keith Thomas, while aware of the risk of evoking 'a fuzzy nostalgia for some imaginary merry England', nevertheless describes the disfunction between 'the neighbourly conduct required by the ethical code of the old village community and the increasingly individualistic form of behaviour which accompanied the economic changes of the sixteenth and seventeenth centuries'.[15] David Underdown, while noting that '[w]e should not sentimentalize the pre-capitalist village community', argues that in the sixteenth and seventeenth centuries communal ideals and 'important unifying bonds' of 'still functioning communities' were compromised by 'profoundly unsettling social and economic changes'.[16] Most recently, Robert Tittler, while '[t]reading ever so carefully, so as not to invoke an antiquated picture of happy townsmen cavorting around the maypole in some mythical past', has argued for 'an overall shift in the ... political culture of a good many [post-Reformation] urban communities' from 'something close to an ethos of community' to 'something closer to conventional notions of 'oligarchy'.[17]

In each of these scenarios, the rhetorical and idealised normative codes of medieval social relations are contrasted not with the rhetorical and idealised normative codes of early modern social relations, but with their practice and experience. The result, despite the caveats, is a paradigm of transition which ignores the fact that medieval settlements were stratified, conflictual, demographically unstable, and integrated into national institutional structures long before the perceived developments of the early modern period. Community in these instances represents not a substantive way of living so much as a process of change. Its analytical force is *retrospective* and allusive, and emanates from what that tells us about events thereafter. In contrast, historians of the 'county community' have explored the literal and *substantive* existence of *Gemeinschaft*. 'Pre-modern' England has been styled a 'loose confederacy' of autonomous, organic, socially cohesive, and essentially discrete counties governed by insular and incestuous groupings of gentry. The English Revolution was essentially a clash between this *Gemeinschaft*-type 'localism' and the forces of *Gesellschaft*, in particular the demands of a centralising state. The whole paradigm was founded on a particularist and personified conception of community. According to Alan Everitt (the paradigm's most influential exponent), while no

> community of course leads a wholly independent life ... yet each ... has a life of its own. It will be influenced by national and metropolitan developments; but it will respond to them in its own way, drawing on its own traditions, its own absorbing historical experience, whenever it is faced with a new challenge or a new opportunity.[18]

It is worth differentiating between not only these retrospective and substantive evocations of *Gemeinschaft*, but also the approaches that have supplanted them. The assumptions informing the revisionist 'county community' paradigm have been exploded primarily by post-revisionist political historiography. Clive Holmes has pointed to the extended social and intellectual connections of the English provincial gentry (the social group with whom 'the community' is conflated); the reciprocity and interpenetration – rather than mutual exclusion – of county and central government; and so the gentry's participation 'in a national political culture'.[19] Work by Ann Hughes on Warwickshire and Mark Stoyle on Devon has questioned the typicality of the 'communities' – such as Everitt's Kent, John Morrill's Cheshire and Anthony Fletcher's Sussex – upon which the model was initially based. Drawing mainly on the ecological and cultural typographies developed by David Underdown, this work has also emphasised the social, political and ecological diversity within county jurisdictions.[20] In particular, network analysis has confirmed on a systematic basis that people were connected with many different groups both at any one time and over the course of their lives. Indeed, on the basis of social linkaging across time and space – focusing in particular on marital connections, the distribution of surnames, and dissenting networks – Charles Phythian-Adams has argued that local history must 'subordinate "community" to a more appropriate, lesser, place than it once used to occupy conceptually, within newly-acknowledged, wider structures'.[21] Drawing on French local history, he terms these structures 'local societies' and 'cultural provinces'. However, as with Christine Carpenter's critique of the late medieval 'county community', the concept of community Phythian-Adams seeks to 'subordinate' is the *Gemeinschaft*-type paradigm initially developed by Everitt. In fact the data assembled by his students, far from subordinating community, is a timely reminder that historians need to reinvigorate the concept in order to examine the many different types of association and modes of communication in which people participated.

This is suggested by developments in medieval and early modern historians' approaches to the term. *Gemeinschaft* as a tool of early modern retrospection has been exploded by medievalists themselves. As Craig Muldrew observes in chapter 9 below, medievalists now perceive the 'medieval community' not as an actual harmonious and co-operative entity so much as sets of precepts and practices that sought the promotion of co-operation towards certain ends.[22] Community, as a state of interpersonal relations, did not preclude conflict. On the contrary, conflict was intrinsic to such relations, and the precepts and practices of community were invariably crystallised through attempts to resolve or contain it.[23] This echoes the importation of an alternative concept of community, based upon the 'community study', into early modern studies.[24] This regards community 'more simply ... [as] a certain kind of social science practice, namely the concentration on small groups, bounded in one way or another, as units of research'.[25] However, for historians of the 'community study', it is the conflict and power themselves – rather than processes of reconciliation – which are of most interest. For Robert Scribner, the

> study of communities in the late medieval and early modern period is of great importance because it opens up a sense of the dynamic nature of social and political relationships within the urban and peasant worlds. That dynamic, however, can be understood or recovered, not by focusing on a single overarching concept, but rather by paying attention to competing discourses and strategies of power.[26]

According to David Sabean, what is 'common in community is not shared values or common understanding so much as the fact that members of a community are engaged in the same argument ... in which alternative strategies, misunderstandings, conflicting goals and values are thrashed out'.[27] As Ulinka Rublack reminds us, 'the chances of making claims in this argument were not equally distributed': if, as many historians have either claimed or implied, 'what makes community possible is the fact that it involves a series of mediated relationships', then a range of factors influenced their mediation and so the dynamics of community. Mediating forces included 'property – the access to resources, the apportionment of rights and claims, and the acceptance of obligations and duties'. Similarly 'status mattered, and so did gender. There were limits to what could be said. And anyone who challenged the notion of community itself could be forcefully silenced; communal speech and argument were regulated.'[28] In the words of Keith Wrightson, the early modern parish 'was in many ways a community, an association of neighbours, a unit of identity and belonging, a primary group – but one perennially defined and redefined by processes of inclusion and exclusion'.[29]

The 'community study', then, at least at the micro-level of a village or parish, provides insight into how 'larger processes were experienced in particular local societies, how they impinged upon individual lives, and how the varied responses which they occasioned helped to shape their outcomes'.[30] It gives the historian access to the places where people lived and the contexts 'in which national demographic, economic, administrative and ... ideological changes both coincide and interact' in a socially meaningful and (as important) in an observable manner.[31] While the analytical intimacy such studies provide has confirmed the early modern period as one of significant change, it is no longer depicted as the transition from *Gemeinschaft* to *Gesellschaft*. What was particular about the later sixteenth and seventeenth centuries was 'an intensified interaction between the locality and the larger society, which drew together provincial communities into a more closely integrated national society and at the same time introduced a new depth and complexity to their local patterns of social stratification'.[32] Early modern communities were not so much eclipsed by 'society' and 'the state', but were socially, economically and culturally realigned both within and without. As Patrick Collinson puts it, they were 'part and parcel of the developing historical process itself'. Rather than describing the English Reformation in terms of linear progression, Collinson uses the metaphor of an hourglass: the reconstitution of community involved its temporary contraction by which it was redefined rather than expunged.[33] Consequently 'community was not something "pre-modern", unchanging, structural, but was constructed, [and] changed over time'; there occurred not 'a collapse of community, but its articulation in different forms, reflecting the working of social polarisation as society filled out at the bottom'.[34] Similarly, later sixteenth- and seventeenth-century state formation was welcomed and appropriated by different social groupings within communities.[35] Political integration and social stratification 'reinforced local communities and strengthened the hands of local elites and petty office-holders', thereby changing the dynamics of social and cultural relations within them.[36] Communities were present, so to speak, amidst the turmoil of their own refashioning.

In stripping community of its *Gemeinschaft* connotations, micro-historical 'community studies', like post-revisionist critiques of the county community, have highlighted how other processes – such as class conflict and consciousness, state formation, ideological conflict, or the reproduction of patriarchy – were aspects of, rather than antithetical to, community and communal relations. In most studies, these relations remain bound in the first instance by a geographically and jurisdictionally defined sense of 'place'. However, as the geographer John A. Agnew has argued, while community and place are often compatible, they are by no means coterminous.[37] From a historical perspective, community cannot be regarded merely as a function or accident of a person's residence within a parish, borough, or county boundary, and (more appositely) their appearance within the historical records generated by those jurisdictions. The techniques of network analysis provide an alternative and complementary way of assessing social grouping and association: of correlating the skeletal, connective outlines of community across space as well as the imperatives of proximity and residence within place. Most importantly, in the analysis both of networks and place, the conceptual assault on *Gemeinschaft* as an interpretative principle should not preclude consideration of the cultural and symbolic significance of community to particular people in particular places at particular points in time: it is not simply a function of structured relations or skeletal connections. While retaining a sense of these factors, there is also the need to regard community as at once an expression and a source of identity and meaning.[38]

Post-structural analysis, which highlights the symbolic and perceptual aspects of belonging, suggests that the relationship between community and person – in terms of symbolic representation and personal identification – was a complex and multifarious process. For example, Anthony Cohen has defined community as 'a resource and a repository of meaning' which people construct 'symbolically'.[39] Community is both the production of boundaries and social distance against 'the outside world' and 'a masking symbol to which its various adherents impute their own meanings'. As such, the 'symbolism of community ... speaks simultaneously for the collectivity to those on the other side of its boundaries, and to each of its members who refract it through their individual sense of belonging'.[40] This, Cohen argues, is as true for adolescent urban teenagers or Irish fisherman as it is for south London householders, Devonshire farmers' wives, or suburban activists in northern England. A sense of place could in itself be integral to communal identity, or to what Timothy Jenkins terms 'local particularity'. This he defines as 'territoriality' – how people relate to, and draw meaning from, landscape, buildings, physical boundaries; 'personality' – the sets of locally shared (and contested) assumptions and expectations about what it is to be a person in relation to others; and 'local history' – the layers and ridges of collective memory.[41] However, as Cohen notes, 'members of a community can make virtually anything grist to the symbolic mill of cultural distance, whether it be the effects upon it of some centrally formulated government policy, or matters of dialect, dress, drinking, marrying or dying'.[42] As such, community, whether of place or network, was a process of symbolic production: the means by which relationships, actions, artefacts, events and representations were invested with meaning. Thus, just as Andy Wood has shown how concepts of the law and custom inculcated class consciousness among England's free miners, so Daniel C. Beaver has explored the symbolic power of religious ritual in engendering both social cohesion and political loyalties.[43]

Four points follow from this. First, that 'the symbolic' is intrinsic, rather than juxtapositionary, to material relations and conditions. Second, that all people – not simply artists or masters of ceremonies – create and interpret 'symbols'. Third, that even the most apparently mundane occurrences and things – whether seating arrangements at table or church, the dynamics of gossip, or a style of footwear – are at once expressive, demarcatory and significations of power. Finally, analysis of the 'symbolic' provides the means by which historians can break the bounds of community in terms of locality and geographical propinquity. Indeed, such analysis highlights the ways in which community can exist as a powerful rhetorical concept – a symbolic entity in its own right. As such, it establishes yet another definition of community – this time not even primarily predicated on the involvement of people – as a symbolic, or 'imagined' category which can operate at a national, or even global, level.[44]

Referring to the medieval 'county community', Carpenter has suggested that it 'is time to abandon the word and to begin some serious investigation of how the gentry saw both themselves and their role within the polity and how others saw them'.[45] Even this brief survey of the conceptual ramifications of the term would suggest that community, once relieved of its ideological baggage and revealed in all its diversity, provides a perfect means of doing just that. The chapters of this volume, each different in terms of disciplinary background and topics of interest, illustrate not only the singular narratives but also the parallels and connections suggested by the concept. They are nominally grouped into sections on communities of networks, place and rhetoric. The types of networks examined include the circulation of humanist manuscripts in Essex and London; the matrix of medical practitioners in the metropolis; the links between provincial Catholic gentry; and the sociability of Samuel Pepys. The chapters on place explore the rural parish community and its redefinition; metropolitan criminals in their social and cultural contexts; the survival of civic community in the late seventeenth century; and the shift from 'negotiated' to 'architectural' communities over the course of the period. Finally, the construction of rhetorical communities is illustrated by mid-Tudor links between nationalism and language theory; by the emergent concept of the 'public' in claims to political legitimacy; by 'town–gown' symbolism as a precarious source of stability; and by journal correspondence as the construction of knowledge. However, these are not rigid typologies: all three, to a lesser or greater degree, inform each of the portraits that are painted and stories that are told. William Blundell, as Margaret Sena illustrates, was part of a Catholic community defined by its sense and experience of 'persecution', its sharing of topical and pointed ballads, and the provision of exclusive institutions like a burial ground. Paul Griffiths's anatomy of metropolitan crime is as much an exploration in networks, representation and labelling as in the boundaries and margins of place. And, as Cathy Shrank shows, the quest for order through a national vernacular was the intellectual agenda of a community of scholars well aware that identity was forged through language. However, all chapters display a similar appreciation of the subtleties, resonances and diversity of community.

As, too, did contemporaries. Early modern definitions of community, in particular those in seventeenth-century dictionaries, point towards as broad a conceptual canvas as those discussed above and below. It is worth briefly surveying this canvas, if only to emphasise the conceptual similitude that nineteenth-century definitions of the term have obscured. The dictionaries provide something of a definitional narrative of community. This is based partly on the fact that, as dictionaries became more sophisticated and more commercially competitive over the course of the century, definitions in general became more extensive. However, there are also suggestions of at least two conceptual reconfigurations involving the word: one at the beginning of the seventeenth century, and one at the beginning of the eighteenth. In Robert Cawdrey's 'A Table Alphabeticall', published in 1604, the word 'communitie' was paired with the word 'communion' and defined as 'fellowship', so implying that community and communion were the temporal and spiritual equivalents of the same conjoining process.[46] This coupling was never to occur again. In 1616 John Bulloker, in the most influential definition of the century, defined communitie as 'fellowship in partaking together'.[47] However, communion was no longer part of the equation: the temporal and spiritual – community and communion – had been separated.[48] The word 'commonalty' underwent a similar undressing. In 1604 it denoted 'common people, or commonwealth'. By 1616 it had become simply 'the common people', depoliticised in the way that community was desanctified.

More continuous – indeed, increasingly emphatic – was the suggestion, implied by the verb 'partake', that communities were created through participation: community was not a given entity, but was rather constructed through the recurrent decisions and actions of people. For example, by 1656 Blount was defining community as 'a participation, fellowship, or society; good correspondency, neer familiarity one with another', and gave as his example 'a corporation or company incorporate'.[49] Two years later, in 1658, Edward Phillips defined community as 'injoining in common or mutual participation'.[50] In these definitions, community was connected not so much with geographical place as with the institutions within a place that facilitated 'mutual participation'. On the other hand, phrases like 'good correspondency' and 'neer familiarity one with another' suggest emotional rather than simply institutionalised relationships. Moreover the overt masculinity of 'fellowship' had been replaced by an emphasis that anticipated Blount's 1674 definition of commune as 'that which belongs to one as well as another, common, publick'.[51] This in turn resonated with Shakespeare's abstracted use of the term in *Henry IV* to describe how royalty might be made ordinary and devalued through over-exposure:

> as the cuckoo is in June
> Heard, not regarded, seen, but with such eyes

As, sick and blunted with community
Afford no extraordinary gaze.[52]

Its pejorative connotations from a monarchical perspective contrast with John Locke's positive adoption of the same abstracted sense of the term to denote 'reason'. Locke argued that man, 'being furnished with like Faculties, sharing all in one Community of Nature, there cannot be supposed any such *Subordination* among us, that may Authorize us to destroy one another'.[53]

On the other hand, as late as 1695 a non-abstracted sense of the word 'society' remained an equivalent rather than an antithetical designation to community. For example, in the Phillips edition of that year, community was defined as 'common or mutual participation. A society of men inhabiting in the same place. Pious foundations for support of several persons under a regular manner of life are called communities – Hospitals, colleges, companies, guilds.' In the same edition, society appeared as: 'an assemblying of several people in one place, on purpose to assist one another in business. Also a particular tye between some persons, either for interest, out of friendship, or to live a Regular life. Also company joyn'd together in study of some Art or Science'.[54] The Royal Society, by definition, was also a community, while the York dissenter and benefactor Lady Sarah Hewley, when ruminating in the early 1690s on the condition of the dissenting community in York, observed that 'God hath taken away severel of our sosiety heare, and thos that upholds it are very ould, weke and inferme'.[55] By 1706 society had become 'company, conversation, civil intercourse. Fellowship, friendship – company of several persons joyn'd together for some common interest, or to assist one another in the management of any particular business.' However, it was the definition of community which showed most change. Whereas before the word had referred to 'a society of men inhabiting in the same place', it now designated 'a body of men united in civil society for their mutual advantage – as a corporation, the inhabitants of a Town, the companies of Tradesmen'. Society – or at least 'civil society' – had become both general and abstract; community, while it retained some sense of institutional organisation, was local, specific, and explicitly related to place.[56]

In fact this potential for difference was already present in the writings of Locke some thirty years earlier. When not philosophising about 'reason', Locke usually used 'community' and 'society' interchangeably to denote the conceptual space between the (propertied) private and 'political power': as he wrote in *Essays on the Law of Nature* I, 'there are two factors on which human society appears to rest ... a definite constitution and the state and form of government, and ... the fulfilment of pacts. Every community among men falls to the ground if these are abolished.'[57] However, on another occasion, when defining the word 'commonwealth', he stressed that he meant 'not a

Democracy or any term of Government, but an *Independent Community* which the *Latines* signified by the word Civitas, to which the word which best answers in our Language is *Common-wealth*, and most properly expresses such a Society of Men, which Community or Citty in English does not'. This was because 'there may be subordinate communities in a Government; and city amongst us has a quite different notion from commonwealth'.[58] While this anticipates later definitions of society and community, it should not obscure the different and often overlapping ways in which the terms were defined at the time: ways which were dependent not necessarily on 'a moral value' or a particular place – though it may imply those factors – so much as 'common or mutual participation' and 'good correspondency'. Such inferences in turn point us towards the concept of communication, or the manner in which people, as Cawdrey put it in 1604, 'make partaker, or give part unto'.[59]

Community, then, was something done as an expression of collective identity by groups of people. It occurred over periods of time, with shifting emphases and boundaries – both for the community and for the person. One community – and a person's attachment to it – did not preclude the simultaneous existence of others: indeed, the power of the concept is in the attention it draws to the overlap in representations, practices and identities. As a process, therefore, community may be approached as a combination of six constituent parts. First, the institutional arrangements, practices and roles that structured it. Second, the people who did it, did not do it, did not want to do it, were excluded from doing it. Third, the acts and artefacts – whether communicative or material – which defined and constituted it. Fourth, the geographical places in which it was located. Fifth, the time in which it was done and perpetuated. And, sixth, the rhetoric by which it was legitimated, represented, discussed, used and turned into ideology. In these senses, the chapters which follow are an attempt to return to early modern under-standings and practices of community, rather than to impose late twentieth-century concepts on to the past.

NOTES

1 Raymond Williams, *Keywords: a vocabulary of culture and society* (London, Fontana, 1976), p. 23.

2 Conal Condren, *The language of politics in seventeenth-century England* (Basingstoke, Macmillan, 1994), pp. 106–7.

3 Christine Carpenter, 'Gentry and community in medieval England', *Journal of British Studies* 33 (1994), 340–80; Charles Phythian-Adams, 'Introduction: an agenda for English local history', in *id.* (ed.), *Societies, cultures and kinship, 1580–1850: cultural provinces and English local history* (London, Leicester University Press, 1993), pp. 19-21; Alan Macfarlane, 'History, anthropology and the study of communities', *Social History* 5 (1977), 631–52.

4 Williams, *Keywords*, p. 76.

5 George A. Hillery, Jr, 'Definitions of community: areas of agreement', *Rural Sociology* 20, (1955), discussed by Colin Bell and Howard Newby, *Community studies: an introduction to the sociology of the local community* (London, Allen & Unwin, 1971), p. 29. See also pp. 21–53.

6 For a recent reiteration of the former see Alan Everitt, 'The local community and the great rebellion', in R. C. Richardson (ed.), *The English civil wars: local aspects* (Manchester, Manchester University Press, 1998); for its formulation in relation to towns see Roger Howell, 'Neutralism, conservatism and political alignment in the English revolution: the case of the towns, 1642–49', in John Morrill (ed.), *Reactions to the English civil war, 1642-49* (Basingstoke, Macmillan, 1982). For a critique of the latter see Lyndal Roper, '"The common man", "the common good", "common women": gender and meaning in the German Reformation commune', *Social History* 12 (1987), 1–22, p. 7.

7 Jenny Kermode, *Medieval merchants: York, Beverley and Hull in the later Middle Ages* (Cambridge, Cambridge University Press, 1998), pp. 12–13.

8 Robert Scribner, 'Communities and the nature of power' in *id.* (ed.), *Germany: a new social and economic history, 1450–1630* (London, Arnold, 1996), p. 293.

9 E. P. Thompson, *Customs in common* (Harmondsworth, Penguin, 1991), pp. 12–13; Andy Wood, 'Custom, identity and resistance: English free miners and their law, *c.* 1550–1800', in Paul Griffiths, Adam Fox and Steve Hindle (eds), *The experience of authority in early modern England* (Basingstoke, Macmillan, 1996).

10 Similarly the late twentieth-century emergence of 'community politics' is qualititatively different from national or formally organised local politics. Williams, *Keywords*, p. 75. See also C. J. Calhoun, 'Community: toward a variable conceptualization for comparative research', *Social History* 5 (1980), 105–29.

11 Scribner, 'Communities', pp. 291–2. See also Richard M. Smith, '"Modernisation" and the corporate medieval village community in England: some sceptical reflections', in Alan R. H. Baker and Derek Gregory (eds), *Explorations in historical geography* (Cambridge, Cambridge University Press, 1984), p. 154.

12 Ferdinand Tönnies, *Gemeinschaft und Gesellschaft* (Darmstadt, Wissenschaftliche BuchGesellschaft, 1979). See also David Harris Sacks, 'The corporate town and the English state: Bristol's "little businesses", 1625–41' in Jonathan Barry (ed.), *The Tudor and Stuart town: a reader in English urban history, 1530–1688* (Harlow, Longman, 1990), pp. 299–302.

13 Scribner, 'Communities', p. 292; Smith, 'Modernization', p. 152.

14 Max Weber, *Economy and society: an outline of interpretive sociology*, ed. Gunther Roth and Claus Wittich (Berkeley CA, University of California Press, 1978); R. H. Tawney, *Religion and the rise of capitalism: a historical study* (Harmondsworth, Penguin edition, 1990). For more extensive discussion of these themes see Chapters 6 and 9 below.

15 Keith Thomas, *Religion and the decline of magic: studies in popular beliefs in sixteenth- and seventeenth-century England* (Harmondsworth, Penguin, 1991), p. 672; Smith, 'Modernization', p. 141.

16 David Underdown, *Revel, riot and rebellion: popular politics and culture in England, 1603–60* (Oxford, Oxford University Press, 1985), pp. 17–18.

17 Robert Tittler, *The Reformation and the towns in England: politics and political culture, c. 1540–1640* (Oxford, Clarendon Press, 1998), p. 13.

18 Alan Everitt, *Landscape and community in England* (London, Hambledon Press, 1985), p. 9. See also Roger Howell, 'Newcastle and the nation: the seventeenth-century experience', in Barry (ed.), *The Tudor and Stuart town*.

19 Clive Holmes, 'The county community in Stuart historiography', in Richard Cust and Ann Hughes (eds), *The English civil war* (London, Arnold, 1997), p. 229.

20 See, e.g., Underdown, *Revel, riot and rebellion*; id., 'The problem of popular allegiance in the English civil war', *Transactions of the Royal Historical Society*, fifth series, 31 (1981), 69–94; Ann Hughes, *Politics, society and civil war in Warwickshire, 1620–60* (Cambridge, Cambridge University Press, 1987); id., 'Warwickshire on the eve of civil war: a county community?', *Midland History* 7 (1982), 47–72; Mark Stoyle, *Loyalty and locality: popular allegiance in Devon during the English civil war* (Exeter, University of Exeter Press, 1994).

21 Phythian-Adams, 'Introduction', p. 21.

22 See, e.g., Susan Reynolds, *Kingdoms and communities in western Europe, 900–1300* (Oxford, Clarendon Press, 1997).

23 Tittler, *Reformation*, pp. 15–17.

24 The best introduction to the genre remains Bell and Newby, *Community studies*. The classic application of the concept in English early modern historiography is Keith Wrightson and David Levine, *Poverty and piety in an English village: Terling, 1525–1700*, second edition (Oxford, Clarendon Press, 1995).

25 David Sabean, *Power in the blood: popular culture and village discourse in early modern Germany* (Cambridge, Cambridge University Press, 1984), p. 27.

26 Scribner, 'Community', p. 320.

27 Sabean, *Power in the blood*, pp. 29–30.

28 Ulinka Rublack, *The crimes of women in early modern Germany* (Oxford, Oxford University Press, 1999), p. 2; Sabean, *Power in the blood*, p. 28.

29 Keith Wrightson, 'The politics of the parish', in Griffiths *et al.*, *Experience of authority*, p. 12.

30 *Ibid.*, p. 36.

31 Smith, 'Modernisation', p. 144.

32 Keith Wrightson, *English society, 1580–1680* (London, Hutchinson, 1982), p. 224.

33 Patrick Collinson, *De Republica Anglorum, or, History with the politics put back* (Cambridge, Cambridge University Press, 1990), pp. 17–18; id., *The birthpangs of Protestant England: religious and cultural change in the sixteenth and seventeenth centuries* (Basingstoke, Macmillan, 1988), p. 69.

34 Sabean, *Power in the blood*, p. 29; Ian W. Archer, 'The nostalgia of John Stowe', in David L. Smith, Richard Strier and David Broughton (eds), *The theatrical city: culture, theatre and politics in London, 1576–1649* (Cambridge, Cambridge University Press, 1995), p. 25.

35 Wrightson, 'Politics', p. 27; Michael J. Braddick, 'State formation and social change in early modern England: a problem stated and approaches suggested', *Social History* 16, (1991), 1–17.

36 Collinson, *Republica*, pp. 17–18; Ian W. Archer, *The pursuit of stability: social relations in Elizabethan London* (Cambridge, Cambridge University Press, 1991).

37 John A. Agnew, *Politics and place: the geographical mediation of state and society* (London, Allen & Unwin, 1987), pp. 62–71. For his extremely suggestive three-tiered definition of place – as 'locale', 'location' and 'structures of feeling' – see pp. 26–8.

38 See Jeffrey C. Alexander and Steve Seidman (eds), *Culture and society: contemporary debates* (Cambridge, Cambridge University Press, 1990), especially pp. 199–217.

39 Anthony P. Cohen, 'Of symbols and boundaries, or, Does Ertie's greatcoat hold the key?', in *id.* (ed.), *Symbolising boundaries* (Manchester, Manchester University Press, 1986), p. 17; *id.*, *The symbolic construction of community* (London, Routledge, 1989).

40 Cohen, 'Of symbols', pp. 13, 17.

41 Timothy Jenkins, *Religion in everyday life: an ethnographic approach* (Oxford, forthcoming); Keith Wrightson, 'Northern identities: the *longue durée*', *Northern Review* 2 (1995), 25–35, p. 30.

42 Cohen, 'Of symbols', p. 17.

43 Wood, 'Custom', p. 279; Daniel C. Beaver, *Parish communities and religious conflict in the Vale of Gloucester, 1590–1690* (Cambridge MA, Harvard University Press, 1998).

44 The classic statement remains Benedict Anderson, *Imagined communities: reflections on the origin and spread of nationalism* (London, Verso, 1983).

45 Carpenter, 'Gentry and community', p. 380.

46 Robert Cawdrey, *A table alphabeticall* [1604] (Amsterdam, Thedrum Orbis Terrarum, 1970).

47 John Bullokar, *An English expositer: teaching the interpretation of the hardest words used in our own language* (London, 1616).

48 For a classic exposition of this process see John Bossy, *Christianity in the West* (Oxford, Oxford University Press, 1985).

49 Thomas Blount, *Glossographia, or, a dictionary interpreting all such hard words* (London, 1656).

50 Edward Phillips, *New world of words* (London, 1658).

51 Blount, *Glossographia*, fourth edition (London, 1674).

52 William Shakespeare, *Henry IV*, ed. David Bevington (Oxford, Oxford University Press, 1987), I, iii, ll. 74–6.

53 John Locke, *Two treatises of government*, ed. Peter Laslett (Cambridge, Cambridge University Press, 1993), p. 271.

54 Edward Phillips, *New world of words* (London, 1695).

55 James Raine (ed.), *Brief memoir of Mr Justice Rokeby* (London, Surtees Society, 1861), pp. 10–11.

56 For a fuller exploration of these processes of change see chapters 6, 8 and 9 below.

57 John Locke, *Political essays*, ed. Mark Goldie (Cambridge, Cambridge University Press, 1997), p. 87.

58 Locke, *Two treatises*, p. 355.

59 Cawdrey, *Table*.

Part I

Networks

Chapter 2

Reconstructing manuscript networks: the textual transactions of Sir Stephen Powle

Jason Scott-Warren

Over the course of the 1980s and 1990s, scholars working on the early modern period, and especially on its literature, became aware of the ongoing importance of manuscripts as a medium of textual transmission, long into the period conventionally dubbed 'the age of print'. The older medium has been shown to have persisted in many forms, of which the least unsettling to our preconceptions is the manuscript for presentation, the text handwritten as a gift for a particular dedicatee. These luxury objects bear an obvious relation to their medieval precursors as we most commonly imagine them, via, say, the image of the Ellesmere Chaucer. More exciting, because harder to accommodate, is the world of 'informal' manuscript transmission which has recently been opened to view. Diverse kinds of written material circulated among the literate classes on loose sheets, in makeshift pamphlets and in blank-paper books. This phenomenon was probably pan-European, but there appears as yet to be nothing in Continental scholarship to rival the surge of interest witnessed in British, American and Australian studies.[1]

While that interest has given rise to some fine empirical work documenting the geography, economics and career structures of scribal activity, it has been underwritten by theoretical concerns, particularly as these impinge upon questions of authorship and reading. If all readings are appropriations, conditioned by the cultural situation of the reader, then the process of appropriation is nowhere more visible than in the manuscript medium. Reading and writing here converge: to own a text, you sharpen your pen, mix your ink, and start to copy. In practice, texts in manuscript prove highly malleable; a poem which circulated widely will tend to appear in many different versions, varying in verbal details or bearing witness to wholesale revision. Such a poem might well attract flattering imitations or damning ripostes, which would then circulate alongside it. If 'the author' is (as Foucault claimed) not a given but a historical construct, the manuscript medium demonstrates just how weak its influence could be in the early modern period.[2] In many cases, transcripts of poems offer no record of authorship, and where they do, their ascription is often problematic. Lacking any 'authoritative' points of origin which might circumscribe their meaning, it is tempting to view such texts as collaborative social productions.[3] For a long time the vagaries of the manuscript text were left to editors, who studiously brushed them under the carpet as they set about embalming the corpus of their particular name-author. Recently, however, it has been suggested that we should bring these vagaries to the forefront of a project called 'the social history of writing'.[4] Adapting some celebrated historical slogans, one might want to think of it as 'literary history from below' or as 'literary history with the reader put back in'. This chapter aims to demonstrate that 'community' provides a key concept which can mediate between the often antipathetical disciplines of social history and text studies, thus making this project something more than a fantasy of interdisciplinarity.[5]

The idea of community, central to some of the most ambitious projects of social history, is also an idea with which anyone working on early modern manuscript circulation has to grapple. Communities are brought into being through shared practices; a manuscript community is a group of people who bond through the exchange of handwritten texts. But how are we to conceive of such communities? Scholars have tended to employ a range of terms as if they were straightforwardly interchangeable; manuscript communities are by turns 'spheres', 'circles', 'peer groups', 'elites' or 'coteries'. More creatively, they have imagined 'concentrically widening circles of readers', or (rather eerily) have pictured texts passing through 'veins of circulation' which outsiders 'tap into'.[6] At this point I wish to propose that the most useful concept for thinking about manuscript communities, both as they existed historically and as they were perceived by individual members, is that of the network.[7] Bringing this term to the analysis of communities for the first time, J. A. Barnes offered the following definition:

> Each person has a number of friends, and these friends have their own friends; some of any one person's friends know each other, others do not. I find it convenient to talk of a social field of this kind as a *network*. The image I have is of a set of points some of which are joined by lines. The points of the image are people, or sometimes groups, and the lines indicate which people interact with each other.

Although, in the opinion of Alan Macfarlane, this idea has not buttered the parsnips of social historians engaged in the full-scale reconstruction of historical communities, I hope to demonstrate that the open-endedness of the idea makes it considerably more relevant to the study of manuscript communities than the alternative terms, which (as I shall demonstrate) all overemphasise closure and exclusivity.[8]

But the same factors which render manuscript circulation interesting in theory make it hard to study in practice, and the reconstruction of past manuscript networks is fraught with difficulties. Manuscripts can seem to be so impersonal as to resist all but the most general of attempts to contextualise them. The manuscript collections of verse which ought to yield most to interdisciplinary enquiry are a case in point, since usually they offer no evidence as to their early ownership or the locale in which they were collected. Henry Woudhuysen estimates that around 230 miscellanies survive from the period before 1640; of those, thirty were probably compiled in Oxford, fourteen in Cambridge and eleven at the Inns of Court, while fourteen were household collections.[9] Although very rough, these figures leave more than two-thirds of extant miscellanies homeless. Furthermore, as Harold Love points out, 'the fact that most personal miscellanies rarely record the circumstances of receipt of particular items, and almost never those of further transmission, disguises their dynamic quality as points of transit within networks of copying'.[10] Given these factors, two approaches are possible. The first is to gather a group of demonstrably related manuscripts and to examine the relations between them, using any contextual details one can find to build up a picture of their probable owners and of the interchanges which gave rise to words on pages. The second is to home in on an exceptional manuscript, one of the very few which *do* record circumstances of receipt and onward transmission. In what follows I pursue the latter course.

The two manuscripts at the centre of my case study are Tanner 168 and 169 in the Bodleian Library in Oxford, familiarly known as the commonplace books of Sir Stephen Powle. That designation is misleading. A commonplace book is a book in which textual fragments are arranged under subject headings for ease of recall.[11] By contrast, these are miscellanies, into which items have been entered haphazardly; information retrieval is facilitated by an index at the end of the second volume. The two folio volumes, each containing more than 200 leaves, are continuous – the original pagination of Tanner 169 picks up where that of Tanner 168 leaves off – and their contents appear to have been compiled over two and a half decades, beginning around 1596 and tailing off around 1622. Although they are clearly closely related, these are only two out of ten Tanner manuscripts which contain texts formerly in Powle's possession; one of the others (Tanner 309) is a substantial letter book with many materials relating to his travels. So full was Powle's self-documentation in these collections that they enabled Virginia F. Stern to write his biography, published in 1992 as *Sir Stephen Powle of court and country*.[12]

So who was Powle? Born *c.* 1553, probably in Great Ilford, Essex, he was the youngest of three surviving sons of an important administrative official, the Clerk of the Crown, Thomas Powle, and Jane Tate of Waxham, Norfolk. Stephen was educated at Oxford, Cambridge and the Middle Temple, where he qualified as a barrister but developed a healthy dislike of the common law, preferring Calvinist theology and the liberal arts. Breaking off from his studies, he embarked on travels which took him to Geneva to hear the preaching of Théodore de Bèze; to Basel, where he paid a visit to Erasmus's study; then on to Strasbourg, Heidelberg, Nuremberg and Frankfurt. This was the first of three European journeys he undertook between 1579 and 1588. The second was to the court of the Calvinist duke, Johann Casimir, at Heidelberg, whence Powle as Agent of the Queen sent back newsletters to the Lord Treasurer, William Cecil. The third took him to Venice, where he stayed for a year, writing newsletters for the Secretary of State, Francis Walsingham. Two years after his return, early in 1590, he married Elizabeth Woodhouse Hobart, a widow hailing from the same Norfolk parish as his mother; she was to die less than a year later, giving birth to twins neither of whom lived to see their first birthday. By late 1593 Stephen had married again, to Margaret Turner Smyth, a wealthy widow and mother of ten, in whose lands at Blackmore in Essex he was to settle. In 1596, after several years of subsistance on piecemeal favours, his career took off. Powle first became Deputy Clerk of the Crown, taking his aged father's place in all but title. Then, in 1601, five months before his death, 'Old Tom Powle' surrendered to his son his office as one of the Six Clerks of the Court of Chancery; Stephen continued in the post until 1607. He was knighted by King James in 1604. The years between his retirement and his death were outwardly uneventful, save for service as Justice of the Peace for Essex and Middlesex. Outliving Margaret Smyth, Powle married for the third and final time in 1623, to another widow, Lady Anne Wigmore. This occasioned a move to the parish of St Margaret's, Westminster, where Sir Stephen and Lady Anne were buried within a year of one another, in 1630 and 1631 respectively. The process by which Powle's manuscript remains came into the hands of Thomas Tanner (1674–1735), Bishop of St Asaph and a great antiquarian, and so eventually passed with his collections into the Bodleian, remains obscure.[13]

The outward uneventfulness of Powle's retired years is belied by the activity documented in his miscellanies. Before turning to these, however, it is worth asking two preliminary questions. First, why was he so careful to preserve documents? Collections like Powle's are so common that particular explanations may be superfluous, but two factors are potentially relevant here.[14] The first is humanism, with its emphasis on the textual hoarding of commonplaces gathered from reading for redeployment in speech and writing.[15] From stray references and annotations we can be sure that Powle kept a number of collections which have not survived, including commonplace books properly so called. He tells how, when God sent him to study scripture at Oxford, he strove 'to yeilde a reason of my fayth, by collectinge all places that might make for the confirmation thereof: at which time I enriched my store with these noates digested into common places' (309.80^r). He refers to 'Master Gainsforde preachinge in the Midle Temple anno 1578', directing the reader to 'Se my common place booke titulo peccatum' (under the heading of 'sin') (246.17ʳ). Powle even kept a 'book of *simples*' into which he put a sprig from a tree growing in the churchyard at Basel, 'for the strangnes thereof' (309.133ᵛ).

A second factor which might have fuelled Powle's collecting was his work as Clerk of the Crown and as an official in the Court of Chancery. Both posts were bureaucratic in the extreme. Among the tasks performed by the Six Clerks were the filing of pleadings (the statements which initiated Chancery suits), the gathering of responses and depositions from witnesses, and the enrolling of the court's final decrees.[16] The livelihood of a Chancery official was founded upon the safe storage of documents. So it is relevant to note that most of the first volume of Powle's miscellany, Tanner 168, is taken up with business-related transcripts, collected between Powle's assumption of his father's duties in 1596, and about 1604. Commissions, oaths, pardons, writs, letters patent; such items were presumably copied for their specifics as well as for the general guidance they might offer on points of procedure. Only after this business section does the manuscript break up and become genuinely miscellaneous. Although predominantly a letter book, Tanner 169 became the repository for a random assortment of documents which Powle had been collecting, probably as small pamphlets or 'separates', over the previous thirty years, as well as for new materials which are entered in roughly chronological order.[17]

My second preliminary question is why Powle stands out from the general run of compilers. Why did he trouble to document the date, provenance and even, on occasion, the onward circulation of the texts he copied? Part of the explanation may lie with his active brand of Calvinism, which encouraged diary-keeping and autobiographical writing.[18] This is best exemplified by an autobiographical fragment which Powle wrote after the death of his first wife in 1591, headed:

> This Meditation followinge is a thanksgiuing to the Almightie for all his spirituall & temporall blessings, wherin is breefly sett downe the whole course of his life, made ⟨early⟩ in a morning before day ⟨and begonne allmost at midnight⟩ in his bedde at Clay Hall in Essex 10th Martij. 1590 on these wordes of ⟨the⟩ Psalmist. Media nocte surgam ad confitendum tibi Domine. (309.79ᵛ)

Time and place are precisely specified in order to replicate a scriptural gesture.[19] This impulse towards contextualisation, nurtured by Powle's spiritual discipline, may well have fed into his miscellanies. Beyond that, the fact that he was himself a scribally publishing author must have made a difference. He made particularly detailed contextual notes on his copy of 'The Soules secret Meditacion', a discourse of spiritual consolation which he sent to a female friend in despair in 1592, as if he anticipated a wider readership for the book and did not want anyone to be ignorant of its author's name.[20] And in one isolated instance a clarificatory note in Tanner 169 addresses a reader as 'you', as if Powle anticipated readers even of his miscellanies.[21] But in many cases the scrappiness of Powle's notes on provenance suggests that these were merely personal memoranda, notes of things which interested him. At an extreme is Powle's note that *Leicester's commonwealth* had been copied for him 'by my red hedded madde manne'.[22] The scribe remains unidentified.

This chapter explores some of the key features of early modern manuscript networks by taking Powle's contextual details to the archive in search of more information, and then returning to reread his textual traces in the light of that knowledge. Inevitably, the illumination I offer is glancing and tentative. I nonetheless hope that it will be of interest to both literary critics and social historians, and will encourage others to work towards a more close-grained understanding of the circumstances in which early modern texts lived and moved.

On 18 October 1605 Powle penned a set of 'Problemes of Judges Habetts'. Why are their caps square and black? Why are their robes red, or sometimes purple? Why furred in white? Why lined with silk? Why are they hooded? And so on. The answers to these questions are unexciting. Each aspect of the judge's clothing is made to symbolise a different aspect of the profession: the rectitude, zeal, uncorruptibility and sensitivity which are the prerequisites of the job. Only when it is asked, 'Why be their Robes lardge, wyde, pleyted and of great Compasse?' and the answer comes back, 'To signifie thereby that they ought to be men of great Capacitie, to comprehend all causes', does one detect a hint of irreverence. At the end of the piece, Powle subscribed:

> my yesterdayes conceipt of the habitt of
> oure Englishe Iudges: 19 october 1605
> Sent to master Iohn Clapham //// Your fellowe and frende
> Stephan Powle:
>
> (168.207ʳ)

Clapham was Powle's 'fellowe' at this time because he too was a Six Clerk. This establishes the 'Problems' as a work-related piece, designed to be passed between colleagues who might enjoy its gentle mocking of another of the professions occupying Westminster Hall.

John Clapham himself tells us a good deal more about this workplace. For he was also a writer, who between 1589 and 1591 had published a translation from Amyot's Plutarch and a Latin poem about Narcissus. In 1602 the first version of his *History of England* appeared in print, and shortly after taking up his Chancery office in 1603 he completed a digest of Elizabethan history.[23] Dedicating a manuscript of that history to Sir Thomas Hesketh, Attorney of the Court of Wards and Liveries, Clapham contrasted his past reclusiveness with his present public employment, telling his addressee no longer to pity his solitariness, 'by reason that I am sorted in society with a competent number of honest, kind, and learned gentlemen'. He claimed that he had completed his text hastily, and that it would be his last, 'for I must now purge my brain of all historical and poetical fantasies'.[24] But his new workplace was not quite the literature-free zone he had imagined.

Five days after he sent Clapham his 'Problemes of Judges Habetts', Powle fired off another piece, entitled 'Why a man is said to be the head of his wyfe' (169.4^{r-v}). It was, he noted, a 'half howers conceipt sent to my goode frende, Master Clapham'. Like the earlier text, this is an exercise in over-reading, offering three divine, three natural and two conjectural justifications for this commonplace. So, for example (a conjectural reason), a man is called the head of his wife because heads have eyes to see, memories to retain and tongues to speak, and because wives must use their husband's heads, not their own. A wife must not speak, Powle writes, because 'her mouthe is shutt vpp by all lawes, ⟨and not⟩ to speake in any publicke assemblye'. But, at this point in the manuscript, a woman *does* speak. Powle provides a marginal note: 'A foolish wooman sayed: yf my husband be the headde then I wilbe the cappe, and by that meanes aboue him.' The way this sharp riposte is handled is revealing; branding the woman 'foolish', Powle quite arbitrarily disallows the marginal voice a place in his game. Wit is strongly marked as masculine. Furthermore, like the piece on judge's habits, this treatise shows internal signs that it was designed to be circulated among colleagues in Chancery. The second 'natural' reason why a man is called the head of his wife is

> Because in the head, *Tanquam in arce, collocatur thesaurus scientiarum* [as in a Tower is placed the treasury of knowledges], wherewith man ought to be furnished, the better to be able to command and directe: the woman by nature is to obey. And the tower is the sup*er*emynent parte of the Cittye. as the head is of the bodie.,

The reference to the city betrays the local significance of this passage. The London life of a Six Clerk was an itinerant one, led between the Court in Westminster Hall, the Lord Chancellor's residence at York House near Charing Cross, the clerks' offices off Chancery Lane and, whenever ancient documents were called for, the Tower of London.[25] The Tower did indeed contain a treasury of knowledge for these officials, and the wit of Powle's treatise draws upon that shared professional geography. Not only is his humour gendered, it is humour in uniform. So it is doubly exclusive, doubly constitutive of a sense of community.

In sending his demonstration of male superiority to Clapham, Powle was also instructing a newly-wed in the proprieties of household government. A little less than a year before, on 28 November 1604, Clapham had obtained a

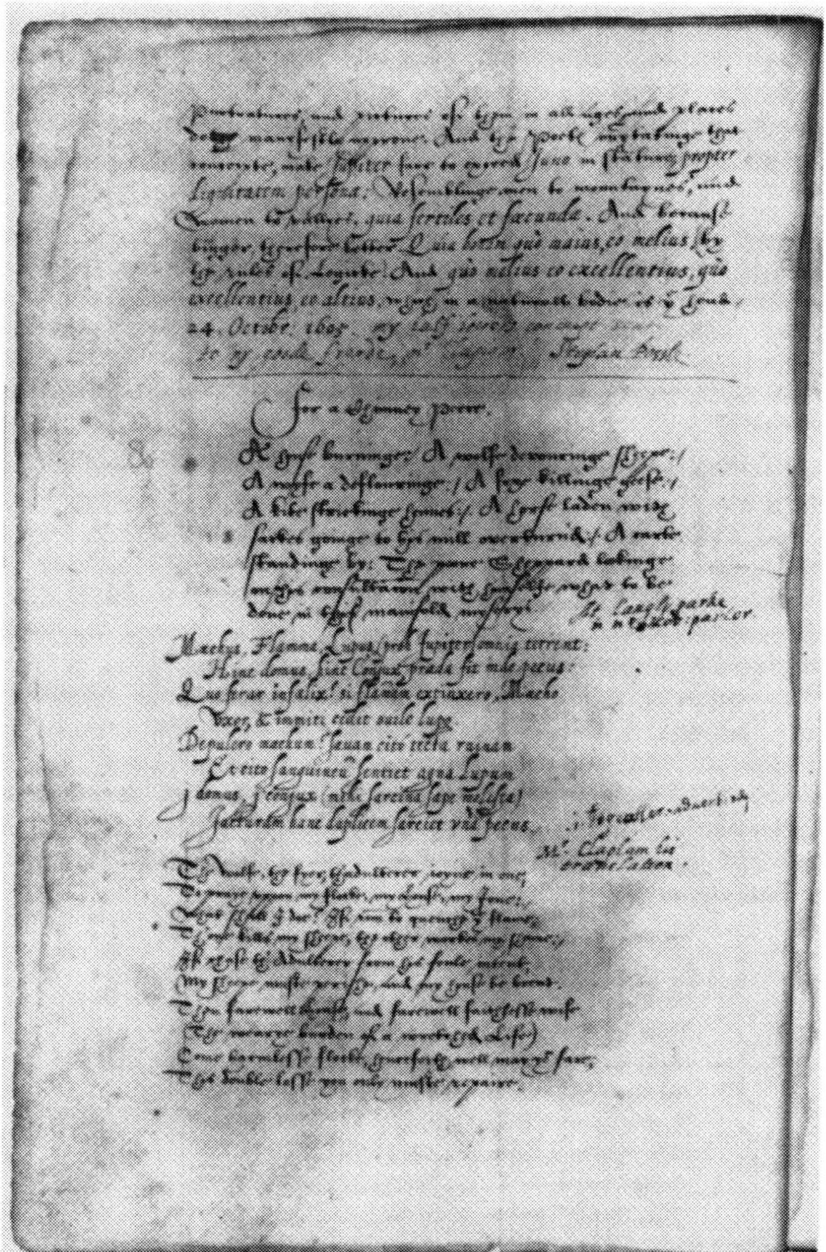

Figure 2.1 'For a Chimney Peece' (Bodleian Library, Tanner MS 169, fol. 4ᵛ)

licence to marry Anne Kidderminster, 'Maiden', at the church of St Botolph Aldgate.[26] Standard accounts of Clapham's life, unaware of this licence, assume that he was married earlier, on the basis of a statement in the dedication to his history of the reign of Elizabeth (dated 26 July 1603). There Clapham admits to Hesketh that he has bought the office of Six Clerk at a high price:

> But as I have played the part of an unwise merchant that hazards all his wares in one ship; so, like a man that reserves not himself for second fortunes, I have in the selfsame vessel embarked my own self, I mean my life, which ought to be dearer unto me than my worldly substance ... And if yourself of your own gentleness and wonted love to me, will either excuse me or afford me a favourable censure, I trust that my wife and children shall never complain to you of my unadvised dealings therein.[27]

The marriage licence demonstrates that the 'wife and children' who will benefit from Clapham's wise gamble in purchasing a Six Clerkship were at this time entirely notional. In fact, Clapham would find his wife through his work. Anne was the daughter of Edmund Kidderminster, who had been a Six Clerk since 1591.[28] This information serves to frame the text which follows 'Why a man is said to be the head of his wyfe', which is undated, and entitled 'For a Chimney Peece' (169.4^v; reproduced in Figure 2.1).

The work is an applied emblem. It first describes an image, showing 'A house burninge:, A wolfe devouringe sheepe:, A wyfe a deflouringe' and a catalogue of further disasters, surveyed by a 'poore Sheppard' who has evidently failed badly in his duty of household government. Accompanying Latin verses represent 'his consultacion with himselfe what to be done in this manifold myserys', and the translation below it is obligingly supplied by 'Master Clapham':

> The Wolfe, the fyer, th'adulterer ioyne in one,
> To praye vppon my flocke, my House, my Ione:,[29]
> What shall I doe? If runn to quenche the flame;
> Th'one kills my sheepe, the other workes my shame:,
> If chase th'Adulterer from his foule intent,
> My sheepe muste perishe, and my house be brent.
> Then farewell House, and farewell faithlesse wife
> (The wearye burden of a wretched Life)
> Come harmlesse flocke, henceforth well may you fare;
> This double losse you only muste repaire.

The emblem furnishes a conversation piece of the kind that probably formed a recognisable genre in Tudor and Stuart painting; it provokes its viewers to disagree with the shepherd's decision, and so to initiate a genteel debate.[30] The likely viewers are pinned down by a marginal note which tells us that this chimney piece actually existed, 'At langly parke in M*aster* Ked: parlor'. 'M*aster* Ked:' is Edmund Kidderminster, and Langley Park was his country house at Langley Marrish in Buckinghamshire.[31] So this piece has been produced between a father- and son-in-law duo, who are also colleagues, and transmitted by them to another colleague, Stephen Powle. Given that history, the shepherd's choice appears particularly pointed. For he opts to rescue his sheep – his livelihood – in the hope that they will 'repair' the double loss of house and wife. Although it is a game, the work which the emblem undertakes is remarkable; it raises the spectres of cuckoldry and male failure in order to assert male autonomy, an autonomy which is secured through work. For this reason it might have been valued by Powle, whose marriage to a wealthy widow preceded his acquisition of a personal income. Here again, manuscript circulation is predicated upon male bonding and the exclusion of 'foolish' women.

The remaining dealings with Clapham documented in Powle's miscellany relate to less specific concerns. There is a couplet from Fulke Greville's play *Mustapha*: 'Treason is like a Cocatrices eies / First sees then kills: but firste seene dies' (169.43[r]). This widely disseminated fragment is here subscribed '29 November 1606. M*aster* Clapham from M*aster* Foucke Greuill'. Whether Clapham received it direct from the author is unclear. What is certain is that in 1606 the primary context of the couplet would have been the Gunpowder Plot of the previous November. There is also a copy of the former Lord Treasurer Burghley's remedy for the gout, dated 23 June 1609 (169.78[r]). This was, Powle notes, 'Given to mee by M*aster* Clapham and approved by M*aster* Wilkinesone'. Clapham was Burghley's onetime clerk, and perhaps his secretary, and Richard Wilkinson was another Six Clerk. Here we have evidence of the testing of remedies in the workplace. Finally, from the same day as the 'Problemes of Judges Habetts', there is a prayer, written by Powle, beseeching God to make his journey to heaven speedy and direct. This was 'Referred by the highest coorte to the consideration of M*aster* Clapham' (168.207[r]). Powle evidently took his *contemptus mundi* religiosity to work with him, encouraging his colleagues to put their earthly court in a spiritual perspective.

Thus far we have seen how texts could bond a community, fostering values which were tailored to the particular situation in which its members found themselves, and allowing individuals to make their mark on the group through the materials that they introduced for its consumption. But the concept of the network proposes that such loosely defined communities are always open-ended, giving on to myriad other, heterogeneous groups. When a text moved between two communities in a network – from, say, a workplace to a neighbourhood – it was contested, adapted and reappropriated.

In or before 1606, Edmund Kidderminster gave Powle a set of Latin verses which he translated and transcribed in his miscellany (169.68[v]):

> A wanton wench sit⟨inge⟩ on bedde close by a Doctors syde:
> Did aske him, wheather Eauen or Morne, weare best venerian tyde
> His answeare was: The sweetest tyme, is eauninge in the night
> But out of doupt, the holsomst tyme, is mornings first day light.
> With that she clapt her hands and sayed; Before all wor[l]dly wea⟨l⟩th
> let me haue eau[n]inges darke delightes, lett me haue mornings health

The notes preceding this poem chart disagreement as to its authorship:

> Owld M*aster* Ked*derminster* gaue me thease verses followinge which he sayed weare made by a learned wooman in Latin: ⟨but Do*ctor* Franke my tenant sayed he [*sc*. Kidderminster] made at the request of a fine lady⟩

Dr Isaac Frank was a tenant on Powle's property, probably purchased around 1606, in the hamlet of Mile End and the parish of Stepney.[32] Since he is Powle's neighbour rather than his colleague, his scepticism about the poem's provenance is presumably based on mere instinct: for some unstated reason he refuses to believe that the lines were written by a woman. This kind of scepticism was endemic in manuscript networks. Since it was often impossible to trace claims of provenance back beyond the immediate contact, doubts about provenance proliferated. Despite their differences, both accounts of the poem's genesis testify to ambivalence about 'learned women' and 'fine ladies'. We may hazard that the poem derived its interest from the way it exploited conflicting male reactions to female sexuality, as something both titillating and threatening. Powle himself seems to have found the Latin version a little too accepting of the woman's appetites, so the 'bella puella' mutates into 'A wanton wench' in his translation. (Does the first line parody a prettier poem beginning, perhaps, 'A fair young maid sitting alone close by a river's side'?) The presence of doctors both within and without the poem licenses the speculation that Dr Frank's response is also a form of interpretation. His opinion of the poem's authorship deflects the barely veiled eroticism of the doctor–patient relationship on to Kidderminster and the poem's imagined female commissioner. The episode demonstrates how intricately a text could implicate readers as it passed between them.

That Dr Frank was in a position to offer an opinion on this poem implies that Powle either gave or showed it to him, and suggests that more than just a sense of dynamism is missing from the average verse miscellany. A multitude of face-to-face encounters and a world of oral commentary are implicit in the system but are largely irrecoverable from its textual traces. While the letters that Powle wrote in this period (as reproduced in his miscellany) are directed to an extended family residing in distant counties like Glamorganshire and Staffordshire, these individuals do not figure at all in the networks of manuscript circulation, which instead comprise colleagues, proximate kin, neighbours, tenants and servants.

One leaf of Powle's miscellany (169.140ʳ) offers a particularly clear idea of the potential richness of a text's social life, although in this case the text is oral rather than written (see Figure 2.2). We see it travelling along a route which Powle must have travelled many times, as his affairs took him from Blackmore in Essex via Stratford-by-Bow to Mile End, thence via Aldgate into London, and back again. Powle first notes that an Essex neighbour, a 'Master Buttlor of Tooby', 'tould me his Sonne hath a Stone brought from the East Indies called Lapis nephriticus of a greene collor'; this reputedly cured 'the stone in the bladder & raynes' when worn on the left wrist. The Mr Butler in question was probably John Butler, member of a Bedfordshire gentry family, and a Justice of the Peace in Essex; this information may well have been communicated to Powle at the sessions. Powle had Butler's claims confirmed at Mile End by a professional, his friend Dr Frank, who 'did read vnto me a booke called Crato in folio, in Latin, that did mention the lyke'. (Several books purveying the medical wisdom of Johannes Crato von Crafftheim might fit the bill.) Frank also ventured his opinion as to whether or not the stone should actually touch the flesh. Next Powle consulted his old friend Sir Walter Ralegh, at this time imprisoned in the Tower on charges of treason, who produced another book, possibly Bairo's *Secreti medicinali,* 'that commendeth admirably this stone it must be a darke grenish color'.[33] Once again the Tower, home to Ralegh's library of over 500 volumes, turned out to be a treasury of knowledge. The sequence concluded in a gift, Powle recording that 'This stoane Sir W. Rawlegh did geaue mee which I keepe as a J[e]well. 1613'.

The memorandum and its accretions provide a model for the kind of interchange which must have been taking place in relation to all kinds of texts, not just medical, and for the variety of different interests which might be brought to bear on them. While Butler's interest in medical matters may well have been personal (he died in 1614) and while Dr Frank's was professional, Ralegh's had a self-advertising edge.[34] Another medicine of which he told Powle, this time for the dropsy, required '2: ounces of Sassafrasse rootes from Virginia' (169.140ᵛ), a prescription which asks be read in relation to Ralegh's continuing efforts to win his release from prison to undertake further explorations in the New World. Like letters, medical receipts bearing a famous name and exotic ingredients, set adrift on the currents of manuscript circulation, might be used as a means of creating demand and of swaying public opinion.[35] Powle's manuscript networks remind us that names could function in much the same way, since Isaac Frank's daughter was called 'Casia', after a variety of cinnamon which early travellers to the West Indies had found growing there in abundance, 'and of no lesse goodnesse, then that which the phisitians minister for such as be diseased with the ague'. A physician-father draws on an exotic medicament to promote the circulation of his daughter.[36] Given these considerations, it is apt that John Butler's oral text

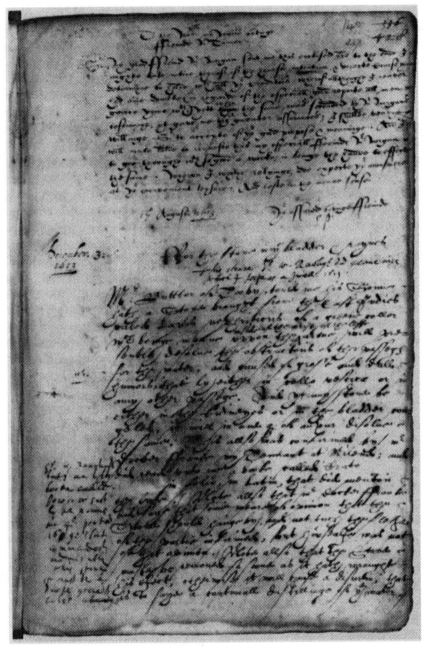

Figure 2.2 A remedy for the stone (Bodleian Library, Tanner MS 169, fol. 140ʳ)

should eventually crystallise into the healing jewel *lapis nephriticus*. Early modern texts were objects, circulating alongside things as solid as medical ingredients and as apparently intangible as the reputation of a courtier or the name of a marriageable woman.

The themes I have discussed in this chapter converge in the textual transactions surrounding Katherine Smyth, granddaughter of Powle's second wife, Margaret. Katherine makes her first appearance in Powle's collections when he transcribes a letter which he wrote in 1620 to his neighbour Thomas Lucas, of St John's, Essex, with whom she was a servant.[37] She has fallen between two stools, Powle claims,

> for shee hauinge beene supported by the countenance of seruice in Your howse for somm feawe yeares past; and hauinge beene vphoulden, and underpropped somwhat also, by my petty (yet well wishing) gracing of her. Now neuerthelesse relying on vs boathe; she is fallen, to the ground of boathe our displeasures. (169.195ᵛ).

Lucas's displeasure, because she has won the love of his son; Powle's displeasure, because she has turned down two worthy matches which he had proposed for her. Powle says that he will overlook her faults if Lucas will forget her want of duty. The next letter in the miscellany shows this one up for what it is: a sleight, masking Powle's desire to further Katherine's relationship with young Thomas Lucas. The letter is ghost-written by Powle for his granddaughter. 'Her' addressee is Samuel Harsnett, Bishop of Norwich, to whom she appeals 'as my Lord Chancellor herein', asking him to bring her new master round to her love match (169.195ᵛ–96ʳ).[38] Harsnett was a friend of Lucas senior, who in 1604 had presented him to the rectorship of Shenfield in Essex. The argument of the letter is that the marriage is a *fait accompli*: witnesses, licences and rings are all in place as evidence that they are effectively married. The letter was never sent, and Katherine was evidently dismissed and separated from Lucas, for the next letter in the series is sent from Powle to his recently widowed sister, Lady Cheyney, at Drayton Beauchamp in Buckinghamshire, offering Katherine as a servant. Her abilities are itemised, and she is objectified as a gift, 'this assured signe and pledge of my brotherly loue', 'the Iewell out of my loue I offer you' (169.198ᵛ). There is no note of what became of this scheme.

The final item in this sequence is a poem in four stanzas, headed 'Thes verses weare geauen to my daughter Kate by yonge master Tyffin of wakes hall in Essex 1622' (169.199ᵛ). Wake's Hall, in the north Essex village of Wake's Colne, was a long way from Powle's house at Blackmore, in Chelmsford hundred. But his wife's family owned land there, and until his death in 1621 Powle's brother-in-law John Smyth lived at Crepping Hall in Wake's Colne.[39] We may infer that Katherine was living with relations in north-east Essex when she received the four stanzas from William Tyffin, at the time about nineteen years old and the heir to considerable estates. These stanzas offered her a warning:

> Beware (faire maydes) of musky Courtires oathes:
> take heed what guifts, and fauiours you reciue:
> lett not the fadinge gloase, of silkin cloaths:
> dazell your vertues, or your fame bereave
>   for loose but once, the holde you have of grace:
>   who will regard your fortunes, or your face:

Although they are here unattributed, these verses are ascribed to Josuah Sylvester (c. 1562–1618), better known as translator of Du Bartas's *Semaines*.[40] They go on to outline the dire consequences of surrendering one's virginity to courtiers and monarchs: 'begin with Kinges, to subiects thou wilt fall: / from Lorde to Lacky, and at last to all'. They probably also offer a textbook example of the changing valences of manuscript texts moving between different communities. Three years earlier, in November 1619, Tyffin had entered the Middle Temple, a locale to which this poem is eminently suited and from which it may well have come.[41] Mounting an onslaught on the hypocrisy of courtiers, it would have fallen in easily with the rivalry which existed between the royal court and the Inns of Court. Taken down to the country, a text which had bonded a community of men becomes a highly charged gift from a man to a woman, assuring her of his trustworthiness – unlike a courtier, the Inns of Court man will take the tree if he takes the fruit. That is how it must have appeared to Powle, as he copied it into his miscellany with a careful note about its provenance.[42] But if Tyffin was interested, he did not continue so. In 1628, or shortly thereafter, he married Elizabeth, daughter of Richard Harlakenden of Earl's Colne.[43]

Why did Katherine Smyth give Sir Stephen young master Tyffin's poem? Framed by the miscellany, the piece has both local and general interest; it is at once a fashionable acquisition and a chapter in an ongoing family saga. Whatever her motives, the case makes the point that the circulation of manuscripts was more than a matter of elite male bonding. Despite their deliberate exclusion from the texts I examined earlier, the role of women was far from negligible. On a sheet of rough notes at the end of Tanner 169, Powle recorded a Latin word game and a spell for ridding oneself of the cramp, both learnt in 1593 'of Mistris Smith widdowe whoame I hoape to marry' (169.231ʳ). A charm which the Earl of Gowry supposedly had in his pocket when (in the King James version) he plotted to kill the Scottish king in October 1600 was, Powle records, 'deliuered my wyfe by ould Baldwen oure soliciter'.[44] Margaret Smyth also brought with her a stock of medical prescriptions and a printed mid-Henrician Bible, from which Powle copied a controversial prologue. And she brought with her Katherine Smyth, who expanded Powle's textual network as he worked to make her a match.

Even the servants, clerks and scribes that Powle set to work copying and checking his manuscripts had a part to play in the gathering and onward dissemination of their contents. For example, what is probably the most venerable item in the miscellany, a rhymed Latin poem by the eleventh/twelfth-century poet Hildebert of Lavardin, was marked 'Geauen me by my seruant Leycroft' (169.63'). Although it is difficult to determine the social status of Powle's servants, at least one, Tobias Dobby (169.189'), was a graduate of St John's College, Cambridge, which he had entered as a sizar, the poorest grade of student.[45] So, in theory, the huge reservoir of manuscript material circulating at the universities could have been opened to Powle through subordinate members of his household.

This chapter has outlined some of the key features of early modern manuscript networks and the huge variety of texts which passed through them. Within pre-defined communities (institutions, localities, or kin groups), texts could nurture a sense of communal identity, by means of their local references, their in-jokes and their pointed exclusions. As they moved between communities, texts came under pressure and were explicitly or implicitly rewritten to serve new interests. Their meanings were contested, their texts were altered, or they were transformed in order to be put to entirely new uses. Texts in manuscript were objects, gifts to be 'geauen', and they circulated alongside fame, reputation, precious objects and women. The concept of the network, of the community which opens on to other communities, is vital because in its open-endedness it reminds us of how great could be the variations of status in manuscript exchanges. Male coteries existed, but household, neighbourhood and kinship links cut across these cosy enclaves. Universities, Inns of Court, the court, the coffee houses – all the institutions within which manuscript communities have been shown to have flourished – were riven by hierarchies which are all too easily overlooked. The points of transition between networks are the sites on which the social history of early modern writing will be written.

NOTES

I am grateful to members of the Cambridge Interdisciplinary Renaissance Seminar and the York Renaissance Seminar, to Steven W. May and to fellow contributors to this volume for comments on earlier versions of this chapter.

1 Margaret Ezell, *The patriarch's wife: literary evidence and the history of the family* (Chapel Hill NC, University of North Carolina Press, 1987); Harold Love, *Scribal publication in seventeenth-century England* (Oxford, Clarendon Press, 1993); H. R. Woudhuysen, *Sir Philip Sidney and the circulation of manuscripts, 1558–1640* (Oxford, Clarendon Press, 1996). A journal for *English Manuscript Studies 1100–1700* was initiated in 1989.

2 Michel Foucault, 'What is an author?', in Josué V. Harari (ed.), *Textual strategies: perspectives in post-structuralist criticism* (Ithaca NY, Cornell University Press, 1979).

3 For an exploration of this complex issue see Marcy L. North, 'Queen Elizabeth compiled: Henry Stanford's private anthology and the question of accountability', in Julia M. Walker (ed.), *Dissing Elizabeth: negative representations of Gloriana* (Durham NC, Duke University Press, 1998).

4 This idea is developed by Arthur F. Marotti, *Manuscript, print, and the English Renaissance lyric* (Ithaca NY, Cornell University Press, 1995).

5 On the resistance of social history to 'high culture', including literature, see Adrian Wilson, 'A critical portrait of social history', in *id.* (ed.), *Rethinking social history: English Society 1570–1920 and its interpretation* (Manchester, Manchester University Press, 1993), p. 26.

6 Arthur F. Marotti, reviewing Love, *Scribal publication*, in *Modern Philology* 93 (1996), 381–7; Steven W. May, 'Manuscript circulation at the Elizabethan court', in *New ways of looking at old texts: papers of the Renaissance English Texts Society, 1985–91* (Binghamton NY, Medieval and Renaissance Texts and Studies, 1993), 273–80, p. 275.

7 Love, *Scribal publication*, especially pp. 190, 209.

8 J. A. Barnes, 'Class and committees in a Norwegian parish', *Human Relations* 7 (1954), 39–58, p. 43; Alan Macfarlane, Sarah Harrison and Charles Jardine, *Reconstructing historical communities* (Cambridge, Cambridge University Press, 1977), pp. 18–22.

9 Woudhuysen, *Sidney*, p. 157, drawing on Peter Beal, *Index of English literary manuscripts* I, *1450–1625*, 2 parts (London, Mansell, 1980).

10 Love, *Scribal publication*, p. 80.

11 Anne Moss, *Printed commonplace-books and the structuring of Renaissance thought* (Oxford, Clarendon Press, 1996).

12 Virginia F. Stern, *Sir Stephen Powle of court and country: memorabilia of a government agent for Queen Elizabeth I, Chancery official, and English country gentleman* (Selinsgrove PA, Susquehanna University Press, 1992). Stern provides a catalogue of Powle manuscripts in appendix A. References to the Bodleian Tanner manuscripts are hereafter supplied parenthetically in my text. In transcriptions, contractions and suspensions have been expanded and supplied letters italicised. Insertions are indicated thus: ⟨...⟩.

13 Stern, *Powle*, pp. 181–2.

14 Love, *Scribal publication*, pp. 197–203.

15 On humanist practices of 'gathering' and 'framing' see Mary Thomas Crane, *Framing authority: sayings, self and society in sixteenth-century England* (Princeton NJ, Princeton University Press, 1993).

16 Henry Horwitz, *Chancery equity records and proceedings, 1600–1800: a guide to documents in the Public Record Office* (London, HMSO, 1995), pp. 13–20; W. J. Jones, *The Elizabethan Court of Chancery* (Oxford, Clarendon Press, 1967), pp. 119–35.

17 A rough count established that Tanner MS 169 contains 166 items, around eighty-nine of which are letters, of which seventy-one are written by or to Powle himself. There are twenty-four poems, twenty-one treatises/orations and twenty medical prescriptions.

18 See Tom Webster, 'Writing to redundancy: approaches to spiritual journals and early modern spirituality', *Historical Journal* 39 (1996), 33–56.

19 Psalms 119.62, 'At midnight I will rise to give thanks unto thee because of thy righteous judgments' (King James Version).

20 Tanner MS 246. The work has an 'Argument' which appears to address this wider readership, and in 1608 Powle added to the title page a note which clarified the circumstances of the text's production. The addressee of 'this discourse in the forme of a longe letter' was one Cordell Maye; she was the daughter-in-law of Matthew Hutton, then Bishop of Durham, with whom she was staying when Powle sent her the treatise. It seems likely that Powle's display of Calvinist theology was implicitly addressed to Hutton.

21 Alongside a ghost-written letter Powle wrote, 'This letter thus reformed by mee my ealdest brother Master Thomas Powle did write as from him sealfe diuised to a frende of his many yeeres after my fasshioninge the same as yowe see' (169.43ᵛ).

22 Tanner MS 169, fol. 32ʳ. Powle notes that his copy of *Leicester's commonwealth* was copied out of Sir William Cornwallis's manuscript; it is followed by several of Cornwallis's 'paradoxes'.

23 Charles Martindale and Colin Burrow, 'Clapham's *Narcissus*: a pre-text for Shakespeare's *Venus and Adonis*?', *English Literary Renaissance* 22 (1992), 147–76; E. P. Read and C. Read (eds), *Elizabeth of England: certain observations concerning the life and reign of Queen Elizabeth by John Clapham* (Philadelphia PA, University of Philadelphia Press, 1951). On literary production and clerkship, including Six Clerkship, see Woudhuysen, *Sidney*, pp. 66–76.

24 Read and Read, *Elizabeth of England*, pp. 29–30.

25 Jones, *Chancery*, p. 6.

26 J. L. Chester and G. J. Armitage (eds), *Allegations for marriage licences issued by the Bishop of London* I (London, 1887), p. 292.

27 P. W. Hasler (ed.), *The House of Commons, 1558–1603*, 3 vols (London, HMSO, 1981) I, p. 609; Read and Read, *Elizabeth of England*, pp. 10, 28.

28 T. D. Hardy, *A catalogue of Lord Chancellors, Keepers of the Great Seal, Masters of the Rolls, and principal officers of the High Court of Chancery* (London, Butterworth, 1843), pp. 106–7.

29 'Joan', a generic and unflattering name for a wife.

30 See, e.g., Karen Hearn (ed.), *Dynasties: painting in Tudor and Stuart England, 1530–1630* (London, Tate Gallery, 1995), pp. 98–9 (cat. 50).

31 See Kidderminster's 1607 will, PRO (now F[amily] R[ecords] C[entre]) PROB 11/110 (92 Huddlestone), of which his wife Anne was sole executrix.

32 Frank's first name is given in his daughter's marriage licence; see note 36 below. William Le Hardy (ed.), *County of Middlesex: calendar to the sessions records*, new series, IV, *1616–18* (London, Radcliffe, 1941), 35, records an indictment against Dr Frank of Stepney for failing to maintain the highways. An Isaac Francke matriculated pensioner from Trinity College, Cambridge, in the Easter term of 1574 and took his B.A. from Clare, 1575–77; J. A. Venn and J. Venn, *Alumni Cantabrigiensis*, part I, vol. 2 (Cambridge, Cambridge University Press, 1922) p. 173.

33 Bairo is item 211 in Walter Oakeshott, 'Sir Walter Ralegh's library', *Library*, fifth series, 23 (1968), 285–327. 'Friend' may be too strong a word; in 1590 Powle thanked God for

preserving him from 'my bedfellowe at the Inns of court (and many yeeres companion) riotous, lascivious and incontinent *Rawlegh*' (309. 80ᵛ–81ʳ).

34 Butler's will is FRC, PROB 11/123 (2 Lawe). It lists four sons: Sir Oliver, Nathaniel, James and John, and a son-in-law, George Digbie.

35 See Kenneth Fincham and Peter Lake, 'Popularity, prelacy and puritanism in the 1630s: Joseph Hall explains himself', *English Historical Review* III (1996), 856–81.

36 Richarde Eden, trans., *The history of trauayle in the West and East Indies, and other countreys lying eyther way, towardes the fruitfull and ryche Mollucaes* (London, Richard Iugge, 1577), fol. H1ʳ. Powle's unfamiliarity with the name is indicated by the fact that he spelt it 'Kesie' when ghost-writing a love letter for his servant Dick Hoskyn to send to her (169.42ʳ). For 'Casia', see her marriage licence, in J. L. Chester and G. J. Armitage (eds), *Allegations for marriage licences issued by the Bishop of London* II (London, 1887), 14 December 1616.

37 Lucas was the father of the writer and natural philosopher Margaret Cavendish, Duchess of Newcastle (1623–73).

38 Harsnett was the author of *A declaration of egregious popish impostures* (London, Iames Roberts, 1603), discussed in Stephen Greenblatt, *Shakespearean negotiations* (Oxford, Clarendon Press, 1988), chapter 4.

39 See his will; E[ssex] R[ecord] O[ffice] (Chelmsford), D/ACW 6/261. ERO (Colchester), D/DYz (2) and (3) document land transactions between Tyffins and Smyths in the 1590s.

40 On Sylvester see Susan Snyder (ed.), *The divine weeks and works of Guillaume du Salluste, Sieur du Bartas, translated by Josuah Sylvester*, 2 vols (Oxford, Clarendon Press, 1979) I, 4–32. The poem is B357 in Margaret Crum, *First-line index of English poetry, 1500–1800, in manuscripts of the Bodleian Library, Oxford*, 2 vols (Oxford, Oxford University Press, 1969).

41 H. A. C. Sturgess, *Register of admissions to the Honourable Society of the Middle Temple* (London, Butterworth, 1949), 13 November 1619. Tyffin is described as 'grandson (nepos) and heir of William T[yffin] of Colnewake'; the will of the older William is ERO (Chelmsford), D/ACW 8/59, dated January 1617. On the culture of the Inns see Arthur F. Marotti, *John Donne, coterie poet* (Madison WI, University of Wisconsin Press, 1986).

42 A similar narrative probably attaches to Powle's copy of 'The lowest trees have tops', a lyric now ascribed to Sir Edward Dyer. Powle's copy is headed 'Verses given as I suppose by Master Lea to Lant; intimating, that secret loue speakes little. ⟨but sithence I did vnderstande that they weare Sir W. Rawleighs verses to Queene Elisabeth; in the beginninge of his fauoures⟩' (169.192ᵛ). The identities of Lea and Lant remain mysterious; for speculations see Woudhuysen, *Sidney*, p. 161. However, Powle elsewhere (169.147ᵛ) records 'my daughter Lantes medicine' for clearing the sight, suggesting that she too is a daughter or granddaughter of Margaret Smyth.

43 ERO (Chelmsford), D/DH VI. B. 8, 15. This was probably the same Richard Harlakenden who conferred the living of Earls Colne upon the diarist Ralph Josselin in 1641; Alan Macfarlane, *The family life of Ralph Josselin, a seventeenth-century clergyman: an essay in historical anthropology* (Cambridge, Cambridge University Press, 1970), p. 17.

44 Tanner MS 169, fol. 141ᵛ. This may have been Humfrey Baldwin of Springfield, near Chelmsford, described in his will as 'one of the procurators of the Courte of Arches and Deputy Register of the same Courte', FRC, PROB 11/25 (part 2) (61 Rudd), proved 1612.

The official account of the Gowry conspiracy mentions 'a little close parchment bag, full of Magical characters, and words of inchantment' found in the traitor's pocket, but it does not offer a text of the charm; *The Earle of Gowries conspiracie against the Kings Maiestie of Scotland* (London, Valentine Simmes, 1600), fol. C2ᵛ. See further Steven Mullaney, *The place of the stage: license, play, and power in Renaissance England* (Chicago IL, University of Chicago Press, 1988), chapter 5.

45 Venn and Venn, *Alumni Cantabrigiensis* I, ii, p. 48.

Chapter 3

Defensive tactics: networking by female medical practitioners in early modern London

Margaret Pelling

The primary relationships explored in this chapter are those between unlicensed medical practitioners, the London College of Physicians, and between the 'irregulars' themselves. Tactics involve manoeuvring in the presence of the enemy. The term is being used here because the evidence for discussion is from confrontations – often but not always face-to-face, and of a semi-legal character – with men on the accusatory side, and a mixture of men and women on the other. However, the intention is also to arrive at some assessment of strategy, that is, the longer-term aims, conscious or otherwise, which can be constructed at a distance from the enemy. Whether the tactics in question can accurately be seen as purely defensive, as implied by my title, is ostensibly true, but perhaps less true in practice, in terms of the balance of disadvantage, rather than advantage, on either side.

'Networking' is a more problematic term to have chosen. It is the concept of community that is being addressed, and there will be no consideration here of network theory as such. However, it could be argued, on a commonsense basis, that the two now overlap. The notion of community, widely but variously used in post-war sociology,[1] seems to have been deployed by early modern historians primarily in three contexts: first, the contrast between medieval and post-Reformation society, which incorporates debate over the shift from communalism to individualism; second, the contrast between rural and urban society in the context of urbanisation and, later, industrialisation, which tends to share ground with the first; and third, the notion of a county community, a hierarchically structured grouping which nonetheless possesses a geographical integrity and a common cause, or interest, in terms of national politics.

Some historians are still prepared to use the term 'community' in a pragmatic sense simply to describe a place, or an ethnic minority group.[2] However, recent work has devoted considerable effort to depriving 'community' of most of its obvious attributes.[3] Thus our new communities are not static, they can encompass the mobility which characterises early modern English life. They are not created simply by geographical boundaries; in fact they can be mental, not physical. They are not homogeneous, and, if heterogeneous, they are not necessarily socially well integrated. Mere propinquity does not create a community, and neither does gender. Above all, community can be no synonym for harmonious relations. Some of the argument is, often tacitly, about the difference between necessary and sufficient factors. Few historians of England have gone as far as Sabean, whose German villagers are tied together by hatred and by banding together against an enemy within, but the consensus now seems to prefer a notion of community which depends on interaction, which is at least partly negative, and which works, in Wrightson's terms, by processes of inclusion and exclusion.[4] Much the same seems to apply to the term 'neighbourhood', which like 'community' combines ideology with geography, but on a smaller, more literal scale, and with the advantage of its being a term in contemporary use. Unlike community, 'neighbourhood' identifies a contemporary ideal, albeit one which could be appropriated by classes or factions.[5]

Since community has been purged of its physical and literal attributes, and also of any sense of a shared programme which can be taken for granted rather than constantly recreated, and since the emphasis is now (perhaps not surprisingly at the beginning of the twentieth-first century) on the processes of communication and interaction, it would seem that communities and networks have a good deal in common. With respect to my own material, which derives from early modern London, the deconstruction of community has a paradoxical effect. According to the old definitions, it would be very hard to claim that my female protagonists at least could represent a community of any kind, except by virtue of being all female. The revision of the notion of community, however, reopens the whole question.

Those concerned are the female 'irregulars' accused by the College of Physicians in the years 1550–1640 of practising physic in the London area without the college's permission.[6] The college's powers were conferred by statute, and resembled the rights of search and supervision exerted by the London craft and trade companies. However, the college only gradually acquired the ability to impose effective sanctions, and its decisions were constantly vulnerable to challenge or indifference. 'Irregulars' is a convenient label, but it reflects the college's point of view, and cannot be seen as defining the activities or integrity of these practitioners. The irregulars were not confined to the true empirics, but included substantial numbers who belonged to the other medical corporations in London, the Society of Apothecaries (which, under the aegis of the college, emerged as a company separate from the Grocers in 1618) and the Company of Barber-Surgeons, of middling status but one of the most numerous and widely distributed of the London crafts. The Apothecaries and the Barber-Surgeons were well integrated in civic life, and their members shared in the attributes conferred by male citizenship. The college on the other hand avoided civic responsibilities and had only weak links with civic sources of male authority. The protracted historical process of professionalisation has ensured that the collegiate physician is seen as securely seated at the apex of the health-care pyramid. The broad base of the pyramid, then as now, consisted of the care provided mainly by women, either as family members or outside the household. However, sheer numbers, from the point of view of medical elites, have been interpreted only as proving their case against the proliferation of illicit practitioners and the gullibility of patients. For the historian, the numerousness of the irregulars is important, but also significant is their variety, and the way in which ill people chose practitioners according to a 'hierarchy of resort', but without necessarily observing the hierarchy suggested by the pyramidal structure of orthodox practice.

That physicians were opposed by perfectly respectable apothecaries and barber-surgeons tends to be overlooked, reflecting the tendency of contemporary polemic and satire to link physicians, women and empirics. Historians have long revelled in the invectives directed against empirics, and also in the irreverence directed against orthodox practitioners – but often for the wrong reasons in historical terms. Historiographically, medical practitioners have been subject to a false polarity between 'ineffectual' on the one hand and 'maligned' on the other. Such polarities have also plagued the much-discussed issue of whether, and how, female practitioners were forced out of medicine during the seventeenth century. Many excellent contributions have sought to modify this simplified picture, but it seemed to me that one missing element consisted in the problems caused for male practitioners, especially physicians, by the gender connotations of the work they did and the contexts in which that work was carried out. Suggesting that male physicians suffered from chronic gender as well as status anxieties was aimed not at redistributing sympathy but rather at explaining why physicians behaved as they did, and why their contemporaries behaved as they did towards them. The physicians' efforts at establishing an identity had much to do with defining professional and middle-class *mores*, but behind this apparent success lay a long, arduous process in which their efforts could do more harm than good.[7]

All types of male practitioner can be seen as affected by gender-related disadvantages, but for physicians the problems were particularly acute. It was not simply a matter of its being easier for women to intrude into physic, but rather that the work, work context and work-related attributes of physicians too closely resembled those of women. Medicine is a particularly pointed case of this gender effect, but the same approach could be applied to other areas of work – the division of labour within the textile trades, for example, or within agriculture and animal husbandry. There is enough evidence to suggest that, even in old age, when tasks more ambiguous in gender terms were taken on, an early modern man was more likely to end up dependent on spinning done by his wife and their children than he was to spin himself. More interesting perhaps are those areas, like medicine, where men's work incorporates, or appropriates, forms of work carried out by women or associated with feminine attributes.

This case is best supported by literary, iconographical and biographical evidence, rather than records of actual practice. Evidence of medical practice is ubiquitous in early modern sources, but it is usually scattered and often cryptic or terse. Most casebook evidence relates either to a specific type of practice, especially astrological physic, or is either polemical or selective on social or intellectual grounds. This is not a disqualification, but it is a limitation. With respect to female practitioners, most of what we have derives from gentlewomen or above – valuable, but narrowly based, and relatively detached from the world of women's work.[8] This evidence effectively relates only to what was officially sanctioned, however partially, by male elites. The invisibility of female practitioners below the gentry level is illustrated by the findings of Ronald Sawyer, who analysed the medical cases of the astrological physician, Richard Napier.[9] Napier lived most of his adult life as the parish incumbent of the north Buckinghamshire village of Great Linford, and, while his contacts with London were extensive, his physical and social context, recorded in great detail in his case notes, might be expected to have every claim to community status. Sawyer concluded moreover that proximity was the most important factor in a villager's initial choice of practitioner. Nonetheless he found, again, that only gentlewomen were recorded in any detail. A number of local women were clearly active and significant as practitioners, but they remained shadowy and even nameless. Many irregulars are made visible by the denunciations of their competitors, but the proximity of a ferocious medical polemicist, John Cotta, failed to reveal much about the base of the pyramid. Even the local midwives were difficult to identify with any certainty.[10] Other sources, created by corporations rather than by individuals, give us some insight into the role of women in medical poor relief, but this, somewhat erroneously, has the effect of reinforcing the stereotypes about women's practice below the gentry level.

Hence the value of an extensive series of hostile interactions between male and female practitioners, as recorded in the Annals of the London College of Physicians. It is necessary to concentrate here on female practitioners; the whole population of female patients and witnesses cannot be considered. As already suggested, 'non-collegiate' might be a more accurate description than 'irregular' of those the college saw as its opponents. The college comprised a small, tight, would-be homogeneous group aiming at hegemonic control of a metropolitan world of rampant pluralism in medical practice. The college's own criteria of admission were so exclusive that the exclusion of women is in no way remarkable. It is more revealing to look at the attributes of the other irregulars who were male, to see how much women could lack and still be medical practitioners. The male irregulars could be variously members of the college (eventually), university-trained, ordained, literate in Latin and other languages, familiar with the Inns of Court, freemen or trained by apprentice-ship, licensed by a bishop, protected as members of royal, noble or diplomatic households, and able to enter into contracts and bonds on their own behalf. All these attributes involved connections which could provide means of defence, and women were ostensibly deprived of virtually all of them. Moreover, many male irregulars were mobile, not because they were wandering mountebanks, but because they were in London temporarily while they carried out business or pursued a law suit. Women also came to London for these purposes, but it seems clear that female irregulars – or at least those pursued by the college – were more likely to be fixed in London than were the males.

It is necessary at this point to provide some overall parameters. Over the period in question, 1550–1640, the college pursued a total of 714 irregulars, of whom 110 (15·4 per cent) were women. Some irregulars were summoned repeatedly but never seen; for others there were protracted, often face-to-face confrontations over decades. Of the 110 women, thirty-nine were summoned but never seen; only six appeared in person three or more times before the college. In between are the majority, who made one or two personal appearances before the college but who might have been the subject of rather more entries in the Annals as the college tried to pin them down. The extreme case was the 'west-end' practitioner Mrs Payne, for whom there were sixteen entries over a period of fifteen years. Over this time she managed to limit her appearances in person to three. Mrs Payne's methods of deflecting college summonses included promising co-operation, sending excuses, writing what the college called absurd letters, and simply failing to turn up.[11] A tabulation by gender and year of initiations, or the first hostile contacts between the college and irregulars, shows no startling differences in the proportions between males and females over time.[12] The 1580s are the only period for which I have located something like a 'scare' about old women intruding into medicine, but this is also the period at which the college's records begin to improve. There are two apparent peaks, in 1612 and 1627, but I have found no evidence of gender-specific concern in these years except a hint around 1627 that Charles might have patronised female practitioners.[13] It is also possible to construct a chronology by gender for the amount of time the college spent on the irregulars, estimated in terms of numbers of entries. Here again, but more markedly, the female irregulars are represented by a fairly consistent baseline, while the time spent on male irregulars fluctuates more dramatically. This and other measures suggest that a male practitioner was more likely to be re-arraigned by the college on a further charge, and in general likely to take up more of the college's time, than a female. Whether this means the college was more successful in deterring female practitioners is a matter needing careful interpretation. With respect to outcomes, it is first necessary to note that the college was rather better at recording punishments, ranging from fines to imprisonment, than it was at recording verdicts, so the latter have to be inferred from the former. Interestingly, there is not a great difference between men and women in the proportions found guilty of unlicensed practice – women were slightly more likely to be found guilty, at 51 per cent of their 'actions' or separate cases, as compared with 47 per cent for men. It must be stressed that the other half can be classified not as *not-guilty* outcomes, but rather as 'inconclusive'. With respect to punishment, again the differences by gender are not striking. In each case, about a third were not punished (although they might be admonished or warned), a third were fined, and a third were punished by other means, including imprisonment. Men were slightly more likely than women to be given punishments involving fines, and women were slightly more likely than men to be let off without punishment. This apparent equality with respect to outcomes is itself worthy of note, since it might be expected either that women would have got off much more lightly, or that they would be more readily pinned down as offenders and subjected to exemplary punishment for ideological reasons.

The *process* of initiation, that is, how irregulars came to the attention of the college, cannot be explored here,[14] but it should be emphasised that the college was not a regulatory body which was informed by agencies or individuals whenever irregular practice occurred. Instead, the college's proceedings were based on a combination of its own information-gathering, information laid by members of the college, requests by outside bodies including the courts, information laid by other irregulars, and, last but not least, those using the college's powers to pursue their own ends. The college was seen by Londoners not as the first and last port of call when they had a grievance against a practitioner, but as one recourse among many. The contractual basis of much practice at the time meant that the means of redress was the same as in other areas regulated by the right of one individual to take another to court. The college was effectively co-opted into this method of regulation of affairs between patient and practitioner. Women constituted a significant presence in two main areas of initiation: as irregulars informing on other irregulars, of which more later, and as connections of patients, particularly wives complaining on behalf of husbands. It has to be added, however, that in the majority of instances it is not clear how initiation took place.

Any notion of community, however attenuated, must consider issues of location and status or class. Both in this case are complicated by lack of information. The college identified irregulars by parish or locality in some cases, and in two cases the woman had no other known identity.[15] However, only thirty-four women (31 per cent) can be attributed to a particular parish; rather more (forty-two) to a particular ward. There is a degree of concentration in two wards, Bridge Without (including Southwark), and Faringdon Without, to the west. Before inferring the presence of communities of practitioners, however, we have to recall that this is over a period of ninety years; there is also little reason to believe that practitioners practised according to geographical boundaries. Both wards are predictable localities in this context, Bridge Without in terms of its association with prostitution and lack of regulation generally, and Faringdon Without in terms of the location of the college itself and its tendency to look westwards. If parishes rather than wards are plotted, the women are located peripherally: there are none in the central City parishes, a few just within the Walls, and more in a ring of the larger extra-mural parishes.

With respect to status – marital as well as occupational and social – the most notable point is that the college described twenty-one of the female irregulars only by their names. Sixteen more appear simply as 'Mrs.' and two as Goody or Goodwife. Only ten were described as, or can be inferred to have been, widows; of these, three were observed to remarry. Thirty-six more were apparently married women, whose husbands' occupations were occasionally given (tailor, broker, innkeeper, joiner, apothecary, barber-surgeon). Thirty-four women, including twenty-five given no definite marital status, can be associated with some occupation, but this includes the college's label of 'empiric' as well as midwives and others who appeared to practise medicine on a fairly regular basis. Almost no occupations unrelated to medical practice are recorded of the female irregulars in the Annals. In quantitative and occupational terms, therefore, the college is not illuminating about the world of women's work, and in this, of course, it is typical of most records constituted by male authority. It is even less assiduous, or at least less successful, than might be expected in tracing husbands who might be held responsible for their wives' activities. It could be inferred that one reason for this was the college's complicated but determined attempt to isolate itself from the world of craft and manual labour – complicated, because of the manual taint attached to all medical work, and because of the equally determined intrusion into physic by apothecaries and barber-surgeons. The assumption being made is that most of the women concerned came from the artisan class or lower. This remains an inference, but one striking absence in the Annals is any reference to the practice of physic carried out by gentlewomen. It seems likely that a gentlewoman who practised in the country might also on occasion practise in the town, but if this phenomenon existed, the college ignored it. References are made to gentlewomen patients and informants, but not to gentlewomen practitioners.

This is not the only major absence in the college's pursuit of female irregulars. It was, of course, entitled to pursue only those suspected of practising physic, although this is not so restrictive a category, given that even tooth-drawers might give their patients medicines to take internally.[16] Moreover, the overlaps between food, drink and medicine, and the habitual involvement of women in all three, would further broaden the population at risk.[17] It is extremely difficult to estimate the size of this population, but one very rough estimate suggests that there might have been at least 300 women practising medicine in a more or less public manner in London over the ninety-year period, of whom the college failed to notice two-thirds.[18] It is valuable to know anything about as many as 110 female practitioners in a single centre, but this does not give us the base of the metropolitan pyramid of practice, and it is likely that there were at least as many female irregulars as there were men, even though women were more or less excluded from the grocers', apothecaries', and barber-surgeons' corporations just as they were, more categorically, from the college.

Quantitative measures, though necessary, tend also to be lumpen, and attention should also be paid to individual cases. Three main kinds of defensive tactic on the part of the female irregulars may be considered: first, the resort to patronage; second, the existence and extent of a network between male and female practitioners; and third, whether there was a network among female irregulars themselves, reflecting female domains of practice. For all three tactics, but for patronage in particular, we need to note not just the presence but the possible deployment of stereotypes.

One contemporary (and enduring) stereotype held that women were more often ill, and made more frequent use of practitioners, than men. Stereotypes which the college deployed were, first, that it was almost helpless in the face of the brazen proliferation of empirics; second, that old women intruded into medicine; and third, that women, including gentlewomen, were irresistibly attracted to irregular practitioners. The ambiguity of 'attraction' here is intentional, since contemporary comment regularly added sex to the equation. One famous example is the astrological practitioner and protégé of Buckingham (and of his mother), John Lambe, murdered by a London crowd in 1628. One accusation flung at Lambe was that he used charms to procure innocent women for Buckingham's sexual enjoyment.[19] Six months before his death, Lambe was examined by the college at the request of the Bishop of Durham, whose physician Lambe had claimed to be. The college noted of Lambe that his reputation 'had been on the lips of everyone for some time, due to his knowledge of magic, astrology and of other mystic sciences. For which reason he was esteemed by not a few women of rank and was supported on a generous scale at their expense'.[20] Although subscribing to this view, the college rarely substantiated it in particular cases; no reproachful letters to noble-women were inscribed into the Annals over this period. It is worth noting that, on another occasion, the college, possibly with relief, concluded that charming was one thing and the practice of physic another.[21] The only female patrons who impact on the Annals for this period, besides Elizabeth, are Lady Howard, and the Countess of Warwick, both on behalf of male irregulars.[22]

So much for women as patrons. What about patronage networks involving women practitioners? Patronage, especially by the monarch and members of the Privy Council, was an almost intractable force in respect of male irregulars, but it had less influence with respect to females. Only five appear to have had high-ranking patrons. One, yet again, was Mrs Payne; another, Margaret Kennix, who is first mentioned in the Annals as 'a certain ignorant foreign woman' living in Seacoal Lane, was protected by Elizabeth, through Walsingham, as a woman practising simple medicine among the poor and the sole support of an impotent husband and family. Walsingham accused the college of 'hard dealing' towards Kennix, and threatened that such treatment would 'procure further inconvenience therby to yourselfs then perhaps you would be willing shoold fall out'. To give the college its due, it sent a delegation bearing a letter extremely deferential in tone but holding to its position, after which there is no further record.[23] A third woman, like Kennix, uncannily echoes topographically defined figures found in contemporary literature: Mrs Wood-house lived in 'Hogginton' (Hoxton), and claimed to diagnose pregnancy successfully, and to restore bewitched people. However, she was also known as 'the woman of Kingsland', and may have been connected with the lazar-house there; she also prescribed physic, and advised on bloodletting. Six years after the first entry about Mrs Woodhouse, the college resolved to embark on legal proceedings against her. For this, interestingly, they sought the permission of the Lord Treasurer, whom they knew to be currently employing her. He made the revealing response that he was happy for the college to proceed, as Woodhouse had finished treating, in the country, his daughter Lady Montague's dislocated joint, and he no longer needed her services.[24] Here the college's posture of deference is more marked, as is the double standard cheerfully embraced by those in power. Although such cavalier treatment was probably also meted out to male irregulars by their patrons, it seems less likely that a female irregular could establish a secure longer-term connection with a well-placed patron except, possibly, as his mistress. This conclusion perhaps reinforces the earlier supposition about the comparatively low social status of most female irregulars. Social distance did not in the least inhibit the upper classes from using such practitioners, but did limit the amount of protection offered by this relationship.

In a few instances, however, we find something like middling forms of patronage: this brings us to the second tactical area, that of networking between male and female practitioners. The college's own criteria involved a grey area in which practice could be carried on if supervised by a collegiate physician, and female as well as male irregulars took advantage of this. This overlaps with the tactics used by women within a system in which ultimate responsibility was thought to rest with their male connections. Women could thus use patronage networks indirectly, like Mrs Plomley, whose husband was a musician in the King's chapel. This talisman appears to have worked even after the husband died. Mrs Plomley had the male world working for her in other respects: the college found the complainant, a woman, 'querulous and peevish'.[25] In a very few cases, there is the possibility that a female irregular was dealt with leniently because she was related to, or even being employed by, a collegiate physician.

In respect of female–male tactics involving kinship, father–daughter relationships are not so much in evidence as spousal and sibling connections. There are instances both of husbands taking the blame for their wives and of wives shifting the blame on to their husbands, especially if the husband was absent or dead. A few women, like Mrs Arundell, alias Powell, wife of the 'remarkable and well-known impostor' Roger Powell who put up bills and practised in markets, seem to have suffered as a result of the high profile of their husbands; Mrs Powell was, however, supported by a farrier, Mr Hodgeson.[26] An interesting sibling example is Agnes King (alias Tannikin Kommick), who achieved a degree of protection because the Bishop of London and others were prepared to write on behalf of her in association with her brother, also an irregular, Toby Simson.[27] A woman who used the male world and male stereotypes thoroughly was Joan Thumwood. She pleased the college in two ways: she confessed, and she asked for mercy. Moreover, she claimed only to practise among children and infants, an area of practice which collegiate physicians preferred to avoid. Her husband entered into a bond of £20 for her; his own pleas for mercy reduced this by half. Joan's self-defined world of female practice did, however, intersect with the male. Her husband was a member of the Barber-Surgeons' Company, and his pleas on her behalf were supported by three fellow members. Interestingly, both the male Thumwoods in the Company were pleading poverty a few years later.[28] Joan, like some other female irregulars, could have become the effective breadwinner in her family. Others besides Joan, and Mrs Powell, were supported in their appearances before the college by men, whether as patients, neighbours or co-practitioners. As what should be seen as the natural complement to this, female irregulars cited male sources for either their medicines or their mode of practice. Given the frequent impossibility of tracking down these sources, it hardly mattered whether this was a process of claiming protection or of transferring blame. That deflection, like flat denial, could be a successful tactic is indicated by an exasperated aside in the single entry about Rebecca Owen: 'she layes it on his Master [that is, the accuser's master]; So is it double posted, and now nothing donne'.[29]

By comparison with male irregulars, women's actual voices are rarely inscribed even indirectly into the Annals, although their utterances are not infrequently labelled in some way, especially if they could be charged with criticising collegiate physicians. Nonetheless, there is enough in the cases already cited, where many women seem to be calling on the male world for protection, to suggest resistance and even agency. This brings us to the third tactical area: do the Annals reveal a female world of practice, and was this capable of more, or less, resistance to the college's hostility?

It is clear, first of all, that the qualities of anonymity and invisibility which characterise women's work historically could to some extent become advantages in a context such as this. Second, there were areas of practice around women's bodies which the college definitely avoided, of which midwifery is the best defined, but which also seem to have included witchcraft and magic, where the college was brought into cases rather than initiating them. Midwifery is the only area for which the Annals record an institutional form of collective action on the part of female practitioners. But, however much still the concern of women, midwifery was an area of practice which was publicly regulated and in which its practitioners were called upon to perform public functions.[30] Similarly a mixture of public and private was a growth area in which women seemed to be expanding their role, namely the treatment and management of infectious disease. Here again women could either act autonomously or establish a niche for themselves in association with male practitioners, for example in applying mercurial unction to female sufferers from venereal disease. However, as is shown by the almost immediate emergence of negative stereotypes of the plague nurse, these essential and semi-public roles were rapidly circumscribed and made to look as unattractive as possible.[31]

Of particular interest in terms of the dynamic between women and the college was purging. This was a fundamental technique in the physician's armoury which survived the decline of Galenism until well into the twentieth century. It was also a polluting function of the body which for the early years was handled by women, and which for all age groups was intimately connected with the female role in caring, food provision and self-medication.[32] The college's task was the almost impossible one of establishing a distinction between publicly and privately induced forms of purging – hence a wealth of detail in the Annals about numbers of stools, etc. – and of distancing purging as induced by a college fellow from purging induced by a woman. A responsibility staring the college in the face, but which on the whole it may have preferred not to recognise, was that of identifying purging which was intended to induce abortion. Again, these cases tended to be brought to the college rather than the college seeking them out. Assisting the college to some extent, but also indicating the overlap between male and female practice, was the fact that female irregulars in no way restricted themselves to herbs and simples, although a few tried to *excuse* themselves on these grounds. They also bought from apothecaries compounds of antimony and other metals, later described by the collegiate apologist Goodall as 'the most dangerous, venenate and fatal' of all medicines.[33]

Thus, although it is apparent that there existed a stereotype of female practice which was used defensively by both sides, as well as niche areas of female specialism, it is not clear that there was something called female practice which was enough to create an occupational community or even a network, except in the problematic case of midwifery, where an occupational community existed at the cost of being implicated in male networks of authority. A last point to be considered is the extent to which female irregulars came to the college's notice only because they were informed upon by other female irregulars. This is a phenomenon familiar from witchcraft trials, and was of course also an inevitable feature of a society which depended for its policing on the duty of neighbours, enforced or otherwise, to give each other away.[34] In such a context (and the college was sometimes explicit on this point), information became a kind of currency, interchangeable with fines. Like medical practice itself, informing crossed gender boundaries. In the case of the elderly and long-established practitioner Mrs Scarlet, it was her husband who informed on another female irregular, Mrs Sharde, accusing her of giving purges to procure abortion. Mrs Sharde, who claimed a male source of expertise and had two male backers prepared to ask for her to be admitted to practice, informed in her turn upon a third female irregular, Anna Baker.[35] Sometimes it can be inferred that the informing was done to eliminate local competition, as when Mrs Wright was informed on by an apothecary's apprentice, who claimed people flocked to her daily. A kind of negative neighbourhood effect is observable with Anne Hodge of Southwark, a blind woman married to another irregular, David Hodge, who, interestingly, was identified by his accuser as 'the blind woman's husband'. Anne Hodge, unusually, informed on three other irregulars, all women and all 'neighbours of hers'.[36] Although Anne Hodge may have been eliminating rivals, it would be wrong to exclude the possibility that she, a blind woman cut off from many areas of female employment, offered their names in desperation as a defensive tactic against fining or other punishment by the college.

In conclusion, how useful is the concept of community in respect of the actors highlighted by this series of confrontations, given that we have redefined community to mean something like network? Early modern London may be envisaged as a matrix, in which the connections extend horizontally and vertically. The connections are capable of carrying both negative and positive impulses. The college is best seen as a tight-knit but rather lonely corner of the matrix, by its own choice supported mainly by connections upwards which sometimes worked and sometimes did not. With respect to the female irregulars, the college was attempting, often because of impulses coming to it from other directions, to make holes in a part of the matrix at or below its own level, but with which its visible connections were mostly non-existent. Occasionally its conscientious but rather dim probing lit up a part of the matrix where the mesh was close because of factors like geographical location or ethnicity. More complicated, and possibly even more important, was the *invisible* matrix of mentality, of stereotypes, associations, memory, rumour and talk. This can be envisaged as existing alongside the other in all its dimensions, but as making different connections and as being in certain crucial areas denser and more entangling. Thus one can see the collegiate physician positively enmeshed in a network of invisible connections with the female irregulars. His work was like theirs, his vices were like theirs, even his virtues as an individual practitioner resembled those of women. As fast as the college tried to cut these connections they were reformed by satire, gossip and the realities of early life and everyday experience. The female irregulars them-selves were similarly but even more densely enmeshed, partly because of their occupation, but mostly simply because they were women. Some can be seen using such connections defensively, or even turning them to advantage. For the female irregulars, the invisible matrix determined more than did the visible, but this did not prevent them trying, at least as individuals, to build up something more substantial. Like the college, but not by their own choice, their connections with the visible matrix were relatively few but well used.

A final case in illustration. Avis Murrey, summoned before the college in 1626, proved to be the wife of a surgeon whom she falsely claimed to be dead. This gave her claims to a male source of expertise, and to the rights, albeit limited, of the craftsman's widow. Her accuser was a Scottish woman, Isobella Huchinson, the wife of the King's perfumer. Murrey said she was advised by one Blackwell of St Thomas's Hospital, and that she bought purges from an apothecary. She was told to bring in Blackwell's bill to substantiate her defence. At the next meeting, however, all the college could record was that Murrey, Isobella Huchinson and another woman 'made a great dispute here to no purpose'. About a month later the complainant Huchinson returned, to make a cryptic concession towards Murrey. That Huchinson was using her husband, and Murrey the parts she could grasp of the male network, is I hope obvious. What can be inferred, further, is that the female protagonists were all Scottish – still a likely kind of ethnic network at the end of James's reign – and that once things became heated the college was unable to understand a word they said. The college, having had to admit the Scots as honorary English, or

'British', following James's accession, would be chary of admitting this.[37] Instead, it hid behind a stereotype about the confusion and unreliability of women's speech. It was Avis Murrey who effectively came out on top: she deflected punishment by the college using sheer female obfuscation – aided, it should be noted, by some gesture from Huchinson, who had at least, using the college, made Murrey pause. The college, for its part, shied nervously away from female clamour, claiming not to understand it – aware, as it could not fail to be, that its own skills were reducible by contemporaries to talk, and mere opinion.

NOTES

I am grateful to the audience at a 'Gender and History' seminar in Oxford in October 1999 for their comments. I also wish to acknowledge the assistance of Frances White in the preparation of this chapter.

1 Colin Bell and Howard Newby, *Community studies: an introduction to the sociology of the local community* (London, Allen & Unwin, 1971).

2 See, e.g., Beat Kümin, *The shaping of a community: the rise and reformation of the English parish* (Aldershot, Scolar Press, 1996).

3 Cf. David Underdown, 'Community and class: theories of local politics in the English Revolution', in Barbara C. Malament (ed.), *After the Reformation: essays in honour of J. H. Hexter* (Manchester, Manchester University Press, 1980); Richard M. Smith, '"Modernisation" and the corporate village community: some sceptical thoughts', in Alan R. H. Baker and Derek Gregory (eds), *Explorations in historical geography* (Cambridge, Cambridge University Press, 1984); Joyce Ellis, 'A dynamic society: social relations in Newcastle-upon-Tyne, 1660–1760', in Peter Clark (ed.), *The transformation of English provincial towns, 1600–1800* (London, Hutchinson, 1984); Gervase Rosser, 'Communities of parish and guild in the late Middle Ages', and Nick Alldridge, 'Loyalty and identity in Chester parishes, 1540–1640', both in S. J. Wright (ed.), *Parish, church and people* (London, Hutchinson, 1988); Miri Rubin, 'Small groups: identity and solidarity in the late Middle Ages', in Jennifer Kermode (ed.), *Enterprise and individuals in fifteenth-century England* (Stroud, Sutton, 1991); Christine Carpenter, 'Gentry and community in medieval England', *Journal of British Studies* 33 (1994), 340–80.

4 David Sabean, *Power in the blood: popular culture and village discourse in early modern Germany* (Cambridge, Cambridge University Press, 1984); Keith Wrightson, 'The politics of the parish in early modern England', in Paul Griffiths, Adam Fox and Steve Hindle (eds), *The experience of authority in early modern England* (Basingstoke, Macmillan, 1996), especially pp. 11–12.

5 John Bossy, 'Blood and baptism: kinship, community and Christianity in western Europe from the fourteenth to the seventeenth centuries', in Derek Baker (ed.), *Sanctity and secularity: the church and the world* (Oxford, Oxford University Press, 1973); D. V. Kent and F. W. Kent, *Neighbours and neighbourhood in Renaissance Florence* (New York, Augustin, 1982); Annabel Gregory, 'Witchcraft, politics and "good neighbourhood" in early seventeenth-century Rye', *Past and Present* 133 (1991), 31–66; Paul Griffiths *et al.*, 'Population and disease, estrangement and belonging, 1540–1700', in Peter Clark (ed.), *The Cambridge urban history of Britain* II, *1540–1840* (Cambridge University Press, Cambridge, 2000).

6 For greater detail on what follows see Margaret Pelling, *The strength of the opposition: the College of Physicians and irregular medical practitioners in early modern London* (Macmillan, forthcoming). See also *id.*, 'Thoroughly resented? Older women and the medical role in early modern London', in Lynette Hunter and Sarah Hutton (eds), *Women, science and medicine, 1500–1700* (Stroud, Sutton, 1997).

7 See Margaret Pelling, 'Compromised by gender: the role of the male medical practitioner in early modern England', in Hilary Marland and Margaret Pelling (eds), *The task of healing: medicine, religion and gender in England and the Netherlands, 1450–1800* (Rotterdam, Erasmus, 1996).

8 See, for example, Linda Pollock, *With faith and physic: the life of a Tudor gentlewoman* (London, Collins & Brown, 1993); Lynette Hunter, 'Women and domestic medicine: lady experimenters, 1570–1620', in Hunter and Hutton, *Women, science and medicine*.

9 Ronald C. Sawyer, 'Patients, healers and disease in the southeast Midlands, 1597–1634' (unpublished Ph.D. dissertation, University of Wisconsin, Madison, 1986). For Napier see also Michael MacDonald, *Mystical Bedlam: madness, anxiety and healing in seventeenth-century England* (Cambridge, Cambridge University Press, 1981).

10 Sawyer, 'Patients, healers and disease', pp. 146–92, 196.

11 London, Royal College of Physicians, Annals (hereafter Annals), entries between 6 November 1607, pp. 202 ff., and 15 April 1622, p. 152, especially pp. 207, 7 (3 March 1609), 18 (11 December 1609), 19 (12 January 1610). All page references are to the transcript/translation of the Annals, now available on microfilm. I am grateful to the President and Fellows for permission to quote from the Annals.

12 All tabulations appear in full in *Strength of the opposition*.

13 Pelling, 'Thoroughly resented', pp. 67–8, 80–2; Annals, 12 February 1627, p. 220.

14 This is the subject of a chapter in *Strength of the opposition*.

15 Annals, 1 October 1596, p. 103.

16 *Ibid.*, 22 December 1627, p. 214.

17 See Margaret Pelling, *The common lot: sickness, medical occupations and the urban poor in early modern England* (London and New York, Longman, 1998), especially pp. 38–62.

18 Pelling, 'Thoroughly resented', p. 71.

19 *DNB*, article 'John Lambe'.

20 Annals, 18 December 1627, p. 241.

21 *Ibid.*, 16 March 1627, p. 222.

22 *Ibid.*, 7 August 1601, p. 136; 6 August 1596, p. 102.

23 *Ibid.*, 22 December 1581, pp. 5A–7.

24 *Ibid.*, 3 July 1596, p. 101; 14 September 1602, p. 149; 17 September 1602, p. 150.

25 *Ibid.*, 19 February 1608, p. 209. Mrs Plomley was first summoned (unavailingly) 30 March 1607 (p. 193); by July she is described as a widow.

26 *Ibid.*, 30 September 1594, p. 89; 12 April 1611, p. 30. For Roger Powell see 25 September 1590, p. 70; 3 September 1591, p. 73.

27 *Ibid.*, 5 July 1623, p. 171; 11 July 1623, p. 172.

28 *Ibid.*, 22 December 1581, p. 6; 12 January 1582, p. 8; 25 January 1582, p. 8; London, Barbers' Company, Barber-Surgeons' Hall, Minutes, 10 March 1590, 27 March 1597. My thanks to the Master and Wardens for permission to quote from the Minutes.

29 Annals, 3 May 1616, p. 83.

30 *Ibid.*, 10 January 1617, p. 94; 21 February 1617, pp. 95–6; 3 July 1617, pp. 98–100; Hilary Marland (ed.), *The art of midwifery: early modern midwives in Europe* (London and New York, Routledge, 1993); Adrian Wilson, *The making of man-midwifery: childbirth in England, 1660–1770* (London, UCL Press, 1995).

31 Margaret Pelling, 'Nurses and nursekeepers: problems of identification in the early modern period', in *id.*, *The common lot*; Richelle Munkhoff, 'Searchers of the dead: authority, marginality, and the interpretation of plague in England, 1574–1665', *Gender and History* 11 (1999), 1–29.

32 See Pelling, 'Compromised by gender'; Heinrich von Staden, 'Women and dirt', *Helios* 19 (1992), 7–30.

33 Charles Goodall, *The College of Physicians vindicated* (London, 1676), p. 116.

34 Cf., for example, Diane Purkiss, 'Women's stories of witchcraft in early modern England: the house, the body, the child', *Gender and History* 7 (1995), 408–32; J. A. Sharpe, 'Witchcraft and women in seventeenth-century England: some northern evidence', *Continuity and Change* 6 (1991), 179–99.

35 Annals, 6 December 1588, p. 54; 18 April 1589, p. 57; 13 July 1599, p. 124.

36 *Ibid.*, 9 October 1607, p. 201; 5, 12 February 1619, pp. 119–20; 24 September 1619, p. 130.

37 *Ibid.*, 7 April 1626, pp. 203–4; 2 June 1626, p. 205; 7 July 1626, p. 207; 3 January 1606, pp. 179 ff.

Chapter 4

William Blundell and
the networks of Catholic dissent
in post-Reformation England

Margaret Sena

One of the most persistent claims within current historiography on post-Reformation Catholicism maintains that politically the English Catholic gentry were relatively quiescent. By no means his most salient point, this was certainly the view offered in John Bossy's *English Catholic community, 1570–1850*. For Bossy, the disestablishment of Catholics under Elizabeth I inspired a generation of activists to oppose the Protestant regime in various ways. But, following a series of abortive rebellions and clerical in-fighting under Elizabeth I, the Catholic provincial gentry settled into a quiet passivism that was distinguishable from the activism of the clerics. By the aftermath of the Gunpowder Plot, the activist spirit had faded and the gentry turned their attention inwards; they concentrated not on toppling the established religious order but instead on reforming their households, supporting their seminaries for the supply of clerics, and creating the 'little parishes' where post-Reformation Catholicism would flourish.[1] This model of introspective seigneurial Catholicism in the provinces has become a commonplace in most accounts. Even Christopher Haigh, one of the most vocal critics of the Bossy thesis, seemed to concede that the Catholic provincial gentry were an introspective group by the early seventeenth century, which Haigh identified as one source of Catholicism's failure.[2]

Recently some cracks have appeared in this edifice as historians have begun to reassess the political role of Catholics. The research of Caroline Hibbard, for example, has exposed a core of Catholic political activists at the court of Charles I, though she distinguished sharply between these characters and Catholic provincial gentry.[3] In a more recent study of Yorkshire, Michael Questier extended such political engagement to the Catholic laity, where he uncovered a coherent circle of Yorkshire papists who sought to undermine the Protestant policies of the Elizabethan regime by supporting the accession of James I. Finally, in a study of Sir Thomas Tresham, Sandeep Kaushik has criticised the rigid distinctions between Catholic loyalism and resistance altogether, speaking instead of a 'range of options' through which even a quintessential Catholic 'loyalist' like Tresham could express political opposition to the Elizabethan regime.[4]

In this chapter, I want to question some of the reigning orthodoxies concerning the supposedly introspective and isolated Catholic gentry. My purpose is not only to move beyond the conceptual limitations of the frustrating categories of 'loyalist' and 'traitor' that Kaushik has identified, but also to raise more fundamental objections against an approach that imposes a set of analytical criteria that seem inappropriate for understanding Catholic dissent under a Protestant regime. Most studies have attempted to gauge the political opposition of the Catholic laity either by looking exclusively for acts of violence or by insisting upon modes of political action practised by those who shared both access and ideology with the established regime. By defining 'political activism' in this narrow sense, historians have missed the other ways that Catholics challenged political power. Likewise, by looking only to institutions and public venues such as Parliament, election addresses and jury charges, they have overlooked the alternative means of expressing opposition to the policies of the Protestant state.

This chapter explores the political outlook and activities of the Catholic provincial gentry by examining the religious networks of William Blundell of Little Crosby in Lancashire. The Blundells are, of course, familiar characters in post-Reformation Catholic history, known both for their staunch recusancy and their rich collection of family papers. More recently they have also been taken to epitomise the isolated and introspective existence which historians have seen as typical of the Catholic provincial gentry. For Bossy, Blundell was the first of a series of post-Reformation Catholic patriarchs who were 'satisfied with the pattern of their lives, intent on country concerns, and convinced that the world would get on all right if only people would let it alone', while for Christopher Haigh, though Blundell clearly 'resisted' the Reformation, his religious outlook and networks appeared to be similarly confined to Lancashire.[5] This chapter takes a very different view of this northern gentleman, arguing that many of Blundell's actions and writings demonstrate a highly engaged, activist role within the underground Catholic church in England. The first section will examine what we can learn about Blundell's political alliances and concerns under Elizabeth I. The second focuses on how these concerns and alliances developed after the accession of James I. My aim here is not to dismiss the interpretative scheme of Bossy's great study, *The English Catholic community, 1570–1850*. Rather, I would like to pose some new questions based on the insights of recent work on religious networks and communities of other groups in England.[6] I would like to suggest that English Catholics can be viewed as a coherent 'community' in more than sociological terms.

William Blundell was born in 1560 as the first son and heir of Richard Blundell, a gentleman whose estate comprised the manor and lands around Little Crosby, a village nestled on the south-western coast of Lancashire.[7] As Haigh showed in his study of the county, Richard Blundell remained in close contact with the former Marian establishment during the first decades of Elizabeth I's reign, despite his early conformity. At least four local parish clerks who renounced their posts in the early 1560s spent time at Crosby Hall, while an informer reported that Richard Blundell had signed an oath of papal allegiance in 1566 with other gentlemen at the request of Nicholas Sander.[8] As Haigh and others have suggested, it is possible that Blundell's connections with Elizabethan exiles marked Little Crosby as a base for seminary priests. Soon after their arrival in the area Richard Blundell sheltered missionaries at his estate, and may have sent William to Douai College for his education.[9] Some of these missionaries, such as James Ford and Robert Woodroffe, were from Lancashire families. Others had taken more circuitous routes to the county. Christopher Small was born in Cornwall, educated at Oxford and ordained at Rheims before arriving in the north.[10] Thomas Bell, the most famous missionary connected with the Blundell estate, arrived from Yorkshire in 1582–83, where he had organised networks of safe houses with other missionary priests.[11]

Whether the Marian priests or the missionaries played a more formative role in shaping the religious life of young William Blundell is perhaps a moot point. What is significant is that, once these clerical connections were established, the religion of the Blundell household was much more elaborate than the simple procurement of Roman rites and sacraments. Our best source concerning the activities of the family during the 1580s is the report sent by Thomas Bell to the Earl of Derby upon his capture in 1592. Bell described a highly social and participatory religion in which several families gathered together at a designated estate, where 'manie tymes 10 to 12 Priestes ... mett ... on one day' and 'great multitudes of people flocked togeather to heare masses'.[12] The events themselves could be lengthy affairs: Bell claimed they consisted of multiple masses 'longe [in] solemnitye', lasting through the afternoon, after which 'preaching [was] annexed thereunto', followed by confessions, discussions about religious matters, and formal reconciliations with Rome.[13] Crosby Hall often served as the meeting place for these clandestine gatherings, and it was there that William Blundell associated with other gentry families from nearby parishes. Edward Stanley, the son of Peter Stanley of More Hall in Aughton parish, travelled to Little Crosby to hear masses and sermons, while Lawrence Ireland of Lydiate was reconciled there.[14] In 1585 there was a grand celebration for William Blundell's marriage to Emilia Norris, daughter of Sir William Norris's heir at Speake, another gentleman suspected of taking a papal oath in the 1560s. Several priests and gentlemen attended the event. It featured a mass, confession for the bride and a wedding sermon preached by Bell.[15]

One could dismiss the ties with neighbouring Catholic gentry and seminary priests as a peculiarity of Lancashire, a place where Protestantism supposedly made little progress and recusant numbers were comparatively high. But there was another feature of Blundell's religious experience that extended his Catholic connections: his imprisonment for violating Elizabethan statutes. Like others in his generation, Blundell spent time in prison for harbouring priests during the 1590s, an experience he described in his commonplace book entitled the 'Great Hodge Podge'.[16] Blundell explained that in 1590 the authorities searched Crosby Hall and discovered the seminary priest, Robert Woodroffe. William and his father were imprisoned at Lancaster Castle, where they remained until Richard's death in 1592. William was released shortly afterwards but taken into custody again when new evidence of his missionary connections surfaced in Bell's report. He was sent to London and examined before Archbishop Whitgift and later imprisoned at the Gatehouse prison until 1595.[17]

Some historians have recently drawn attention to prisons as important centres of missionary evangelism, where lax regulation occasionally allowed Catholic priests and lay zealots to create sites of 'religious activity and conflict' during their confinement.[18] Blundell's experience at Lancaster Castle supports the picture of close associations between Catholics in the prisons. At Lancaster Castle William and his father met two gentlemen already recognised by the mission leadership as lay heroes: Henry Latham of Mosborough, whose flight from Lancashire in 1585 had earned him recognition in the *Concertatio Ecclesiae Catholicae in Anglia*, and Richard Worthington of Blanscough, the father of the future president of Douai College.[19] Richard Blundell had described a close relationship between these gentlemen prisoners, referring to Worthington as 'one of our deare friends' and expressing concern about Latham's health.[20] And while Blundell never elaborated on his company at the Gatehouse, the authorities transported him to London with Henry Latham.[21]

More important, Blundell described his experience in prison in the same ideological terms as other self-professed Catholics in the 1590s. Though Blundell wrote his narrative retrospectively, it is significant that he referred to his imprisonment in the 1590s as 'persecution' for adherence to the Catholic religion.[22] 'Persecution' was an important theme in the polemical campaign waged by Catholic political activists against the Protestant regime. Writers like Robert Parsons and Thomas Hide frequently criticised the Queen's government for 'persecuting' Catholic subjects solely on the basis of their religion. And, while they paid special attention to the treason laws, these writers defined 'persecution' as any statute which deprived subjects of their goods or liberties for religion.[23] That Blundell and other lay people also employed these concepts in the 1590s suggests they held the same ideological concerns as the missionaries.

By the mid-1590s Blundell had established diverse networks as institutional supports for his participation in this illegal religion. His local network of priests, gentry families and their servants conformed – but was not limited to – the standard model of provincial Catholicism. Yet Blundell also had extensive personal and intellectual connections with Catholics across England. An important event took place at the close of Elizabeth I's reign which neatly illustrates how much Blundell relied on these networks. In 1598 the Privy Council directed officials in the provinces to collect payment from the kingdom's wealthiest recusants for the supply of the Queen's light horse regiments in Ireland.[24] Royal messengers delivered notification letters with little difficulty in other counties. In Lancashire, however, armed bandits assaulted them. When local authorities searched the homes of those scheduled to pay the light horse levy, they could locate only four of the twenty-five persons named in the letters. A party led by Sir Richard Mollineux, John Nutter, parson of Sefton, and Richard Vaughan, the new Bishop of Chester, searched Crosby Hall but could not locate William Blundell.[25] Instead they arrested Emilia Blundell, who, for the next six months, was repeatedly examined and imprisoned at Sefton and Chester. In May 1599 she also fled the county while in the custody of her brother, Edward Norris.[26]

Several historians have interpreted these events as a local conflict between Crown officers and a dominant faction of recusant gentry that included William Blundell.[27] In his escape from the county Blundell undoubtedly relied upon his local networks of support, after all. He admitted to hiding 'secretly att Countrie houses some 3 quarters of a yeare' before leaving Lancashire, and several other clues suggest co-operation with his friends and kin. Some of the other fugitives, like Henry Lathom, Blundell knew personally from his experience in prison. Others were acquaintances from the days of clandestine worship in the 1580s.[28] The central figures in Blundell's networks were his in-laws, the Norrises. Emilia Blundell had been at the home of William Norris, her brother, when she escaped the region, while tenants at her home estate were suspected of violently attacking several figures instrumental in the pursuit of William Blundell and the other fugitives a few years before.[29]

At the same time, these local networks offered protection and support in other counties, for the events make little sense without the context of this gentleman's connections with the broader networks of Catholics that existed by the 1590s. Thus, from connections through family and friends in his county, Blundell was able to travel safely between country houses as far away as Wales and Staffordshire.[30] He also seems to have had some connections in London. In his autobiographical narrative he described a five-week stay in the capital during his unsuccessful efforts to receive a pardon from the Queen.[31]

Aside from the networks of papists in Lancashire and other places, it was Blundell's commitment to the ideological community of Catholics that informed his decision to flee the authorities. We can learn something about his motives from a ballad he wrote and copied into the 'Great Hodge Podge'. He called his song 'a dittie ... made upon the persecution made in Sefton parish, Especially by Vahon Bishop of Chester, and Nutter, parson of Sefton'.[32] For Blundell, his pursuit by Richard Vaughan and John Nutter represented scenes adapted from the ecclesiastical script of persecution of the early Christians, and in which missionaries had often exhorted lay people such as Blundell to suffer 'temporal afflictions' or else to flee.[33] Casting the Lancashire clerics into the roles of Diocletian and Nero, Blundell protested that authorities pursued him solely for his 'conscience' in religion:

> Youe that present are, take of us some pitie,
> who in dolefull wyse shew our greiffe in songe,
> Mourne with us a whyle, yee that hear this Dittie
> Made to moane ourselves of receaved wronge,
>
> ...
>
> for our Conscience sake, they pursue or take
> those whom they suspect or knowe
> Ancient truthe affectinge new fond faithes reiecting,
> such to prisons they do hale[34]

Besides drawing parallels between his experiences in Lancashire and the 'persecution' of the early Christians, Blundell maintained that his experience was shared by other Catholics in England. His use of the collective voice in this song conveyed a distinct sense of the shared experience of a community of Elizabethan Catholics, moving his discussion from personal tragedy to collective refrain:

> Husbands and their wives parted are a sunder
> parents severde are from their children deare;
> servants men and mayds forced are a number
> service newe to seeke, God, not they, knowes wheare.[35]

Like the clerical polemicists, Blundell combined criticism of the regime's policies with bold assertions that Catholicism represented the 'true religion' of England. He articulated the point most clearly in references to St Austin of Canterbury, a character who symbolised the legitimate Roman succession to Canterbury in the Romanist interpretation of English ecclesiastical history.[36] In lines reminiscent of Campion's epitaph, Blundell directly equated his legal problems with the maintenance of St Austin's religion:

> all the countrie talketh
> everie way one walketh
> what in Sefton wee endure

> for no strange opinion
> but that ould Religion
> Austin planted here most sure[37]

The various Catholic networks that Blundell created during the reign of Elizabeth I point to the same tenuous relationship with the Protestant government that scholars have repeatedly emphasised in discussions about other dissenting groups in this period. On the one hand, the extensive support networks and strong ideological commitments reveal a coherent community of English Catholics opposed to the Queen's government and policies. And yet to label Blundell a representative of a Catholic opposition to the Elizabethan government would be too simplistic. Blundell may have opposed the Queen's officials in Lancashire, but he also tried unsuccessfully to secure a pardon from the Queen's council in London, surely a sign of his commitment to operating within the political process. It was only when this strategy failed that Blundell decided to wait for the Queen's death in hope of favour under the new Stuart regime.

Some historians have posited an important shift in the political sensibilities of the Catholic gentry under the early Stuarts, claiming that provincial gentlemen successfully imposed their own strictly pastoral version of the English mission against the potentially subversive aims of the clerics. And yet, in Blundell's experience, these were the years when he truly established himself as a recognised leader of Catholics. In part, he achieved this reputation through his work as a propagandist and proselytiser. Although this gentleman could list only a single printed broadsheet among his published works, Blundell was a poet whose verse was 'published' in the scribal medium.[38] Aside from the 'persecution dittie', there are seventeen additional ballads that Blundell wrote and copied into the 'Great Hodge Podge'.[39] Before looking at the circulation of these ballads, let us first consider their message.

Many of the ballads borrowed heavily from the arguments, positions and conflictual language employed by contemporary Catholic polemicists. One of the most prominent of Blundell's arguments asserted that the nation should return to the Church of Rome because it was the 'true religion' of England. He denounced the doctrines of the Church of England as heretical and false, representing Protestantism as a religion of sectarian novelty. In one song he exploited the familiar refrain of 'welladay' to lament the state's religious policies:

> Alacke Walladay, Walladay, & Walladay,
> Alacke & Walladay, Lord for thy pitie,
> Alacke & Walladay, lay wee our mirth away,
> let us do watche & pray in towne & Citie
>
> ...

> Gods Churche is nowe reprovde walladaye walladaye
> gods Churche is nowe reprovde, Lorde for thy pittie
> gods Church is nowe reprovde, fonde faithes & sects are lovde
> wherby gods wrath is movde in towne & Citie[40]

It was common in Catholic controversial literature to refer to all Protestants as 'sectaries' in order to emphasise the unity within the Roman communion and, conversely, the heretical break that Protestants had made from that union. Catholic writers often pointed to internal disputes within the Church of England as evidence of their heresy. In the remaining verses of this song, Blundell made similar charges about the national church:

> These sects thoughe they discorde, walladaye, walladaye:
> these sects thoughe they discorde Lorde for they pittie
> these sects thoughe they discorde, father all one gods worde.
> O turne theire harts good Lorde, in towne & Cittie
>
> …
>
> All broods of everie secte walladaye walladaye
> all breeds of everie sect lorde for thy pittie
> all broods of everie secte, hould sure them selves electe
> gods Lawes tho they reiecte in towne & citie[41]

In another ballad Blundell returned to the theme of 'persecution', although here the accusations against the Protestant regime were not drawn specifically from his experiences in Lancashire during the 1590s. Blundell voiced instead more general complaints about the unjust imprisonment of Catholics throughout England:

> Wee Catholiks tormented sore, with heresies fowle railinge tonge,
> with prisons, tortures, losse of goodes, of lands yea lyves, even theeves amonge,
> doo crave with harts surcharg'd with grieffe,
> of thee (Sweet Jesu) some relieffe[42]

Again, Blundell directly equated those prosecuted under the regime's anti-Catholic statutes with the upholders of true religion. Suffering under such prosecution directly enlisted one in the ongoing struggle between the forces of true faith and the forces of heresy:

> Our cause is thyne, and thyne are wee
> whoe from thy truth refuse to slyde
> our faithe thy trueth, true faith the cause
> for which these garboyles wee abyde
> true faith I say, as plaine appears
> to all whoe shutt not eyes and ears
>
> To all whoe shutte not eyes and ears
> gainst fathers scriptures, Church, and thee;
> whoe built thy church as Doctors all,

> with scriptures playnlie doe agree
> not soone to falle upon the sande
> but on a Rocke, stile sure to stande[43]

Blundell called for national religious change once more in what is probably his most famous work, a ballad that began with the opening line 'the tyme hath been'. Less overtly polemical than those discussed above, the verses in this ballad operated instead as a series of neat antitheticals between the 'old' and 'new' religion:

> The Tyme hath been wee hadd one faith
> And strode aright one ancient path
> The tyme is now that each man may
> See newe Religions coyn'd eich day
>
> Sweet Jesu with thy mother mylde
> Sweet Virgine mother with thy childe
> Angells and Saintes of each degree
> redresse our Contrees miserie[44]

It is tempting to interpret this ballad as a nostalgic plea for Marian religious policies. But we should recall that Blundell was born in 1560, and thus had no personal recollection of religion under Mary. Like his clerical contemporaries, Blundell employed words like 'novellers' and 'new' to undermine Protestant claims to ecclesiastical antiquity, an important mark of a true Christian church. Thus the following verses did not merely support a 'return' to the old religion. They upheld key points of Roman doctrine, ecclesiology and soteriology. On the important controversial question of whether Roman sacraments conveyed grace directly, for example, Blundell insisted:

> The tyme hath been men did beleeve
> gods Sacraments his grace did give
> they tyme is nowe men say they are
> uncertaine signes and tokens bare
> Sweet Jesu, &c.[45]

Similarly, on the issue of clerical marriage and the support of female religious orders, he argued:

> The tyme hath been, men would live chast
> and soe could maids, that vowes had past
> the tyme is nowe that gifte is done
> new gospellers such gifte have none
> Sweet Jesu, &c. [46]

What held Blundell's poem together and made it sound like a collective petition was the refrain that punctuated every stanza. And despite the semantic instability of a word like 'country' in this period, its inclusion alongside the previous critiques concerning specific aspects of the Church of England suggests that Blundell's lines articulated a national plea to change the state's religious policies:

> Sweet Jesu with thy mother mylde
> Sweet Virgine mother with thy childe
> Angells and Saintes of each degree
> redresse our Contrees miserie[47]

Who was the audience for these ballads? The refrains which repeatedly enjoined listeners to 'redresse our contries miserie' or to 'watch and pray in towne and citie' encouraged participation, indicating that Blundell's ballads were likely performed before a larger audience than the members of his own extended household.[48] Although it would be very difficult to reconstruct the social composition of that audience, we do know that the songs were accessible to the more humble levels of society. Sung ballads were a 'socially inclusive' medium for contemporaries, even though few would identify them as a genre exclusive to the 'people'.[49] Can we tell anything about the occasions on which these ballads would have been sung? Blundell copied the songs alongside other religious carols, so it seems probable that they were intended to be sung on feast days. We have at least one contemporary report of non-liturgical singing at feast day gatherings from the biographer of the Benedictine missioner Ambrose Barlow. In the 1620s he described Christmas celebrations in which Catholics 'spent the night modestly and devoutly, sometimes in prayer before the altar, otherwiles singing devout songs by the fireside'.[50] To be sure, Barlow was famous for his mission among the rural poor, but the fact that Blundell utilised a form like the ballad to broadcast the positions of the misssionary leadership shows how committed Catholics identified closely with the aims of their evangelising priests.

There was also a point when Blundell's audience ceased to be strictly limited to his locality, for some of his poetry did eventually find a wider audience. By the 1630s his verses on 'the tyme hath been' were circulating widely in manuscript. The poem found its way into the verse miscellany of the Yorkshire gentlewoman Margaret Bellasis, while another reader copied out Blundell's verses in the form of a pocket manuscript.[51] A decade earlier, the Laudian bishop Richard Corbett assumed his audience's familiarity with Blundell's poem enough to rely on its opening line as a synonym for popish nostalgia:

> But since of late Elizabeth
> And later James came in
> They never daun'd on any heath
> As when *the time hath bin*[52]

It would be difficult to trace precisely how Blundell's ballad made its way to the Bellasis household or to readers who copied out the verses. The Bellasis family was a notable Catholic family in Yorkshire, but we should be careful not to assume too much of a 'secret society' of Catholics.[53] As Bellany has noted in his study of politically charged verse libels, the transmission of sensitive material was helped along by entrepreneurial distributors but also through informal social contact as friends shared news and information with one other.[54] But if Blundell's views are indicative of those being expressed privately, there were political implications behind the gatherings of provincial Catholics described in Bossy's *English Catholic community.*

Blundell enhanced his local reputation as a lay leader through other activities as well. In 1611 he ordered his tenants to enclose a portion of his estate known as the 'Harkirke' to provide a burial ground for recusants when local clerics began to refuse them at parish churches.[55] His motives were apparently connected with his own notion of maintaining a godly community of Catholics. As he explained in a private account, 'havinge hearde that Catholicke Recusants were prohibited to bee buried at their Parishe Church, bethought mee (myself through God's grace beinge also a Catholique) where were best to make readie in this my village of Litle Crosbie a place fitt to burie such Catholiques either of myne owne howse or of the Neighbourhoode as should departe this lyfe duringe the tyme of these troubles'.[56] By 1629 more than eighty people had been buried there.

It is important to understand how Blundell's local prominence exceeded the 'seigneurial' duties normally ascribed to Catholic gentleman. The burial register he kept indicates that his reputation clearly extended beyond his own neighbourhood; the Harkirk drew people from towns and parishes along the Merseyside. The friends of Richard Holland carried his body some six miles from Prescot after his own parish clergy refused it. Another group transported bodies from Orrell and Thornton, while others trudged seven miles from Liverpool to Little Crosby.[57] Even those who saw the Harkirk as a dangerous institution in the service of popery confirmed its local fame. In the 1620s the parson of Sefton noted that local papists called the Harkirk the 'new church yard', while some of his parishioners admitted creeping on to Blundell's estate at night to 'see the grave stones and other monuments which ... [they] had often heard reported of'.[58] Blundell also seems to have carved out his position in direct opposition to the roles that Protestant conformists could play in county government as local clergy, Parliament men or 'godly' magistrates. Thus, where delivering a jury charge or parliamentary election address was not a possibility for this recusant gentleman, Blundell continued to play an important role in his locality as someone who provided support and assistance to Catholics.

For all his campaigns to promote his religion among the lower orders in neighbouring parishes, Blundell retained a keen interest in the religious and political struggles between Protestants and Catholics in England in the 1620s. References in the pages of the 'Great Hodge Podge' indicate that Blundell was aware of events taking place in his home county as well as in London and on the Continent. To illustrate the point, I would now like to examine three in more detail.

One of the items Blundell copied into the 'Great Hodge Podge' was a newsletter or 'separate' entitled 'A true relation of the falle of the howse at Blackfreers', containing a detailed report of the collapse of a roomful of people attending a Jesuit sermon at the French ambassador's residence at London in 1623. As Alexandra Walsham has shown, this event generated much discussion among contemporaries. For many zealous Protestants the accident appeared to be a sign of God's providence against the papists during the tense negotiations for a marriage treaty with Catholic Spain.[59] Catholic polemicists also joined in these debates over the religious and political meanings of this event, although John Floyd's *A word of comfort ... concerning the late lamentable accident ... in the Black-friars* is the only known Catholic printed work.[60]

Like Floyd's tract, Blundell's 'true relation' reprocessed this event into a confirmation of the Roman church and its missionaries, though the author cast aside scriptural justifications and focused instead on the details of the accident itself. Thus where Protestant accounts had described the priest Robert Drury processing mechanically into the room and reading the gospel, Blundell's account described Drury's sermon as a highly charged, evangelical event:

> To relate unto you with what spirite & religious zeale the goodman endeavoured to ingraffe in his harts true Christian virtue and pietie, goeth farre beyond my Colde expression ... hee had only ended the first poynt when as the whole Auditorie seemed to dissolve into teares and as divers who escaped have tould mee sithence, you might have hearde a generall sighing and knocking of breasts throughe the whole Company: an evident signe of the working of Gods holy spirite.[61]

From this point, the author proceeded to the crux of this contested event: the accusations circulating among Protestants that the Jesuit preacher, Robert Drury, had provoked God's vengeance by maligning their religion before his death. One rumour circulating among Protestants contended that Drury had mocked the recent death of a London minister, Thomas Sutton.[62] The author of Blundell's letter knew of these reports and explicitly denied them. 'So farre was hee from medling with Mr. Suttons death (as some falsly surmised) or using iniurious speeches against Protestants or their Religion,' he explained, that Drury had been instructing his audience to 'make actes of Contrition' in the moments before the room collapsed.[63] The defence of Drury's sermon was accompanied by a general rehabilitation of the missionary priests killed in the accident. The author described Drury's learning as 'singular', while noting that William Whittingham was called 'the poore mans Priest' by those who knew him best.[64] The separate concluded by relating incidents where God's justice could be seen working in the favor of Catholics, in France in 1608 and at Wells under Elizabeth I.[65]

Another letter in Blundell's collection, 'the Copie of lettre sent to Mr. Lewes, preacher at Ormschurche ... Concerning his late book against the Masse', dealt more with local personalities.[66] 'Mr. Lewes' mostly likely referred to John Lewis, one of the King's preachers at the nearby parish of Ormskirk, while his 'book against the Masse' was probably his 1624 publication, *Melchizedech's antitype ... with a scrutiny of the mass*.[67] The copy purported to be a letter sent to John Lewis by a 'Protestant frend', who wrote offering constructive criticism on *Melchizedech's antitype*. Following the initial pleasantries, however, this letter degenerated into vitriolic censure of the book. The main thrust of the author's complaint was that *Melchizedech's antitype* overflowed with errors and mistakes. At several points, Lewis had 'disent[ed] from the undenyable assertions of our ... much more learned, Protestant brethren'.[68] Where Lewis had attacked the Roman mass and the presumption of Romish clerics, the author berated Lewis that his point was 'only a Chimericall Idea begotten and borne of your owne brayne to rayse your booke (the Papists will say) to some Omnipotent volume'.[69] In his attempt to refute transubstantiation, the author corrected Lewis again. 'As Mr. Whittaker sayth,' he explained, 'wee only dispute of the *manner* of the presence of Christs body.'[70] The 'Protestant frend' concluded bluntly that John Lewis should 'let the world take notice of you for an active Gallant, since it Cannot for a deepe Divine'.[71]

Blundell also copied a ballad entitled 'The Invention of the new ghospell', a song that mercilessly lampooned Martin Luther. Luther may appear to be a surprising object of ridicule in the 1620s, but this song would have carried an important ecclesiological message for contemporaries. As Anthony Milton and others have pointed out, Martin Luther loomed large in the debates over succession between the institutional churches of England and Rome, and Catholic writers frequently attacked Luther as a foreign interloper whose followers had taken over the English church.[72] Attacks upon the 'religion of Luther' implied a series of criticisms against the legitimacy of the English national church. In Blundell's ballad, a foolish and angry Martin Luther stumbles across 'the new ghospell' of Protestantism:

> Shall I tell you by what slighte
> the new ghospell Came to lighte?
> which before never did appeare
> in our worlds wyde hemisphere.
>
> Luther, tooke a great displeasure
> and was angrie owte of measure,

to his passions wholy bent,
thus hee shapt a male content.

...

For on pleasure & delighte
hee had fixte his appetites:
on the earthe bending his looke
headlong thus his waye hee tooke.

hee could not well see the Waye,
for the worlde had litle day
all were in obscuritie,
in the mist of Papistrie.[73]

This theme was continued throughout, as the ballad proceeded to deride the Lutheran tradition of clerical marriage as the convenient rationalisation for the Reformer's selfish lust for Katherine Von Bora. What would have enhanced the sarcasm of this message for contemporary audiences was its setting to the familiar tune of 'shall I wrastle in despayre', a melody that normally accompanied a popular love ballad.[74] Sung to this tune, the basis of clerical marriage in the Protestant churches was reduced to a trifling love story between a fallen monk and nun:

[Lances] eyes, that pierceth stones,
hee had; for hee made noe bones
to pierce quyte the Cloysters walls
& his Catherin owt hee Calls

her veyle too, hung in her eyes.
whereupon Luther once espyes
offe he takes it, & then shee
saw the light as well as hee.

Doe not then the truthe denye
being made cleare the mistie skye
& the ghospell by this slight
being thus strangelie brought to light.

Whylst hee view'd his lovely Catherin
whom hee deem'd for venus patern,
did not Luther then see more
then could all the world before?[75]

Who was responsible for sending these items to Blundell? Although precise authorship is difficult to determine, the arguments they contain suggest that all three were written by committed Catholics. The Blackfriars separate and the Luther ballad explicitly defended the Roman religion as the true religion of England. And, despite some contradictory appearances, the Lewis libel was probably penned by a Catholic as well. Of course, libels written against ministers had become commonplace in English towns and parishes in the 1620s.[76] But the particular strategy of refuting opponents with quotations taken from their own brethren had been popularised by the Catholic polemicist 'John Brereley, Priest'.[77] Thus while it is conceivable that a 'Protestant frend' actually wrote to John Lewis, it is more likely that the author intended this letter as a public airing of the divisions among English Protestants. It is quite probable, then, that all Blundell's letters were written by Catholics. There is no reason to assume clerical authorship of all three of the letters, although the author's extensive knowledge about the careers of Drury and Whittingham suggests that a missionary priest wrote the Blackfriars separate.

What is more significant for our purposes is not only that Blundell retained his missionary contacts in this period, but that his communication networks ultimately extended beyond clerics ministering in Lancashire.[78] Blundell never explicitly described how he acquired these newsletters and separates, but all three of the items discussed show signs of wider circulation. The Lewis libel contained a note that 'the incorrectness ... proceeds from the absence of the author and the want of a better scribe', while the Blackfriars author directed his energies towards a more public audience, writing 'for the edification of all devoute Catholickes [and] satisfaction of all moderate Protestants' and for a recipient familiar enough with London personalities to understand the references made to the minister Thomas Sutton.[79] The Luther ballad mimicked the format of a broadside ballad and employed a recognisable tune that encouraged wider circulation.[80]

Beyond the significance of his extensive clerical networks, Blundell's collection of letters in the 'Great Hodge Podge' suggests an awareness of national politics that is not often attributed to provincial Catholics. Of course, when compared with the 'news' collections kept by Protestant figures such as William Davenport or Walter Yonge, it is clear that Blundell's interests were vastly different. Noticeably absent from the 'Great Hodge Podge' are the parliamentary speeches, the court gossip or the reports of state trials which are the more obvious indicators of political awareness. Nevertheless, it would be wrong to interpret Blundell's interest in the Blackfriars accident, the reputation of the minister John Lewis or a ballad about Martin Luther as simply an 'introspective' or 'narrow' interest in national religious politics. One can read the Blackfriars letter as words of support following the collapse of the Spanish match, while his attention to the Lewis libel reflected not only Blundell's interest in local scandals and ecclesiastical politics, but also the role that this Ormskirk minister played in publishing *Melchizedech's antitype* in the polemical campaigns against papists in 1624 following the 'blessed revolution' in English politics. Again this underlines that while Blundell's political concerns do not readily conform to the issues most familiar to early Stuart historians, this gentleman was nevertheless engaged in national discussions about religion and politics.

There is little explicit evidence of Blundell's personal disappointment after the failure of negotiators to incorporate some measure of English Catholic toleration into the French marriage treaty of 1624. But certainly it is telling that, when violence did erupt again at Little Crosby, the occasion was the arrival of the local authorities to prosecute the reactivated laws against recusants. For Blundell, this entailed the confiscation of his cattle. In 1627, when local authorities arrived at Blundell's estate to confiscate his property, an armed struggle broke out between his tenants and the sheriff's men. As a result of this violence, Sir Ralph Assheton, the sheriff of the county, summoned Blundell to Star Chamber for inciting a riot and maintaining the Harkirk burial ground.[81] Like his troubles in 1598, Blundell's struggles with the local authorities represented a battle not between the government and Catholics in monolithic terms, but between Assheton, a notable puritan gentleman, against the papist Blundell, who now found himself on the defensive.[82] But with the rise of such anti-puritan figures in the Caroline government, the tide soon turned against Assheton. The opportunities created by Charles I's commitment to order soon manifested itself in a variety of ways that benefited Blundell. First, though Assheton eventually won his suit and Blundell was ordered to pay a large fine of £2,500, Lord Weston later reduced the amount to £250. Blundell also benefited from the Wentworth Commission, which enabled him to compound his debts, ensuring that Crosby Hall would pass to his grandson William Blundell, the future Cavalier, in 1638, since Blundell's eldest son and heir, Nicholas, had suffered an early death.[83] Though we know little about the early career of William Blundell the future Cavalier, his inheritance probably aided his entry into a public career which his grandfather never enjoyed. When King Charles I allowed papists to join his forces against the Scots, Blundell's grandson readily enlisted himself and, in doing so, continued his grandfather's attempts to reintegrate Catholics into the political life of England.[84]

In conclusion, Blundell appears as an engaged, active member of this community of English Catholics. His activist, zealous notion of the true Catholic religion translated into a direct (and sometimes violent) battle with his Protestant enemies. His position assumed a number of roles: as a violent resistor of arrest, as an evangelist for his religious opinions, as makeshift rector for his burial ground, and as a producer and consumer of news and information concerning his religion. These were subtle strategies that allowed him to challenge the Protestant regime outside the more familiar institutions of political expression that excluded this gentleman, like the assize court speech, the election address, and the parliamentary oration. In fact, one could draw an instructive parallel between Blundell's actions from the 1590s onwards with puritan motives and strategies during the 1630s, when the absence of a parliamentary forum and restrictions on preaching forced many to conduct campaigns of godly reform through private discussions and illicit preaching.[85] While we cannot point to any overt resistance to the continued Protestant policies of the Elizabethan and Jacobean regimes, it remains difficult to support the view that Catholics like Blundell confined their interests simply to matters of personal toleration.

For the reader who would point to Blundell's atypicality, some points must be made. We would be wrong in assuming that Blundell represented a monolithic Catholic oppositionist force. Blundell was clearly a zealot, but his activism is nevertheless instructive in pointing to the variegated range of political stances that this could encompass. Of course, some might argue that Blundell hailed from Lancashire, from a county where Catholic networks were thick on the ground and which produced a more congenial setting for Blundell's activities than elsewhere. I would first suggest that the example of William Blundell demonstrates just how heated these confessional battles in that county could be, while the evidence of manuscript circulation points to a much wider world of co-religionist communication than the area around Little Crosby.

The picture of gentry Catholicism that emerges from this study is thus not the religion confined to households, sacraments, fast and feast. It began with these, but extended those duties, assuming supplementary structures like ballad preaching, separate writing, burial ground maintenance. I want to suggest that such activities reveal a religion that resembles less an English Catholic separatist community and more a loosely organised threat to the regime, hindered though it was by the logistical problems of operating under a Protestant regime. Whether we can accurately describe that opposition as resembling more closely the political choices represented by the contemporary solutions of confessional pluralism offered by tolerationist solutions (as the French Huguenots), or an English church that followed ultramontane or episcopal models of Roman church government, or whether this gentleman could have preferred his kingdom to have been reconquered by Spanish imperial forces, is probably impossible to say. We can say, however, that the politically engaged model of provincial gentry Catholicism goes a long way to explain the networks of lay Catholics to whom the Jesuits appealed in 1639 for contributions against the Scots.[86]

NOTES

Versions of this chapter were presented at the Religious History of Britain seminar at the Institute of Historical Research and at the Conference on the Long Reformation at Princeton University. I am grateful for all the participants' insightful questions and comments, and especially to Peter Lake, Michael Questier and Robert Crews, who generously helped to edit various drafts.

1 This characterisation is based on John Bossy, *The English Catholic community, 1570–1850* (London, Longman, 1975); *id.*, 'The character of Elizabethan Catholicism', *Past and Present* 21 (1962) 39–59; *id.*, 'The English Catholic community, 1603–25', in Alan G. R. Smith (ed.), *The reign of James VI and I* (London, Macmillan, 1973). Bossy has since modified some of his views in 'Unrethinking the Wars of Religion', in Thomas A. Kselman (ed.), *Belief in history: innovative approaches to European and American religion* (Notre Dame IN, University of Notre Dame Press, 1991).

2 While Haigh's early work stressed the need to understand the effects of networks and legal status in community formation, his later essays focus on refuting other aspects of Bossy's thesis. Cf. Christopher Haigh, *Reformation and resistance in Tudor Lancashire* (Cambridge, Cambridge University Press, 1975), chapters 15–17, 19; *id.*, 'The fall of a church or the rise of a sect? Post-Reformation Catholicism in England', *Historical Journal* 21 (1978), 181–6, with *id.*, 'From monopoly to minority: post-Reformation Catholicism in England', *Transactions of the Royal Historical Society*, fifth series, 31 (1981), 129–47; *id.*, 'The continuity of Catholicism in the English Reformation', *Past and Present* 93 (1981), 37–69; *id.*, 'Revisionism, the Reformation and the history of English Catholicism', *Journal of Ecclesiastical History* 36 (1985), 394–406.

3 Caroline Hibbard, *Charles I and the Popish Plot* (Chapel Hill NC, University of North Carolina Press, 1983); *id.*, 'The contribution of 1639: court and country Catholicism', *Recusant History* (1980) 16, 42–56.

4 Michael Questier, 'The politics of religious conformity and the accession of James I', *Historical Research* 71 (1998), 14–30; Sandeep Kaushik, 'Resistance, loyalty and recusant politics: Sir Thomas Tresham and the Elizabethan state', *Midland History* 21 (1996), 37–72.

5 Bossy, *English Catholic community*, pp. 94–5; *id.*, 'The English Catholic community, 1603–25', p. 102. Haigh did not specifically discuss William Blundell but see his remarks about the family in *Reformation and resistance*, pp. 282–3.

6 Jacqueline Eales, *Puritans and roundheads: the Harleys of Brampton Bryan and the outbreak of the English civil war* (Cambridge, Cambridge University Press, 1990); Margaret Spufford (ed.), *The world of rural dissenters* (Cambridge, Cambridge University Press, 1995).

7 William also had two younger brothers, James (who died young) and Richard, and a sister, Jane. See *The visitation of the County Palatine of Lancaster ... made by Sir William Dugdale* [1664–65], ed. F. R. Raines, Chetham Society, new series, 84 (Manchester, Simms, 1872), p. 37.

8 Haigh, *Reformation and resistance*, pp. 250–1, 247–68. For the discussion of the oath see *ibid.*, pp. 250–1. The other gentlemen who signed the oath were Sir Richard Mollineux, Sir William Norris and John Mollineux. The Marian priests associated with Crosby Hall were John Peele alias Pycke, James Darwen, Peter Jackson and Thomas Williamson. See *ibid.*, pp. 250, 255–7 (Darwen, Williamson); F. Tyrer, 'The recusant Blundells of Crosby', *North-west Catholic History* 4 (1972–73), 27–51 (Peele).

9 Haigh, *Reformation and resistance*, pp. 277–9. The Douai College diary includes the arrival of a twenty-year-old youth named Blundell in 1580, quoted in Gibson, *Crosby records*, p. ix.

10 These names are taken from 'Copy of the information sent to the Earl of Derby by the apostate Bell [1591]', *Archives of the Archbishop of Westminster*, A Series, vol. 4, no. 38 (Westminster Cathedral Archives, Series A Film, Wakefield, Micro Methods, 1965), fol. 433. See also Anstruther, *Seminary priests* I, p. 122 (Ford), p. 319 (Small), p. 385 (Woodroffe).

11 For Bell's clerical career see *ibid.*, pp. 29–30; Michael Questier, 'English clerical converts to Protestantism, 1580–96', *Recusant History* 20 (1991), 455–77; Haigh, *Reformation and resistance*, pp. 288–9.

12 'Copy of the information sent ... by the apostate Bell', fol. 429, and (describing masses at the estate of Edward Standish), fol. 445.

13 *Ibid.*, fols 429, 433, 435.

14 *Ibid.*, fols 433, 434.

15 'Copy of the information sent ... by the apostate Bell', fols 433, 451. Blundell's wedding date is given in F. Tyrer, 'The recusant Blundells of Crosby' II, *North-west Catholic History* 6 (1979), 1.

16 L[ancashire] C[ounty] R[ecord] O[ffice], 'Great Hodge Podge', fols 202–5, reprinted in Gibson, *Crosby records*, pp. 21–4, 31–40. For comparative statistics see P. McGrath and J. Rowe, 'The imprisonment of Catholics for religion under Elizabeth I', *Recusant History* 20 (1991), 415–35.

17 'Great Hodge Podge', fol. 202.

18 Peter Lake and Michael Questier, 'Prisons, priests and people', in Nicholas Tyacke (ed.), *England's long Reformation, 1500–1800* (London, UCL Press, 1998), p. 204.

19 Joseph Stanley Leatherbarrow, *The Lancashire Elizabethan recusants*, Chetham Society, new series, 110 (1947), p. 70.

20 'Great Hodge Podge', fol. 115.

21 *Ibid.*, fol. 202.

22 Cf. *ibid.*, fols 202–5, with Sir Alexander Culpepper's account in Bodleian Library, Tanner MSS 118, fols 129ᵛ–135ᵛ, partially reprinted in Christopher Buckingham 'The troubles of Sir Alexander Culpepper of Goudhurst', *Cantium* 2 (1970), 5–8.

23 A similar point is expressed in Peter Lake and Michael Questier, 'Agency, appropriation, and rhetoric under the gallows: puritans, Romanists and the state in early modern England', *Past and Present* 153 (1996), 64–107.

24 A[cts of the] P[rivy] C[ouncil], ed. J. R. Dasent, vol. 29 (London, HMSO, 1905), pp. 635–6, 111–12, 117–18, 131–2. For background see F. X. Walker, 'The implementation of the Elizabethan statutes against recusants, 1581–1603' (unpublished Ph.D. dissertation, University of London, 1961), especially pp. 382–5; William Raleigh Trimble, *The Catholic laity in Elizabethan England, 1558–1603* (Cambridge MA, Belknap Press, 1964), pp. 177–252.

25 *APC*, vol. 29, pp. 111–12, 117–18, 219–20, 302; S[tate] P[apers] D[omestic], *Elizabeth I*, 12/274/25, 12/266/18I, 12/266/18II; *Calendar of the manuscripts of the Most Honorable Marquis of Salisbury*, ed. M. S. Giuseppi (London, HMSO, 1902), vol. 9, p. 398; *Calendar of state papers, domestic series, 1598–1601*, ed. H. F. Brown and M. A. E. Green (London, HMSO, 1869), p. 7.

26 LCRO, Blundell of Little Crosby (DDBl) MSS 30/2, fol. 1; 'Great Hodge Podge', fol. 114.

27 See, e.g., Haigh, *Reformation and resistance*, pp. 327–32, especially p. 330; F. Tyrer, 'The Recusant Blundells of Crosby' III, *North-west Catholic History* 7 (1980), 1–5; Leatherbarrow, *Lancashire recusants*, pp. 139–51.

28 The fugitive names are taken from *APC*, vol. 29, p. 220; *SPD, Elizabeth I*, 12/266/18II.

29 Haigh, *Reformation and Resistance*, pp. 328–30.

30 'Great Hodge Podge', fol. 202ᵛ.

31 *Ibid.*, fol. 202ᵛ.

32 *Ibid.*, fol. 141. The song itself is undated, but the reference to Richard Vaughan as Bishop of Chester establishes the date of these events as no earlier than 1598.

33 *The New Testament of Jesus Christ* (Rheims, John Foigny, 1582), annotation on 1 Peter 4:17, p. 663; annotation on Acts 12:18, p. 325.

34 'Great Hodge Podge', fol. 202ᵛ.

35 *Ibid.*, fol. 141ᵛ.

36 R. Parsons, *A treatise of three conversions of Englande from paganisme to Christian religion*, 3 vols, unpaginated [St Omer], 1603–04.

37 'Great Hodge Podge', fol. 141ᵛ. Cf. Blundell's lines with the verses in [Thomas Alfield], *A true reporte of the death & martyrdome of M. Campion Iesuite and prieste*, sig. E2ᵛ.

38 Harold Love, *Scribal publication in seventeenth-century England* (Oxford, Clarendon Press, 1993); Arthur F. Marotti, *Manuscript, print, and the English Renaissance lyric* (Ithaca NY, Cornell University Press, 1995). On Blundell's broadsheet see D. R. Woolf, 'Little Crosby and the horizons of early modern historical culture', in Donald R. Kelley and David Harris Sacks (eds), *The historical imagination in early modern Britain: history, rhetoric and fiction, 1500–1800* (Cambridge, Cambridge University Press, 1997), pp. 103–4.

39 'Great Hodge Podge', fols 125ᵛ–144, in which Blundell is named as the author on fol. 144. Blundell's verse is discussed in Louise Imogen Guiney, *Recusant poets: from St Thomas More to Ben Jonson* (New York, Sheed &Ward, 1938), pp. 285–9.

40 'Great Hodge Podge', fols 136ʳ⁻ᵛ.

41 *Ibid.*, fol. 136ᵛ.

42 *Ibid.*, fol. 142.

43 *Ibid.*, fols 142ʳ⁻ᵛ.

44 *Ibid.*, fol. 137ᵛ.

45 *Ibid.*, fol. 137ᵛ.

46 *Ibid.*, fol. 138.

47 *Ibid.*, fol. 137ᵛ.

48 On the ballad refrain see Natascha Wurzbach, *The rise of the English street ballad, 1550–1650*, trans. Gayna Walls (Cambridge, Cambridge University Press, 1990), p. 74.

49 Tessa Watt, *Cheap print and popular piety, 1550–1640* (Cambridge, Cambridge University Press, 1991), pp. 3, 13.

50 W. E. Rhodes (ed.), *The apostolical life of Ambrose Barlow, O.S.B*, Chetham Society, new series, 63 (1908), p. 10.

51 'Verse miscellany of Margaret Bellasis', BL, Additional MSS 10,309, fols 148ᵛ–49ᵛ; 'Collections of William Cole', BL, Additional MSS 6402, fols 120ʳ⁻ᵛ.

52 R. Corbett, 'A Proper New Ballad Intitled the Faeryes Farewell, or, God-a-Mercy Will', in H. R. Woodhuysen (ed.), *The Penguin book of Renaissance verse* (London, Penguin, 1992), p. 44 (emphasis in original).

53 J. C. H. Aveling, *Northern Catholics: the Catholic recusants of the North Riding, 1558–1790* (London, Chapman, 1966), pp. 228–9, 273–5.

54 Alastair Bellany, '"Rayling rymes and vaunting verse": libellous politics in early modern England, 1603–28', in Kevin Sharpe and Peter Lake (eds), *Culture and politics in early modern England* (Stanford CA, Stanford University Press, 1993), p. 291.

55 Bossy, *English Catholic community*, pp. 143–4. The most detailed account is given in Woolf, 'Little Crosby', pp. 93–132.

56 Gibson, *Crosby records*, pp. 69–79, 45–62.

57 *Ibid.*, pp. 69–70, 72, 75, 77.

58 PRO, STAC 9 1/2, fols 17ᵛ, 19, 21.

59 Alexandra Walsham, '"The fatall vesper": providentialism and anti-popery in late Jacobean London', *Past and Present* 144 (1994), 36–87.

60 J. Floyd, *A word of comfort, or, A discourse concerning the late lamentable accident ... in the Black-friars at London* ([St Omer, English College Press], 1623).

61 'Great Hodge Podge', fol. 4. Cf. William Gouge, *The extent of Gods providence* (London, 1631), pp. 395–6; *The fatall vesper* (London, 1623), sigs C4–D2; John Chamberlain to Joseph Mead, 23 October 1623, BL, Harleian MSS 389, fol. 372; W. C., *The dolefull evensong* (London, 1623), sig. B2, although the last author admitted that Drury 'discoursed with much vehemency', sig. B4.

62 Walsham, 'Fatall vesper', p. 47.

63 'Great Hodge Podge', fol. 4.

64 *Ibid.*, fols 4ᵛ, 5.

65 *Ibid.*, fol. 5ᵛ. Cf. Floyd, *A word of comfort*, pp. 27–33.

66 'Great Hodge Podge', fol. 7.

67 J. Lewis, *Melchizedech's antitype, or, The eternall priesthood and all sufficient sacrifice of Christ* (London, 1624).

68 'Great Hodge Podge', fol. 7.

69 *Ibid.*, fol. 7.

70 *Ibid.*, fol. 7ᵛ (emphasis added).

71 *Ibid.*, fol. 11.

72 Anthony Milton, *Catholic and reformed: the Roman and Protestant churches in English Protestant thought, 1600–40* (Cambridge, Cambridge University Press, 1995); Michael Questier, *Conversion, politics, and religion, 1580–1625* (Cambridge, Cambridge University Press, 1996).

73 'Great Hodge Podge', fol. 3ᵛ.

74 Claude Mitchell Simpson, *The British broadside ballad and its music* (New Brunswick NJ, Rutgers University Press, 1966), pp. 653–4.

75 'Great Hodge Podge', fol. 3ᵛ.

76 Adam Fox, 'Ballads, libels and popular ridicule in Jacobean England', *Past and Present* 145 (1994), 47–83; Bellany, 'Rayling rymes'.

77 The identity of the best-known practioner of this style, 'John Brereley, Priest', has been

established as James Anderton of Lostocke in Lancashire. His death in 1613 eliminates his authorship here. See A. F. Allison, 'Who was John Brereley? The identity of a seventeenth-century controversialist', *Recusant History* 16 (1982), 17–41. On 'leaked letters' see Kenneth Fincham and Peter Lake, 'Popularity, prelacy, and puritanism in the 1630s: Joseph Hall explains himself', *English Historical Review* III (1996), 856–81.

78 Blundell's Jesuit contacts in this period were John Layton and John Worthington, both buried in the Harkirk in the 1620s. See Gibson, *Crosby records*, p. 75. Blundell kept informed about the parameters of the French marriage treaty in October, 1624. See 'Great Hodge Podge', fol. 204.

79 *Ibid.*, fol. 7.

80 *Ibid.*, fol. 6ᵛ.

81 PRO, STAC 9 1/2.

82 R. C. Richardson, *Puritanism in north-west England: a regional study of the diocese of Chester to 1642* (Manchester, Manchester University Press, 1972), p. 127.

83 'Warrant to Sheriff for payment to Wm. and Jane Blundell, 2/3 estate, 5 Sept 1634', LCRO, Blundell of Little Crosby (DDBl) MSS 30/11, unfoliated.

84 On the Cavalier's pre-war career see *Cavalier: letters of William Blundell to his friends, 1620–98*, ed. Margaret Blundell (New York, Longman, 1933), pp. 1–9.

85 Ann Hughes, 'Thomas Dugard and his circle in the 1630s: a 'parliamentary–puritan' connexion?', *Historical Journal* 29 (1986), 771–93.

86 Hibbard, 'The contribution of 1639'.

Chapter 5

———◆———

Social networks in Restoration London: the evidence from Samuel Pepys's diary

Ian W. Archer

She is grown so great, I am almost afraid to meddle with her; she is certainly a great world, there are so many little worlds in her ... I am sure I may call her a gallimaufrey of all sciences, arts, and trades.[1]

Historians of the early modern metropolitan area have adopted a number of approaches to the problem of its constituent 'communities'. Among the most fruitful has been the analysis of the geography of a variety of social relations to determine the strength of neighbourhood ties. Thus Jeremy Boulton has looked at the choice of marriage partners, bondsmen, overseers and witnesses to wills to show how householders in the early seventeenth-century Boroughside district of Southwark were linked by a network of neighbourly obligations and interactions to constitute a 'local social system'. This approach encourages us to conceive of the metropolitan area as a patchwork of neighbourly sub-communities, although it leaves open the question of how they related to each other, and whether there was any transcendent sense of metropolitan identity.[2] Other historians, developing the notion that community entails some sense of emotional attachment, have pointed out that communities in a city as complex as London were not necessarily geographically bounded: in a city as institutionally complex as London, guilds could be a focus of social and business interaction for Londoners from dispersed localities. This approach has encouraged us to think of individual Londoners as belonging to a variety of interlocking communities (parishes, wards and guilds), each of which generated loyalties, the intensity and mobilisation of which would vary according to context.[3] Another group, looking at the social topography of the city, has pointed to the increasing differentiation between a commercial city core, a fashionable West End based on Westminster, and the poorer suburbs to the north, east and south. While this approach has a more fully developed understanding of the impact of social differentiation (perhaps underestimated in both the previous

approaches), it has sometimes fostered the tendency to think of the constituent parts of the metropolitan area as being socially homogeneous, playing
down the pockets of poverty in the West End, or the continuing presence of
wealthier households in the suburbs.[4] It has also encouraged the view present
among some political and literary historians that the metropolis constituted a
mutually antagonistic City and Court. This is certainly a view present within
many of the period's literary products, notably the Jacobean drama of cuckoldry,
but its invocation runs the risk, as Malcolm Smuts and Susan Whyman have
pointed out, of reductionism, oversimplifying more complex patterns of social
interaction between citizens and gentlemen.[5]

The one-sidedness of these various approaches is reinforced by the difficulties of the sources. The exploration of local social systems is heavily dependent
on the evidence from wills. Quite apart from the difficulties of comprehensive
record linkage within the metropolitan area, wills are inherently limited as
guides to the relative importance of different types of social relationship. As
David Cressy has pointed out, they were intended to fulfil a specific and
limited purpose, namely the transmission and settlement of property at death,
and, given the strong claims of the immediate nuclear family on resources, it
is hardly surprising that its members predominate.[6] Those like myself who
have argued for the strength of institutional loyalties, whether to parishes or
guilds, also run the risk of their answers being archivally determined: if one
goes to the records of parishes and guilds one is bound to find individuals
relating to them and interacting with each other within their institutional
frameworks. As for relations between citizens and courtiers, too much of the
argument has been based on assumptions derived from literary sources, too
little on the day-to-day transactions of the historical subjects.

The historian is left wishing for sources from individual subjects, recording
a more representative range of their social transactions than the fragmented
materials usually consulted. Such sources are in fact available in the form of
diaries, and their potential has not always been fully realised, perhaps because
of the problem of the typicality of any individual.[7] In this chapter I shall use
the diary of Samuel Pepys as a guide to his social relations. Rather than
recording every one of Pepys's social transactions I have concentrated on the
people with whom he dined, supped or drank in two sample years, 1660 and
1666.[8] Considerations of space mean that the discussion is confined to
relations with individuals outside the immediate familial circle. I do not,
however, wish to deny the primacy of the household. In the year 1666 Pepys
dined at home on 264 of the 346 occasions for which he recorded his eating
place. He only rarely ate alone and was usually accompanied by what he
described as 'my people' (i.e. unspecified servants and his wife). But this
chapter's main concern is with Pepys's wider connections, with the people
brought into the household on the 120 occasions on which guests are recorded

as having been present in that sample year, with the people with whom Pepys socialised when invited to dinner in the households of others (forty-eight occasions in 1666) or with friends in taverns (thirty-one occasions).[9] The chapter is concerned with establishing the social milieu in which Pepys operated and the ways in which it changed under the impact of the author's upward social mobility. It hopes to shed light on some of the categories of community analysis above by looking at the geographical extent of the subject's relationships, at the degree to which City and Court connections intersected in the diarist, and at the importance of relations of kinship.

As we have seen, historians have put considerable emphasis on the parish as a focus for local identity. Pepys did not hold Daniel Milles, the minister of his parish church, St Olave's Hart Street, in very high regard, and until 1667 he was a rare visitor to the Pepys household.[10] Nor did Pepys hold parochial office, usually seen as one of the key forces for local integration, during the diary period. At times he felt contempt for his neighbours, declaring in 1667 that 'I will practise that I will have nothing to do with any of them'.[11] And yet in 1668, on nineteen of the twenty-seven Sundays on which he attended religious services, he was present in St Olave's. The church came to play an important role in his professional identity because of the special gallery which had been constructed for the navy officers in 1660.[12] He seems to have enjoyed the parish's Ascension Day dinners in which he participated in 1667, 1668 and 1669. 'All the parish almost' was present, and Pepys with his Navy Office colleagues enjoyed the 'good discourse' among the neighbours, 'they being most of them very able merchants as any in the city'. The tavern at which these dinners were held, the Dolphin on the junction of Mark Lane and Tower Street, was, after Rawlinson's on Fenchurch Street, Pepys's most regularly visited eating and drinking place.[13] He enjoyed the company of fellow parishioners and merchants, Sir Richard Ford, Thomas Andrews, John Lethieullier, Robert Knightly and the Bateliers. William Batelier, a wine merchant and 'a pretty man, understanding and well discoursed', who lived opposite Pepys on the north side of Crutched Friars, enjoyed dancing with him, supplied him with wine, procured books and Nanteuil prints for him from France, talked of witches and spirits and of the tricks of his trade, and advised the diarist on the form of a letter to the Duke of York. Batelier's sister Mary was a linen draper, 'my ... pretty seamstress in the Royal Exchange', from whom Samuel regularly made purchases, and she was often at social gatherings in the Pepys household. Elizabeth Pepys's companion, Mary, in the years 1664–66 was the daughter of fellow parishioners, William and Nicola Mercer, and widow Mercer provided lodgings for Will Hewer, the diarist's office clerk and later friend.[14] There can be little doubt that Pepys would have been a very familiar figure around the parish, but his local loyalties were not incompatible with activities over a much wider area.

We can get an idea of the topography of Pepys's social transactions if we look at the location of the places in London and Westminster at which he ate, drank and shopped. He visited numerous taverns, alehouses and coffee houses, often to socialise with friends and gather news, sometimes to transact business. He divided his time between the City and Westminster, but concentrated his visits on certain locations within those areas. Pepys rarely ventured into the less fashionable northern, eastern and southern suburbs (save when visiting his kin or on his way somewhere else). Within the city walls the establishments he patronised were overwhelmingly concentrated in the south-east, in the area near the Navy Office where he lived, and bounded by Fenchurch Street, Fish Street and Thames Street (17 per cent), and in the city-centre streets focused on the Royal Exchange, namely Cornhill, Lombard Street and Threadneedle Street (19 per cent). Although he occasionally patronised establishments in the western area within the walls, including Paul's churchyard, these visits were infrequent. More striking is the cluster of eating and drinking places he visited around Fleet Street and Chancery Lane near his father's house in Salisbury Court (12 per cent). The largest number of establishments he patronised, however, was in Westminster, in the area around the Old and New Palace Yards and along King Street (37 per cent). This was close to where Pepys lived at the time the diary opened, but he continued to be drawn there by the demands of his job and in pursuit of the pleasures of the West End. Another significant cluster was located a little farther north in the area centred on Charing Cross (7 per cent). Pepys's social life was therefore 'bi-polar', with social transactions focused on both the West End and on the commercial heart of the old city. This reflected his position as a naval administrator whose offices were located between the heart of central government in Westminster and the dockyards at Deptford and Woolwich; it also reflected his position as a professional with aspirations to participate in fashionable society but whose job demanded regular contact with mercantile contractors as well as government ministers.[15]

The pattern of Pepys's shopping expeditions tells a similar story. Although we cannot subject the material to comparable statistical precision, because Pepys is often vague about the location of the shops he patronised, enough can be identified to allow some impressionistic conclusions to be drawn. What is striking is how little of Pepys's shopping was centred on the immediate neighbourhood of the Navy Office. His shoemaker, William Wootton, resided in Fleet Street; his tailors, William Langford, Nicholas Penny and William Pym, in Salisbury Court, Fleet Street and the Strand respectively; his wife's tailor, John Unthank, at Charing Cross; his mercer, John Bennet, in Paternoster Row. His favoured booksellers operated out of St Paul's Churchyard (Joshua Kirton) and Duck Lane (William Shrewsbury). Pepys paid regular visits to the fashionable retail complexes located in the Royal Exchange and its rival, the

New Exchange, in the Strand, mainly for haberdashery, fashion accessories and mercers' and drapers' goods. He also maintained strong customer loyalty to some of the women traders in Westminster Hall, particularly with Ann Mitchell, a bookseller of ephemera, and Betty Lane, a linen draper, the latter of whom was one of his mistresses. It is a pattern which reflects the nature of occupational and retailing concentrations in the city, and the location of the most fashionable outlets. The western suburban parish of St Dunstan in the West had a high concentration of tailors, catering to the quality end of the market; St Paul's Churchyard housed no fewer than twenty-three booksellers at the time of the Great Fire; the small booths in the Exchange were ideal for the sale of fashion accessories and trinkets, and they were places where the elite gathered to exchange news and gossip. But the pattern of Pepys's shopping was also determined by considerations of customer loyalty. A limited number of outlets were used for any given product, and key tradesmen – 'my tailor', 'my shoemaker' and 'my bookseller' – were returned to time and again. Sometimes Pepys would drink with the shopkeepers who supplied him; Unthank's was a favoured rendezvous for meeting up with his wife; others, like William Wootton, with whom he exchanged theatrical gossip, were valued for their knowledge of affairs about town.[16] The development of these strong relationships of patronage between shopkeepers and their customers reflected both the need for the customer's insurance against potentially fraudulent tradesmen and the fact that much business was conducted on credit.[17]

The breadth of the area of Pepys's sociability and shopping calls into question the degree to which mobility within the metropolitan area was hampered by poor communications. Although Pepys encountered traffic jams of up to an hour and a half, he could abandon his hackney and travel by boat, and he was capable of traversing London and Westminster at some speed.[18] In the course of one by no means untypical day Pepys journeyed both westwards to Whitehall and eastwards to Greenwich, and found time for five social calls.[19] On other days he was quite capable of journeying back and forth between his house in Seething Lane and Westminster on two occasions.[20] He often went on foot, suggesting that such mobility would not have been out of the question for those of more modest means. Pepys's movements also reveal the operation of a society which was still in its essentials 'face-to-face'. While travelling through the city streets membership of the elite was signalled by dress and to some extent by mode of transport. Pepys would regularly 'bump into' friends and acquaintances in the city streets: 'seeing my neighbour Mr. Knightly walk alone from the Change ... I did invite him home with me', 'so back homewards, and seeing Mr Spong, took him up', 'having ... discoursed with Mr Hooke a little whom we met in the street', 'going abroad ... I met my late Lord Mayor ... and went with him by water to White-hall'.[21] The elite congregated at certain fixed points like the Royal Exchange, the New

Table 5.1   The social backgrounds of Pepys's companions, 1660 and 1666

| | No. of 'interactions' (No. of individual subjects in brackets) | | |
| | 1660 | 1666 | |
Social category	Males	Males	Females
Total interactions	833 (277)	384 (128)	186 (56)
Public servants	209 (59)	122 (31)	15 (4)
'Men of business'	107 (6)	13 (6)	5 (3)
Other household servants	19 (10)	5 (2)	–
Lawyers	42 (8)	6 (3)	6 (1)
Clergy	41 (20)	13 (3)	–
Medical professions	35 (9)	11 (6)	9 (1)
Military	97 (31)	28 (9)	17 (5)
Politicians	54 (10)	84 (22)	25 (7)
Country gentlemen	25 (14)	17 (3)	–
Merchants	45 (23)	102 (29)	25 (11)
Tradesmen and shopkeepers	104 (36)	39 (16)	56 (14)
Cultural services	29 (19)	11 (9)	15 (2)
Kin	140 (27)	55 (11)	29 (8)
Status unclear	60 (36)	3 (3)	14 (9)

Notes Some individuals appear in more than one category, e.g. navy officers who were also politicians. Comparisons between overall numbers of individuals with whom Pepys socialised in the two years should be treated with caution because of his more abstemious drinking habits in 1666.

Exchange, Westminster Hall and the nearby Palace Yards, and St James's Park, and although the gathering places in the city had a more mercantile character than those in the West End, there were plenty of points of overlap between them. Furthermore, although extending over a wide area, Pepys's social centres were concentrated on specific points within the metropolitan area: there were certain taverns and coffee houses where he was likely to find people of his acquaintance. The 'anonymity' of London life is not one of the lasting impressions of the diary.

As mentioned, to determine the social milieux in which Pepys moved, the people with whom he dined, supped and drank in two sample years were analysed. Although one can sometimes infer the presence of other companions, individuals are counted only when Pepys *explicitly* states that he dined, supped or drank with them. Only one entry has been allowed for any individual on any one day, to avoid the possible distorting effect of Pepys's tours of alehouses and taverns with a shifting body of companions. The method is not exhaustive, for he sometimes gives only generic accounts of those present: 'much and good company', 'a great company of my lord's friends'.[22] Nor can one always be sure that the persons recorded as being present were actually the ones with whom he conversed rather than simply those with whom he was most impressed. Pepys clearly enjoyed hobnobbing, but he was never backward in being forward, and the diary probably gives a reasonably reliable indicator of the different social milieux in which he operated. Pepys's female acquaintances, who have been analysed for 1666 only, and who are probably under-represented in the diary for reasons which will become apparent, have been separately classified according to the status of their fathers or husbands.[23] The results of the survey are given in Table 5.1.

Pepys's circumstances changed dramatically over the diary period. At its outset he was serving as clerk to George Downing, teller of receipt in the Exchequer, and as man of business to Edward Mountagu. His earnings were in the region of £50 per annum, 'esteemed rich, but endeed very poor'.[24] The transformation in his fortunes came about through his association with Mountagu, who played a key role in the Restoration. Pepys acted as his secretary on the voyage to bring back Charles II, affording the diarist the opportunity to be presented to the King and the Duke of York, and impressing Mountagu with his indispensability. Mountagu was elevated to the earldom of Sandwich, appointed vice-admiral of the fleet, and Master of the Wardrobe, with the award of lands to the value of £4,000 per annum. In the course of the voyage Mountagu had promised Pepys that they would 'rise together'. He was as good as his word, for he secured Pepys the post of the Clerk of the Acts to the Navy Board and a deputyship in the Privy Seal Office. The clerkship of the acts gave Pepys a salary of £350 per annum, and the opportunity to gain more through fees and perquisites.[25] His rate of accumulation accelerated: estimating his estate at £25 at the beginning of he diary, already by the end of 1660 it was £300. His finances were improved by the outbreak of the second Dutch war in November 1664 and his securing of the post of treasurer to the Tangier committee in March 1665. His estimated wealth rose from £1,205 on the eve of the war to £6,900 shortly before the peace in July 1667. Whereas he had been spending £7 per month on household needs in 1662, by the end of 1666 he was spending £100 per month.[26] At the beginning of the diary period he had only one servant; by its end his household comprised a waiting woman, three maids, a footboy and a coachman.[27] He could now consider himself 'able to live with comfort, though not with abundance'.[28]

It is clear that many of Pepys's social transactions in both periods occurred with members of what we have come to recognise as the 'middle class', defined as 'independent trading households', men who had to use their skills in business and the professions or who traded with the products of their hands.[29] Pepys was a familiar figure among his fellow public servants and among merchants and tradesmen within the city; he also counted among his friends members of the clerical, legal and medical professions. But the category 'middle class' conceals as much as it reveals, because the data do not make clear the degree of differentiation within its constituent groups: in particular the category of public servants is very elastic. Pepys's own income in 1660 makes him in economic (if not cultural) terms a very marginal figure for inclusion in a middle class the income threshold of which has been defined at £100 per annum in the later seventeenth century.[30] His life-style in 1666 with expenditure at £1,200 per annum put him in a different league. In 1660 Pepys's social milieu was emphatically that of the clerks and men of business who thronged Westminster and who serviced both central government and the private needs of politicians and aristocrats. His closest associates were other members of Sandwich's household, notably Edward Shipley, his steward, Henry Moore, his man of business, Will Howe, a clerk, and John Creed, a secretary and Pepys's principal rival for his master's favour. Another prominent group was the lower-ranking clerks in government service, people of a similar status to Pepys himself. In 1660 they included clerks in the Exchequer like Jack Spicer and John Hawley; under-clerks to the council like Will Symons, Peter Llewellyn and Samuel Hartlib junior; council messengers like Thomas Doling; and clerks in Chancery like James Chetwind. During 'Cromwell's time', Pepys tells us, he with other 'young men used to keep our weekly clubs' at Wood's tavern in Pall Mall: Symons, Llewellyn, Hartlib, Chetwind and Doling were all among those who regularly attended. These men were closely linked: the Hartlibs were neighbours of the Pepyses in Axe Yard, and Chetwind was married to Will Symons's sister.[31]

As his social standing improved he found himself ill at ease with his former companions. Meeting a group of his erstwhile fellow clerks in January 1664, he remarked that it was 'sorry company and the discourse poor'; the only comfort Pepys could now find in the company of men like Samuel Hartlib junior was 'to bless God to find the difference that is now between our condition and that heretofore'.[32] By 1666, although there were still many merchants and tradesmen in his social circle, the public servants with whom he predominantly associated were men of considerable political clout in their own right. As Clerk of the Acts, Pepys acquired accommodation in the Navy Office in Seething Lane, and lived cheek-by-jowl with some of his colleagues.

The four principal officers were entitled to lodgings within the Office: the treasurer, Sir George Carteret (as a man with interests at court) resided off-site, but Pepys lived in close proximity to the surveyor, Sir William Batten, the comptroller, Sir John Mennes, and also one of the commissioners, Sir William Penn. With all these men there were professional and personal tensions. Batten he considered to be corrupt, inefficient and married to an ill-tempered wife, Mennes was incompetent and Penn a man 'of very mean parts but only bred a seaman'.[33] But professional and domestic arrangements meant that there were frequent occasions of social interaction between them. Something of the intimacy enforced by their domestic arrangements is captured by Pepys's description of the diversions of a summer's evening: 'it being very hot weather, I took my flagilette and played upon the leads in the garden, where Sir W. Penn came out in his shirt into his leads and there we stayed talking and singing and drinking of great draughts of claret and eating botargo and bread and butter till 12 at night'. Batten, Penn and (to a lesser extent) Mennes hosted dinner parties 'with all our families' both at their lodgings in Seething Lane and at their houses in Walthamstow, and Pepys reciprocated (albeit not as frequently). Penn accompanied the Pepyses on their jaunts to Islington, Mile End, Bartholomew Fair and Hyde Park, and to the theatres; at Batten's Pepys enjoyed music and singing with the actress Mrs Knip.[34]

Pepys's colleagues enjoyed considerable political influence. Batten was MP for Rochester, Mennes a gentleman of the privy chamber, and Penn an intimate of the Duke of York. Sir George Carteret was Vice-Chamberlain and a key ally of Clarendon. Sir William Coventry, a navy commissioner from 1662 to 1667, to whom Pepys gradually attached himself, enjoyed considerable political influence at court through his position as secretary to the Duke of York. Through his membership of the Committee for Tangier from 1662, Pepys worked in collaboration with Sandwich, Carteret, Coventry, Albemarle and Peterborough. The combination of his connections with a high-ranking Restoration politician like Sandwich, the demands of his job for attendance on various Whitehall and parliamentary committees, and the role of the Duke of York as Lord High Admiral, gave him an entrée to the world of high politics. He was never a courtier, but he had many opportunities both to observe and to find out what was going on.

What I particularly want to stress is the degree to which men like Pepys mediated between the worlds of the Court and of the City. It is true that it is hard to detect a distinct set of civic values in Pepys's mental world. He only occasionally attended civic functions. Although he had enjoyed a 'very great dinner and most excellent venison' with the Lord Mayor and aldermen after the sessions, he found the Lord Mayor's feast a dull affair, 'being wearied with looking upon a company of ugly women'.[35] Although he was a regular guest at Trinity House dinners, and he maintained an interest in the affairs of his old school (St Paul's), which was under the tutelage of the Mercers' Company, he was only present at livery company functions on two occasions during the diary period.[36] The fact that Pepys's participation in events such as these was limited does not undermine the basic point about the strength of his trading connections because by the later seventeenth century many merchants were similarly detaching themselves from the paraphernalia of civic office and ritual.[37]

His work for the Navy Office brought him into contact with many merchants, and his relations with them contain an element of business calculation. The timber merchant Sir William Warren was the man favoured by Pepys against William Wood, Batten's man, and by allowing Warren a near monopoly in the supply of timber to the navy from 1664 Pepys also prospered. Warren was 'the friend I have got most by of most friends in England but the king'.[38] But if profit was one consideration, another was the quality of their 'discourse'. There were plenty of dullards among the merchants he encountered, including Sheriff William Hooker, 'a plain ordinary silly man', William Cutler, hemp merchant, 'a prating man', and most insistently and scathingly Sir John Robinson, the lieutenant of the Tower, 'a talking, bragging bufflehead'.[39] Shared cultural interests generated the relations of real warmth, and the diary is interesting on the degree of participation by mercantile groups in virtuoso culture. Pepys appreciated Warren not only for his business sense, 'a miracle of cunning and forecast in his business', but also for 'his excellent discourse and advice', 'his discourse being very great and his brains also', 'understanding seven times more than ever I thought to be in him'. Warren was at his ease among the virtuosi, entertaining Pepys, Viscount Brouncker (the navy commissioner, courtier and mathemetician), Dr Walter Charleton (a royal physician) and Commissioner Peter Pett, all fellows of the Royal Society, to a venison pasty at the Pope's Head tavern and listening with interest to Charleton on the subject of vegetarianism.[40] Thomas Hill, the agent of the Houblons in Lisbon, and Thomas Andrews, a neighbour in St Olave's Hart Street, were both involved in the victualling of Tangier, but they also joined Pepys for regular musical entertainments, 'most excellent pretty company; so pleasant, ingenious, and harmless, I cannot desire better', and serious discussion, 'pretty discourse, very pleasant and ingenious'. Hill moved among the political arithmeticians Graunt and Petty, and was capable of 'the rarest discourse about Rome and Italy' or more generally (and pessimistically) 'of most things of a man's life and how little merit doth prevail in the world but only favour'.[41] Hill was close to his employers, the Houblons, a family trading to France, Spain and the Mediterranean, headed by James senior, for whose five sons Pepys developed an extraordinarily high regard: 'a set of the finest gentlemen that ever I met with all in my life', 'their discourses (having been all abroad) very fine', 'a fine sight it is indeed to see these five brothers thus loving one another, and all industrious merchants'.[42] Another neighbour, later a fellow of the Royal Society, Sir Richard Ford, was involved in navy contracting, but was respected by Pepys as 'a very able man of his brains and tongue, and a scholar'.[43] About another contractor, the hemp merchant Captain George Cocke, who hosted numerous dinner parties at which Pepys was present, he was more ambivalent. He was garrulous, 'a conceited man but of no Logique in his head at all', and he had an enormous capacity for drink, 'the greatest epicure that is', but Pepys found his company 'most excellent'. Cocke could talk interestingly on Poland (of which he had first-hand experience) and on Roman history; he was elected a fellow of the Royal Society in 1666; he was a major source of political news (both foreign and domestic), perhaps because of his friendships with Clarendon's secretaries and with Viscount Brouncker; and he shared Pepys's interest in the theatre and singing. At the end of 1665 Pepys remarked that 'I have never lived so merrily ... as I have done this plague time, by my Lord Brouncker's and Captain Cocke's good company'.[44]

Pepys's cultural interests in music, the theatre and science broadened his social acquaintance. Pepys admired the actor Henry Harris for being 'a very curious and understanding person in all, pictures and other things', and he was a welcome guest.[45] Among the physicians with whom he regularly socialised were James Pearse, the chief naval surgeon of the day, and Timothy Clarke, one of the royal physicians. Clarke talked with Pepys about plays and philosophy and recommended reading matter.[46] In 1660 Pepys had sought intellectual stimulation in the meetings of the Rota Club, where he heard James Harrington.[47] By 1664 he was increasingly in the company of the virtuosi, and in February 1665 he was elected a fellow of the Royal Society, and he attended meetings occasionally thereafter.[48] As his own circumstances improved he was able to host dinner parties bringing together men of taste, like that on 19 July 1668 for which he assembled Samuel Butler, the author, Samuel Cooper, the miniaturist, John Hayls, the portrait painter, and Richard Reeve, optical instrument maker.[49]

Networks like that of Pepys connecting City and Court must have been critical in the circulation of news and information.[50] The political system continued to rely on informal connections of a sort which made leaks inevitable. The Duke of York complained of Sir Richard Ford that he could not keep a secret, and further 'that it is so much the part of a merchant to be guilty of that fault that [he] is resolved to commit no more secrets to merchants of the Royal Company'.[51] Pepys had sources of political gossip in his court patrons and the MPs of his acquaintance. With royal physicians like Pearse he discussed 'all the businesses of the court – the Amours and the mad doings that are there'. He was also plugged into the networks of city news through his regular visits to the Exchange, his mercantile friends and his schoolfellow Jack

Cole, from whom 'a man may know the temper of the city ... he being of a general conversation and can tell how matters go'.[52] Moreover, Pepys's network linked people of different religious persuasions. Declaring himself 'a sceptique' in religion, he was a conformist, but one who does not seem to have found the Duke of York's Catholicism a problem.[53] His mentor in business matters, William Warren, was an anabaptist; one of the politicians he most respected, Baron Crew, lost influence at the Restoration because of his Nonconformist sympathies; Pepys's own surgeon, Thomas Hollier, was vehemently anti-Catholic and his stationer, John Cade, a presbyterian.[54]

A very important feature of Pepys's social milieu was the role of kin. In 1660 and 1666 16·8 per cent and 14·3 per cent respectively of the recorded social interactions with males (using the above limited criteria) were with members of his kin. A significant number (11·8 per cent and 10 per cent) of these were with people outside his immediate family circle (i.e. his father and brothers).[55] Twenty-five named male kin members outside the nuclear family enjoyed drinks or meals with the diarist in 1660, and nine in 1666. Among the frequent callers on Pepys's hospitality were his brother-in-law, Balthasar St Michel; his maternal uncle, the blacksmith Thomas Fenner; William and Anthony Joyce, tallow chandlers, who had married Fenner's daughters, and William Wight, fishmonger, the half-brother of Pepys's father. When visiting Cambridge, Pepys would pay calls on his cousin, a tailor and woollen draper, John Angier, or he would visit his more exalted Cambridgeshire kin, his great-uncle Talbot Pepys of Impington, and his sons.[56] Family gatherings could bring together distant kin. On Twelfth Night 1660 Pepys went with his father, his two brothers and sister to a supper given by his cousin, Thomas Strudwick of Snow Hill in Holborn, a confectioner married to the daughter of Sir Richard Pepys, Lord Chief Justice of Ireland under the Commonwealth; also present were another cousin, the pewterer Benjamin Scott and his wife (another of Sir Richard's daughters), and members of the Drawater family who had married into the Strudwicks.[57]

One of the most noticeable features of Pepys's kin is the degree to which they stretched over a broad social spectrum, which would have contributed strongly to community. Pepys owed his own advancement to his cousin the Earl of Sandwich, through whose connection by marriage with John, Baron Crew of Stene, he gained familiarity with the Crews, 'the best family in the world for goodness and sobriety'.[58] Other kin of social prominence included his great-uncle Talbot Pepys, of Impington, and his son Roger, who succeeded his father as Recorder of Cambridge in 1660 and served as MP in the Cavalier Parliament. There were several other lawyers among the kin group: another son of the Cambridge patriarch, Dr John Pepys, was a civil lawyer and a fellow of Trinity Hall, Cambridge, who arbitrated in the dispute over the Brampton estate; John Turner, in whose house in Salisbury Court Pepys had his lithotomy in 1658, was the Recorder of York from 1662 and a king's serjeant from 1669. Other relatives were businessmen. Among them were a cousin, Thomas Pepys, and William Wight, free of the Fishmongers' Company but operating as a general merchant and worth £4,000 at his death in 1672. There were numerous lesser tradesmen among Pepys's kin. His own father, John Pepys, was a tailor (admittedly one of some substance living in a three-storey house in Salisbury Court, and presumably the beneficiary of a genteel clientage) who had married Margaret Kite, a woman of obscure origin who had been a washmaid in her youth. When his father inherited the Brampton estate on the death of Samuel's uncle Robert in 1661 he ascended in social status, taking on the role of modest country gentleman, but the tailoring business was taken on by his younger son, Tom, who lived in a house taxed on four hearths in Bride Lane. We have already encountered Uncle Fenner the blacksmith, the Joyce brothers, tallow chandlers, Strudwick the confectioner and Scott the pewterer. His mother's kin (with whom Pepys had more tenuous relations than with his father's kin) seem to have been of particularly low social status.[59] Of the funeral of his aunt Kite, who was a butcher's widow, Pepys remarked that 'besides us and my uncle Fenner's family there was none of any quality but poor raskally people'.[60]

As that last remark suggests, Pepys's social ascent made him more embarrassed to be in the presence of his poorer kindred. Dining with the Joyces, he remarked, 'how sick was I of the company, only hope I shall have no more of it a good while'. His uncle Fenner had remarried 'a pitiful, old, ugly, illbred woman in a hatt, a midwife', and their relations were 'sorry mean people'. At Uncle Fenner's funeral Pepys was struck once more by the 'pitiful rout of people'. Balthasar St Michel he found to be a preposterous individual whose social aspirations were incompatible with his humble circumstances: 'he stands upon a place to be a gentleman that may not stain his family, when God help him, he wants bread'.[61] But Pepys also acknowledged his obligations to his relatives. It is perhaps not surprising that Samuel should have been so involved in efforts to set his brothers and sister up in the world. He worked hard to find a wife for his feckless brother Tom; he was involved in negotiations with at least seven potential husbands for his sister Paulina before terms were reached with the Huntingdonshire farmer, John Jackson; he watched over his brother John's Cambridge undergraduate days, and in 1670 secured him preferment as the Clerk of Trinity House. But the obligations of the ties of wider kindred were also keenly felt. When Lettice, one of his maternal aunts, visited in September 1667 he records that 'I made as much of them as I could such ordinary company; and yet my heart was glad to see them, though their condition was a little below my present state to be familiar with'. For his aunt Kite he performed the services of an executor.[62] Pepys assisted Anthony Joyce in securing contracts to supply tallow to the navy and was willing to lend him money when he got into financial difficulties after the Fire; when the poor man drowned himself, Pepys worked hard to prevent the forfeiture of the estate to the Crown.[63] For all that he feared Balty's importunity ('I shall not be able to wipe my hands of him when I once concern myself of him'), Pepys did use his influence to secure him the place of naval muster master in the summer of 1666 and of deputy treasurer of the fleet sent to the West Indies in 1667.[64] In addition to the connection with Sandwich, Pepys was himself the beneficiary of various forms of kin support. His cousin Roger, the MP for Cambridge, was a regular visitor and source of legal advice. He advised in the dispute over Robert Pepys's estate, and about possible land purchases, and arranged Paulina's marriage settlement. Although of a country persuasion in politics, he was prepared to give his cousin advice on his defence before the parliamentary committee on miscarriages.[65]

Although Pepys's wife complained of her limited acquaintance,[66] the diary calls into question the notion that men and women inhabited separate spheres in this period, for Pepys's sociability was by no means completely masculinised.[67] Of the 120 occasions in 1666 on which guests are recorded as being present for dinner in his house, we learn that on fifty-six days his named companions were (his wife and the servants apart) exclusively male, on thirty-eight occasions mixed, and on twenty-six occasions entirely female. Likewise when dining at the homes of friends and colleagues in that year the company was exclusively male on twenty-five occasions, and on twenty-six occasions mixed. In taverns he was in male company on seventeen occasions, in mixed company on six occasions, in female company twice, alone twice, and in uncertain company on four occasions. It is likely that the presence of women is underestimated in the dinners Pepys records. When he dined at home his wife was usually present, but he does not consistently record the presence of spouses at the houses of his acquaintances.

Pepys's female companions were to a large extent determined by the pattern of his male acquaintance, and there does not seem to have been an overt effort to keep politics out of the conversation in mixed groups, at least at the level of the social elite. He and his wife were welcome at Lady Sandwich's table, where Samuel discussed matters both of politics and of trivia like 'the beauty of men and women'.[68] Abigail Williams, Lord Brouncker's mistress, seems to have enjoyed a peculiarly privileged position, joining her husband at city taverns where he met Navy Office colleagues and merchants. In 1660 Pepys was often in the company of the wives of his fellow bureaucrats, and later he shared tables with the wives of his Navy Office colleagues. Perhaps those of lesser social status (particularly the pretty tradesmen's wives who were welcome guests at his house) enjoyed less privileged access to the topics of male discourse. In 1666 the female company he enjoyed most was that of Mary Batelier, sister of the neighbouring wine merchant; Mary Mercer, his wife's companion; Mrs Pearse, the surgeon's wife; and Mrs Knip, the actress. These women would join the Pepyses on their 'grand tours' to Islington, and in singing and dancing. As Samuel commented, 'music and women I cannot but give way to, whatever my business is', but at times politics intruded, for Mrs Pearse was present when her husband discoursed with Pepys on 'all the businesses of the court'.[69] There is, of course, an important exception to the proposition that Pepys's female companions were determined by his attachments to males, and that is his dealings with his mistresses, who were women of lower status than himself, like Mrs Bagwell, the carpenter's wife, or Betty Martin and Doll Powell, the linen drapers of Westminster Hall. Pepys's relationships with these women was exploitative, but the women involved may not have been entirely lacking in agency. They used their associations with Pepys to gain favours: Betty Martin worked to get her husband a place as a purser, and Mrs Bagwell secured the position of master carpenter for her husband. Sexual favours were part of the currency of patronage.[70] The pattern of Pepys's relations with women thus reinforces some of our earlier themes: the ways in which he linked City and Court, and the ways in which his social connections covered a wide range of the social spectrum.

Historians are developing an interest in the question of the degree to which a metropolitan identity can be said to have existed in the early modern period. The identity of Londoners was arguably fractured by the variety of communities which made up the greater London area. Londoners had always felt ties towards parishes and guilds, not necessarily incompatible with civic loyalties, but arguably more important to them in practical terms. But as the metropolitan area grew the city became ever more fragmented. The old city incorporated no more than a quarter of the metropolitan population in the later seventeenth century as a result of suburban expansion, and the suburbs had radically different characteristics from each other as well as from the commercial core. London became more socially polarised as suburban development fostered a greater degree of residential segregation. But the study of individuals such as Pepys enables us to see the ways in which these constituent communities could be linked. Pepys's kin connections extended his social network over a broad social range; his employment located him in Westminster, the old city, and in the riverside parishes to the east of the city; and he linked the potentially divergent elites of City and Court. If we are to explore the ways in which a metropolitan identity was created it will be by looking more closely at the brokering roles of men like Pepys rather than by the institutionally bounded approaches which have characterised our efforts thus far.

NOTES

1 D. Lupton, *London and the Countrey Carbonadoed and Quartered into Severall Characters*, in *The Harleian miscellany: a collection of scarce, curious, and entertaining pamphlets and tracts, as well in manuscript as in print*, 12 vols (London, 1808), IX, p. 312.

2 Jeremy Boulton, *Neighbourhood and society: a London suburb in the seventeenth century* (Cambridge, Cambridge University Press, 1987), chapter 9; Derek Keene, *Cheapside before the Great Fire* (London, Economic and Social Research Council, 1985); Peter Earle, *A city full of people: men and women in London, 1650–1750* (London, Methuen, 1994), pp. 171–8.

3 Ian W. Archer, *The pursuit of stability: social relations in Elizabethan London* (Cambridge, Cambridge University Press, 1991); Steve Rappaport, *Worlds within worlds: structures of life in sixteenth-century London* (Cambridge, Cambridge University Press, 1989); Joseph P. Ward, *Metropolitan communities: trade guilds, identity and change in early modern London* (Stanford CA, Stanford University Press, 1997).

4 Michael J. Power, 'East and west in early modern London', in E. W. Ives, R. J. Knecht and J. J. Scarisbrick (eds), *Wealth and power in Tudor England: essays presented to S. T. Bindoff* (London, Athlone Press, 1978); *id.*, 'The social topography of Restoration London', in A. L. Beier and Roger Finlay (eds), *London, 1500–1700: the making of the metropolis* (Harlow, Longman, 1986); *id.*, 'The east London working community in the seventeenth century', in Penelope Corfield (ed.), *Work in towns, 850–1850* (Leicester, Leicester University Press, 1990); Lawrence Stone, 'The residential development of the West End of London in the seventeenth century', in Barbara C. Malament (ed.), *After the Reformation: essays in honour of J. H. Hexter* (Manchester, Manchester University Press, 1980); R. Malcolm Smuts, 'The court and its neighbourhood: royal policy and urban growth in the early Stuart West End', *Journal of British Studies* 30 (1991), 117–49; Julia F. Merritt, 'Religion, government, and society in early modern Westminster, c. 1525–1625' (unpublished Ph.D. dissertation, University of London, 1992).

5 Douglas Bruster, *Drama and the market in the age of Shakespeare* (Cambridge, Cambridge University Press, 1992); Lawrence Venuti, *Our halcyon dayes: English pre-revolutionary texts and post-modern culture* (Madison WI, University of Wisconsin Press, 1989); John Twyning, *London dispossessed: literature and social space in the early modern city* (Basingstoke, Macmillan, 1998); David L. Smith, Richard Strier and David M. Bevington (eds), *The theatrical city: culture, theatre, and politics in London, 1576–1649* (Cambridge, Cambridge University Press, 1995); Smuts, 'Court and its neighbourhood'; Susan E. Whyman, 'Land and trade revisited: the case of John Verney, London merchant and baronet, 1660–1720', *London Journal* 22 (1997), 16–32.

6 David Cressy, 'Kinship and kin interaction in early modern England', *Past and Present* 113 (1986), 38–69.

7 But see Alan Macfarlane, *The family life of Ralph Josselin, a seventeenth-century clergyman: an essay in historical anthropology* (Cambridge, Cambridge University Press, 1970); Amanda Vickery, *The gentleman's daughter: women's lives in Georgian England* (London, Yale University Press, 1998). Other sources which might be subjected to a similar analysis to that attempted here are the letters of the mid-sixteenth-century family of merchants, the Johnsons; the accounts of Edward Alleyn, the theatre entrepreneur; and the so-called 'obituary' (a list of the dates of death of close friends) of Richard Smyth, a legal official in seventeenth-century London: Barbara Winchester, 'The Johnson letters, 1542–52' (unpublished Ph.D. dissertation, University of London, 1953); W. Young, *The*

history of Dulwich College, 2 vols (London, Bumpus, 1889); Aileen Reed and Robert Maniura (eds), *Edward Alleyn: Elizabethan actor, Jacobean gentleman* (London, Dulwich Picture Gallery, 1994); *The obituary of Richard Smyth, Secondary of the Poultry Compter*, ed. H. Ellis (Camden Society, old series, 44, 1849).

8 R. C. Latham and W. Matthews (eds), *The diary of Samuel Pepys*, 11 vols (London, Bell & Hyman, 1971), hereafter cited by volume number and page references only.

9 For the household, see X, pp. 193–7.

10 III, pp. 134–5; VIII, pp. 248, 437, 540, 564; IX, pp. 24, 184, 219, 220, 260, 406.

11 VII, p. 105.

12 I, pp. 232, 225, 230, 233, 254, 289, 295.

13 II, p. 106; VIII, p. 218; IX, pp. 179, 559.

14 For Andrews and Ford, see below pp. 85–6; II, pp. 239–40; VII, pp. 31–2, 278, 280 (Knightly); VII, pp. 15–16, 43, 110, 135, 199, 200, 228, 230, 233, 238, 240, 246, 249, 256, 258, 265, 322, 358, 360, 362–3, 379, 380, 403, 404 (Bateliers, social references for 1666); VI, pp. 70–1, 76, 338; VII, pp. 228, 358; VIII, p. 421; IX, pp. 249, 304, 427, 428, 450–1, 453, 464 (Bateliers, specific references); VI, pp. 316, 328, 338, 339; VII, pp. 35, 41, 322 (Lethieullier); V, pp. 229, 256, 257, 265, 267; VII, pp. 18, 44, 53, 54–5, 72, 78, 81, 84, 108, 110, 111, 113, 117, 126, 128, 129, 133, 142, 152, 167, 170, 172, 176, 181–2, 183, 195, 198, 199, 205, 212, 216, 227, 228, 230, 240, 246, 267, 412 (Mercers).

15 X, pp. 70–2, 416–28; XI, pp. 62–3, 280–3; Robert Ashton, 'Samuel Pepys's London', *London Journal* 11 (1985), 75–87.

16 I, pp. 59, 88, 223; II, p. 195; III, p. 204; IV, pp. 239, 347, 411.

17 Cf. Craig Muldrew, *The economy of obligation: the culture of credit and social relations in early modern England* (Basingstoke, Macmillan, 1998).

18 II, p. 231; III, p. 160; V, p. 307; VII, pp. 367, 369; X, p. 454.

19 VI, p. 94.

20 VII, p. 123, pp. 155–7; IX, pp. 221–3.

21 VII, pp. 31, 218–19, 239, 393.

22 I, pp. 303, 318, 323.

23 The status of too many women was unclear for analysis in 1660. Defining women in terms of their husbands' status is problematic because it can occlude the real nature of Pepys's relations with them. See the problem of his mistresses, discussed below.

24 I, p. 2; X, p. 131.

25 I, pp. 167, 170, 187, 194, 196–9, 205, 221.

26 I, p. 32; II, p. 1; V, p. 310; VIII, p. 245; X, p. 136.

27 X, pp. 193–4.

28 IX, p. 529.

29 Shani d'Cruze, 'The middling sort in eighteenth-century Colchester: independence, social relations, and the community broker', in Jonathan Barry and Christopher Brooks (eds), *The middling sort of people: culture, society, and politics in England, 1550–1800* (Basingstoke, Macmillan, 1994), pp. 181–3.

30 Peter Earle, 'The middling sort in London', in Barry and Brooks (eds), *Middling sort.*

31 I, p. 208; II, p. 127; IV, p. 10; V, p. 50; VI, pp. 147–8; VII, p. 375; X, p. 60.

32 V, p. 30. Cf. II, p. 51; V, pp. 41, 330; VII, p. 53.

33 V, p. 293.

34 For examples, see II, p. 115; VII, pp. 69–70, 189, 261, 267, 280, 282, 283, 287, 422; VIII, pp. 196–7, 485; IX, pp. 57, 88, 184, 193, 202.

35 II, p. 203; III, p. 240; IV, pp. 294–5, 354–6; VIII, pp. 319–20.

36 I, p. 177; II, p. 119; III, pp. 17–18, 29, 43, 93, 103–4, 110, 115–16, 160, 187, 190, 246; IV, pp. 71, 125, 148, 184–5, 209, 343; V, pp. 15, 94–5, 172–3, 186, 210, 290; VI, pp. 35–6, 48, 84, 155; VII, pp. 50, 72, 381–2; G. G. Harris, *The Trinity House of Deptford, 1514–1660* (London, Athlone Press, 1969) (Trinity House); I, p. 44; IV, p. 33; V, pp. 37–8 (St Paul's School); I, pp. 18–19, 186–7; Thomas Girtin, *The golden ram: a narrative history of the Clothworkers' Company, 1528–1958* (Clothworkers' Company, privately printed, 1958) (livery companies).

37 Nicholas Rogers, *Whigs and cities: popular politics in the age of Walpole and Pitt* (Oxford, Oxford University Press, 1989), pp. 16–18.

38 III, pp. 118–19, 160, 187, 190, 246; IV, pp. 422–3; V, p. 271; VI, p. 226; VII, p. 402. Cf. the victualling merchant Sir Denis Gauden: IV, pp. 23, 26, 242, 244–5, 337; V, p. 271; VI, pp. 25, 171, 172–3, 251, 253–4, 322; VII, pp. 29–30, 373; IX, p. 33.

39 IV, pp. 77–8, 341; VI, pp. 328, 331.

40 IV, pp. 223–4; VII, pp. 1, 223–4, 402.

41 IV, p. 12; V, pp. 35, 83, 124, 215–16, 293, 332, 337; VI, pp. 32, 44, 125, 285; VII, pp. 64–5, 125.

42 VI, pp. 336–7; VII, p. 36, 64, 370.

43 IV, p. 77.

44 III, pp. 154, 362, 355–6; V, p. 300; VI, pp. 92, 199, 227, 282, 290, 342; VII, pp. 18, 34, 38, 68, 72, 364, 404, 408; VIII, pp. 68–70.

45 VIII, pp. 28, 29; IX, pp. 12, 128, 134, 138, 175, 218–19, 289.

46 I, pp. 72, 134, 236; III, p. 230; VIII, pp. 58–9, 156, 159.

47 I, pp. 3, 14, 17, 20–1, 24, 61.

48 X, pp. 361–8.

49 IX, p. 265.

50 Dagmar Freist, *Governed by opinion: politics, religion, and the dynamics of communication in Stuart London, 1637–45* (London, Tauris, 1997); Ian W. Archer, 'Popular politics in sixteenth and early seventeenth-century London', in Paul Griffiths and Mark Jenner (eds), *Londinopolis: essays in the cultural and social history of early modern London* (forthcoming, Manchester University Press).

51 V, p. 300.

52 Examples from 1666: VII, pp. 142 (Exchange); 286–7, 317–18, 375, 402 (Cocke); 416 (Ford); 323 (Colvill, a goldsmith banker); 420 (Cade, stationer); 99–100, 314–15, 399–400 (Pearse, surgeon); 191–2 (Francis Finch, MP); 356–7, 376 (Sir Thomas Crew, MP);

387 (Lord Crew); 307, 334–5, 354–5, 369–70, 383 (Sir George Carteret); 411–12 (Brouncker); 342–3 (Bellasys); 352–3 (Sir Stephen Fox). For Cole see III, pp. 133, 254.

53 I, p. 141; IV, pp. 164–5. For his Anglicanism see I, p. 289; II, p. 171.

54 X, p. 469 (Warren); IX, p. 164 (Crew); V, p. 256; VIII, pp. 586, 587; IX, p. 16 (Hollier); VII, p. 240 (Cade).

55 It should be acknowledged that the very large number of occasions on which Pepys dined with his patron's household distorts the figures for 1660. If they are excluded the proportion falls from 11·8 per cent to 6·3 per cent.

56 I, pp. 67, 69; II, pp. 146–7; III, p. 217.

57 I, p. 10. Cf. I, pp. 29–30, 54, 205, 252.

58 VII, p. 356.

59 Ralph Houlbrooke, *The English family, 1450–1700* (Harlow, Longman, 1984), pp. 56–7.

60 II, p. 179.

61 I, p. 177; II, p. 205; III, pp. 13, 16, 62; V, p. 158; VII, pp. 169, 366.

62 VII, p. 46; VIII, p. 442.

63 III, p. 68, 96, 111.

64 II, p. 164; VI, pp. 140, 271, 318; VII, pp. 82, 87, 90, 111, 154; VIII, pp. 15, 19, 130, 131, 141, 142, 148–9, 154; IX, p. 248.

65 II, pp. 145, 147; III, pp. 113, 218, 253, 263; IV, pp. 28, 34, 35, 41; VIII, pp. 261, 493, 496, 517; IX, pp. 18–19, 55, 56, 61, 64–5, 95, 113, 162.

66 IV, p. 9.

67 Robert B. Shoemaker, *Gender in English society, 1650–1850: the emergence of separate spheres?* (Harlow, Longman, 1998).

68 I, pp. 303, 314, 320.

69 I, pp. 69–70; VII, pp. 99–100.

70 V, pp. 242, 285, 286, 338; VI, p. 55; VII, pp. 50, 75, 218; VIII, p. 97 (Martin); IV, p. 266; V, pp. 65–6, 163; VI, pp. 39–40; VIII, pp. 39, 95 (Bagwell).

Part II

Place

Chapter 6

A sense of place? Becoming and belonging
in the rural parish, 1550–1650

Steve Hindle

> In the fallen world, communities (patterns of interaction) are endlessly dying and
> being born. The historian's job is to specify what, at a given moment, is changing
> into or being annihilated by what.[1]

Rural communities obviously have long and highly localised histories, over
the course of which custom, circumstance and human agency have
incrementally shaped the nature of social relations.[2] In this sense, local
communities have been constituted both by a long-term *historical* process of
structuration and sedimentation, in which successive waves of political,
economic and cultural development have subtly remoulded the contours of
belonging; and by short-term *generational* processes of adaptation and
assimilation, in which, over the course of the life cycle, individuals and their
families were absorbed into, and ultimately departed from, networks of
association. In early modern England both types of process were fundamentally local and, in their most intimate and familial manifestations,
essentially parochial: the parish was *the* locale in which community was
constructed and reproduced, perhaps even consecrated. This is not, of course,
to deny that the parish was incorporated into more extensive social, economic,
political and religious structures, overlapping and intersecting with wider
communities of friendship, credit, patronage and faith.[3] It is, however, to
insist that the corporate character of societal development was most obviously
manifested in the lived experiences of people working and worshipping in
close proximity to one another. If, as the new sociology insists, society is a
process constantly reproduced by its members, then in early modern England
the parish was *the* arena in which structure, ritual and agency combined to
create and maintain (and perhaps even to challenge) a highly localised sense of
belonging.

If community was a *process*, moreover, it was also an *ideal*, the highly
prescriptive norms of which – quietness, charity, credit, honesty, consensus –

are often so vociferously rehearsed in the sources that historians become almost deaf to their cadences. This chapter, however, is premised on the view that the early modern English parish, like all communities, had both margins and boundaries, and that becoming a member of, and belonging to, the parish community were transactions which entailed the negotiation of relativities of status and of space. In short, the maintenance of parochial harmony was predicated on the internalisation of a sense of 'place', both in geographical and in social-structural terms. The parish was not only a territorial and juris-dictional entity, it was also a social, economic and moral hierarchy.[4] Since an infinite community is by definition a contradiction in terms, 'community' necessarily implied exclusion. Outsiders were 'strangers' not only in the sense that they originated beyond the physical boundaries of the community but also because their behaviour or reputation cast them beyond the pale of a moral consensus.[5] This chapter illuminates the transformation, under the impact of wider economic, political and ideological changes in the late sixteenth and early seventeenth centuries, of those local processes of inclusion and exclusion through which communal life was structured. In the brief space available I want to suggest that five trends – the institutionalisation of poor relief; the restriction of residence to settled 'inhabitants'; the restruc-turing of parish governance; the ever tighter regulation of customary use rights; and the oscillation of a religious policy which defined the relationship of parishioners to the rituals of Christian fellowship – redrew the parameters of belonging in the community of the parish, a redrafting to which the poor in particular were subject. Whereas they had once claimed their rightful place at the heart of the corporate community of Christian worship, the poor were now simply given (put in) their place, and an inherently marginal and dependent place at that.[6] As the timeless equilibrium 'between people and land, labour and repose, peasant and lord, king and kingdom, production and consumption, custom and circumstance' which had been idealised in commonwealth rhetoric was eroded by the weight of social and economic practice, the parochial sense of place became ever more rigidly defined and articulated.[7]

As both Alan Macfarlane and Richard Smith have argued, most discussions of community are influenced (often subconsciously) by notions of 'decline', a tradition which Smith traces back to those classical notions of transition between the stark dichotomies formulated by the founding fathers of sociology.[8] The genealogy traced by Smith is not, however, the only source of the notion of community as it is employed by modern historians. R. H. Tawney in particular drew his model of early modern social and economic change from those sixteenth-century moralists who were themselves pre-occupied with the replacement of the values of commonwealth with those of commodity and covetousness.[9]

Some models of social change are, of course, artificially linear (although that is often how processes of change are perceived by contemporaries). Far from suggesting an irreversible decline in communal identity, however, I want to suggest that rural communities were actually forged anew in this crucible of change. The physical and moral thresholds of the parish community were *reinforced* in this period. The results of the recasting of the local social drama were ambiguous. On the one hand, the margins of the parish became both deeper and wider, fostering increasing self-consciousness among those who were made to feel excluded, both morally and economically, from the local community: this was the 'dark parish' of 'poor delvers and day labourers', dismissed by their betters as 'pilferers Backbyters hedge breakers and myscheveous persons'.[10] On the other, as the meaning of community narrowed, chief inhabitants – the *parochiani meliores et antiquiores* – began to regard themselves not merely as representatives of the local community but actually as that very community. Thus while the parish officers of Layston (Hertfordshire) regarded themselves as 'the principal members of this little commonwealth', and those of Constantine (Cornwall) as the 'law-makers of the commonwealth', vestrymen elsewhere in rural England were increasingly describing themselves, and were described by others, simply as 'the parishe'.[11] The recasting of community, then, implied that traditional values of solidarity and reciprocity remained, and perhaps even thrived, but in more socially restricted ways. Indeed, the ethos of community increased *within* certain groups (especially among those ratepayers and office-holders who regarded themselves as the 'better sort' of the parish) even as it diminished *between* them (and especially between the 'better' and the 'worser' sort). How did this complex process come about?

WELFARE

The institutionalisation of welfare under the terms of Tudor legislation delegated enormous discretionary authority to parish officers and others of middling status in deciding the criteria of belonging in the local community and in allocating those entitlements which were its most significant prerogatives. Serious structural problems had emerged in the English economy by the late sixteenth century and their perceived providential origin provoked a flood of governmental and ecclesiastical exhortations to charity by the rich and repentance among the poor. Because the Protestant debate over the causes of poverty turned upon perceptions of human failings, the need for a discriminatory classification of the poor was all the greater. From the mid-sixteenth century onwards, then, Protestant ethics of civility and obedience found expression in the social, economic and spiritual life of the parish. Most conspicuously, novel attitudes towards the poorest members of the community crystallised in the notorious 'Slavery Act' of 1547.[12] Whereas the earlier legislation of 1531 had been concerned with the consequences of idleness, the regime of Protector Somerset turned its attention specifically to idlers and to the source of their perversion, and offered an expanded definition of vagabondage. The savage punishments – including branding and slavery – stipulated in the statute were reflective of Calvinist anthropology, especially in the extent to which the rigour of moral discrimination between the deserving and the undeserving reflected the theological distinction between the elect and the reprobate. Although these provisions were sufficiently draconian to render the statute virtually unenforceable, they symbolised the attenuation of the communal ideal. This was, moreover, only the first of many statutes culminating in the Elizabethan poor laws of 1598–1601 in which more calculating notions of charity were introduced into the community of the parish.[13]

The age-old distinction between the idle and afflicted was therefore reinforced by sixteenth-century thinkers to whom it was axiomatic that the impotent should be maintained. Attitudes to sturdy beggars were, however, complicated by an emerging awareness of distinctions among the idle, and especially of the presence of a large number of labouring poor: those who were willing but unable to find work. By the late sixteenth century, therefore, the tripartite classification of the poor – the impotent, the thriftless, the labouring – had become orthodox. Welfare legislation enshrined three enduring principles: that the vagrant were to be whipped, the impotent relieved and the unemployed found work. In all these respects, the unit of obligation and control was the little commonwealth of the parish, which effectively became a welfare republic, the moral and physical boundaries of which had to be effectively policed. Of course, the ancient settled poor of the parish lay at the heart of the community and were accordingly treated benevolently and sympathetically by their rate-paying neighbours.[14] But if the local community was compassionate, its compassion had a hard edge, and the realities of relief at the margins (where communities are always tested and new social identities formed) were grudging, mean and tainted by fear and suspicion.[15]

It fell to parish overseers and to the ratepayers and vestrymen who elected them to take the crucial decisions through which entitlement was allocated.[16] As the anonymous author of *An ease for overseers of the poore* of 1601 put it, overseers had a 'political' role: 'to be governors of the poore'.[17] The overseer was 'to have charge over the poore as the shepearde over his sheepe': 'to employ by worke, to relieve by money, to order by discretion the defects of the poore'. Those fit for the office were men of 'wealth, wit and good conscience'. It was recommended that overseers should ideally be 'subsidie men', or failing that 'substantiall men', for only they had the 'grace and majestie', 'circumspection', 'respect' and 'countenance to controll'. The overseer should also be a man of sufficient wisdom, distinguished by his 'experience of the laws', to be worthy of the 'honour of the office'. Only the foolish would scorn him, while the discreet would fear him, for 'the office of the overseere extendeth farre', consisting particularly 'in taxing contributions for the reliefe of the poore and in the discrete dispensation and ordering thereof'. Welfare legislation therefore specified the conditions under which the poor could be relieved and granted enormous discretion to those who enforced it. The calculus of entitlement was complex. A charge of 1623 empowered parish officers to report any idle labourer in order that magistrates could commit them to bridewell; to ascertain every weekend which of the poor had work for the next week, and to supply materials on which they could be employed; to ensure that pauper children were taught knitting and spinning; and to make twice-weekly searches for suspected night-walkers and pilfered goods. Most tellingly of all, however, overseers were not only to punish, but also to withhold poor relief from, all beggars and pilferers. The money thus saved would be used to reward those inhabitants who informed on pauper delinquency, at the rate of 6*d* a time.[18]

The poor, then, even the deserving poor, should know their *place*, both in the geographical sense of their parish of settlement and in the social-structural sense of their relation to their betters. The vestry of Swallowfield (Wiltshire) perfectly summed up the priorities of ratepayers when in 1596 they noted their desire that 'all shall do their best to helpe the honest poore, the blynd, the syck, the lame & diseased persons'. This bald statement of the charitable imperative found its counterpoint in the injunction that the poor should bear their lot with patience and fortitude. Charity was to be tempered with regulation: 'such as be poore and will malepertlye compare with their betters and sett them at nought shalbe warned to live and behave them selves as becomethe them'. If the poor failed to show due deference, they were to be reviled as 'comon disturbers of peace and quyetnes' and 'reformed by the severitie of the lawe'.[19] Discretionary decisions about entitlement to relief lay at the heart of all institutional charity in early seventeenth-century England. And as Lord Chief Justice Holt was subsequently to remark, 'What is *discretionary* but a softer word for *arbitrary*?'[20]

SETTLEMENT

Failure to defend parish boundaries imperilled the traditional notion that charity began at home and moved outward to kindred and neighbourhood. The worst-case scenario was that at Layston, where the rector complained in 1636 that twenty years of unregulated migration had allowed at least eighty welfare scroungers to infiltrate the parish, exhausting the resources of poor rates and endowed charity alike.[21] This fear of 'poor strangers crept amongst us' was ubiquitous until a federal co-ordinating structure for welfare republics was established in 1662, when the settlement laws clarified the conditions of local entitlement. Even into the eighteenth century, decisions about parochial responsibility were controversial and might entail 'exclusion crises' during which 'strangers', single mothers or newly married migrant couples were hounded across parish boundaries.[22]

Exclusion could also take more indirect forms, occurring even where poor migrants merely threatened to become a drain on parochial resources. In 1598 the Constantine vestry compelled all landlords to maintain lodgers and their prospective families at their own expense; in 1650 it insisted that irresponsible landlords should be rated for the poor 'not according to their ability' but 'according to the damage and charge' which they 'bring the parish unto by their folly'. A census taken at a parish meeting in North Nibley (Gloucestershire) in 1614 bracketed unauthorised inmates and strangers alongside pilferers, idlers and bastards. The vestry of Boxford (Suffolk) agreed in 1608 that lodgers would be permitted only with the prior consent of six chief inhabitants and with bonds of indemnity, an order repeated with stiffer penalties in 1625. At Hexham (Northumberland) in the 1630s the vestry insisted on the expulsion of inmates, to prevent 'prejudice and damage' to the town should this 'beggarly brood fall into poverty'. At Bedale (North Yorkshire) in 1642 fourteen days' notice to the vestry was required before strangers could be accommodated. In 1654 the vestry of Frampton (Lincolnshire) ordered fines of £20 for any householder taking lodgers without either the consent of the vestrymen or 'competent estate and sufficient bond given by the stranger that comes in to save the town from charge'. At Holmpton (East Yorkshire) the 'booke of instructions to be kept by the minister and strictly put in execution by the constables' begins with a declaration of the categories of rogues by statute. At Sigglesthorne (East Yorkshire) an 'exclusion order' was made 'by the inhabitants' as late as 1700. In early eighteenth-century Coleshill (Berkshire) the parish vestry ordered that no labourer was to be employed unless he was a parishioner, with a fine for offending employers.[23] The orders of 1630 for the good government of the parish of Aughton (Lancashire) prohibited parishioners from accepting single pregnant women as lodgers. In some parishes, such as Lytham (Lancashire) in 1627, the prohibition even extended to parents who offered house room to their unmarried pregnant daughters.[24]

Such regulations represent the unwelcoming, not to say the unwelcome, face of community, a countenance which frowned most severely on the 'imprudent' sexual and marital practices of the migrant poor. Although the inhibition of pauper marriages was strictly illegal, it seems to have been widespread in the period before the 1662 settlement laws clarified the ambiguities of entitlement to parish relief among young married couples. It was achieved either by the raising of objections at the calling of the banns, *viva voce* in the chancel of the parish church (as at Frampton in 1654), thus leaving little or no imprint in the historical record; or by having a quiet word with the minister beforehand, discouraging him from calling the banns in the first place (as at Swallowfield in 1596). Whatever the real identity of those who made objections, they were almost always cloaked in the language of community: those objecting are described as 'the parishioners', 'the inhabitants' or the 'parish'.[25]

GOVERNANCE

As might be expected, questions about membership of the community of the parish raised other questions about the criteria of belonging, the most important of which turned on participation in the decision-making process: who had the right to decide who belonged to the community? Parish elites answered this question in the petitions they submitted to the ecclesiastical hierarchy requesting that attendance at, and voting rights in, parish meetings should be restricted only to the better sort of inhabitants. The incumbent and churchwardens were rewarded with a bishop's faculty, an authoritative document whereby the oligarchic structure of parish governance was formally established or confirmed as a 'select vestry'.[26] The vicar-generals' books of the diocese of London contain forty-two such faculties, each of them effectively a parish constitution, over the period 1601–62. Thirty of these documents date from the period 1611–37, and a further eleven from 1660–62.[27]

Although faculties stipulated rules and regulations specific to each vestry, it is clear that as early as the 1610s a generic formula had been adopted to justify the circumscription of participation in parish affairs. In Ealing (Middlesex), for instance, parish meetings had allegedly been characterised by 'much disorder', both in 'taxing men indiscreetly by the consent of the inferior sort of people' and 'in disorderly placing of many in the church contrary to their rank and degree'. At Isleworth (Middlesex) audits had apparently been undermined by the dissent of the 'evil disposed and others of the inferior and meaner sorte of the parishioners'. At Twickenham (Surrey) such dissent had been all the more significant because 'the meaner and inferior sort of the multitude were so far the greater in number'. At Chigwell (Essex) the admitting of 'the parishioners of all sorts' to the church meetings had created confusion and disorder, since so many of them were 'ignorant or weak in judgement and others were not so readie to yield to that which the better sort of the parishioners would determine and agree upon'. By the 1620s faculties uniformly referred to the need for church business to be 'dispatched and done peaceably with discretion and in good order'. At Islington (Middlesex) parish business had customarily been determined 'by the parishioners and the better sort of inhabitants without contradiction' until 'of late certain refractorie and contentious persons of mean condition had endeavoured to resist and hinder the good determinations and proceedings' at vestry meetings.[28]

The wave of faculties issued at the Restoration are particularly interesting for the light they throw on parish government during the revolution. The 'late unhappy wilfulness and disorder in this kingdom' had, it was alleged, provoked 'irregularity in the management and dispatch of affairs relating to the good of the parish', specifically 'remissness and neglect in things necessary', 'heate and violence in other things less requisite' and 'faction in all [others] by the meaner sort of people who have least interest and little judgement'. Despite the good intentions of those who were of 'far better rank and condition', business 'had been carried tumultuously rather by number than by worth'. In 'the late times of distraction', it seems, all had 'claimed a liberty' to attend parish meetings, and 'the multitudes that soe mett were often so disorderly and tumultuous that nothing could be quietly and peaceably determined but with so much confusion and disorder' that the business in hand was obstructed and the peace breached.[29] In all these cases, both before 1637 and after 1660, successive chancellors of the diocese granted permission for the canons of the Church of England to be breached. The 'ancient custom' of the church stipulated that anybody 'rated toward the poor in the parish had from time to time a voice in the election of the church officers and hath been admitted to the church meetings'.[30] But where tumult, faction and popularity threatened to undermine the good governance of the parish, the right to attend was restricted. In this way, the select vestry became an institutional surrogate for the community it was supposed to serve.

CUSTOM

The pressures of immiseration and population turnover which encouraged parish elites to employ the calculus of welfare entitlement also forced them into the stricter regulation of less tangible communal resources. Disputes over the timing and scale of tithe payments, for example, reflect conflicting claims to the yield of land and livestock, and the depositions given in church courts reflect striking differentials between people of different social rank not only in their knowledge of ownership but also in the means by which that knowledge was acquired. Although custom offered a rhetoric through which the legitimacy of particular claims might be rehearsed and the harmony between individual and communal interests reasserted, it was an idiom in which both language and vocabulary became increasingly freighted with the interests of the ancient propertied inhabitants. This was true both in the central courts of equity, where the Barons of the Exchequer and Masters in Chancery increasingly tested customary claims against notions of reason, and in local manorial courts, where use rights were subject to intensive regulation. The fear of encroachment provoked manorial authorities into the reinforcement of communal boundaries, especially in those cases where parochial responsibility for the poor was superimposed on more ancient and complex inter-commoning arrangements between adjacent communities. Thus the copyholders of the five hamlets of Ashchurch (Gloucestershire) agreed in 1575 that the unregulated use of 160 acres of pasture customarily shared between them was 'inconvenient'. Instead they chose to allot to each of the hamlets a portion of the pasture 'according to the condition or quality of everyman's copyhold'. This decision implied the fragmentation of an older customary economy in the particular interests of the leading tenants of each hamlet.[31]

One of the best documented episodes of the reification of localised rights in property relates to the woodland parish of Caddington on the Hertfordshire–Bedfordshire border, where customary tenants had claimed since the thirteenth century 'to take freely in the woods according to the nature of their holdings'.[32] Although restrictions on wood collection have been taken to imply that 'the value of common rights in woodland should not be overestimated', unauthorised felling was evidently widespread. The attempts of the manorial court notwithstanding, the Wood had been cleared of timber by the turn of the century, a trend reflected by the increasing application of the term Caddington Common to what had once been called Caddington Great Wood. Manorial orders now turned to the restriction of cutting and carrying away of ferns for fuel, to the regulation of grazing and to the punishment of trespass.

Fears that strangers were taking advantage of Caddington common rights are reflected in late Elizabethan manorial orders: non-tenants were prohibited from pasturing cattle in 1575 and again in 1593, and there were further regulations about wood-cutting and hedge-breaking by 'out-townsmen' in 1579. Fines for illegal grazing on the common by non-residents were raised to 20d in 1594, to 2s in 1596 and to 2s 6d in 1604. By 1609 the concern to regulate 'the uses of waste' had become particularly intense: 5s fines were ordered for any illicit removals of mould or chalk. Some of these regulations were enforced against tenants as well as out-townsmen. Stints, stipulated at five sheep for each acre of fallow in 1594, were reduced to one in 1628. There is also evidence of similar concern with squatters, cottagers and inmates. Fines of 3s 4d were ordered in 1578 for lodging more than two tenants in a cottage. In 1610 the manorial court prohibited the letting of cottages to 'strangers'; in 1611, 10s fines were ordered for taking inmates; and in 1612 a penalty of £5 was stipulated for any lodgers at all. Presentments under the 1589 inmates statute date from 1597, and there were at least twenty-two orders for the removal of lodgers, involving over forty 'strangers', in the period 1615 to 1635, at least one of them attracting the attention of the county bench. The law was also growing steadily more difficult to enforce: the manorial court was insisting on indemnity bonds by 1632, and by 1636 there were prosecutions for failure to remove lodgers. The illegal erection of cottages also provoked a wave of concern, with eight prosecutions in 1615 alone. Both in limiting the growing numbers of inmates and cottagers, and in having difficulty in removing them, Caddington was typical of many early seventeenth-century sylvan and pastoral communities. The 'tragedy of the commons' led inexorably to an 'exclusion crisis'.

Piecemeal restrictions of the kind carried out in Caddington must have been very common elsewhere, and were particularly intense after enclosure. The lords of the manor of Honidene (Sussex), Richard Sackville, Earl of Dorset, and Edward Bergavenny, wrote to the homage in July 1622 explaining that 'whereas by our warrant and your consent' Chaylye Common had already been 'divided and allotted to every one according to their severall interests', they intended to confirm the arrangement at the next manorial court. They had nonetheless heard that 'strangers having no right of common there doe labour by indirect meanes to hinder' the enclosure 'tending to the mutuall prejudice of lord and tenant alike'. They resolved to force the enclosure through and to fulfil the promises of compensation made by their steward but also to punish any further misdemeanours committed by 'forreyners or others'.[33] Indeed, this sense that foreigners should be prevented from exploiting local common rights had been bolstered by an authoritative judgement at common law in 1607. In *Gateward's Case* the Justices of Common Pleas ruled that rights of common might be claimed only by copyholders or leaseholders, to the exclusion of cottagers, on the basis that customary right inhered not in persons but in houses of husbandry. In thus reifying or materialising intangible use rights the judges contributed to the process whereby cottagers and squatters were denied access to common wastes in the interests of the ancient settled tenants of the community.[34] And all this, of course, is to say nothing of enclosure, the most obvious means whereby the customary balance of communal resources might be tipped in favour of the propertied. Perhaps as much as 18 per cent of the land in the south Midlands, much of it located in pastoral areas, was enclosed in a 'second great wave' of agrarian change between 1575 and 1674. Despite governmental optimism that 'enclosure by agreement' might adequately compensate the propertyless, the marginal poor were often browbeaten or simply ignored in the process of hedging and ditching communal space.[35]

RITUAL

As David Underdown has argued, ritual reveals important features of the social, religious and political identity of the community. But, he insists, 'ritual is not merely reflective of society, it is itself a feature of the social order, part of the way the social structure is articulated and communicated and hence fit into a web of language and gesture rather than being simply the consequence of fixed and material features of a society'.[36] This is most obviously true of those rites of passage – baptism, churching, marriage and burial – through which the processes of becoming a member of, and departing from, the community of the parish was structured. The public rituals of the parish church represented phases in a ceremonial system through which individual religious identity was symbolically represented in its wider social context. Communion was, therefore, a collective rite in which the symbols of fellowship were consciously and unconsciously manipulated. This ritual, like those of baptism and marriage, was performed in the parish church and explicitly depended upon the parish as its social referent. To this extent, changes in the form of the ritual both reflected and symbolised changes in the structure if the parish community.

In particular, the stylistic innovations in parochial religion insisted upon by Archbishop Laud in the 1630s had profound implications for the nature of the local community. The Laudian emphasis on 'the objective qualities of the sacred, its immanence in the fabric of the parish church and its unique concentration in the fixed communion table' led to the attempt to enforce a 'circle of order' which circumscribed access to the heart of Christian worship.[37] The removal of communion tables from the nave to the upper end of the chancel, and the construction of a boundary of altar rails around them, was the liturgical equivalent of the enclosure of the common fields, depriving the community as a whole of its traditional right to the resources of the supernatural economy. Whereas their Jacobean predecessors had huddled around the communion table, only the more prosperous Caroline parishioners who sat in the front pews now had unrestricted sight and hearing of the celebration of communion. A ritual which had once expressed social solidarity now smacked of religious fragmentation, with poorer parishioners in the rear pews distanced from the heart of the ceremonial system. Laudian church discipline therefore designated insiders and outsiders just as effectively in the local community as it did in the communities of realm and cosmos.

Ritual also characterised the inversionary customs of the festive calendar through which the community was brought together in an atmosphere of carnival and celebration. Among the most remarkable descriptions of late sixteenth-century communal sociability are the reminiscences of Francis Taverner, lord of the Hertfordshire manor of Hexton. Writing in 1625 in a tone that conveys both nostalgia and condescension, Taverner recounted the 'strange kind of pastyme and jollities' of the Hocktide feast, sports which had continued (along with 'maying feasts' and 'plays of Robyn Hood and Little John') into the 1560s, and which he felt 'these nicer tymes of ours would not only despise but also account ymmodest if not prophane'.[38] The revellers gathered atop the highest hill in the parish on Hock Monday morning, and played 'pulling at the pole'. Opposing teams played tug-of-war with 'a long and very strong ashen pole' which the women tried to pull down the hill and the men sought to keep erect. The 'waggishe' men frequently let go, so that the women 'fell over and over with their coats about their ears'. When the women triumphed, they would push the men 'into the ditches and brooks' and would 'baffle and besmeare' any of 'the weaker men they could master'. When the pole was eventually brought to the market cross, the women 'provided good cheere' and 'a great number of people' feasted together in the town house 'without any affront or dislike taken at any hand'. A collection was then taken, and the proceeds were split between the poor of the parish and the church-wardens. In the afternoon there was further sport in the 'play close', where if the women 'toke any of the weaker men prisoners they would use them unhaplye inoughe'. Taverner thought that the 'pulling at the pole' represented 'deliverance from the Danes', a local victory achieved by the women of the parish by beating the enemy 'with poles and beesoms', 'kicking them into the kennelles and bemyring their faces, and that with all manner of hockerie and scorne unto them'. It is particularly significant, however, that Taverner chose to emphasise that Hexton Hock was 'solemnised' by 'the best inhabitants', who annually elected two officers to provide the ale and govern the feast. In deliberate imitation of churchwardens' staffs, these hockers carried 'large birtchen brooms'. 'Many of the inhabitants, both men and women, and amongst them the most substantiale of them', scripted the performance of the inversion ritual, casting the community in its appointed role.[39]

Rituals such as these have had their apologists, both among historians and contemporaries. Historians, especially those influenced by functionalist anthropological thinking, have argued that they acted as societal safety valves, temporarily encouraging inversion, misrule and other games of role reversal, in the longer-term interests of reaffirming the hierarchical principle.[40] Similarly positive assessments were not unknown to contemporaries: William Piers, Bishop of Bath and Wells, argued in 1633 that Sunday revels were 'highly valued for the civilising of the people, for their lawful recreations, for composing differences by making of friends, for increase of love and amity, as being feasts of charity, for relief of the poor, the richer sort then keeping open house and for many other reasons'.[41] Although such views should not be uncritically accepted, festive customs were clearly of immense social, economic and cultural significance. By legitimating the local calendar, defining and preserving the physical and moral limits of the local community, and structuring the values, beliefs and rights which formed the framework of everyday experience, revels affirmed social solidarity within the context of local power relations.[42]

One particular festive ritual, the beating of the bounds of the parish at Rogationtide, also served the purpose of reaffirming the spatial boundaries of the community. As is well known, the perambulation was 'a corporate manifestation of the village community', both reflective, and constitutive, of a sense of belonging to the parish.[43] Although perambulation was the one form of religious procession to survive the Reformation, it is nonetheless significant that the following century saw considerable controversy over entitlement to participate in the festivities. The Archdeacon of Berkshire insisted as late as 1615 that perambulations should be kept by ministers 'with a sufficient number of the parishioners of all sorts, aswel of the elder as younger sort, for the better knowledge of the circuits and bounds of the parish'.[44] From as early as 1559, however, clergymen were enjoined to walk the parishes as they were accustomed, but only 'with the curate and the substantial men of the parish'.[45] This restrictive stipulation was reiterated in successive visitation articles by Elizabethan and Jacobean bishops. Archbishop Grindal's articles for the province of York required in 1571 that Rogations, commonly called gang days, should be carried out only by 'the parson, vicar or curate, churchwardens and certain of the substantial men of the parish'.[46] As might be expected, restrictions on participation were not merely social-structural, they were also geographical and jurisdictional. Thus Bishop Howson of Oxford stipulated in 1628 that the numbers walking be 'restrained and limitted by the minister and the church-wardens and some other substantial men of your parish', in order that perambulations 'be not overburthensome', 'especially with out-commers from other parishes'.[47] Like wakes and church ales, it was feared Rogationtide drinkings might all too easily tempt the migrant poor of adjacent parishes to take advantage of hospitality. By definition, however, perambulations were designed to promote social and spatial awareness of the boundaries of the parish community, and were therefore exclusive occasions.

RECASTING THE COMMUNITY

The ethos of community was one of charity, neighbourliness and reciprocal obligation. Ideally, it should encompass all the members of the 'little commonwealth' of the parish. Everyone, insisted the chief inhabitants of Swallowfield in 1596, ought to 'do his best to end all strifes w[hi]ch shall happen between neighbor and neighbour be they poore or Rytche'.[48] This fundamental Christian injunction to 'love thy neighbour as thyself' necessarily implied, as John Rogers of Dedham (Essex) urged in 1632, that 'true love must be common: one *another*.' Neighbourly love, he argued, 'is in the plurall number and shewes a communitie; that we must not love one, or two, or a few, but all, and especially all that feare God. Love communicates itself and is not engrossed to a few ... yea we must love the meanest that fear God and not neglect them. The meanest member of the body is regarded by the greatest.'[49] But although it carried enormous ethical weight, the ideal of neighbourliness was just that – an ideal.[50] As the foregoing discussion has suggested, the realities of social and economic differentiation in the century after 1550 ensured that the vision of neighbourliness became fragmented and marginalised, and was perforce restricted to certain degrees and sorts of inhabitants, among whom the habit of political association strengthened the parochial sense of place.

If the community of the parish became oligarchic, it was, above all, a *male* oligarchy. Since the primary qualification for participation in the parochial decision-making process was discretion, it necessarily followed that women were excluded, since their lack of education rendered them unfit to exercise it.[51] Although there were undoubtedly powerful female networks of mutuality and support which might provide a refuge from patriarchy, and although women might exert considerable influence in the construction and maintenance of communal opinion over matters of honour and reputation, the political culture of the rural community was by definition dominated by substantial male inhabitants.[52] Indeed, in their wish to be 'estemed to be *men* of discretion, good Credett, honest Myndes & Christian lyke behaveour one towards an other', male chief inhabitants undoubtedly envisaged themselves as 'the parishe'.[53] Just as their deployment of rhetorics of differentiation and dissociation testifies to the role of the better sort in classifying and constructing the moral community, the policies which they enacted demonstrated their ability to dictate the geographical boundaries of the parish. In their role as the policemen of migration, in the piecemeal enclosure of rural England to which they contributed and from which they benefited, in their pre-eminence in the rituals of Rogationtide through which the perimeters of the parish were committed to collective memory, the chief inhabitants of rural communities turned the landscape into emptiable space, and dictated the order of human territoriality.

As the hierarchy of belonging in the rural parish became ever more narrowly based, the continuum of belonging underwent a similar process of contraction. But both developments might actually be constitutive of new communal identities and attitudes. After all, the realities of exclusion were not simply linguistic. Just as their participation in the decision-making process fostered increasing self-consciousness among the parish elite, the poor were made all too aware of their place as strangers and subordinates. The better sort were well aware of their capacity to cleanse the commonwealth: 'in a town when chief men hold together', asked John Rogers of Dedham in 1632, 'what evil can stand against them? What good may they not effect?'[54] The poor were no less conscious of the sources of their strength: an Essex labourer inciting over 100 of his neighbours from Hatfield Peverel and Ulting to forcibly 'fetch out corn enough for all' in the summer of 1594 asked, 'What can riche men do against poor men yf poore men ryse and hold toguither?'[55]

By the mid-seventeenth century the parochial sense of place had become widely diffused throughout the social structure. It found official expression in the six income bands and corresponding dress codes of the sumptuary legislation, which was rehearsed in royal proclamations, reiterated from the pulpit, and represented in clothing and comportment. Most famously, under the terms of the 1571 'Cap Act', the poor were made to dress for deference, thereby precluding the potential 'confusion of all degrees' which contemporaries feared as 'the most pestilent canker in a commonwealth'.[56] In death, too, the rich exercised their prerogatives to distinguish themselves from the poorer neighbours, not only by electing to be buried in the chancel of the parish church, but also, after 1666, by forfeiting a £5 levy to a good cause – the poor of the parish – entitling themselves to be buried other than in a woollen shirt, shift or sheet.[57] Death may have been a great leveller, but status and wealth were visible even beyond the grave. The confidence with which the propertied exempted themselves from the obligation to bury their kin in woollen, and the increasing tendency of doles to the poor to be distributed only on the condition that paupers 'trouble not' the households of the deceased at funerals, reflect a long-term process of cultural polarisation whereby local elites withdrew from communal affairs. Indeed, the separation of the ruling class from their social inferiors was arguably even more marked in death than it had been in life: in the delay between death and burial, in the clothing in which they were wrapped, in the geography of interment, in the iconography of commemoration, and in the hospitality which followed, the propertied firmly grasped one last opportunity to assert their social and economic privileges.

There were other potent markers of social distinction, not least of which were those co-ordinates on the social maps of responsibility, entitlement and precedence: the poor rate assessment, the custumal and the church seating plan. The poor, and especially the migrant poor, were relegated to the margins of all three maps: flitting through constables' account books only as vagrants bribed to pass on their way; repeatedly fined in manorial court rolls for encroaching on the waste; shunted in pew plans to viewpoints, perhaps even the belfry or the gallery, remote from altar and pulpit alike. In these senses, to borrow Gerrard Winstanley's resonant phrase, the poor were 'hedged out' of the community: denied automatic access to welfare in cash and kind; excluded from the communal perquisites of the customary economy by quickset and fences; and distanced from the symbolic heart of the community by box pews and altar rails.[58] All of which makes even more urgent Edward Thompson's famous (and, as yet, unanswered) question: 'How did a society whose manifest ideology was paternalism feel from below?' In answering it, we must remember that belonging, like other entitlements, was conditioned by inequalities of wealth and power.[59] These inequalities endowed the propertied even with the right to redefine the very *meaning* of community, as the most famous contemporary apologist for the subordinate recognised. 'The heart of covetousness,' insisted Winstanley, 'swells most against community, calling community a thief, that takes other men's rights and property from them.'[60]

NOTES

1 William Hunt, *The puritan moment: the coming of revolution in an English county* (Cambridge MA, Harvard University Press, 1983), p. 131.

2 Brian Short, 'Images and realities in the English rural community: an introduction', and Joan Thirsk, 'English rural communities: structures, regularities and change in the sixteenth and seventeenth centuries', both in Brian Short (ed.), *The English rural community: image and analysis* (Cambridge, Cambridge University Press, 1992).

3 Cf. Richard M. Smith, '"Modernisation" and the corporate medieval village community in England: some sceptical reflections', in Alan R. H. Baker and Derek Gregory (eds), *Explorations in historical geography* (Cambridge, Cambridge University Press, 1984).

4 Keith Wrightson, 'The politics of the parish in early modern England', in Paul Griffiths, Adam Fox and Steve Hindle (eds), *The experience of authority in early modern England* (Basingstoke, Macmillan, 1996), p. 19.

5 David Levine and Keith Wrightson, *The making of an industrial society: Whickham, 1560–1765* (Oxford, Oxford University Press, 1991), p. 280.

6 Compare medieval attitudes to poverty elaborated in Geoffrey Shepherd, 'Poverty in *Piers Plowman*', in T. H. Aston, P. R. Coss, C. Dyer and J. Thirsk (eds), *Social relations and ideas: essays in honour of R. H. Hilton* (Cambridge, Cambridge University Press, 1984), and David Aers, '*Piers Plowman*: poverty, work, and community', in *id.*, *Community, gender and individual identity: English writing, 1360–1430* (London, Routledge, 1988), with the late seventeenth-century position described in A. L. Beier, '"Utter strangers to industry, morality and religion": John Locke on the poor', *Eighteenth-Century Life*, 12 (1988), 28–41.

7 Joyce Oldham Appleby, *Economic thought and ideology in seventeenth-century England* (Princeton NJ, Princeton University Press, 1978), p. 3.

8 Alan Macfarlane, *Reconstructing historical communities* (Cambridge, Cambridge University Press, 1977), pp. 14–16; Smith, '"Modernisation" and the corporate medieval village community', pp. 150–61.

9 R. H. Tawney, *Religion and the rise of capitalism: a historical study* (1926; London, Penguin, 1990), especially pp. 140–96. This view (and that of those historians who followed him) is explicit not only in More's *Utopia* but also in Robert Crowley, 'An information and petition against the oppressours of the pore commons of this realme' [1548], in J. M. Cowper (ed.), *The select works of Robert Crowley*, Early English Text Society, Extra Series, 15 (Oxford, Oxford University Press, 1872), pp. 151–76; and Hugh Latimer, 'Last sermon preached before Edward VI, Lent 1550', in G. E. Corrie (ed.), *Sermons by Hugh Latimer*, Parker Society (Cambridge, Cambridge University Press, 1844), pp. 239–81.

10 BL MS Harley 787, no. 11; Steve Hindle, 'Hierarchy and community in the Elizabethan parish: the Swallowfield articles of 1596', *Historical Journal* 42 (1999), 835–51, p. 850.

11   Hertfordshire R[ecord] O[ffice] D/P 65/3/3, pp. 328, 338; Cornwall RO DD P39/8/1, unfoliated (resolutions of 10 June 1598, 20 October 1650).

12   C. S. L. Davies, 'Slavery and Protector Somerset: the Vagrancy Act of 1547', *Economic History Review*, second series, 19 (1966), 533–49.

13   Paul Slack, *Poverty and policy in Tudor and Stuart England* (Harlow, Longman, 1988), pp. 113–37.

14   Tim Wales, 'Poverty, poor relief and the life cycle: some evidence from seventeenth-century Norfolk', and W. Newman-Brown, 'The receipt of poor relief and family situation: Aldenham, Hertfordshire, 1630–90', both in Richard M. Smith (ed.), *Land, kinship and life cycle* (Cambridge, Cambridge University Press, 1984).

15   Steve Hindle, 'Exclusion crises: poverty, migration and parochial responsibility in English rural communities, c. 1560–1660', *Rural History* 7 (1996), 125–49.

16   The following discussion summarises Steve Hindle, 'Exhortation and entitlement: negotiating inequality in English rural communities, 1550–1650', in Michael J. Braddick and John Walter (eds), *Order, hierarchy and subordination in early modern England and Ireland* (Cambridge, Cambridge University Press, forthcoming).

17   The following discussion is based on *An ease for overseers of the poore: abstracted from the statutes, allowed by practise, and now reduced into forme, as a necessarie directorie for imployinge, releeuing, and ordering the poore* (Cambridge, 1601), pp. 3, 5–7, 14.

18   Bodleian Library MS Tanner 73, fol. 390.

19   Hindle, 'Hierarchy and community', p. 850.

20   Holt KB 680, cited in D. E. C. Yale (ed.), *Lord Nottingham's Chancery cases* I, Selden Society 73 (London, Quaritch, 1954), p. xlvi.

21   Hindle, 'Exclusion crises', p. 133.

22   Steve Hindle, 'Power, poor relief and social relations in Holland Fen, c. 1600–1800', *Historical Journal* 41 (1998), 67–96; *id.*, 'The problem of pauper marriage in seventeenth-century England', *Transactions of the Royal Historical Society*, sixth series, 8 (1998), 71–89.

23   Cornwall RO DD P39/8/1, unfoliated (resolutions of 10 June 1598, 20 October 1650); GPL MS 16526, fol. 99; Suffolk RO FB77/E2/3 (ordinances of 28 March 1608, 17 April 1625); Peter Rushton, 'The poor law, the parish and the community in north-east England, 1600–1800', *Northern History* 25 (1989), 132–52, p. 140; North Yorkshire RO PR/BED 2/1, unfoliated (resolution of 1 July 1642); Hindle, 'Power, poor relief and social relations', pp. 89–90; EYAS PE 19/12, unfoliated EYAS PE 144/23, unfoliated (resolution of 18 February 1700); Peter Clark, 'Migration in England during the late seventeenth and eighteenth centuries', reprinted in Peter Clark and David Souden (eds), *Migration and society in early modern England* (London, Hutchinson, 1987), p. 235.

24   Lancashire RO QSB/1/70/48; DDC1/1141.

25   Hindle, 'The problem of pauper marriage'.

26   Beat Kümin, *The shaping of a community: the rise and reformation of the English parish, c. 1400–1560* (Aldershot, Scolar Press, 1996), p. 252.

27   L[ondon] M[etropolitan] A[rchives] DL/C/338–344.

28   LMA DL/C/340, fols 47^v–49, 129, 130^v–31, 184^v–85; DL/C/341, fols 149^v–50, 162–63, 163^{r-v}; DL/C/343, fols 86^{r-v}.

29 LMA DL/C/344, fols 128–29^v, 205, 207^v–09^v, 210–11^v, 213^v–14, 214^v–16.

30 LMA DL/C/343, fol. 106.

31 Daniel C. Beaver, *Parish communities and religious conflict in the Vale of Gloucester, 1590–1690* (Cambridge MA, Harvard University Press, 1998), p. 32.

32 Steve Hindle, 'Persuasion and protest in the Caddington Common enclosure dispute, 1635–39', *Past and Present* 158 (1998), 37–78, pp. 50–2.

33 East Sussex RO SAS/ABER 27, fol. 16.

34 Roger B. Manning, *Village revolts: social protest and popular disturbances in England, 1509–1640* (Oxford, Oxford University Press, 1988), pp. 85–6, 311, 315; E. P. Thompson, *Customs in common* (London, Merlin, 1991), pp. 121–2, 130, 132–3, 136, 138–9.

35 Robert C. Allen, *Enclosure and the yeoman: the agricultural development of the south Midlands, 1450–1850* (Oxford, Oxford University Press, 1992), pp. 30–2; Hindle, 'Persuasion and protest', p. 41.

36 David Underdown, *Revel, riot and rebellion: popular politics and culture in England, 1603–60* (Oxford, Oxford University Press, 1987), p. 44.

37 Beaver, *Parish communities and religious conflict*, p. 159.

38 BL MS Additional 6223, fols 11^v–14.

39 Sally-Beth MacLean, 'Hocktide: a reassessment of a popular pre-Reformation festival', in Meg Twycross (ed.), *Festive drama* (Woodbridge, Boydell & Brewer, 1996), pp. 233–41.

40 Mikhail Bakhtin, *Rabelais and his world* (English trans., Bloomington IN, Indiana University Press, 1965), pp. 74–6; Peter Burke, *Popular culture in early modern Europe* (London, Temple Smith, 1978) pp. 199–204; Michael D. Bristol, *Carnival and theatre: plebeian culture and the structure of authority in Renaissance England* (London, Routledge, 1985), pp. 26–39.

41 PRO SP 16/250/20.

42 Hunt, *The puritan moment*, pp. 132–3; R. W. Bushaway, 'Rite, legitimation and community in southern England, 1700–1850: the ideology of custom', in Barry Stapleton (ed.), *Conflict and community in southern England: essays in the history of rural and urban labour from medieval to modern times* (Stroud, Sutton, 1992), pp. 124–30.

43 Keith Thomas, *Religion and the decline of magic: studies in popular beliefs in sixteenth- and seventeenth-century England* (London, Weidenfeld & Nicolson, 1971), p. 65.

44 Kenneth Fincham (ed.), *Visitation articles and injunctions of the early Stuart church* I, Church of England Record Society I (Woodbridge, Boydell & Brewer, 1994), p. 132.

45 P. L. Hughes and J. F. Larkin (ed.), *Tudor royal proclamations* II, *1553–87* (New Haven CT, Yale University Press, 1969), p. 122.

46 W. H. Frere (ed.), *Visitation articles and injunctions of the period of the Reformation* III, *1559–75*, Alcuin Club Collections XVI (London, 1910), p. 264.

47 Fincham (ed.), *Visitation articles and injunctions* I, pp. 197–8.

48 Hindle, 'Hierarchy and community', p. 850.

49 John Rogers, *A treatise of love* (London, 1632), p. 91.

50 Eamon Duffy, *The stripping of the altars: traditional religion in England, 1400–1580* (New Haven CT, Yale University Press, 1992), p. 95.

51 Sara Mendelson and Patricia Crawford, *Women in early modern England, 1550–1720* (Oxford, Oxford University Press, 1998), pp. 50, 56–7.

52 Steve Hindle, 'The shaming of Margaret Knowsley: gossip, gender and the experience of authority in early modern England', *Continuity and Change* 9 (1994), 391–419; Bernard Capp, 'Separate domains? Women and authority in early modern England', in Griffiths *et al.*, *The experience of authority*.

53 Hindle, 'Hierarchy and community', p. 851 (emphasis added).

54 Rogers, *A treatise of love*, p. 46.

55 J. S. Cockburn (ed.), *Calendar of assize records: Essex indictments, Elizabeth I* (London, HMSO, 1978), nos. 2579–80. For other examples see Joel Samaha, 'Gleanings from local criminal court records: sedition among the "inarticulate" in Elizabethan England', *Journal of Social History* 8 (1975), 61–79; Peter Clark, *English provincial society from the Reformation to the Revolution* (Hassocks, Harvester Press, 1977) p. 250; J. A. Sharpe, 'Social strain and social dislocation, 1585–1603', in John Guy (ed.), *The reign of Elizabeth I: court and culture in the last decade* (Cambridge, Cambridge University Press, 1995), pp. 199–200.

56 13 Elizabeth I, cap. 19 (1571); N. B. Harte, 'State control of dress and social change in pre-industrial England', in D. C. Coleman and A. H. John (eds), *Trade, government and economy in pre-industrial England* (London, Weidenfeld & Nicolson, 1976), p. 137; W. P. Baildon (ed.), *Les reportes del cases in Camera Stellata, 1593–1609* (London, privately published, 1894), p. 57. For prosecutions see PRO CHES 21/1, fol. 154ᵛ (April 1591).

57 Alan Hunt, *Governance of the consuming passions: a history of sumptuary law* (Basingstoke, Macmillan, 1996), pp. 323–4.

58 Gerrard Winstanley, 'A new-year's gift for the parliament and army', in Christopher Hill (ed.), *Winstanley: The Law of Freedom and other writings* (Cambridge, Cambridge University Press, 1983), p. 201.

59 Edward Thompson, 'The crime of anonymity', in Douglas Hay *et al.*, *Albion's fatal tree: crime and society in eighteenth-century England* (London, Allen Lane, 1975), p. 304. Cf. Hindle, 'Exhortation and entitlement'.

60 Winstanley, 'A new-year's gift', p. 196.

Chapter 7

Overlapping circles: imagining criminal communities in London, 1545–1645

Paul Griffiths

The underworld was a world apart.[1]

I touched all sides, and nobody knew where I belonged.[2]

DRAWING EDGES

I imagine communities in early modern London as a shifting sequence of overlapping circles. Overlapping because the communities I have in mind constantly touched at points of intersection, dispute, or compromise. Circles because, despite these overlaps that make it difficult for us to think of 'pure' categories or communities, I am anxious to retain crystal-clear senses of shared experiences and interests among the vagrants, thieves, brothel-keepers and pimps who are my principal protagonists.

London was a city of overlapping circles and this disarray was a root cause of its tensions. The city map was complicated by crisscrossing jurisdictions. Wards and parishes overlapped, trespasses made explicit in boundary contests; obstructive liberties remained, sapping the patience of legislators. The people, too, were a many-sided mass. This diversity was tamed by concise cuts that split people into convenient polarities like settled and rootless or citizen and criminal. Societies are imagined along boundaries like these that signify difference as well as uncertainty. Foucault calls this 'the principle of elementary location or partitioning'; the construction of 'confused, massive or transient polarities' to locate 'presences and absences'.[3] These 'ideological' cuts[4] helped to disseminate senses of inclusion and exclusion. In such ways it was hoped that policy and policing would fashion criminals as dishonest, distant, and different outcasts.[5]

The 'underworld' was one such cut. A long line of (mostly literary) scholars have turned the pages of contemporary pamphleteers like Harman, Dekker or Greene, to uncover a tightly graded, organised criminal underworld in early modern London.[6] In so doing, they tell a tale of two cities: the settled, conventional city and its mirror image, the 'parallel [underworld] culture'. One scholar writes that criminals were 'no longer ordinary men of their times', but an alien troop set apart by their mobility, promiscuity, and vocabulary; an actual 'anti-order', no less.[7] Just like contemporary pamphleteers or policy-makers, generations of scholars have imagined crime through boundaries: putting people in tightly sealed pockets of insiders and outsiders. To some extent, historians do much the same thing if they pass judgement on the reality, or otherwise, of a criminal underworld in early modern London without thinking more deeply about how circles of citizens and criminals overlapped.

Mary Douglas writes that 'all margins are dangerous': what disturbs governors are 'half' or incomplete identities, or border crossings. It is here, at the margins, where insider meets outsider, that difficulties can ensue. Douglas notes that there is 'energy' in 'margins and unstructured areas'.[8] Drawing boundaries is a reassuring and satisfying gesture because it defines a problem and limits it to a particular place. The criminologist Tannenbaum writes that the community 'cannot deal with people whom it cannot define'. Uncertain presences are unsettling. Imagine the panic in London Common Council, then, when it was reported that 'sundry lewd and ydle persons' had committed 'divers outrages' in 1603, who 'cannot well bee described but by viewe and sight of them'; or in the next year as reports circulated of a pack of 'lewde and dangerous' lurkers 'who cannot yet be described by any particular markers whereby they may be noted'.[9]

Magistrates felt far more comfortable when suspects had traceable bio-graphies and good reason to be in London. Above all, it was restless move-ment, imprecision or nothingness that was depicted in descriptions of threatening existences. Time after time, suspects were charged with 'not havinge any certyne or knowne trade of life', or with being unable to supply 'good accompt of howe they doe lawfullie live' or 'lawfull cause of theire repaire or abode'. In a nutshell, judicial examinations tried to piece together the facts of lives. Suspects were questioned about their 'ordre of lyfe' or 'qualities of livinge'. Thomas Dekker's 'inquisitor' asked the following questions of women he spotted out late at night. 'Where have you been so late? ... Are you married? ... What's your husband? ... Where lie you?' Elinor Death was questioned at Bridewell in 1603: 'And beinge demaunded wheare she dwelt saithe she doth not knowe, and being asked what maintenance she hathe to live uppon she cannot showe anie just matter.' As a result, the court ruled that it 'appeareth plainlie' that 'she liveth as an idle vagraunt, lewdlie, and disorderlie', and punishment followed swiftly.[10]

Boundaries were never more valued than in the late sixteenth and early seventeenth centuries, when it was felt that they were under pressure. Now, at the precise point when they seemed fallible and frail, boundaries and moralities were emphatically asserted. The interpretation of crime and its seemingly spiralling sources was a cause of deep concern in Guildhall and Whitehall. The swarm of criminals who, like parasites, fed off the citizens' hard graft were the topic of the day in word and print. Pamphleteers cautioned that this was no passing phase on a road to recovery; crime was in all corners and it was a highly organised challenge to the well-being of society. Preachers blasted delinquents from their pulpits. Politicians passed an endless stream of orders to curb the menace. But their warnings never ceased, and they escalated in both tone and number over the century 1545–1645.

Common Council was sure about the scale of difficulties in 1610, declaring that '[e]xtraordinary assemblies flocke and meete togeather to committ outrages and other dangerous attempts'. 'The city is exceeding full' was the cry in 1627.[11] Quite striking are emphases on present time and first-hand experience. Damaging dangers are here and now: 'badde' people 'daily arrive' in London; vagrants 'dailie swarme' and 'dailie hunte' in all parts of the city.[12] Vagrants swarmed everywhere, more 'than at any tymes heretofore hath been seene', Common Council regretted in 1609. Thirty years later, little had changed: 'in every mans observation the streetes of this citty are very much pestered with [vagrants] ... as if there were noe lawes at all'.[13] Over and over again, until it was a ritual bleat, magistrates voiced horror at the swarms of vagrants like locust clouds descending on the city.

And it was not just a vagrant rush that raised daily dread: a fleet of other testing dangers knocked the city off balance. Soaring crime was by now a perennial lament: 'offences dayly more and more abound by reason that the citty groweth dayly more populous', the Court of Aldermen moaned in 1609.[14] London's immoral face was now more plain to see – 'bawds and the practice of bawderey increaseath and raineth muche in this citty', the Bridewell governors complained in 1621, trying to nudge the Court of Aldermen into moral combat.[15] Alehouses as well as vagrants cropped up in 'exceeding numbers'. Alleys appeared to turn off to all points of the compass, giving shelter to threatening 'sorts'. Greedy landlords divided rooms into ever smaller spaces, squeezing in impossible numbers of inmates. Several streams rushed across the city far too fast to dam up – traffic, human traffic, rumour, noise.[16] Even worse, physical barriers were breached: doors, windows or holes dotted the walls, parts of which were crumbling. It seemed that steeply rising crime and a galaxy of other horrors were eroding civic prestige.

This decay and disarray are what rulers sought to describe and contain. The city was a messy, moving mass, but it could be tamed by imagining stability in the form of compliant citizen communities or observed boundaries. It was also useful to turn *detective* and *discover* communities, their origins, people, and shape. This is why a monsoon of criminal labels fell on rootless and threatening existences. It is also why the authorities kept counting people as never before from the second half of the sixteenth century. A census is a political instrument, a possession of knowledge: it counts but also classifies, and gives identity and shape to hitherto faintly seen problem groups.[17] The number of these political numerations rocketed towards the turn of the seventeenth century: full-scale counts of wards or parishes were frequently set up; problems like inmates, Catholics or the poor, as well as troubling institutions like new buildings or alehouses, were added up; beggars and fishwives were badged and registered in steps to prune their numbers. Counting, labelling, licensing, marking, and discovering were inevitable political outcomes in this city of more than usual motion.

People were split into neat compartmentalisations through boundaries, and not just by governors. The most basic fracture was that dividing citizen and the unfree. Citizenship was a political, economic and social badge; a stamp of hard graft, sound conduct, and belonging that was evidence to counter slanders and grade character. One citizen heaped scorn on his Star Chamber opponent, 'a sleight fellow of little or noe credit'; but he was 'a householder of staid condicon and one of the liverie of his companie'. Another, in the same forum, expected respect because he was 'an ancient citizen'.[18] It was deeply wounding to hurl insults; even more so when jibes like beggar, pickpocket, thief, or whore put people on the criminal fringes. A bunch of priests sneaking along 'Prests Alley' after dark were said to be 'more lyke theeves than true men'.[19] The upright citizen is very visible in orders to still the city's hustle and bustle. He (it is nearly always he) is a householder who pays rates, holds office, and follows sound religion. He is among the cream of the community and is 'well disposed', 'honest', 'substanciall', 'able', or 'discreet'. Victims of theft were usually described as 'the good and best sorte of people'. Unlike the rootless and footloose criminal, citizens were 'ordinarie tradesmen' with a 'certaine place' in the metropolitan maze.[20]

At the opposite point of the compass to the 'best' people was the 'beast'. One 'common vagabond' was labelled 'an unruly idle beast'.[21] What emerged more vividly at the close of the sixteenth century was a sense of crime as both a cause and a consequence of the fast-growing, filthy, and smelly city. Into this mere square mile was compressed a galaxy of criminal and environmental horrors that were twinned through explanatory theories. Criminals threatened not just order, but the air, health, and beauty of the city too. Small wonder, then, that vocabularies implying contagion and contamination were extended to criminals as well as to plague, disease, dirt, foul smells, and the body.[22] The pox, too, was a mark of dirty infamy, and a real threat to citizens when it was felt to be contagious.[23]

Like rag-gatherers digging up heaps of rubbish or inmates squeezed into single rooms, vagrants infected the city and its citizens with their crimes and sores. To make matters worse, another mark of vagrancy was its dirty smell, a real risk when it was felt that infection passed through the air. It was said that Peter Harris, a 'comen roge' and 'idell vacabonde', was 'a nasty filthy man and stanke so as no man was able to abyde the ayre of him'. Beggars buzzing around St Paul's were said to be 'a very greate annoyance and noysome in smell'.[24] It is no accident that streets were ordered to be swept free of dirt and vagrants in the same sentence. One order referred to human 'refuse and vagabond people'.[25] In a polluted city where it was felt that crime was an infectious urge, and that criminals infected citizens, environmental understandings of crime proliferated and made good sense.

Even more unsettling was the understanding that there were ways of life on the edges. The written words of the courts referred to the 'vagrant', 'loose', or 'pilfering life'. Suspects were accused of appearing *like* loiterers, vagrants, or whores. Nothing was more troubling than reports of 'lewd, idle and wicked persons who flock to the city and maintain themselves by robbery and cosening', or 'the loose, rogishe and dissolute people which dailie live by thefte, coseninge and other badd and ungodlie meanes'.[26]

Other moral commentaries deliberately depicted threatening existences in terms of suspicious movement, secret manoeuvres, or hidden and therefore unknown actions. Suspects were said to have loitered, lingered and lurked in 'private' places. They were spotted on streets 'ranging', 'roving', 'shifting', or 'straggling'. Thomas Tosser, 'a vagrant pilferer, was 'taken skulkinge att Anthomes Ordinary whence things latelie have been stollen'. A constable 'watched' Ellen Holder 'skulking' for an hour in the street. A warrant was issued for Thomas Haskins, alias 'Little Tom', 'a creeper in at windows', in 1603, while Rose Bent and Elizabeth Owen were called 'stragglyng naughty packs'.[27]

Activity at the edges was depicted in records of policy and prosecution as sly, cunning, and underhand. John Parker was called 'a vagrant who frequenteth shoppes and warehouses slylie of purpose to steale'. Thomas Morgan was 'an ydle masterles man and pryer into houses to pilfer'. One 'ruffian' moved about 'cunninglie'; other shady people were 'crafty', hatching plots 'privily', making 'secret moves', or 'shrowding' dubious dealings.[28] Shadows added menace. Senses of 'otherness' have geographies too. Suspects lurked in 'secret corners', dark passages, obscure, private, remote, and 'unknown places' where light, regulation, and citizens' routes did not reach. Quite typical is the description of the 'malicious practises of divers lewde and wicked persons ... which doe lurke and hyde themselves in close and secrett manner ... livinge by wicked and ungodlye meanes'.[29]

In such ways, then, magistrates constructed boundaries that depicted separate worlds, moralities, and geographies. Their tactical insistence that citizen and criminal were in practice distinct categories was rooted in their perception of a city stretched to bursting point. In these tense and testing times it was felt that sweeping socio-economic change was challenging the existing, perceived nature of London and citizenship. The city seemed never stable; the rights of citizens were plucked away by the creeping intrusion of foreigners; perceptions of the city continued on a downward slide, culminating in the plea to the Crown in 1632 that 'the freedome of London which was heretofore of very great esteeme is growne to be [of] little worth'.[30] One defence of civic identity that took several forms was to beef up the image of citizenship; one of these forms was the neat partition between citizen and criminal. Yet there were few reassurances or still points at these boundaries. Worse still, the cancer was spreading inside the walls of the city. Boundaries are in some respects comforting, locating unpleasant things. It was hoped that distances between citizen and criminal would furnish support and solace. But just how great were such distances; and in what senses can we discuss criminal communities? It is to these issues that I will now turn.

CRIMINAL COMMUNITIES?

The evident distortions of a constructed 'underworld' or calculated political boundaries do not mean that we should limit criminal communities to a minor role in early modern London. Instead of a parallel criminal universe, we should hunt for the jigsaw pieces that, when put together, show associations or networks of criminals.[31] Bronislaw Geremek writes that 'one theft does not make a thief', and indeed many claimed that they robbed 'in meare necessity for want of victualls', or that 'they did it for poverty', before disappearing from the records for ever.[32] But in the capital, if nowhere else, a degree of planning, sociability, and lodging networks protected and encouraged thieves and others – despite John McMullan's assertion that 'Bridewell court records in London show no organised crime'.[33] Yet the weekly sittings of this court enable us to trace suspects for long periods in its records. Repeated allegations of begging, pilfering, or street-selling are backed up by plentiful evidence of criminal solidarities (and their limits), safe houses, and shared skills and techniques.

Bawdy houses supply good evidence of long-term offending. Contemporaries, after all, called commercial sex a 'trade'. It was said that husband and wife Gilbert and Margaret East 'cherishe ... ill rule in their house ... and live by it'; that John Shaw had 'no trade ... to lyve by but bawdrye'; that Richard Wattwood 'hath none other lyvinge' but the bawdy house he had kept 'theis viii yeres'; that Black Luce 'is a vilde bawde and lyveth by it'; and that the pimp Henry/Harry Boyer 'is a very bawde and comon and useth yt daylie'.[34] Earnings were well beyond the wildest dreams of day labourers. One Maye's wife of the Three Tons (without Aldgate) had earned £100 'by bawdry within these 3 yeres'. John Shaw's wife scooped £4 10s in a single night. Weekly rents paid by resident women were as much as 20s. Small wonder, then, that bawds were reported to be 'welthye' and 'seemed very riche' and that pimps picked up 'muche money'.[35]

None of this is solid evidence of an underworld, though records report a degree of collectivity and longevity in relations between criminals. It is apparent that a large number of alehouses and other houses were safe ports of call for vagrants and thieves. These welcoming staging posts provided resting places, food and drink, places to meet, swap talk, hatch plots, and fence stolen goods. In 1616 the King lectured the mayor and aldermen, saying that '[t]here would be no theeves if they had not their receipts' like 'base victuallers' who had 'nothing else to live by' but keeping 'houses of haunt and receipt' for cutpurses, vagrants, rogues, and deer, horse and sheep stealers.[36]

Many such alehouses were amphibious sites where citizen and criminal rubbed shoulders. They certainly gave criminalities an enduring sense of well defined place. One Bridewell deponent gave information that 'a great nomber' of cutpurses 'lye commonly every Satturday night in a barne at the further ende of Tuttle Street'; that cutpurses also lodged 'at an alehouse beyond the Blewe Anker in Warwick Lane'; and that 'a gret number of cutpurses lye every Saterday at night in another barne betwene Lambeth Marshe and the Bishop of Carlisle's house with dyverse whores thear with them'. Other reported meeting places of cutpurses included houses in 'Tuttle Streete in Westminster', Long Lane, White Cross Street (where 'cutters and hackers' meet), Kentish Street, St Nicholas Shambles ('by Ive Lane'), Fleet Street, Pepper Alley, 'a vitler at St Mary Hill' (where cutpurses 'have good cheare and spend all ther money'), the Three Footstools at St Katherines, the Blue Boar along Thames Street, and 'a sellar under a barbor' next door to St Thomas's Hospital.[37]

Few London spaces were untouched by problematic presences: vagrants, thieves, inmates, nightwalkers and idle, lewd, masterless, and suspicious people found shelter across the city or beyond the walls. William Fleetwood provided a list of 'harboring howses for maisterles-men, and for such as lyve by thefte and other such like shifts' in the city and its suburban fringe.[38] Nine 'fine' residents of St Clement Dane grumbled about a long barn which was 'a receptacle' for 'great numbers of rogues and vagabonds'. The watch disturbed the regular rest of seven vagrant women at 'the Fleet privie'; Luce Winter, a 'vagrant queane ... confessed that she useth to lye at Heyvery Barne neare Islington whether resorteth manie vagrant queanes and roges', including London Stone and Black Jack. In 1586 it was reported that 'rogues and vagabonds oftentimes lodge in the night' on Tower Hill, 'and burn straw to warm themselves'. The Smithfield sheep pens provided comfort for 'rogues, vagabonds, and lewd and masterlesse people ... in the night season'. Fleet Street residents moaned about the 'comen doore' of a divided building which 'is comenly left open' at night, 'whereby the entrie thereof is a comen receptacle for rogues'. Vagrants were frequently found squatting in cellars. On occasion, ballad singers or jugglers were spotted in pairs or larger groups. And we even find a vagrant wedding and see the couple toasted by their best vagrant friends. William Johnson and Cuthbert Wood, 'olde vaccabonds', were presented at Bridewell in 1562. The pair were picked up 'at the weddinge of Agnes Artors and Richarde Sailisburye, gestes of this house', at a house along Turnagain Lane. The couple 'were maried in Sepulchres Churche' and after drank and danced with 'a number of the vacabonds and harlotts of this house'.[39]

Cutpurses, pickpockets, and nips toured markets, scouting possibilities. Fairs were hunting grounds for beggars or thieves; St Bartholomew's Fair was a tense time when policing was stepped up. The Exchange, as the epicentre of London commerce, was much visited by vagrants, nightwalkers, lace clippers, and street traders setting up alternative exchanges, selling fruit, birds, poultry, dogs, plants, trees, 'and other commodities', blocking merchants' paths, 'curseinge and swearinge', sitting 'att unlawfull houres in the night tyme', raising quarrels.[40] The bridge across the Thames carried a stream of people and chances for cutpurses, pickpockets, and pilferers to track targets. Church congregations were a packed and predictable quarry, and cutpurses, pick-pockets, pilferers, and beggars rubbed shoulders with worshippers. Paul's Cross offered other sabbath-day plunder, and the cathedral and its precincts were a promising patch for beggars, street-sellers, thieves, and vagrants: it was a 'common passage and thorowfaire for all kinde of burden bearing people', the authorities lamented in 1598, and 'a daily receptacle for roges and beggars to the great offence of religious mynded people'.[41]

Other word badges of criminal pluralities included accessory, accomplice, agent, bailer, bulk, comforter, companion, confederate, consort, crew, messenger, receiver, runner, setter, sharer, solicitor, spy, stall or supporter. It was said that nine drinkers at the Three Footstools were cutpurse 'comforters'; that Richard Wilson, 'a helper' of cutpurses, 'goeth like an agent', grabbing 'parte of ther gaynes'; that Katherine Norris kept 'stout watch when any officer cometh neare [a Shoe Lane bawdy] to give warning to the rest'; that John Thorowgood 'badd' three boys to cut purses and 'wolde stande afore them' while they did it; and that an alehouse keeper in Pepper Alley 'oftentymes' treated cutpurses to food and drink, and 'sette' William Tuckes to cut purses on the bridge, scooping 4s.[42]

Another worry was household corruption, such as parents steering their children towards a thieving career, or servants dipping into their master's funds at the beck and call of others. It was 'reported' that the mother of Alice Gregory, a young pilferer, was also 'a comon pilferer and teacheth her this trade'. A constable alleged that Solomon Evans was 'a pickpocket vagrant', and that 'he hath foure brothers all of that profession'. John Atkinson, 'a loyteringe fellowe', was said to 'entize' his daughter 'to be naughtie to pilfer and picke', pocketing the pickings. Criminals fell in love: in 1606 Bridewell's minister was instructed not to 'marry any prisoner within this hospital' without prior permission. Anne Bailey and her 'late husband' were serial pickpurses. Magdalene Dutton, 'a vagrant woman', who was noticed 'idling' through markets in 1629, was 'wife to Dutton the comon pickpocket'.[43] Skills were passed on, sometimes from one generation to another. In other scenes we encounter senior scholars like the 'principall cozener' mentioned at Bridewell in 1579. It was alleged that Elizabeth Bristow, 'a beggar' prosecuted in 1560, was 'a common norissher and bringer up of children in beggery'. A joiner's son charged with 'cuttyng a purse in Saynt Anthonyes Churche' said that a serving man 'enticed and taught hym the manner of cuttyng a pursse'. Robert Everett boxed his servant's ears 'for that he cold not picke churche boxes so conyng as he wolde have hym'.[44]

Evidence of pooled wisdom and in-house training also included an array of tools, tricks, or the sort of expertise suggested by titles like creepwindow or shopcreep. Thieves bumped into luckless folk at busy spots. A vagrant was seen 'justiling a woman whilest another stole away her ring'. A ballad singer followed 'that course to drawe company for his master to picke purses'. A bunch of 'very lewdly and idelly disposed' people selling ballads, almanacs, and pamphlets 'confederated themselves with cutpurses' to 'openly singe balletts in the streets to thentente to drawe together multitudes of people to heare them', so that 'their followers' might work unseen. A vagrant cutpurse 'pulled out a pynne from a coache wheele in Cheapeside of purpose to cause the wheele to goe of intente to drawe companie together to worke his purpose'. A thief forced open a stall 'when the night carte went by' as 'he thought to have done it and not to be heard by any', and Barbara Orton 'was found to have false pocketts in her petticoate'.[45] The special tools of the trade confiscated at Bridewell included cutpurse knives, picklocks, a hook 'made fitt to pilfer clothes' through windows, 'an yron instrument to breake open a doore', false dice, 'instruments' for snatching hats off heads, files, wire, 'a bonche of keyes of all sortes', and picklock keys. A vagrant was 'suspected to bee a pickpockett having the engines of a thiefe about him'.

Although few past street discourses survive, techniques or tools imply pooled knowledge and this technology is one path to spoken pasts. Recent studies are more sensitive to snatches of thieves' 'cant' in sources other than tricky contemporary glossaries. Cant conversations were linguistic fences, a vocabulary for 'hidden worlds', mostly to do with people or tactics.[46] Nicknames, too, help us to spot both criminals and criminal activity. They infer given titles, thought up in communities. So it is that we meet Edward Wills, who was 'otherwise called Small by a name the cutpurses call him'; John

Gerrard, 'a common nipp and notorious theefe', who was 'cominly called Buttered Jack'; and Anne Lewis, who 'demeaned herselfe in uncomely beastly sort' at a Blackfriars alehouse, and who was 'usually called Taumikin'.[47]

Nicknames covered most criminal situations depicted in the Bridewell records. We also meet the vagrant beggars Whippet, Irish Nan, Cold Joan, Black Bess, Nan Bradshaw, My Lady will Have All, My Lady Bartfield, Flwellyn alias What You Will, the Lady of Christ's Hospital, Proudfoot, Barefoot, and Blinking Jane; bawds called Black Madge, Black Luce, Long Meg of Westminster, and Pockey Faced Dall; prostitutes called Fair Bess, Little Alice, Little Meg, Little Nan, Scotch Madge, and Flounsing Bess; cutpurses, nips and pickpockets called Bess of the Chest, London Stone, John of Dulwich, Little Tom, Little James, Little Robin, Small Wills, Small Jack of Westminster, Flat Back, Black Jack, Hasty Jack, Jack of the Kitchen, Cowetaile, Crooked Legs, Mowchachoe, and the rather more timorous-sounding Herbert the Ruffian.

Nicknames are a deep-seamed mine for us. They are spoken passports to criminal situations and associations, but they are also open books that say a great deal about sentiments. Nicknames are a clear dig at the upper classes, a badge of ethnicity, an address stamp, an age badge, a swipe at the city (and its institutions), a play on crime labels, a sign of tramping ('foot'), a twist on injuries or blemishes, and a commentary on people of all shapes and sizes. Nicknames also convey senses of distance and otherness beyond the fringes of the city and its settled citizens ('black', 'cold'). As such, they cluttered an already messy identity maze which threatened to become even more tangled as the city grew and altered its shape and character for ever.

Edges of criminal networks are just visible in speech, tactics, or social moments. A baker said 'that he hath ben confettered' with pickpurses in 1560, naming seventeen. 'A bill' was tucked away in a cozener's pocket listing seventeen other cozeners. Knowledge circulated in table talk or chance meetings on streets, reaching all points of the city. Anne Tringoffe said 'that all the world doeth knowe that John Shaw and his wiffe of East Smythfielde are comen bawdes'. People bragged: Francis Castlyn 'advaunted and bragged of his filthines'.[48]

As news about criminalities circulated, images and maps gathered shape; collective memories lodged in minds. Criminal communities had several presences, as literary concoctions that blended fact and fiction, as well as at markets, fairs, and on streets. Judicial records and pieces of legislation also gave theft in particular a collective character. In 1560 the Bridewell governors claimed that Robert Browne 'cannot denye but that he hath been one of the faculty of cutpurses'. In a statute passed in the same decade cutpurses were said to belong to 'a brotherhood or fraternity of an art or mystery'[49] – a good example, it seems to me, of an identification from the point of intersection between the politics of boundaries, the impact of texts, and first-hand knowledge of criminal activity: the list of sites where cutpurses were said to ply their trade appears authentic.[50]

OVERLAPPING CIRCLES

However, despite the signs of shelter and other forms of support and sociability for vagrants and thieves (including shared tricks, tactics, and nicknames), I still feel that it is misleading to relegate offenders such as these to the margins of society. This is partly because, apart from revealing criminal biographies that run for months or years through the records, we know little about the length of criminal careers. Much more visible in the sources are warning signs that we should relax the categories of criminal as drop-out and the citizen as a beacon of upright life. Time after time we come across these imagined strangers moving in circles that overlap. So-called criminals crossed occupational, spatial, familial, or residential borders.[51] All the lines of demarcation defined and defended by governors were potentially passable. A neat split dividing the worlds of criminals and citizens did not exist. Even thieves' cant crossed vernacular boundaries and eventually entered everyday speech.[52]

It is a comfort to imagine crime in specific spaces, and the necklace of 'sinfully polluted suburbs' circling the city was an age-old city lament.[53] Moral geographies put criminalities in certain territories, creating vice monsters in the suburbs or Turnmill Street.[54] But there were few calm spots even at the heart of the city; the din was such in a bawdy house next door to the Guildhall one night that 'my lord mayor hard the noyse'.[55] As we have seen, senses of space overlapped because insiders and outsiders experienced London in similar landscapes, constantly crossing paths on streets, negotiating points of contact at various sites. Busy commercial concourses and other crowd scenes or prominent landmarks carried magnetic properties for people with crime in mind. Here they walked the same city as citizens, even if they moved through streets for different reasons.[56]

Other offenders were able to supply an address or biography that fixed them in London. So the vagrant William Sly claimed at Bridewell that he had 'a house of [his] own'. Another suspect told the governors that he was 'an honest householder'. I 'taketh paines by weedinge to gett a livinge', said vagrant Dennis Wood. The court ruled that the vagrant John Duckett was 'a dweller' in 1608. The vagrant Thomas Jones was allowed to continue his journey home because he 'appeared to be an honest poore waterbearer', while it was said that, 'upon examinacon', Jane Browne 'appeareth to be a poore simple woman who selleth reddishe', and all charges against her were dropped.[57] Many people struggled to cope with dips in luck, and were short-stay marginals trapped on slippery slopes by little-known impersonal forces like trade slumps. We come across begging tailors, 'masterless teachers of youth', nightwalking seamstresses, pimping painters and fishmongers, brothel-keeping cooks, and vagrant servants of the upper class. Queen Elizabeth's wax chandler's wife kept an extremely busy brothel.

Court cases were tests of status, front-line encounters between offenders and the authorities. In many such status trials it emerged that apparently rootless suspects possessed a past of useful work. They had a foothold in London, and some of them were resident ratepayers. Seemingly settled, they were sent home and given another chance. A vagrant 'brought from the bonfier in Cornehill' was a preacher's servant and 'kinsman to alderman Dixies wife'. Frances Withers, 'a woman of lewd conversacon taken in a house suspected', turned out to be Sir William Withers's daughter. A drunk, roaring in 'idle company', was identified as Lady Clifford's daughter. 'An old running bawde' – Mary Lord – was 'kin to [provost] marshal Davis'. Thomas Eustace, the hangman's son, was picked up vagrant three times. It was an awkward moment at Bridewell when a familiar face was dragged in vagrant; she was the daughter of one of the prison's beadles. Ottwell Dobbins was carried to Bridewell 'by his father the bedell' for being 'a ronnegatte and one that will not tarye with anybodye'. The water bailiff's son roamed the streets 'with a sticke noynted with lynt' to lift money from stalls. Other vagrants claimed that they were 'a mans sonne of good fortune' and 'a greate mans daughter'.[58]

Even offenders without a firm footing in the city frequently crossed boundaries because their relations with citizens could possess reciprocal aspects: thieves sold low-price spoils, street-sellers needed customers, citizens felt a warm glow of goodness after helping beggars, the poor pocketed a few coins by lodging recent arrivals in the city. Patrolling edges provided opportunities to parade moralities and boost policing powers.[59] In these limited senses criminals contributed to the good health of the city, setting up economic, social, and physical ties. Another apparent reciprocity was commercial sex. An abridged census of clients provides a miniature portrait of the thousands of encounters between criminals and citizens and their offspring. The names logged in Bridewell records include the sons or servants of the upper classes, the staff of foreign embassies, members of the legal profession, countless merchants, an army of apprentices, and representatives of civic government, including counter clerks, the town clerk's clerk, a Guildhall cloth meter, a Blackwell Hall sealer, a Bridewell wharfkeeper, constables, Alderman River's son, Alderman Pipes's son, Alderman Starkey's apprentice, and Alderman Bond's servant. In as much as bawdy houses satisfied physical longing, and were one route to sexual maturity, circles always overlapped on what Geremek calls the 'fluctuating frontier'.[60]

They also overlapped because over time the authorities built up knowledge about the character and environment of crime. High reoffending, together with the ubiquity, visibility, and therefore predictability of crime, sharpened their sense of offences and offenders, and helped them to construct criminal biographies, to characterise (or label) crimes, and to understand criminal environments in fuller and more nuanced ways. The regular recurrence of names and faces at Bridewell was a clear source of knowledge. The procession of return visits to Bridewell was noted in the court books and the number of previous whippings was passed on to the bench. Such character snapshots became key points in courtroom deliberations. A thief was 'ordered to sett downe in writinge his whole lyfe, falts, and evell behavior' at Bridewell. Clerks leafed through court books to track criminal histories; folio pages listing past crimes were noted and memories reached back. Godfrey Lambright looked 'very giltye' to Bridewell's court in 1578, and it was remembered that he had been charged 'five years sens for lewd liffe'. In 1627 a search was set up for Thomas Coo, who, it was remembered, 'was punished in this house about fifteene yeares agoe'.[61]

The vocabulary of recidivism covers most pages of the court books, especially after the turn of the seventeenth century when the number of 'repeaters' soared. Thousands of suspects were called 'ancient', 'common', 'daily', 'known', 'noted', or 'ordinary' offenders, 'customers', 'guests', or 'professors'. Each time one of these 'repeater labels' was used is a reminder for us that even in what is often thought of as a pre-statistical age, knowledge was accumulated and put to use in court. Offences were counted (or remembered) in this perhaps limited way, and information was stored away to be retrieved when yet another half-remembered face stirred memories. Recidivism and repetition bred familiarity and were key points in the compilation of information.

Front-line officers through face-to-face encounters, tracking, discovering, and arresting offenders, were further sources of knowledge. Marshal Bestney reported that Anne Foster, 'a spy to bawds and a butterfoyst', had 'allwaies of late lived in a bawdy house'. Nicholas Symons said at Bridewell that he was 'a drover and came upp with cattle'. But the marshal knew better, passing on word that he was 'a carrier of news to prisoners in Newgate and a dangerous fellowe'. Two 'bailers' claimed that John Clark 'is a honest boy and newe come out of the countery'. But a constable had a quite different story to tell: 'he is a comon cutpurse', he told the Bridewell court, and he 'hath taken him three severall tymes for pickpursing'.[62] Informers opened more windows on the actions and movements of criminals. Thieves, prostitutes, pimps, and others turned the tables, passing on information about former comrades. In so doing, they nicely illustrate the limits of solidarity.

Largely lost to us are off-the-record meetings, not always required by process and not frozen in manuscript. Chance recordings crop up as spin-offs from other legal moves, and we see officers and offenders sharing meals, bumping into each other on streets, falling into conversation. 'What news at

Bridewell and how is Jane Trosse [a prostitute]?', the pimp Richard Rolles asked Michael Blower, a Bridewell beadle, when the pair met by chance 'at Pauls Gate before Christmas'; the matron 'says she is very sick.' 'She and I have been suer together twelve months and I mean to marry her.' 'You will do well if you do, for I hear she is very sick.' Beadle and pimp then walked together towards the cathedral. Another day, another meeting: Rolles caught sight of Blower and Davy Fowler (another Bridewell beadle) on the street, saying 'he would give them beer if he had money but he had none'. The beadles must have reached into their pockets, for the three sat later raising pots in an alehouse in Crump Alley.[63]

Such conviviality was informal and on occasion was tinged with malpractice. Yet it was not always out of sorts with effective policing – Rolles passed good leads to officers on that day. Blower and Fowler also sat down at the table of the bawd-pimp Thomas Wise, 'being desired to come for Breakfast' on St Steven's Day. Wise chatted idly – 'he was much beholding' to Bridewell's 'honest, wise and discrete' governors, and 'would rather come before them to tell his tale than before any of his parish'. The pimp Henry Boyer also met Blower 'at severall tymes'.[64] Nor did information flow one way only. In convivial moments with officers, shadowing movement in the circles of police and citizens, or in return visits to courtrooms, criminals tapped useful ties and stored knowledge of names, faces, and places; they even impersonated officers. Circles overlapped, sometimes in surprising ways. A 'comon nightwalker' tried to talk her way out of a tricky situation by telling a constable that she was the niece of Bridewell's president. One of Bridewell's 'ancient gessts', Dorothy Woodward, said that a marshal's man 'oftentimes had the use of her bodye' and each day brought her beer at the Hemphouse. Nightwalkers, in particular, had mildly comic and irreverent cross-overs with officers – Dorothy Clifton offered to 'prostrate herself' to a constable who spotted her walking late; Katherine Harris offered 'a pinte of wine to the constable and would have him go to a house where she sayd they might doe anything'; Mary Willins (alias Paris) was spotted 'siezing' a beadle 'making water at the wall'. Another told a constable that he was 'a man of fashion'.[65]

Like crossing streets, boundary-hopping was a day-by-day routine, so spontaneous and deeply sunk in mentalities that it was a near reflex. Early modern London was a city of perpetual transgressions. It is these overlapping circles, 'mediating bridges' or 'border crossings', that expose the vulnerabilties of absolute categories like marginality or the underworld.[66] This 'border energy' is the best test we possess that the margins of the 'underworld' were political and artificial. A flood of criminal labels could not freeze categories like criminal and citizen that were simultaneously sharply defined yet experienced as fuzzy and slippery categories. Criminality or marginality were never static identifications, motionless in time. This word war was one of the defining struggles in this troubled city. In a world of restless motion government sought peace through stable definitions. But this was a mere pipe dream.

Janice Perlman wrote a book called *The myth of marginality* in 1976. Is marginality a myth, a moral commentary about imagined communities? I certainly feel that it is a *tendency*; a *direction* on both sides of the fence – the authorities imagine outsiders when they set boundaries, and they have the pick of the labels. On the other side, people drift, settle, or fall into crime, and teams of like-minded 'confederates' pool sociability and strategies. Nevertheless, these are not free-standing cultures, mere satellites of the citizens' patch. To reiterate, it is the 'energy' at the edges that matters most. Criminalities are moral titles and any person might one day step outside the law. Ostracised marginals move, work, and live in citizens' space. And that is why I imagine these nearly inevitable convergences as overlapping circles, always touching, and in perpetual motion.

NOTES

I must thank John Beattie, Ulinka Rublack and Keith Wrightson for commenting so constructively on earlier versions of this chapter. I should like to dedicate the chapter to the inspiring memory of Bob Scribner, to whom I owe so much. All the issues discussed in this chapter will be more fully described and contextualised in my forthcoming *The first Bridewell: petty crime, policing, and prison in London, 1545–1645.*

1 Vladimir Nabokov, *Lolita* (Harmondsworth, Penguin, 1995), p. 170.

2 Saul Bellow, *The adventures of Augie March* (London, David Campbell, 1995), pp. 132–3.

3 Mary Douglas, *Purity and danger: an analysis of the concepts of pollution and taboo* (London, Routledge, 1966), p. 114; David Sibley, *Geographies of exclusion: society and difference in the West* (London, Routledge, 1995), p. 183; Michel Foucault, *Discipline and punish: the birth of the prison* (London, Allen Lane, 1977), p. 143. See also Iris Marion Young, *Justice and the politics of difference* (Princeton NJ, Princeton University Press, 1990), pp. 59–60, 170; Bronislaw Geremek, *The margins of society in late medieval Paris*, trans. Jean Birrell (Cambridge, Cambridge University Press, 1987), p. 214.

4 Colin Sumner, *The sociology of deviance: an obituary* (Buckingham, Open University Press, 1994), p. 299.

5 See Sibley, *Geographies of exclusion*, p. 183; Lydia Morris, *Dangerous classes: the underclass and social citizenship* (London, Routledge, 1994), p. 157; Florike Egmond, *Underworlds: organized crime in the Netherlands, 1650–1800* (Cambridge, Polity Press, 1993), chapter 1; Ruth Mazo Karras, *Common women: prostitution and sexuality in medieval England* (New York, Oxford University Press, 1996), chapter 5; Geremek, *Margins of society*, chapters 1, 9; Gareth Stedman Jones, *Outcast London: a study in the relationship between classes in Victorian society* (Oxford, Clarendon Press, 1971); Victor Bailey, 'The fabrication of deviance: "dangerous classes" and "criminal classes" in Victorian England', in Robert Malcolmson and John Rule (eds), *Protest and survival: the historical experience: essays for E. P. Thompson* (London, Merlin, 1993).

6 Important recent contributions include Gamini Salgado, *The Elizabethan underworld* (London, Dent, 1977); John L. McMullan, *The canting crew: London's criminal underworld, 1550–1750* (New Brunswick NJ, Rutgers University Press, 1984); id., 'Criminal organization in sixteenth and seventeenth-century London', *Social Problems* 29 (1981), 311–23; Lawrence Manley, *Literature and culture in early modern London* (Cambridge, Cambridge University Press, 1995), especially pp. 341–55; G. M. Spraggs, 'Rogues and vagabonds in English literature, 1552–1642' (unpublished Ph.D. dissertation, University of Cambridge, 1980); Arthur F. Kinney (ed.), *Rogues, vagabonds and sturdy beggars: a new gallery of Tudor and early Stuart rogue literature* (Amherst MA, University of Massachusetts Press, 1990); See my 'The structure of prostitution in Elizabethan London', *Continuity and Change* 8 (1993), 39–63.

7 Quoting Mary Elizabeth Perry, *Crime and society in early modern Seville* (Hanover NH, University Press of New England, 1980), p. 32; Spraggs, 'Rogues and vagabonds', pp. 9, 83.

8 Douglas, *Purity and danger*, pp. 96, 121, 114.

9 Tannenbaum is quoted in Frances Heidensohn, *Crime and society* (Basingstoke, Macmillan, 1989), p. 70; C[orporation of] L[ondon] R[ecord] O[ffice] Jour[nal of Common Council], 26, fols 147, 240ᵛ.

10 CLRO Jour. 25, fol. 124ᵛ; Rep[ertory of the Court of Aldermen] 15, fol. 404; B[ridewell] H[ospital] C[ourt books], consulted on microfilms in my possession, 4, fols 407ᵛ–409; Thomas Dekker, *Lanthorne and candle-light* (New York, The English Experience [585], 1973), fols 42ʳ⁻ᵛ.

11 CLRO Jours 28, fols 63ᵛ, 116ᵛ; 34, fol. 157.

12 CLRO Jours 27, fols 52ᵛ, 422; 28, fol. 84.

13 CLRO Jours 27, fols 319ʳ⁻ᵛ; 26, fol. 82; 38, fol. 308.

14 CLRO Rep. 29, fol. 80ᵛ.

15 BHC 6, fol. 224; H[ouse of] L[ords] M[ain] P[apers] 24 June 1625.

16 Cf. Arlette Farge, *Subversive words: public opinion in eighteenth-century France*, trans. Rosemary Morris (Cambridge, Polity Press, 1994), especially chapters 1–2. And see the words of Thomas Dekker quoted in Manley, *Literature and culture*, p. 363.

17 See Peter Burke, 'Classifying the people: the census as collective representation', in his *The historical anthropology of early modern Italy* (Cambridge, Cambridge University Press, 1987), especially pp. 27, 31–2, 33–4, 35.

18 PRO STAC 8, 121/6; 187/1.

19 G[uildhall] L[ibrary, London] Bridewell Hospital Prisoners' Admission and Discharge Orders, 1691–95, 16/12/1693; PRO STAC 8 85/3; 62/13; 200/22; GL MS 1500.

20 CLRO Jours 26, fols 6–7; 25, fol. 305ᵛ; 27, fols 240ʳ⁻ᵛ.

21 BHC 1, fol. 11.

22 See Sibley, *Geographies of exclusion*, pp. 14, 18–19, 24–5; Thomas A. Markus, *Buildings and power: freedom and control in the origin of modern building types* (London, Routledge, 1993), p. 146 and chapter 5; Alain Corbin, *The foul and the fragrant: odour and the social imagination* (Leamington Spa, Picador, 1994), p. 145; Georges Vigarello, *Concepts of cleanliness: changing attitudes in France since the Middle Ages*, trans. Jean Birrell (Cambridge, Cambridge University Press, 1988), especially chapter 10; Donald Reid, *Paris sewers and sewermen: realities and representations* (Cambridge MA, Harvard

University Press, 1991), pp. 20, 50–1; Joy Damousi, *Depraved and disorderly: female convicts, sexuality, and gender in colonial Australia* (Cambridge, Cambridge University Press, 1997), especially pp. 28, 36, 43.

23 See Jon Arrizabalaga, John Henderson and Roger French, *The great pox: the French disease in Renaissance Europe* (New Haven CT and London, Yale University Press, 1997), especially pp. 173–5 and chapter 9. Cf. Judith R. Walkowitz, *Prostitution and Victorian society: women, class, and the state* (Cambridge, Cambridge University Press, 1980), especially chapters 2–4.

24 BHC 1, fol. 92; GL MS 25/175, fol. 3.

25 CLRO Jours 25, fol. 244; 33, fol. 6^v.

26 BHC 1, fols 81, 180, 182; 5, fols 282^v, 385; CLRO Jour. 25, fols 221^{r-v}, 305^v.

27 BHC 5, fol. 419^v; 7, fol. 95; 4, fol. 369^v; 1, fol. 83.

28 BHC 5, fol. 411; 6, fols 28, 45; PRO STAC 8, 200/13; 274/7; 284/23; CLRO Jours 19, fol. 171^v; 21, fol. 322; 23, fol. 308^v.

29 CLRO Jour. 27, fol. 19.

30 PRO Privy Council Registers 2/42, fols 305–6.

31 Cf. Heather Shore, 'Cross coves, buzzers and general sorts of prigs: juvenile crime and the criminal "underworld" in the early nineteenth century', *British Journal of Criminology* 39 (1999), 10–24, especially pp. 11, 15.

32 Geremek, *Margins of society*, p. 96; BHC 5, fol. 200; 7, fol. 26^v.

33 John L. McMullan, 'Crime, law and order in early modern England', *British Journal of Criminology* 27 (1987), 252–74, p. 265.

34 BHC 3, fols 194, 95^v, 127^{r-v}, 280^v, 102. See also fols 27^v, 101^v.

35 *Ibid.*, fols 328^v, 111, 188, 48, 111, 133^v, 134^v, 122, 279^v.

36 CLRO Jour. 30, fol. 86.

37 BHC 3, fols 3; 34^v, 45^v–46, 167^v, 273; 2, fols 97^v, 95, 181^v; CLRO Jour. 30, fol. 86.

38 T. Wright (ed.), *Queen Elizabeth and her times*, 2 vols (London, 1838), II, pp. 249–51.

39 PRO STAC 8, 212/3; BHC 3, fol. 368^v; 4, fols 410, 411; PRO SP 12/187/20; CLRO Jour. 26, fol. 320^v; GL MS 3018/1, fols 23^v, 25, 26^v, 28^v; BHC 3, fols 359, 362, 392^v; 6, fol. 293^v; 1, fols 192, 192^v.

40 GL MS 4069/1, quoting here fols 41^v, 118^v, 218.

41 GL MSS 25,175, fols 3, 6, 41^{r-v}, 47.

42 BHC 3, fols 273, 273^v; 7, fol. 40; 2, fol. 95; 7, fols 73, 86; 2, fol. 95.

43 BHC 7, fols 48, 78^v; 1, fol. 216; 5, fol. 89; 1, fol. 140; 7, fol. 111^v.

44 BHC 3, fol. 422; 1, fols 52, 41; 2, fol. 22.

45 BHC 7, fols 84^v, 181^v; 6, fol. 243; CLRO Jour. 23, fol. 340; BHC 5, fol. 353^v; 7, fols 44^v, 97^v; 6, fol. 314^v.

46 McMullan, *Canting crew*, pp. 96–7; A. L. Beier, 'Anti-language or jargon? Canting in the English underworld in the sixteenth and seventeenth centuries', in Peter Burke and Roy Porter (eds), *Languages and jargons: contributions to a social history of language* (Cambridge, Polity Press, 1995).

47 BHC 7, fol. 99; 6, fol. 279; 7, fol. 62ᵛ.

48 BHC 1, fol. 91ᵛ; 3, fols 287, 63, 131ʳ⁻ᵛ, 221, 121ᵛ, 359ᵛ.

49 BHC 1, fol. 91ᵛ; 8 Eliz. 1, cap. 4.

50 Criminal pamphlets clearly had some impact on shaping contemporary senses of crime. See Peter Burke, 'Perceiving a counter-culture', in Burke, *Historical anthropology*, pp. 63–75, especially p. 71; McMullan, *Canting crew*, p. 96; Manley, *Literature and culture*, p. 356; Ian A. Bell, *Literature and crime in Augustan England* (London, Routledge, 1991), pp. 21–2.

51 Joseph Ward has argued that differences between citizens ('honest') and non-citizens ('illicit') were extremely thin, and he has also suggested that connections between the City and its suburbs were much less 'antagonistic' than historians have supposed hitherto. Joseph P. Ward, *Metropolitan communities: trade guilds, identity and change in early modern London* (Stanford CA, Stanford University Press, 1997), especially pp. 46, 56, 71, 144, and chapters 1–2.

52 Beier, 'Anti-language or jargon?', pp. 92–3.

53 Thomas Dekker, *The wonderful year* (London, 1603), sig. Di.

54 Laura Gowing, *Domestic dangers: women, words, and sex in early modern London* (Oxford, Oxford University Press, 1996), pp. 72, 100; *id.*, 'Gender, sex, and the freedom of the streets in early modern London', in Paul Griffiths and Mark Jenner (eds), *Londinopolis: essays in the cultural and social history of early modern London* (forthcoming, Manchester University Press); McMullan, *Canting crew*, chapter 4; Geremek, *Margins of society*, chapter 3; Mazo Karras, *Common women*, pp. 14–24; Markus, *Buildings and power*, pp. 23–5.

55 BHC 3, fol. 120ᵛ.

56 Cf. Judith Walkowitz, *City of dreadful delight: narratives of sexual desire in late Victorian London* (London, Virago, 1992), especially chapters 1–2; Young, *Justice and the politics of difference*, pp. 239–40.

57 BHC 4, fols 442, 465; 5, fols 284, 377ᵛ; 6, fols 160, 400ᵛ; CLRO Rep. 14, fol. 263.

58 BHC 6, fols 383, 424ᵛ; 7, fols 21ᵛ, 64, 44, 73; 6, fols 350, 352; 1, fol. 161ᵛ; 3, fol. 350; 7, fols 51, 75.

59 Cf. Bob Scribner, 'The *Mordbrenner* fear in sixteenth-century Germany: political paranoia or the revenge of the outcast?', in Richard J. Evans (ed.), *The German underworld: deviants and outcasts in German history* (London, Routledge, 1988), pp. 43, 47–8.

60 Geremek, *Margins of society*, p. 2. See also Mazo Karras, *Common women*, especially pp. 95–101.

61 BHC 3, fol. 346ᵛ; 7, fo. 24ᵛ.

62 BHC 7, fol. 8; 6, fol. 140ᵛ; 5, fol. 175.

63 PRO STAC 8, B//11/18, Michael Blower, examination; BHC 3, fol. 303ᵛ.

64 BHC 3, fol. 303ᵛ.

65 BHC 8, fol. 173; 6, fols 249ᵛ, 250; 7, fol. 304ᵛ; 8, fol. 104; 6, fol. 39.

66 Douglas, *Purity and danger*, p. 168; Sibley, *Geographies of exclusion*, chapter 3. To be sure, this permanent situation of crossovers has been spotted in other places across the

English Channel at that time, and in London three centuries later. See, e.g., Egmond, *Underworlds*, pp. 40–4; Shore, 'Cross coves, buzzers, and general sorts of prigs', especially pp. 18–21. Perry writes that 'Seville was really two cities' – that belonging to the 'oligarchy' and the 'city of the underworld' – yet she is well aware of their overlap; *Crime and society*, especially chapters 2 and 10, quoting p. 12.

Chapter 8

◆

Citizens, community and political culture in Restoration England

Phil Withington

There is a current interpretative emphasis within early modern urban historiography on the 'twofold, sometimes contradictory character' of England's seventeenth-century cities and boroughs. The first focuses on the city 'as an enclosed stronghold, legally and physically defined through its charters and its walls, with much autonomy from outside authority'. The second conceives of the city as 'a focus for that same outside world, a nodal point in a series of economic, political and cultural networks'.[1] The former approach details the *indigenous, civic culture* of urban settlements, in particular the practice of civic government in relation to socio-economic and religious change. The latter explores the *relativist, urban* roles of cities and towns and the corresponding impact of such roles on the culture of urban settlements themselves. In functional terms both approaches – the indigenous and the relativist – apply to (and overlap within) towns and cities at all times: it was from this often unstable juxtaposition of the two that towns, boroughs and cities derived their composite role as 'places'. However, in so far as early modern studies are concerned, the two have become distinct and chronologically specific. While an indigenous 'civic culture' dominates accounts of towns between the Reformation and the Civil War, a relativist 'urban culture' is regarded as primarily a post-Restoration, 'long eighteenth-century' pheno-menon. The former is conceived of as an aspect of enhanced socio-economic, religious and governmental change and traditionally couched in terms of economic crisis, social polarisation and an intensification of governance. The latter is associated with national (rather than simply metropolitan) urbanisa-tion, related socio-economic and political expansion, and the emergence of a national 'civil society'.

The two most recent narratives of pre- and post-Civil War urban culture are Robert Tittler's exploration of Reformation civic culture and Peter Borsay's examination of 'urban renaissance'.[2] They share a number of similarities. Like

Patrick Collinson and Jonathan Barry, both are interested in urban culture and identity rather than 'distributive economics and consequential social arrangements and readjustments'.[3] As Borsay puts it, they conceptualise the town 'as a special type of place which, by virtue of its generic qualities, moulded experiences and instigated events' rather than towns as 'accidental spaces in which interesting processes and incidents happen to occur'.[4] In their respective quests for an English 'urbanism', Tittler and Borsay focus not on the structural inequalities of urban society but on the cultural propensities of urban elites. While both locate these propensities within broader socio-economic contexts, both also emphasise the cultural dynamism of those elites and the refashioning of manners, association and landscape inherent in such dynamism. Although this is a reaction to what they regard as the overtly sociological and classificatory approach adopted by a previous generation of urban historians, the chronological frameworks which Tittler and Borsay use are nevertheless based on the urban 'social' narratives initially developed by Peter Clark, Paul Slack and others.[5] While Tittler presents pre-1640 urban elites as local freemen acting within – and indeed culturally constructing – a civic context, Borsay argues that the dominant urban milieu after 1660 combined provincial gentry, town-based 'professionals' and 'pseudo-gentry', and prominent citizens culturally distanced from their communal ties. The pre-1640 elites are characterised by their concern for civic governance and privileges; their suspicions of gentry or episcopal encroachments on civic jurisdictions; and their involvement in projects of godly and social reformation. In contrast post-1660 elites are seen to be engaged in the construction of a new and synthetic mode of polite, civil gentility based on provincial purchasing power, cosmopolitan fashions, and expanding national and international markets. While for Tittler the architectural motif of pre-Civil War civic culture was the town hall, its architectural equivalent in the later seventeenth century is the assembly rooms. The former epitomised a process of urban atomisation based on civic autonomy and authority: it embodied not 'a collapse of community, but its articulation in different forms, reflecting the working of social polarisation as society filled out at the bottom'.[6] The latter symbolised a towns's relativist role as both a socio-cultural centre for local societies and a 'space' of assimilation into larger, metropolitan-based urban systems, in the process engendering new forms of 'civilisation, high society and social class'.[7]

This chapter challenges or at least seeks to modify this interpretative disjunction by examining civic survivalism in York during the first three decades of England's post-1660 'urban renaissance'. In so doing it also seeks to refine and extend the concept of culture implicit in much recent urban and political cultural history. An underlying assumption of this chapter is that process and practice – that is, the stuff of traditional institutional and social history – had as much symbolic or cultural significance for contemporaries as heraldry, ceremonies, decorative masonry and propaganda pamphlets. The everyday practice of social relations, and the institutions and processes through which such practice was mediated, offers the best means of recovering the cultural contexts through which individual identities were forged and 'cultural formation, differentiation and subordination' were structured. As Robert Scribner puts it, culture is both 'a system of shared meanings, attitudes, and values, and the symbolic forms (performances, artifacts) in which they are expressed and embodied'.[8] From this perspective, culture was neither a palliative of power nor a form of social control; rather it was substantive to the meaning and articulation of social relations.

With this in mind, this chapter argues that towns during the long eighteenth century should be regarded not simply as urban loci for processes of national class formation but as arenas in which a variety of cultural precepts and practices were sustained, contested, modified and appropriated. By outlining the communal imperatives of citizenship, the chapter shows that civic community remained a particular source of urban identity for those indigenous urban inhabitants who were either able or compelled to participate in civic governance. Such participation has usually been equated with civic office-holding and the perpetuation of oligarchy. However, even a brief outline of the full depth of civic office-holding suggests that participation was more diverse and extensive than historians have traditionally allowed. This is confirmed by an analysis of two other modes of civic participation during the period: the allocation of civic apprenticeships and civic credit. By the former, the children of less wealthy citizens were sponsored by the corporation to learn a trade from city freemen; by the latter, the corporation granted citizens loans on credit, and usually without interest, in order to stimulate or sustain the civic economy.

Both these practices increased rather than decreased in York between 1649 and 1689, and this chapter argues that in conjunction with civic office-holding they helped sustain the structures and boundaries of civic community as a viable source of urban identity and power. Moreover it suggests that the normative *culture* of civic community was not so much oligarchy as civic republicanism, a culture which was predicated on power, inequality and differentiation but which also valued reciprocity, obligation and responsibility. Having outlined and examined these aspects of civic participation, the chapter then argues that, just as historians of the urban renaissance have underestimated the survival of civic community, so historians of Restoration political culture have underestimated the significance of government in general – and civic governance in particular – as a source of organisational and symbolic power within a national context. This second point is examined through the attitudes of York's citizens during the 'exclusion crisis', and in particular the manner in which citizens were mobilised, as a community, against James, Duke of York.

A letter from the aldermen of York to Sir Thomas Widdrington, written in the mid-1660s, offers an initial insight into the persistence of corporatist rhetoric among some of the leading citizens of England's 'second city'. Widdrington, brother-in-law of Lord Fairfax and an architect of the Restoration, served as York's recorder and parliamentary representative during the 1650s. In 1661 he resigned both places but later offered to dedicate his recently completed history of the city to the aldermen and commons. In their letter the aldermen not only rejected his offer but took the opportunity to describe for Widdrington the state in which he had left the city he professed to love – and be a citizen of – but which he was no longer prepared to serve. In the process they drew a clear distinction between the civic community and other urban interests, isolating the city's 'homogeneal and essential members' from other urban inhabitants. Economic hardship made the civic–urban dichotomy all the clearer. The aldermen observed that while 'our whole body is in weakness and distemper, our merchandise and trade, our nerves and sinews ... weakened and become very mean and inconsiderable', other urban interests – 'the earls, dukes, archbishops, deans, prebends and abbots of York' – were 'no homogeneal parts of our body, but only our garnishments, embroideries, and ornaments, and sometimes pricks and goads'.[9]

Two concepts pivotal to their corporatist rhetoric were possession and participation. As their repeated use of the pronoun 'our' suggests, the magistracy were undoubtedly possessive about the body they governed; however, such possession denoted not merely power over that which they possessed but also the unpalatable obligations and responsibilities inherent to such possession. These responsibilities were wrapped up in the immediate social and economic imperatives of civic governance: so far as the magistrates were concerned, the necessity of governance and the exigency of civic office justified those tendencies towards civic authority and autonomy which became culturally normative in the 100 years after 1540. Their conceptualisation of the poor was a case in point. As they pointed out to Widdrington, while 'our poor' were a financial burden, they were also 'our citties' burden. Just as city magistrates were responsible for the material well-being of 'our poor', so 'our poor' required governors to administer their well-being.[10] This relationship in turn legitimated both hierarchical authority among the citizenry and political autonomy without. From this perspective, civic inequalities were pivotal rather than contradictory to the practice of community.

As important was the notion of participation. Just as the magistrates' rhetoric of decay stemmed from their inability to 'keep together our homogeneal and essential members' – including Widdrington – so they were simultaneously contesting the encroachments of vengeful royalist Yorkshire gentry upon civic jurisdictions on the grounds that 'it was never the cittyes minde to loose that ancyent previlege [whereby only elected aldermen became city justices] or to have it intrenched upon, unles those gentlemen would be freemen of the citty, and so by consequences to bear such other office of charge and trouble as wee undergoe'.[11] If the gentry were to wield civic power, they would first have to become citizens and undergo the strains and responsibilities such participation entailed. As seventeenth-century diction-aries also suggest, participation perpetuated and structured civic community as a normative cultural form: if participation ceased, then so would com-munity.[12]

Participation and possession were instigated, in the first instance, through an incorporated city or borough's franchise. In York as in most places the freedom was secured in one of three ways: redemption (whereby the franchise was purchased from the corporation), patrimony (whereby the children of a free household were citizens by birth and inherited the right to practise a city trade) or apprenticeship (whereby an apprentice in a freeman's household earned his freedom after a specified period (usually seven years) of tuition and service). As well as imbuing economic rights – in particular mastery of a trade and access to the city's common land – the franchise also gave access to the privileges and liberties which had been accumulated in a city or borough in the course of the preceding centuries. As such the label 'freeman' was synonymous with the term 'burgess' (denoting freemen of boroughs) and 'citizens' (denoting freemen of cities): it was a form of political as much as social or economic identity. On the one hand this identity meant that, unless an exemption fine had been paid, the citizen was liable to serve the community by holding public office and administering civic services. On the other it meant that poorer or 'decayed' citizens could appeal to their wealthier brethren – usually their public representatives – for civic charity, aid, leases, and so on. While wealthy urban inhabitants who were not citizens were excluded from these communal practices, they were not barred from purchasing and residing in property located in the city. In doing so they became liable for all the usual rates – in particular the poor rate, which was organised by the corporation but collected on a parochial basis – but were disallowed from administering or redistributing wealth. On the other hand recipients of poor relief tended to be established inhabitants of the city jurisdictions rather than vagrants or interlopers. Such inhabitants included 'decayed' freemen, city journeymen and labourers, and their respective households and relicts.

It can be seen, then, that the 'civic' was not a category of class, as Jonathan Barry has argued, but a category of community.[13] Citizenship in later seventeenth-century England denoted not supra-local collectivities defined by shared economic interest so much as the communal association of a range of classes and groupings within delimited geographical and institutional topographies. It conferred contingent privileges, liberties and freedoms – and indeed responsibilities, reciprocities and obligations – rather than universal rights on a range of city inhabitants. Just as Sir Thomas More had written *Utopia* as a citizen of London, so the rejected Sir Thomas Widdrington styled himself a citizen of York.[14] As late as 1689 so did bakers, wine coopers, carpenters, joiners and tailors.[15] While none of these occupied senior civic office – never mind the Speaker's place in Parliament – in 1659 the godly grocer and civic magistrate Stephen Watson left £60 in his will 'to bind eight or less poor citizens children apprentices at good trades with able men'.[16] While 'citizen' could be a precise form of labelling – denoting city freemen and their households – in practice the parameters of its inclusivity were more ambiguous and extensive. For less wealthy, 'decayed' and female citizens in particular, citizenship was predicated on genealogy, kin, residence and inhabitance – and indeed dependence and reliance – as much as on current participation in trade and government.

Civic government, in its institutionalisation of various forms of participation – by men and women, the wealthy and poor, children and adults, dependants and independents, masters and apprentices, conformists and Nonconformists – was the embodiment and apotheosis of civic community. Of these participatory forms, office-holding has received by far the most attention from historians. Such participation has generally been conceptualised in terms of oligarchy. In the process, 'oligarchy' has been deployed in a somewhat uncritical fashion. Oligarchy in contemporary usage was the 'evill and unjust' equivalent of 'good and just' aristocracy, whereby the 'governing of the best men' (an aristocratic form of government) became the 'usurping of a few gentlemen or a few of the richer or stronger sort' (an oligarchic form of government).[17] While such usurpation undoubtedly occurred in England's early modern boroughs and cities, for some historians the term has become a pejorative shorthand denoting either the absence of twentieth-century democracy, the withering of a romanticised medieval commonalty or the inevitable consequence of economic inequality.[18] In contrast, recent social and intellectual historiography would suggest that the normative political cultures of England's seventeenth-century boroughs and cities are best understood as variants of an indigenous republican tradition rather than straightforward bastions of oligarchic power.[19] This civic republicanism was neither necessarily antithetical to monarchy nor a precursor of liberal democracy. Rather it was a participatory and elective culture based upon incorporated privileges which at once calibrated citizens according to those criteria influencing office-holding and distinguished them as a community from 'straingers' and 'forreigners' who were not enfranchised within the city's constitution. Like other modes of English republican thought, it was patriarchal and elitist.[20]

However, unlike them it was not confined (for the most part) to learned texts or the imaginations of classically taught statesmen. Rather it was sustained by practice, providing the conditions in which 'the Englishman could develop a civic consciousness, an awareness of himself as a political actor in a public realm'.[21]

From this perspective, those 'able', 'better' and 'discreet' citizens who, according to civic prescription, were invariably elected to civic office constituted the community's public representatives. Of course, as Peter Clark and others have shown, such representatives were usually the wealthiest, best connected or most energetic citizens: ability was a contingent rather than universal criterion. This should not obscure the fact that civic power was articulated through the structures and languages of civic republicanism, not oligarchy. Such power was inseparable from more general status within the community. Moreover because civic republicanism stressed the civic community's autonomy from external (and in particular gentry) interference as much as internal participation, calibration and stratification, the hierarchies and status quotients inherent in civic community were not easily transferable on to other urban social groupings. These points are illustrated by contemporary usage of the terms 'elite' and 'Mr'. In modern usage 'elite' is a generic term denoting 'the choice part or flower of society or of any body or class of person'. However, in later seventeenth-century York the word referred specifically to civic power and status. As was the case in other elective and corporate-based cultures, 'elites' were those citizens (usually three) put forward by a larger elective body to be considered for public office by a smaller elective body. Out of the three elites, a single citizen would be elected for the place. This was true of parochial offices, such as churchwarden and parish clerk; it was true of offices elected at ward level, such as constables; and it was true of offices in the corporation and magistracy proper, be they those of sheriffs, aldermen (who were also Justices of the Peace) or mayors. Similarly while Borsay regards the title 'Mr' as the new 'marginal assignation' of 'urban gentility' after 1660, in fact in York its conferment remained entirely dependent on election to and occupation of the civic office of chamberlain. This office was occupied by eight young freemen a year and involved responsibility for the city's finances. More important, it was a fiscal and ceremonial rite of passage into civic participation at the executive level and the only means of securing the requisite nomenclature within civic society. As late as the 1730s Francis Drake could observe that:

> As a feather to the place [of chamberlain] the title ... Mr is always prefixed to their names, in speaking or writing to them ever after .... In York, when anyone is called so that has not passed this office, or is of so mean an account as not to be thought worthy of it, [they are asked] '"Mr" quoth 'a, [and] pray who was lord-mayor when he was chamberlain?'

This was, felt Drake, 'an opprobrious question when used in this city by the vulgar'.[22]

Therefore in York membership of 'the elites' was indivisible from civic office-holding and the precepts and practices of civic republicanism. Civic republicanism was in turn the normative ideology of civic community. Moreover different types of office attracted different types of elite across the city's interconnected parochial and guild jurisdictions. The result was a relatively diverse and integrative participatory public which was nevertheless structured according to the types of public office for which citizens were eligible and the kinds of civic power such eligibility secured. This is illustrated by the relationship between wealth and corporate office-holding in York. Using weekly contributions to the poor rate as a wealth index (though the same patterns emerge if hearth ownership is used instead) the average wealth of residents in York in 1671 was 1·34d. This compared with 4·69d among civic office-holders, suggesting a substantial gap between the civic community and its representative public. This representative public – which in 1671 constituted 8 per cent of York's heads of household – was itself calibrated according to wealth. While the most junior office-holders (presentment jurors) averaged only 1·14d, the most senior (alderman magistrates) averaged 12d. For each of the five tiers of office-holding in between, increases in wealth correlated nicely with the nominal gradient of public power, to the extent that the perceived custodians of York's commonalty – the seventy-two members of the legislative common council – averaged 4·52d, almost identical to the wealth of the mean wealth of the public as a whole. In this way, structured civic participation served to approximate wealth differentials across civic society with hierarchies of power, authority and responsibilities within the community's nominal public sphere.[23]

Although civic office was undoubtedly a source of power and status, the community's elected representatives were also trustees of the communal resources, privileges and powers of 'our citty' and the well-being, or commonweal, of their fellow citizens. One manifestation of this trust was the perpetuation and actual increase in the 'charity towards byndinge poore cittizens children apprentices' between 1649 and 1688. This feature of civic governance invoked community in a number of ways. In the first instance, its administration required capital. Given that apprenticeships supplemented poor relief – and so were not usually financed by funds from the poor stock – money was usually acquired through charitable bequests like the one denoted by Alderman Watson. These depended on richer citizens not only leaving money to the city but also entrusting the corporation with the responsibility of both investing (or lending the money at interest) in order to maximise funds and matching particular children with suitable masters or 'dames'. In the second instance, apprenticeships required parents, guardians and occasionally children themselves to petition the corporation for aid. Finally they required city tradesmen and women who were not, on the whole, participants in the city's participatory public to accept poor children into their respective households. This at once brought the tradesmen into a legal arrangement with the city and devolved responsibility for the apprentice on to the master or dame. As such, community was manifested in the mutual participation of at once wealthy, trading and impoverished citizens and the obligations, dependences and reciprocities engendered as a result.

Between 1649 and 1689 the number of civic apprentices increased rather than decreased. In the five-year period 1649–53 sixty-six children secured civic help in negotiating apprenticeship indentures with working and enfranchised households. By 1684–89 the figure had more than doubled to 131. Over the period as a whole, 678 children were placed in households: of these, 77 per cent (522) were boys and 23 per cent (156) were girls (a ratio which was more or less constant over the four decades).[24] While roughly a quarter of apprentices were female, a third of all recorded petitioners acting on behalf of apprentices were women. However, it was not expected that all apprenticeships would lead eventually to the creation of new, enfranchised households. While female indentures usually specified three to six years' service (rather than the statutory seven required for enfranchisement), the majority of apprentices were never able to accumulate the capital necessary to become masters in their own right. For example, in 1671 just under a third of those who became civic apprentices went on to claim their freedom. As such, civic apprenticeships were first and foremost a point of entry into the journeyman ranks, educating the child in a trade so that he or she could later support him or herself through wage labour.

The most common type of training of this sort was in the cloth trades in general, and tailoring in particular (36 per cent in total). This was followed by light and heavy manufacturing (21 per cent); the building trades (13 per cent); and clothworking (11 per cent). After tailors, mariners were the single most likely type of citizen to apprentice a child, especially during the 1670s. Like clothworkers, mariners constituted a minority occupation within the populace as a whole; however, while the former were targeted by civic officers as the key to regenerating York's wealth and controlling poverty, the latter institutionalised the removal of potentially troublesome young men from the civic habitat. Indeed, the mariner John Moore was one of only two citizens to apprentice five or more children over the period (the other being the wheelwright Thomas Adwick). Three citizens – all of them cordwainers – apprenticed four children each, eighteen citizens apprenticed three each, and fifty apprenticed two each. From the perspective of the corporation, a suitable household was one that was not only respectable but also likely to remain creditable for the duration of the apprenticeship. On the other hand, for lowly trades such as clothworking the scheme provided a relatively reliable supply of regular labour. Of those masters and dames to bind three apprentices or more between 1649 and 1689, 74 per cent were in the cloth trades or cloth industries. Two of them – Anne Pinckley, a cordwainer, and Dorothy Preston, a silk weaver – were women.

However, the most significant feature of participation at this level was the fact that both apprentice and master tended to originate from the same city wealth bracket. As such they were representative of that large but usually invisible section of the civic populace (46 per cent of all householders listed in the 1671 hearth tax return) who neither constituted 'the poor' nor were 'able' enough to support, in any material sense, their neighbours on a regular basis. In 1671, of the twenty-seven apprentices bound to a trade, only two – George Johnson and Edmond Edwards – came from households regularly *receiving* poor relief. Both George and Edmond were residents of Monk Ward, the poorest section of the city, and both came from single-parent households: once their indentures were secured, relief payments to their parents ceased. Similarly only four of the twenty-three masters and three dames who took apprentices in that year also *contributed* poor relief.[25] One such master was John Hindle of North Street, a young freemason just establishing himself who paid ¹/₂d weekly to the poor rate for the first time in 1671. He took on his neighbour Thomas Patrick's son, George, for seven years at a cost of £1 10s to the city. Although unable to pay poor relief, Patrick was a working tanner and sometime parish constable. At a very different stage in the life cycle from Hindle was the Bootham taylor William Theakston, who had not paid the rate since 1657 but bound George Palfrayman for four nobles of the city's money in any case. While Patrick was subsequently enfranchised as a mason, Palfrayman never claimed his freedom: whether he remained in York as a journeyman or left to work elsewhere is unknown.

The 'charity towards byndinge poore cittizens children apprentices' increased steadily during a period when York's population is felt to have stagnated if not declined. The chronology of civic loans is somewhat different. The ubiquity of credit relations and their cultural implications represent one of the more important recent themes of early modern social historiography. In an essentially cashless society, in which goods were exchanged on trust or loan, credit was much more than an economic institution. In York, just as the public represented community and the master bound apprentice, so the initiation of credit placed individuals in structured juxtaposition. Credit required the person to cultivate trust, reputation and creditworthiness within his or her sphere of economic interaction; it also inculcated reconciliatory habits which Craig Muldrew has characterised as an 'economy of obligation'.[26] However, the nexus of reciprocities engendered by credit could also be manipulated and controlled: credit may have informed community, but it never dissipated power. It is on this basis that trends in civic credit are interesting.[27] In 1649–53 twenty-one loans were issued by the corporation to the sum of £339. The number of loans increased rapidly at the Restoration, peaking in 1674–78, when fifty-six were issued, to a total of £842. In the five years after 1684 the number of loans returned to mid-century levels, though the gross sum of money leant – £545 – was higher. However, loans were essentially stopped – and outstanding debts cancelled – on the recommendations of a 1688 committee authorised 'to inspect severall bonds in which severall sumes of money and for some considerable tyme ... owing to the citty'. This committee consisted of six 'Tory' aldermen who had recently secured office after the purge of what was widely perceived to be York's 'factious' or 'whig' magistracy.[28]

Like civic apprenticeships, the issuing of civic bonds required several levels of participation. Capital was generated either by bequests to the city or the strategic investment of civic funds. Most bequests were gifted by wealthy citizens; however, the largest civic loan fund had been provided by the London philanthropist Sir Thomas White before the Civil War. White's 'guift' specified that four sums of £25 should be lent interest-free for ten years for the benefit of 'cloth weavers and free cittizens of this citty'. This and other 'publique money' was entrusted to the city's representative public, which both invested funds prudently and distributed bonds to citizens worthy of credit. Investment required merchants and lawyers to entrust 'publique money' in provincial and national credit networks on the city's behalf; distribution involved quorums of aldermen and privy councillors – usually headed by the lord mayor for that year – selecting from the petitioners by poll. However, the likelihood of a citizen securing civic credit was contingent not merely on the predilictions of particular quorums – and indeed on his or her reputation, background and connections – but also the willingness of 'reasonable', 'suitable' or 'able citizens' to come forward as sureties. The most common type of bond – for £10 over two years without interest – required two sureties: 111 were administered between 1649 and 1689. On the other hand, on the seventy-two occasions White's guift was administered, petitioners were required to produce four sureties each.

The contrasts between petitioner and surety are striking. Between 1649 and 1689 clothworkers (34 per cent), cloth traders (22 per cent), victuallers (14 per cent) and manufacturers (15 per cent) most often secured loans. Within these categories clothiers, tailors and bakers were most prominent as debtors. Dealers (8 per cent) and public brokers (5 per cent) were less likely to secure civic credit. While cloth traders and manufacturers tended to monopolise £5 and £10 bonds, clothworkers – thanks partly to the wording of White's bequest – secured 49 per cent of £25 bonds. Moreover in 1659 a consortium of cloth workers secured an interest-free loan of £250 to maintain cloth manufacture in the city. Aside from sums of £500 and £1,000 lent at interest during the later 1660s – both of which generated profits to be reinvested into the city's manufacturing infrastructure – this was the largest civic loan of the period and illustrates a sustained civic commitment (also revealed in patterns of civic apprenticeships) to kick-start industry and 'sett the poor to work'. Moreover, of the twenty citizens who received two civic loans, six were clothiers and five were cloth traders. Similarly two of the six citizens to receive three civic loans were clothiers. In contrast it was dealers (21 per cent) – and in particular merchants – who were most likely to be cited as sureties. While clothworkers (17 per cent) and cloth traders (17 per cent) were next most likely to be cited, it was not clothiers and tailors but the more prosperous tanners and drapers who were most often accepted as 'able citizens'. Moreover urban gentry and non-York residents were increasingly (though still only occasionally) listed as guarantors, although concepts of citizenship continued to be stressed. For example, in 1679 Mr William Roe, schoolteacher at the city school and orphanage in Sherburn, was granted £20 for two years on condition he produced his 'own surety and a freeman' and have the bond 'drawn in the freemans name as principle'. However, this chaffing of community at the edges was less striking than the changing gender dynamic of civic credit. During the 1650s women neither secured nor guaranteed loans. While they remained more or less excluded from acting as sureties, in the years after the Restoration the number of female citizens who secured credit rose to the extent that, by 1679–83, a full third of city debtors were women. Indeed, while Elizabeth Cash and Margaret Hudson both secured two loans apiece, Elizabeth Mitchell was one of only six citizens to secure three.

Far from eclipsing other types of social relationship, civic community as manifested through credit recognised and indeed encouraged a variety of social and ideological groupings as a context for its own practice. For most petitioners the onus was on securing support from more 'able' citizens than themselves. Such contracts might have a neighbourly dynamic, as when Micklegate carpenter Matthew Rason was vouched for by two Micklegate merchants. These associations could be compounded by religious affinity, as when John Humphrey, a Micklegate Nonconformist baker, was supported by two Micklegate merchants who were also Nonconformists. It might involve utilising kin networks, as was the case with the draper Matthew Hotham. Or, as with the clothier Richard Betson, fiscal support might be gleaned from a variety of fellow clothiers, creditors and associates residing both across the city and among the clothiers of Leeds. This practice of community complemented other aspects of citizenship outlined above. Participation in office gave public collateral to inequalities within civic society. Civic apprenticeships not only confirmed the obligations of the public to their poor but facilitated the training – and perpetuation – of the journeymen classes and low-status occupational groups. Civic bonds were part of a wider culture of commerce predicated on trust, reputation and credit; they also provided the means whereby manufacturing and industry were supported in the city. Given the central role of dealing groups – in particular drapers and merchants – in securing credit for clothiers, tailors and manufacturers, it seems likely that, in some instances at least, the same bonds institutionalised the control of capital over economic production. This is a reminder that while civic community was inclusive – in terms of gender, wealth, occupation, and so on – it also structured and perpetuated the inequalities it mediated. Moreover in its utilisation of the investment skills and contacts of merchants and professionals, not to mention its repeated investment in industry, it was amenable to the enhanced commercial contexts of the long eighteenth century. For all the different ways citizens could appropriate, manipulate and use civic office-holding, apprenticeships and credit, civic community remained a normative cultural form in Restoration York.

Having established its ongoing vitality as a participatory social practice, we can now consider briefly how civic community influenced and informed political action during the exclusion crisis, and in particular the pronounced antipathy directed by the citizens against James, Duke of York. Recent political historiography has stressed the complex religious and constitutional configurations which shaped the exclusion crisis.[29] Where attention has been paid to political *organisation*, civic structures have figured prominently as the means by which partisan and national action was facilitated and legitimated.[30] Even within these accounts, partisan politics is treated as distinct and discrete from the realm of government.[31] In York, James epitomised a composite of positions, groupings and attitudes inimical to citizenship; however, he was also resented by citizens in York as a person. Such animosity stemmed in part from James's association with institutional and class interests which were perceived by influential citizens as anathema to the civic community's well-being. However, it was also based on his own subversion of some of the precepts and practices of civic community outlined above, and it is this particular narrative which concerns us here.

The citizens' antipathy was hinted at in the latter part of 1682 by Sir John Reresby, the newly appointed royal governor of the garrison in York, in a letter to his patron at court, Lord Halifax. Reresby explained that:

> the loyall party is much inferior in number to the factious. The first consists of the gentry, clergie, officers and dependents of the Church, militia officers and souldiers, and about a fourth part (as is computed) of the cittyzens; the secound of the Maior and whole magistracy (two aldermen only excepted), the sheriffs and most of the common council, with the rest of that citty.

He explained that 'the factious [do not] soe much exceed the former by reason of principle as influence, ther ever being a great many in such a body that either from fear or interest joine with the strongest, and severall ther have confessed that they darr not act according to their judgements (viz. for the government) for fear of being undone in their trade'. Indeed, it 'is now come to that, that ther is not only a separation of interests, but few doe buy of, or have any commerce but with thos of their own principle'.[32]

In describing partisan conflict in this way, Reresby divided the city into two social spheres which were reminiscent of the aldermen's conceptualisation of the city fifteen years earlier. On the one hand were the indigenous inhabitants – the 'cittyzens' – of York, including both the corporation office-holders and the 'rest of that citty' whom the civic officials were meant to represent. On the other were those urban residents who lived in York but were in no sense citizens, in particular the gentry and members of the ecclesiastical and military professions. The 'loyall party' was more or less synonymous with this urban, non-civic social sphere, the 'factious' with the citizenry. What differentiated Reresby's account from that of the aldermen was that while they regarded the civic matrix as an organic participatory body, legitimated and delimited by mutual socio-economic interests, Reresby conceived it as a nexus of power which could be manipulated by 'stronger' citizens – in this instance for partisan purposes – within the wider urban and national context.

Reresby's depiction of political alignments was designed for official consumption at court and, as such, reflected his own political agenda: namely to reinforce his own, military authority within the city at the expense of the civic elites. Moreover by belittling civic opinion as the product of socio-economic dependence, he not only accused York's leading citizens of abusing their power but robbed other citizens of their political agency and voice. However, viewed from the perspective of civic community, there were very obvious reasons why James had become a civic pariah.

James first visited York in 1665 to escape London and the plague. He returned in 1679 to escape London and 'exclusion'. In 1665 £300 was 'borrowed for the cittyes use' in order to present the duke and duchess with 170 gold pieces (120 for him, fifty for her) and to honour the couple with a civic dinner. While the preparations were elaborate, the profits were kept, for the most part, among the citizens. Gold was purchased from a city goldsmith, grocer-cum-postman and attorney. Martins Micklegate grocers supplied 'sweetmeates and groceryes'. A city butcher provided £17 17s 7d of 'flesh meate'. The city cook prepared the banquet. The wine merchant and alderman Sir Henry Thompson received £31 12s for wine, sherry and sack. Alderman Richard Bawtry, another Martins resident, even had his 'great chamber' decorated by two city painters for 'the Entertainment of his Royall Highness'.[33] The duke's courtiers reported the visit a success.[34] Fourteen years later, the citizens made no provision for his visit. On 4 November – itself an important date in the Protestant calendar – the civic executive 'attended on their Royall highness att Mr Aislabyes house in the Minster Yard' – an ecclesiastical jurisdiction outside civic authority – and made a perfunctory speech.[35] James was not invited into civic space, never mind banqueted in a citizen's house. The snub was sharp enough for the King to write to the Lord Mayor explaining he had 'reason to Expect his Brother should be by all good subjects in your station ... attend[ed] and receive[d] ... in the like manner as he was ... some yeares agoe'.[36] However, the King's warning to his 'subjects' did not prevent the York citizenry from militating, over the next three years, for the statutory exclusion of James from the throne.

The civic 'entertainments' of 1665 had a variety of purposes, not least in convincing James and his brother that a civic populace which had sided against their father in 1642 was now loyal to majesty. The need to reassure was the more urgent given the hostility of other urban interests – such as the local gentry, churchmen and garrison soldiers – to the civic community, and the virulent rumours of insurrection and fanaticism circulating in the north. However, the entertainments had a more specific end. Parliament had recently conferred on James all profits relating to the licence of wine retailing in England's boroughs and cities. This contravened the statutory privilege, extant since the reign of Edward VI, which allowed the city's representative public to issue and profit from eight annual wine licences. Its infringement was damaging to the civic public in that it reduced its ability to regulate directly the consumption of wine within the civic jurisdiction.[37] This threat to governance was compounded by the fact that £50 generated each year by licensing was traditionally 'imployed for the reliefe and maintenance of the poor of the citty (who are very numerous and daily increase) and not for any otherwise'.[38] More obliquely, wine merchants like alderman Sir Henry Thompson (who supplied the liquor for the duke's entertainment) constituted the single most powerful mercantile interest within the city: licensing institutionalised their control over how – and by whom – imports were distributed. However, these issues of revenue and power were inseparable from the symbolic significance of the issue. Licensing had long constituted a crucial aspect of civic self-governance, representing a key attribute of communal regulation in general and godly reformation in particular.

In response to the monarchical incursion into civic community the 'cittye' had initially supported city-licensed vintners in contesting the statute at law. However, James's visit provided an opportunity for direct negotiation. A petition 'touchinge the wyne lycences' was drafted by a committee of eight and presented to James. The citizens agreed 'in all humility to relinquish all their claime and pretence to lycence' as 'a testimony of their unforced service and affections'. They regretted having 'contested in suite ... the interest of your

Royall Highnesse' and stressed that the licences had been defended only because they maintained the poor.[39] The strategy worked. In his written reply, James assured the city 'there shall be noe just reason for any in this citty to complaine' and that 'the poore of this citty ... shall be sensible of his Royal highnesses bounty and goodnesse'. Moreover the city minutes record that James's clerk, 'upon his delivery of his Royal highnesses said answere ... did further deliver by words in the inner Room of the comon hall to the lord mayor and the rest of that court' that James's commissioners would pay '£50 yearly towards reliefe of the poore of the citty' as compensation.[40] If this choreographed display of generosity and obedience provides some insight into the nature of public negotiation at the Restoration, it also shows how a stress on governance and community could engender political consensus. This consensus, hard bought by the citizens, was predicated on James and his commissioners honouring his written and oral word to their poor. He did not. Over the next ten years repeated civic petitions for 'arrears due to the poore' went unanswered and in 1675 'the cittye' began reissuing licences 'to avoide the clamour of the poore'.[41] A language of obligation now legitimated civic opposition to James just as in 1665 it had engendered public conciliation. Moreover by reneging on his promise James had both abused civic trust and jeopardised his credit. In turn civic 'commerce' – and the enlarged role of civic credit within such commerce – suggested sets of values by which James could now be judged.

Such values were revealed in another breakdown in civic credit relations which resulted in Christopher Welburne, a Petergate bookseller, suing his neighbour, the trunk maker William Beeforth, for defamation.[42] Beeforth had come into Welburne's shop to settle a debt. When the size of the debt could not be agreed upon, Beeforth 'in a malitious, mischevious manner ... called the said Welburne a Rogue, A Knave, A Rascall ... and the greatest knave that ever kept shoppe in Petergate'.[43] Deponents supplied definitions. William Pickering explained, 'Rogue is a very scandalous and diffamatory word when spoaken in a scolding angry and mishevious manner ... [and] signifies a man that will stick not att the commission of noe villany ... as understood throughout the citty of York'. A neighbouring mercer explained that 'the generall acceptance of the words Rogue, Rascall and knave when spoken in malitious and mischevious manner is that they signifie A wicked and unjust man and one that has no conscience in his dealings nor sticks at the committing of villany'. Mark Gill, a thirty-year-old goldsmith, confirmed that Beeforth's accusations, once reported, meant he no longer held 'Christ[opher] Welburne in such esteeme and repute as he did before the speakinge of the words nor would he deal with him willingly till he be acquitt from the said aspersion'. However, another neighbour explained that Welburne had always dealt 'justly and honestly': he was 'a man of sober life and conversacon and such a person as could not be prevailed with to do an unjust thing upon no account whatsoever'. Indeed, Welburne's landlord thought him an 'honest, punctuall and faire dealer and tradesman ... sober, very exact and upright in all his dealings ... held in good esteem amongst his neighbours ... [as] reputed within the citty of York'.[44]

These vocabularies, and their normative status 'within the citty', constitute a civic context for understanding exclusion. Moreover the significance of reputation, its construction through rumour and its centrality to commerce suggest the easy insinuation of a national politics still focused on the person into the winks and whispers of social relations within the civic community. James was distrusted for his Catholicism, his political links with long-standing gentry enemies of the York citizenry, and his associations with the military establishment and theories of absolutism. In breaking his 1665 written and oral contract to recompense the city's poor annually in exchange for the monopoly of licensing he ruined his credit further by subverting the practice of civic community and allowing himself to be judged according to the morality of 'rogues' and 'fair dealers'.

The degree of political mobilisation observed by Reresby indicates both the potential depth and the inclusivity of citizenship. Of course such mobilisation within the city had a political impact beyond it, as the same citizens who had 'any commerce but with thos of their own principle' also constituted the city's parliamentary electorate. The citizens of York, like those of most relatively autonomous boroughs and cities, elected exclusionists for each of the three 'exclusion' Parliaments between 1679 and 1682. It was no coincidence that one of their representatives was the wine merchant Sir Henry Thompson, the same Thompson who had supplied the wine for James's visit in 1665. For Reresby, Thompson and the other York MP (the Nonconformist lawyer Sir John Hewley) led the 'eight or ten persons of that citty' by whom 'this nice difference hath been contrived, and is yet industriously mentained'.[45] On the other hand Thompson, in justifying his decision to stand against the court candidate for election as York's parliamentary representative, argued that 'the citty hath long protested they would chuse from amongst themselves, how mean so ever the first vacancy'.[46] Both he and Hewley were men of national standing who, in terms of wealth and connections, were indistinguishable from Sir John Reresby. However, Thompson also participated in York's civic community in a way which gentry like Reresby and royalty like James did not. In so doing, he drew on and represented a culture which was elective, self-governing and politically autonomous, brokering between the civic community of which he was an elite member and those provincial and national groupings of which he was also a member.[47]

Like many historians, Reresby explained the citizens' factious coherence in terms of socio-economic and political 'influence'.[48] The precepts and practices which constituted civic community offer a less condescending and perhaps more fruitful insight into the dynamics of both seventeenth-century civic culture and its relationship to national public life. It is a perspective which resonates with recent excavations of a previously neglected stratum of nineteenth-century liberalism based not on 'individualism, self-help and *laissez-faire*' but on 'community self-government and community representation'.[49] It is also in accord with attempts by Kathleen Wilson, Jonathan Barry and Rosemary Sweet to trace forms of civic survivalism during an urbanising and commercialising long eighteenth century.[50] Aspects of civic community outlined here have included both the possessive, participatory and calibratory dynamics of 'civic republicanism' and those forms of structured dependence engendered through apprenticeships and credit. These practices not only ordered and gave public collateral to urban inequalities but also drew women, children, decayed freemen and low-status tradesmen and producers into the civic nexus. In this way citizenship extended much further than the aldermen's bench, marking the perpetuation, through participation, of civic community. Moreover in utilising practices long current in civil society, such as apprenticeships and credit relations, civic governance was insinuated with and intractable from the realms and expectations of daily 'commerce'.

This is not to suggest that the perpetuation of civic community as a form of participatory practice precluded other forms of association and community. Work on urban environs on the one hand and social identities on the other would suggest that citizens were at once participants in their indigenous civic communities and members of other networks and groupings which both subdivided and transcended civic space.[51] These alternative associations – whether religious, economic, political, intellectual, professional, familial or whatever – could exert simultaneous and sometimes more powerful claims on a citizen's loyalties, affiliations and identities. In this sense, Carl B. Estabrook's claim that England's 'urban and rural spheres' remained culturally discrete until 'the middle decades of the eighteenth century' is overstated, as it acknowledges neither the fluid and sometimes contradictory nature of social identity nor those forms of urbanisation which were altering the contexts within which civic community was articulated.[52] Moreover it overlooks entirely the relativist, 'urban' aspects of urban culture and society. Civic survivalism after 1660 did not require the eclipse of other modes of interaction on the part of citizens – indeed, as patterns of civic credit showed, far from nullifying other forms of collectivity, civic community in York facilitated and depended upon them. That said, it seems equally clear that historians of both urban renaissance and Restoration politics have underestimated the place of civic community in the particular stories they tell. The enduring strength of this community was particularly evident in a place like York, where the tensions inherent in civic social relations could be ameliorated by the proximity of other, unincorporated urban jurisdictions and groupings such as the military, church and gentry.[53] This was especially the case during prolonged moments of tension like the exclusion crisis, when the values and dangers personified by James, Duke of York at once drew citizens into the 'homogeneal parts of our body' and redefined other urban groupings as 'our garnishments, embroideries, and ornaments, and sometimes pricks and goads'. Such moments remind us that civic community remained a potent source of identity and power within an ever more urbanised and integrated national civil society.

NOTES

I would like to thank Keith Wrightson for his comments on earlier versions of this chapter.

1 Ann Hughes, 'Coventry and the English revolution', in R. C. Richardson (ed.), *Town and countryside in the English revolution* (Manchester, Manchester University Press, 1992), p. 69.

2 Peter Borsay, *The English urban renaissance: culture and society in the provincial town, 1660–1770* (Oxford, Clarendon Press, 1989); *id.*, 'The English urban renaissance: the development of provincial urban culture, c. 1680–c. 1760', reprinted in *id.* (ed.), *The eighteenth-century town: a reader in English urban history, 1688–1820* (Harlow, Longman, 1990); Robert Tittler, *The Reformation and the towns in England: politics and political culture, c. 1540–1640* (Oxford, Clarendon Press, 1998); *id.*, *Architecture and power: the town hall and the English urban community, c.1500–1640* (Oxford, Clarendon Press, 1991).

3 Patrick Collinson and John Craig, 'Introduction' in *id.* (eds), *The reformation in English towns, 1500–1640* (Basingstoke, Macmillan, 1998), p. 2; Patrick Collinson, *The birthpangs of Protestant England: religious and cultural change in the sixteenth and seventeenth centuries* (Basingstoke, Macmillan, 1988), pp. 58–9; Jonathan Barry, 'Introduction', in *id.* (ed.), *The Tudor and Stuart town: a reader in English urban history, 1530–1688* (Harlow, Longman, 1990), pp. 32–4; *id.*, 'Bourgeois collectivism? Urban association and the middling sort', in Jonathan Barry and Christopher Brooks (eds), *The middling sort of people: culture, society and politics in England, 1500–1800* (Basingstoke, Macmillan, 1994).

4 Borsay, 'Introduction', p. 2.

5 Peter Clark and Paul Slack, 'Introduction', in *id.* (eds), *Crisis and order in English towns, 1500–1700: essays in urban history* (London, Routledge, 1972); Peter Clark, 'Introduction', in *id.* (ed.), *The transformation of English provincial towns, 1600–1800* (London, Hutchinson, 1984). The juxtaposition is best reflected by comparing the way in which Charles Phythian-Adams and Peter Borsay analyse urban ritual over the period. Charles Phythian-Adams, 'Ceremony and the citizen: the communal year at Coventry, 1540–50', in Clark and Slack (eds), *Crisis and order*; Peter Borsay, '"All the town's a stage": urban ritual and ceremony, 1660–1800', in Clark (ed.), *Transformation*.

6 Ian W. Archer, 'The nostalgia of John Stow', in David L. Smith, Richard Stier and David Broughton (eds), *The theatrical city: culture, theatre and politics in London, 1576–1649* (Cambridge, Cambridge University Press, 1995), p. 25.

7 Collinson, *Birthpangs*, p. 59.

8   Robert Scribner, 'Is a history of popular culture possible?', *History of European Ideas* 10 (1989), 175–91, pp. 181–2.

9   'A sad complaynt by the city of York', in Sir Thomas Widdrington, *Analecta Eboracensia: some remaynes of the ancient city of York collected by a citizen of York*, ed. C. Caine (London, 1897), pp. x–xi.

10 *Ibid.*, pp. x–xi.

11 Leeds Record Office, NH 2443, York aldermen to their parliamentary representatives, 20 February 1662.

12 For dictionary definitions see the introduction above.

13 Barry, 'Bourgeois collectivism?'.

14 More styles himself 'Citizen and sheriff of the Famous City of London'. George M. Logan and Robert M. Adams (eds), *Utopia* (Cambridge, Cambridge University Press, 1998), frontispiece.

15 P. J. Withington, 'Urban political culture in later seventeenth-century England: York, 1649–89' (unpublished Ph.D. dissertation, University of Cambridge, 1998), pp. 45–6.

16 Y[ork] C[ity] A[rchives], E33/583.

17 Sir Thomas Smith, *De Republica Anglorum* (London, 1583), p. 3.

18 See, e.g., J. T. Evans, 'The decline of oligarchy in seventeenth-century Norwich', *Journal of British Studies* 14 (1974), 46–75, pp. 46–7; and Barry, 'Introduction', pp. 24–32.

19 Patrick Collinson, 'The monarchical republic of Queen Elizabeth I', *Bulletin of the John Rylands University Library* 69 (1987), 394–424; id., *De Republica Anglorum, or, History with the politics put back* (Cambridge, Cambridge University Press, 1990); Keith Wrightson, 'The politics of the parish', pp. 25–31; Andy Wood, 'Custom, identity and resistance: English free miners and their law, c. 1550–1800', p. 279, both in Paul Griffiths, Adam Fox and Steve Hindle (eds), *The experience of authority in early modern England* (Basingstoke, Macmillan, 1996); Barry, 'Bourgeois collectivism?', pp. 102–4.

20 Quentin Skinner, *Liberty before liberalism* (Cambridge, Cambridge University Press, 1998); Markku Peltonen, *Classical humanism and republicanism in English political thought, 1570–1640* (Cambridge, Cambridge University Press, 1995); Jonathan Scott, *Algernon Sidney and the Restoration crisis, 1677–83* (Cambridge, Cambridge University Press, 1991).

21 J. G. A. Pocock, *The Machiavellian moment: Florentine political thought and the Atlantic republican tradition* (Princeton NJ, Princeton University Press, 1975), p. 335.

22 *Eboracum, or, the history and antiquities of the city of York* (London, 1736), p. 83.

23 Withington, 'Urban political culture', tables 3.1–3.

24 These and subsequent figures are taken from minutes of the mayor's court complied between 1649 to 1689. Apprentices and their proposed master or dame were recorded once sponsorship had been agreed by the court. See YCA B36–9.

25 Recipients of relief were George Johnson, son of John Johnson, of Trinity Goodramgate; John Cant, of St Cuthbert's; and Edmond Edwards, son of Alice, from St Maurice's. Contributors were William Penrose, the Wilfreds' cordwainer (who bound two apprentices); Lawrence Williamson, North Street carpenter; John Hindle, North Street mason; and Mark Buller, Spurriergate cordwainer.

26 Craig Muldrew, *The economy of obligation* (Basingstoke, Macmillan, 1998), pp. 121–85; id., 'The culture of reconciliation: community and the settlement of economic disputes in early modern England', *Historical Journal* 39 (1996), 915–42.

27 As with civic apprenticeships, civic loans were recorded in the minutes of the mayor's court, and the following figures are based on an analysis of B36 to B39.

28 YCA, B38 fol. 248ᵛ.

29 See, e.g., Tim Harris, *Politics under the later Stuarts: party conflict in a divided society, 1660–1715* (Harlow, Longman, 1993), pp. 7–8; id., *London crowds in the reign of Charles II: propaganda and politics from the Restoration until the exclusion crisis* (Cambridge, Cambridge University Press, 1990), pp. 96–155; Scott, *Algernon Sidney*, pp. 13–14; Steven C. A. Pincus, *Protestantism and patriotism: ideologies and the making of English foreign policy, 1650–68* (Cambridge, Cambridge University Press, 1996). For an account of 'exclusion' which retains a much more pronounced sense of organisation see Mark Knights, *Politics and opinion in crisis, 1679–81* (Cambridge, Cambridge University Press, 1994), pp. 3–16.

30 Gary S. De Krey, 'The London Whigs and the exclusion crisis reconsidered', in A. L. Beier, David Cannadine and James M. Rosenheim (eds), *The first modern society* (Cambridge, Cambridge University Press, 1989); Paul D. Halliday, *Dismembering the body politic: partisan politics in England's towns, 1650–1730* (Cambridge, Cambridge University Press, 1998).

31 While De Krey characterises London's political culture as 'radically libertarian', Halliday settles for a vague and indeterminate notion of 'partisan'. Other accounts have stressed the religious motivations of 'factious' civic leaders. De Krey, 'London Whigs', p. 482; Halliday, *Dismembering the body politic*, p. 178; Judith J. Hurwich, '"A fanatick town": the political influence of dissenters in Coventry, 1660–1720', *Midland History* 4 (1977), 15–57.

32 Sir John Reresby, 'Account of York', in A. Browning, *Memoirs of Sir John Reresby: the complete text and a selection from his letters*, second edition, with a new preface and notes by M. K. Geiter and W. A. Speck (London, Royal Historical Society, 1991), p. 579.

33 YCA, B38, fols 18–19; C26, 1665, 'Expences necessary'.

34 C[alendar of] S[tate] P[apers,] D[omestic], 1664–65, pp. 505, 515, 517, 520, 523, 534.

35 YCA, B38 fol. 162ᵛ.

36 *Ibid.*

37 YCA, B37, fols 164, 172, 180, 189.

38 YCA, B38, fol. 21.

39 *Ibid.*

40 YCA, B38, fol. 23.

41 *Ibid.*, fol. 54ᵛ.

42 Borthwick Institute of Historical Research, D/C CP 1690/5, Welburne c. Beeforth.

43 *Ibid.*

44 *Ibid.*

45 Reresby, 'Account of York', p. 580.

46 B[rynmor] J[ones] L[ibrary], University of Hull, DDFA/39/8, Thompson to Danby, July 1673.

47 Thompson had connections with both Marvell and the second Duke of Buckingham. See BJL, DDFA/39/36; DDFA 39/4.

48 For a recent use of York as an example of mercantile oligarchy see J. A. Sharpe, *Early modern England: a social history, 1550–1760*, second edition (London, Arnold, 1997), pp. 185–6.

49 Eugenio F. Biagini, 'Introduction: citizenship, liberty and community' in *id.* (ed.), *Citizenship and community: liberals, radicals and collective identities in the British Isles, 1865–1931* (Cambridge, Cambridge University Press, 1996), p. 1.

50 Kathleen Wilson, *The sense of the people: politics, culture and imperialism in England, 1715– 1785* (Cambridge, Past and Present, 1995); Barry, 'Bourgeois collectivism?', pp. 109–12; Rosemary Sweet, *The writing of urban histories in eighteenth-century England* (Oxford, Clarendon Press, 1998), pp. 74–100.

51 See, e.g., Charles Phythian-Adams, 'Introduction: an agenda for English local history', in *id.* (ed.), *Societies, cultures and kinship, 1580–1850: cultural provinces and English local history* (Leicester, Leicester University Press, 1996); Joseph P. Ward, *Metropolitan communities: trade guilds, identity and change in early modern London* (Stanford CA, Stanford University Press, 1997), p. 146.

52 Carl B. Estabrook, *Urbane and rustic England: cultural ties and social spheres in the provinces, 1660–1780* (Manchester, Manchester University Press, 1998), p. 279.

53 Withington, 'Urban political culture', pp. 130–75.

Chapter 9

◆

From a 'light cloak' to an 'iron cage': historical changes in the relation between community and individualism

Craig Muldrew

Since the nineteenth century one of the most pervasive discourses about the causes of long-term historical change has concerned the idea that interpersonal relations have moved from a state of relatively localised communal co-operation within the medieval vill and guild to the condition of individualistic materially-accumulating behaviour associated with modern capitalism. This is such a common assumption that it is often used as an explanatory factor in narrative descriptions of historical change without being critically engaged by the narrative in which it is being used. In such discourses the growth of market behaviour is linked with the desire to accumulate more possessions, which in turn created a demand for more goods. This eventually led to an increasing division of labour, more social inequality and alienation as people competed to maximise their accumulation. Of course, there is much truth in this story, but evidence suggests that sixteenth-century households began to accumulate wealth for more negative than positive reasons – out of the hope of financial stability in a precarious economy rather than out of a single desire to maximise wants. But, whatever the reasons for such a complex pattern of economic change, they are generally seen to have led, in a teleological progression, to a state of 'modern' possessive individualism in which each economic actor works to satisfy their own wants rather than acting within a matrix of communal standards. In liberal economics this has been interpreted as a *progression* towards a situation of greater social wealth and individual freedom of choice, while in contrast, much social history has used the rhetoric of a lapsarian fall to describe the same process, as sociable communities dissolved under the pressure of changes brought about by competition to make profits.

This progression has perhaps been most famously described as the move from medieval 'organic' communities of village co-operation and guild solidarity to the contractual, competitive relations of market or 'capitalist' economies, or what Ferdinand Tönnies described as the change from *Gemein-schaft* to *Gesellschaft*. Weber added a further transition, from the social embeddedness of traditional practices to the utility of economic relations, which he described as a move from *Gesellschaft* to *Wirtschaft*.[1] In the last forty years, however, the simple characterisation of medieval communities as harmonious communes has been criticised by many medievalists as a nostalgic idealisation. This criticism has arisen as a result of many detailed empirical local studies of villages and manors. These studies have demonstrated the existence of both co-operation and social conflict, and have produced many debates over the nature of the latter, although most have been over the degree to which conflict could be characterised as class conflict, either between richer and poorer villagers or between lords and peasants.[2] The most extreme argument against medieval community has, however, been put forward by the anthropologist Alan Macfarlane, who in his *Origins of English individualism* claimed that, as far back as the thirteenth century, peasants were 'economically "rational", market-oriented and acquisitive'.[3]

Recently, however, a number of medievalists have begun to investigate the way in which institutions of community actually functioned in practice and have argued for the existence of what may be called a 'non-organic' form of medieval community. John Bossy has shown how Christian theology and the ritual of the social and sacred body promoted a unified identity. The medieval notion of society was of a single Christian community, with man reconciled to Christ and neighbour through communion and belief in the atonement. There was certainly an awareness of conflict through notions of sin in this conception of community, but men were considered to be naturally sociable animals, and conflict was dealt with by overwhelming stress on the activity of reconciliation and the paternalist authority of lordship and the church as the means of maintaining neighbourliness, and providing material and spiritual assistance to others.[4]

Other historians have examined how groups and institutions such as the parish, village, town, guild and realm functioned as communities. Most notably, Susan Reynolds has argued that medieval lay society possessed 'a very homogeneous set of values, which combined acceptance of inequality and subordination with a high degree of voluntary co-operation', whose object was to achieve an harmonious consensus.[5] Miri Rubin has also made a specific investigation of the communal identity of Corpus Christi fraternities and celebrations, examining how personal identities were 'negotiated and manipulated within a grid of social explanation and action within religious ritual'.[6] Similarly, Gervase Rosser has also looked at guilds and fraternity activity in detail and has argued for the importance of the expression of commensality in activities such as feasting as a means of creating relations of trust and co-operation through such group identity. He has argued that 'the categories of nineteenth-century discourse have blinkered modern interpretation' of guild activity, which was part of a social process of work, 'whereby agreements were reached in particular periods and places'.[7] Finally, Christopher Dyer has considered scepticism about the collective nature of peasant society in an examination of the English medieval community and the question of its decline. He has concluded that the village community was never 'an affiliation of equals', and that its effectiveness always depended on hierarchy and the exercise of social control. But despite the fact that the medieval vill never achieved the 'harmonious golden age sometimes claimed for it', in Dyer's view medieval village communities were 'practical and functional' organisations which, far from declining, actually became stronger in the later Middle Ages.[8] Thus there seems to be something of a consensus developing that medieval community should be seen not as the actual existence of continually function-ing harmonious co-operative relationships but rather as the working out of social processes and languages which sought only to *promote* co-operation towards certain ends.

In contrast to such changing and debated notions of community in the medieval period the assumption that the history of economic relations since around 1600 has been a move from co-operation to steadily increasing individualism has not been questioned at a theoretical level to the same degree, despite the fact that many community studies have been undertaken in the past thirty years which show that many forms of co-operation survived even as economic polarisation occurred.[9] One reason for this is that we now have a language of individualism traced back to this period which stresses that we all have interior selves where happiness is located, and interpersonal relations are evaluated as they promote or damage such happiness.[10] As Norbert Elias pointed out as long ago as the 1930s, the very success of the language of radical subjectivity which developed in the nineteenth century, and which sees the individual liberty of selfhood as something dissociated from and *opposed* to communal organisation, has meant that the communal nature of the self has all but been ignored. Elias's great breakthrough was to see that individual autonomous conscience was not an abstract set of mental functions which stood outside history, and that self-consciousness was not an idealistic entity with a history of its own produced through reason in the Hegelian sense.[11] Nor was the individual a political owner of autonomous rights opposed to the force of society as developed by nineteenth-century liberal thought.[12] The individual was rather a product of social history and as much a part of society as any other institution:

> The notion of individuals deciding, acting, and 'existing' in absolute independence of one another is an artificial product of men which is characteristic of a particular stage in the development of their self-perception....

This self-perception in terms of one's own isolation, of the invisible wall dividing one's own 'inner' self from all the people and things 'outside' takes on for a large number of people in the course of the modern age the same immediate force of conviction that the movement of the sun around the earth situated at the centre of the cosmos possessed in the Middle Ages.[13]

As a result of this, community has come to be interpreted as something contrary or opposite to individualism, and the fact that communities were, and are, a set or state of *interpersonal relations* themselves has often been lost. In medieval language, for instance, the condition of a person with an individual conscience in a metaphysical relationship with God, and in worldly relations with their neighbours, was a central ethical concept mediating communal relations. Thus it does not immediately follow that the history of the last 500 years has been a progression away from 'community' towards individualism. Rather, the period has seen changes occur in the way social relations have been interpreted, communicated and mediated between individuals all within a set of overlapping social relations. Society is a state of both co-operation and conflict, and if we have really been on a downward slide towards a state of more and more individual economic competition, then logically industrial societies should be intolerably conflictual, existing in a state of constant Hobbsian civil war as competition completely destroys trust. In fact exactly the opposite has happened, as large-scale corporate social structures have evolved in which people trust a set of minimally calculated standards fairly implicitly, if not without suspicion. People may be increasingly uneasy about the distance which exists between themselves and their governments, bankers, and the corporations which produce consumer products, but most still trust them with a huge amount of authority. Such modern forms of co-operation are very strong and, I would argue, much less conflictual than the more interpersonal forms of co-operation in medieval and early modern society, or are at least able to channel conflict in much more structured ways.[14]

Looking at the trajectory of social interpretation in this way, the question arises as to why modern forms of social organisation are not interpreted in a positive light for promoting co-operation in the same way as 'communities', but are rather ironically presented as uniform rule-based impediments to individual expression and happiness. There is a tremendous paradox in interpretations of the rise of capitalism which see it as the begetter of both 'possessive individualism' and of regimented bureaucracy within 'total institutions' of rational discipline.[15] Michel Foucault even argued that the modern practice of individualism (or 'technologies of the self') was something shaped by disciplinary institutions of modernity. He claimed that the development of individualism had not gone far enough, and towards the end of his life argued for a politics of personal liberation.[16] Given this, it is suitably ironic that, while the origins of modern individualism are commonly traced back to the connection Max Weber made between the Protestant emphasis on individual faith in God and conscience, no phrase of his has retained such resonance in the modern word as that of the iron cage of rational bureaucracy and factory organisation.[17] It conjures up the image of the faceless corporation as an institution where individual initiative, or simple whimsy, is stamped out with the aim of making people undertake repetitive tasks necessary to the functioning of the organisation. Weber had such factors in mind when he described the iron cage, and he blamed the rise of bureaucratic organisations on the utilitarian desire for material wealth, and for him the most characteristic institution was the factory.[18] But bureaucracies have also developed since the nineteenth century to process information, to govern, and to apply specialist knowledge to many tasks, including not only production but education, health and finance, among others.[19] But, whatever their function, it remains true that, together with voluntary associations such as clubs and sports teams, such massive institutions of scale are the most constituent part of modern community in a geographical sense. It is at work, or school, that most people now come across most others they interact with, and neighbourhood as a geographical construct is weak in comparison.

Although this development is a process which has taken place in the nineteenth and twentieth centuries, Weber famously linked the reason for bureaucracy's eventual development, not to social forces, but to the spiritual content of religion and the spread of, as he put it, 'worldly asceticism' in Protestant thought which promoted the disenchantment of the world through work discipline and the forgoing of pleasure to the calling. As he put it:

> when asceticism was carried out of monastic cells into everyday life, and began to dominate worldly morality, it did its part in building the tremendous cosmos of the modern economic order. This order is now bound to the technical and economic conditions of machine production which today determine the lives of all the individuals who are born into this mechanism, not only those directly concerned with economic acquisition, with irresistible force. Perhaps it will so determine them until the last ton of fossilized coal is burnt. In [Richard] Baxter's view the care for external goods should only lie on the shoulders of the 'saint like a light cloak, which can be thrown aside at any moment'. But fate decreed that the cloak should become an iron cage.[20]

This led to rational calculation and accounting, and then to the capitalist organisation of labour, because the same asceticism which frowned on pleasure also frowned on luxury which gave pleasure. Savings were the result of this process, as puritans controlled their desire to enjoy material items while at the same time continuing to work hard – which in turn became investment capital which was used to create rational institutions in the pursuit of more profit.[21] Thus Richard Baxter's 'light cloak' – a moderate increase in consumption of and desire for goods – eventually led to the creation of a world in which the social organisation of capital through savings permitted large-scale institutions to develop. This enabled the production of goods on a massive scale, allowing consumption and capital saving to go on increasing. This in turn created a world of rationalised, alienated work and atomised competitive self-fulfilment in work and material consumption, in which the commensality of community had been lost.[22]

But if we are to think of community as a social process which promotes co-operation and group identity, as suggested in the most recent work on medieval community, these two factors are certainly present in modern industrialised society in very strong ways. There is much co-operation in the way in which modern bureaucracies or institutionalised workplaces function, while local, provincial and especially national governments seek to promote ideas of group identity. If one thing has fallen away from these modern 'processes' of community it is the element of commensality. Feasting, celebration, neighbourliness, local charity and hospitality have been removed, or drastically reduced to certain public occasions or transformed into the bureaucratic provision of entitlements. This is because modern institutions of community are based not so much on cementing and maintaining negotiable relations of interpersonal trust as on financial stability in a competitive environment based on the utility of accounting and thrift to produce profits and continual growth. Commensality, hospitality and entertainment are now largely done on a private voluntary basis removed from public institutions. Thus a tripartite division has taken place. Co-operation and charity have become bureaucratically institutionalised, while communal personal identity has taken the form of a shared national or regional culture combined with a degree of personal choice about the verbal expression of politics and ethics. The practice of the latter, however, is severely restricted by the working of large-scale bureaucracies such as political parties, government agencies and business corporations which implement collective moral agency in our populous societies. At the same time those interpersonal ethics ungoverned by the law, together with hospitality, have become almost entirely privatised.

By interpreting change in this way I wish to dispense with the teleological notion that increasing market competition has created conflict which has dissolved communities, and that modern life can simply be characterised as the condition of a non-communal, individualistic, materially accumulating behaviour associated with modern capitalism. I would rather say that the exact opposite is true: that conflict exists where co-operative bonds are the *most* interpersonal. In such close relations there is the most scope for argument, misunderstanding, disagreement and disappointment. Thus spousal or sexual relations now lead to more disruptive conflict than banking, politics or even labour relations, which are increasingly coming under the techniques of management. Communities have now become structured hierarchical bureaucracies and governmental institutions rather than the mix of formal positions of authority and informal neighbourly and household relations which characterised local communities in the early modern period. Modern forms of co-operation are less conflictual because they are fundamentally based on internalised *self-discipline* for their existence, which promotes the acceptance of managerial authority. Public authority is now also more concerned with those disenfranchised by bureaucratic structures because of lack of employment or because they do not desire to, or have not been educated to, adopt the skills or assumptions of self-discipline needed to work within such institutions, or because they are perceived by managers and police not to posses such attributes, or are excluded on the basis of race, class, gender or culture.

This distinction can be helpfully characterised with a dichotomy between what I have chosen to term 'negotiated' and 'architectural' community. In both medieval and early modern communities interpersonal co-operation and conflict were negotiated by individuals on a one-to-one basis through relations of hierarchy, patronage, contract, marriage, kinship, friendship, geographical neighbourhood, local custom and legal institutions. The main social process in this version of community was bargaining, in which the outcome was agreed upon by all the parties concerned, and society was a continual process of interpersonal bargaining.[23] This also existed in a spiritual form in the theology of reconciliation, which stressed the importance of being at peace with one's neighbours.[24] In addition, the increasing advocacy in the sixteenth and seventeenth centuries of causuistical reasoning as a means whereby individual consciences could make moral decisions was in a sense an internalisation of negotiation.[25]

In contrast, I would term institutions characterised by structured predictability 'architectural', following the extended metaphor Descartes used to describe his sceptical procedure as that of building a new strong house to replace older houses with insecure foundations.[26] Descartes's solitary practice of mental self-examination led to his theory of mind–body duality, and the idea of a more bounded internal self-reflexive mind, but he also advocated it as a means of obtaining stoical self-knowledge and control over the passions.[27] He famously undertook such an adjustment 'shut up in a room heated by an enclosed stove', where he had 'no company to distract me, and having, fortunately, no cares or passions to disturb me'. Thus freed from the passions of social interaction he was free to 'order' his life in better fashion through the use of reason, and become, as he said, a man rather than a child by governing his appetites.[28] Here there is a link forward to Weber, for it was such a concept of reason as self-control which eventually led to the development of rule-based social interaction, whereby political and bureaucratic institutions make rules and people follow them *voluntarily* by controlling themselves, or are coerced into doing so by various means, and are then penalised for failure.[29] Although such 'rules' – things like not swearing at a boss or refraining from taking an afternoon off to go fishing on a whim – may seem similar to a medieval by-law against throwing offal on the street, or being fined for not attending church, there is a crucial distinction between the internalisation of the modern rule and the public nature of previous laws. It is absolutely essential to the modern liberal idea of freedom that the good modern citizen can practise self-control, and authority is seen in a negative sense as being needed only when such control fails. In contrast, in the early modern period public legal authority served the function of self-control and was seen in a positive sense as a means of reconciling individuals who came into conflict because they were more free *impulsively* to do as they wished in what would now be considered a childish sense.

By drawing on Descartes's metaphor I wish to imply that the intellectual basis of such change was developed in the sixteenth century, but actual institutional change took a very much longer time to develop. In the early modern period negotiation continued to flourish as a basis for communal interaction, while institutional structures became increasingly legalistic before becoming bureaucratic. Much religious fraternity and institutional solidarity was of course lost in England after the Reformation, together with religious control over instruments of government. In addition, while guilds survived in London and other towns like York, in many other places they declined, or were actually abolished in towns such as King's Lynn.[30] In addition, a great deal of regulatory action which had been undertaken solely at the village level through manorial institutions came to be augmented or supplemented by nationally organised legal institutions such as assizes and quarter sessions, while new local institutions were created such as the poor law administration. At the same time old institutions such as borough governments and courts were transformed by humanist civic ideals into more prominent institutions with procedure which was similar all over England. What may be said to have been happening in a broad sense was a movement from community being expressed through a large number of local institutions with a religious basis to a much more legalistic community increasingly based as much on civic as on religious identity. In part this was due to the Reformation, but it could not have occurred without the economic changes of the sixteenth century and the expansion of credit which accompanied them.

Such change occurred differently from Weber's model. Historically, of course, there is much which has been criticised in Weber's thought.[31] But Weber was certainly right to show that there was indeed an emphasis in much English Protestant and puritan moralising which emphasised the duty to work and which urged self-discipline, but this did *not* immediately lead in a linear fashion to tensions between production and consumption, or to better, more rational book-keeping and a subsequent increase in savings, ultimately resulting in a more individualistic or a more bureaucratic society.

The evidence of probate inventories and trade figures suggests that the production and consumption of manufactured and imported goods increased quite rapidly in the sixteenth century, and continued to increase throughout the seventeenth and eighteenth centuries. But if we accept that the inflation of the period from 1520 to 1640 was demand-driven rather than a monetary phenomenon, as has been convincingly argued most recently by J. R. Wordie, it suggests that there was more consumption than production, which was especially true of agriculture, which formed the largest section of the economy, where technological constraints on increased production meant prices went up sixfold.[32] Increased consumption led to increased debt loads because there were few individuals who could act as bankers before the end of the seventeenth century. This, combined with the fact that book-keeping was primitive, meant that there was no technological apparatus to hold savings in the form of credit. Since over 90 per cent of the economy was based on credit, most of it sales credit, this meant that the concept and organisation of 'savings' could not evolve before a fairly stable national banking system was developed in the late eighteenth century. Only through the services of the small group of London goldsmiths and scrivener bankers such as Sir Robert Clayton could deposits be made which could form savings. Investment in joint stock companies and in the Bank of England developed from the beginning of the eighteenth century, but before then credit was conceived of in inter-personal terms and was insecure and had to be constantly renegotiated. The saving of cash was termed 'hoarding' and generally considered to be unsociable miserliness which kept a scarce commodity out of circulation. Even early investment was insecure; many bankers defaulted as a result of the stop on the Exchequer in 1672, and a much greater number lost a great deal in the collapse of the South Sea bubble.[33] The result was that, rather than the development of saving in the sixteenth and seventeenth centuries, debt loads increased. Thus, while economic co-operation in the common fields, guild regulation, mutual help and large-scale monastic and aristocratic charity declined as market competition increased, trust, co-operation and reconciliation continued to play a fundamental role in society and the economy in the form of credit and its negotiation, which required hospitality, neighbourliness, forbearance and discretion.

Those who succeeded economically in this world did so by being owed more than they owed others, which led to wealth. This, however, was an intensely social form of wealth difficult to abstract from the local geographical community or, in the case of merchants, from the other merchants they dealt with. But as the geographical extension of credit spread far beyond the local community for many wealthier individuals, the household, *not* the individual, came to be stressed rather than the manor or vill as the fundamental social unit of patriarchal government and economic production for the market. As a result, the 'credit' of individual households and their members came to be interpreted in the moral terms of trustworthiness, and the concept of neighbourhoods of morally competing households became more prevalent than the unified Christian community as theological differences caused religious division.

Also, although many households tried to be thrifty, only a few succeeded, while many more failed – creating the sharp social pyramid of early modern society. Consumption for many was only controlled negatively once they lost credit with their neighbours because they owed too much and they were no longer able to purchase as much on credit. This resulted in disputes over unpaid debts and broken contracts. Most people attempted to solve such disputes through neighbourly reconciliation, but as chains of credit grew more complex, dispute settlement increasingly took the form of litigation in local courts, which had reached unprecedented levels by the beginning of the seventeenth century. This huge amount of litigation also led to much insolvency, or 'breaking', and downward social mobility because of debt. Economic growth in this period was characterised more by insecurity than by secure savings. This was a very severe but also a very public and legal way of limiting consumption, as it was mediated through local civil courts.[34]

Attempts to inculcate a mechanism of self-control in individual consciences to regulate what contemporaries termed 'appetites' took a great deal of time before they had any effect because the replacement of pleasure or happiness gained from immediate satisfaction through consumption, sex or love with the hoped-for future happiness of wealth and stability gained through constant self-inhibition was very hard to square with the most common means of understanding morality and happiness – which were communal rather than personal.[35] Thus, contrary to what Weber proposed, asceticism did not immediately control householders' desires and consequent over-expenditure on goods beyond a small part of the population who were competent book-keepers. The expansion of credit resulted in an intricate system of interpersonal obligations rather than investment capital, and a system whereby economic disputes as well as consumption were resolved communally through public courts. Proceedings in court could lead to a loss of public reputation, and, perhaps most strikingly in terms of consumption, if a defendant was found guilty and forced to a pay a debt the court had the power to order their goods to be distrained, whereupon a bailiff might publicly remove chattels from the debtor's house.

Thus what came into being in the early modern period may be termed the 'juridical community', where group co-operation and dispute settlement of neighbourhoods, villages and guilds was augmented by a set of nationally similar legal institutions whereby disputes could be resolved and co-operation could continue. Manor and borough courts, of course, had played an important role in medieval communities, but the practice of litigation in the sixteenth and seventeenth centuries certainly intensified as did the importance of all sorts of courts, whereby the idea of a civil society of rights, obligations and the sociability of commercial co-operation came to coexist with a weakened notion of Christian community.[36] Perhaps the most crucial change in this process was the elevation of the legal authority of the common law (and magistracy) in national and regional institutions above the authority of lordship and manorial courts as a means of maintaining the social order in a more broadly competitive society.[37] Local customary punishments such as rough music and ducking stools remained in practice, but where customary rights involved property they were sometimes accommodated into the national legal system through equity procedure. Just as often they came into conflict with common law as economic competition and insecurity led more individuals to build their wealth by defining more sharply the *meum* in *meum* and *tuum*.[38] This notion of community also placed much more emphasis on the concept of the equality of potential economic ability and honesty, while maintaining social hierarchy. This was because almost all households were connected to some degree in chains of credit. These structural and linguistic changes occurred so that a much more fluid degree of social and geographical mobility and change could be mediated as marketing activity expanded.

One of the most crucial features of this juridical society was that *public dispute resolution*, both at an informal and at a legal level, remained a fundamental practice which expressed its members' desire to live in a state of communal relations with their neighbours to the degree that reciprocal trust as well as mutual hospitality and civic duty could be maintained. To achieve social harmony many natural personal desires had to be regulated, and, as discussed above, this could be done through a variety of 'informal' public means such as local custom, celebration and ceremony, neighbourly negotiation, as well as through the vastly increased use of contractual legal authority. In addition to such resolution of interpersonal disputes, public authority was also used to discipline misbehaviour in the community, such as drink offences or failure to attend church. Such discipline was also an imposition of public authority, which, as Keith Wrightson has argued, could often be monopolised by wealthier householders who used the offices of quarter and petty sessions to attempt to impose a stricter enforcement of such authority as social problems intensified in the late sixteenth century.[39] This was the primary means of dealing with social tension which was much more important than self-control. It was perhaps less communal than the medieval vill, but still depended on public institutions and authority and the concept of a community based either on Christian love or at least on the minimal trust in promises which Thomas Hobbes saw as the essence of society. The communal nature of such dispute resolution was centred on the concept and process of reconciliation, and as such involved the attempted resolution of disputes *after* they had occurred, first by informal, and then by legal means.

Such means of communal regulation of desires and passions were also a part of many other aspects of early modern life beyond the economic. Litigation over sexuality and sexual insults also multiplied. Sexual behaviour was additionally controlled through groups of friends and family and within the community in the form of reputation, and sexual insults increasingly led to litigation, just as in the case of economic disputes.[40] The reputation and honour of elites were also defended through litigation in the court of Star Chamber, while disputes over marriage contracts and settlements, and inheritance custom often led to some of the most drawn-out and bitter litigation undertaken in the equity courts which could last for years.[41] In addition, disputes over religious practices and other political matters divided town councils, but, as Jonathan Barry has argued, the civic-humanist tradition of active political participation based on classical notions of civic duty to a republican ideal of the *polis,* mapped out by intellectual historians such as Quentin Skinner and J. G. A. Pocock, formed an ideology of 'freedom' in early modern English towns which promoted a culture of 'bourgeois collectivism'. This civic ethos promoted co-operation and reconciliation through participation in town government and institutions.[42] Disputes over religion, taxation, corruption, foreign policy, and, most importantly, legal right, also, of course, occurred in Parliament. The language of reconciliation and the attempts of the members to operate as a community attempting to resolve their disputes can be seen in most debates, but perhaps most obviously in the attempt at the Great Contract of 1610 and in the formation of the Petition of Right in 1628.[43]

Because the emphasis in such processes of reconciliation and litigation was on the resolution of conflict they were characterised primarily by negotiation after it had occurred, more than on following rules to prevent it. This can clearly be seen in the process of reckoning over debts and dispute settlement which took place out of court. In one example of a commercial arbitration concerning £1,300 worth of spoiled goods reported by the diarist Samuel Pepys, a disgruntled merchant, at the end of long negotiations, was willing to settle for £202, only a sixth of his original request.[44] In common law cases this is much harder to observe, because only formal jury decisions were listed in the court records, and the means by which the vast majority of cases were resolved before they came to judgement are not known. But, as Thomas Green has argued, the older idea of self-informing juries was still current in the seventeenth century. The evidence of the notes the judge Sir Dudley Ryder made of civil cases before the Middlesex assizes in the 1750s shows that common law legal process at this date still left wide discretion to juries in commercial disputes where conditional bonds were not involved to discuss such matters as quality of work, profit levels, wage levels and the effect of slander. Evidence from Pepys's diary also shows that jurors were willing to listen to the evidence of litigants outside court.[45] Even in cases involving straightforward monetary debts and sealed bonds, cases could be brought in equity which allowed the judge to apply discretion if it was thought that the exact enforcement of the contract would be unfair to the debtor owing to unforeseen circumstances.[46] In addition, the law of real property could almost be described as an intractably complex system of negotiating the competing claims of manorial custom, willed inheritance, uses and trusts and marriage settlements, which was worked out in equity courts, often at great expense, rather than in terms of absolute rights of alienation.[47] Also, the pleading strategies recorded in equity records, as well as the much smaller disputes recorded by William Hutton in his eighteenth-century Birmingham court of requests, often read like market bargaining, as each side tried to build the best case.[48]

But while this system of communal negotiation combined with juridical legal authority dominated dispute resolution, there was also increasingly an emphasis on self-control based on Christian avoidance of sin, as well as Stoic philosophy's emphasis on virtue and self-knowledge. Although much has been written about the philosophical development of the idea of the self, almost nothing has been done on the social history of selfhood or self-discipline.[49] As noted, Norbert Elias attempted to historicise the process of elite strategies of, and reasons for, self-discipline within the context of medieval and early modern court society. He proposed that the increasing complexity of social institutions in Europe as they developed from feudalism to the absolutist court and then on to modernity occurred concurrently with the development of what he termed, in post-Freudian language, individual drive reduction. He characterised feudal society as one where powerful men competed violently, and in order for the state to develop, he argued, men had to learn to curtail their impulsive behaviour, which could lead to conflict and possibly violence in social situations.[50] In *The court society* he argued that this process took place in Renaissance courts through a process he termed an 'economy of effects'.[51] Court society developed as a result of some feudal lords obtaining a monopoly of power over certain territories, with the power to implement a degree of taxation. To compensate for their loss of territorial power, other feudal magnates joined the monarch's or prince's court, where administration took place, and then came to compete by the rules of courtesy rather than through physical force, to become an influential servant of the ruler. By adapting to the rules of manners and courtesy with regard to the regulation of bodily functions such as spitting or blowing one's nose, and to the regulation of sexual impulses and bodily discharges in the company of others, as well as by the adoption of table manners, courtiers fashioned themselves by internalising self-restraint.[52]

Elias's arguments, however, fall short if we want to know anything about the rest of society which comprised the vast majority of the population of early modern Europe. In an English context Anna Bryson has also examined how concepts of civility and good manners were promulgated and debated far beyond the court, and had an effect on the middling sort through published pamphlet literature.[53] The concepts of self-control and civility were also promulgated more widely in society through the conceptualisation of the mental process of 'reason', which was supposed to act as a form of control over action. Although reason is now thought of primarily as ratiocination or logical thinking in itself, in much early modern thought reason was explained as a process of logical evaluation of action and its *consequences*, to control conflictual passions which could cause discord and melancholy.[54] But this emphasis on reason was primarily intended for those in positions of authority or magistracy. The juridical community and its law needed to be administered and applied by judges, magistrates and governors, who had to be able to keep the passions of greed and revenge in check to avoid the corruption of justice. The early modern answer to the question of who should govern the governors was the advocacy of the rule of reason. As a result, many of the tracts written on the passions were part of that much larger Renaissance body of advice literature which sought solutions to the problems of governing Europe's increasingly complex emerging states by examining Roman republican writings which dealt with similar problems. Thus, as Susan James has shown, many treatises on the passions took over the ancient Stoic tradition which identified the acquisition of self-knowledge with the ability to master passions to prepare a male elite to occupy positions of civil power within the growing legal state.[55] But in addition to this, as the economic unit of the household became more important, so too did emphasis on the patriarchal authority of the household head as a governor of a family. In this context, as Alexandra Shepard has also shown, self-government or 'self-bridling' was often advocated in conduct books as an ideal to be followed by a large proportion of the male population.[56]

But the extent of conflict in sixteenth and seventeenth-century societies combined with the extent of warfare and strife over religion led many to conclude that such reason was still weak in comparison with the passions. Especially in Protestant doctrine, the inability to control the passions was often attributed to the inevitable consequence of the Fall: as punishment for Adam's sins.[57] The result was that obedience to both God's law and public civil law was stressed more than self-control was, and debates over conscience had much to do with the ability of individual souls to follow God's laws.[58] In addition, 'right reason' was seen to be contained in the form of civil laws developed through custom and the making of positive law. This was one of the reasons why many who wrote and spoke about the law in the early seventeenth century argued that all had to obey the rule of law in order for the social order to be preserved.

Thus, despite the increased emphasis on self-government, more reliance was still placed on the law, as in the case of the reformation of manners in the late sixteenth and early seventeenth centuries, which, as noted above, was an intensely legal process which involved prosecution for moral misdemeanours and also the creation of bridewells for minor punishment.[59]

Major change did not take place until the eighteenth century, when litigation of all sorts declined as elites as well as artisans turned to the clubs and societies of the urban renaissance as arenas for the expression of their social identity, and away from the legal ideals and institutions of the juridical community.[60] Here the internalisation of self-control seems to have been much more successful through the adoption of socialised practices of politeness by elites and the middling sort. This took place in voluntary associations, in which the polite pleasure of acts of socialised self-expression in the form of wit (as advocated by the Earl of Shaftesbury through his notion of stoical self-knowledge) played a more important role than self-denial.[61] John Brewer has also shown how eighteenth-century clubs and voluntary associations were increasingly used to negotiate creditworthiness.[62] How much of this new voluntary sociability was made possible because financial tensions about credit were reduced by the spread of good accounting, or how much they helped the middling sort to trust one another, thus reducing the need for litigation, is a question which still needs investigation.[63] But these associations, which were so common in the eighteenth century, are an important part of the story of changes in the relationship of the individual and the community, because they were a new type of communal organisation in which co-operation was not based on geographical proximity, or the inherited organisation of trade guilds, but was created by individual men with similar 'interests'. Such organisation was made possible by the fact that these men felt they could trust one another outside the hierarchical authority structures of older communal associations.[64] This new type of trust based on self-control also led to radical scepticism about the ability to judge trust. As Edward Hundert has argued, it led to concerns that self-control could actually be used to hide a 'real' personality behind an 'acted out' public persona. This stands in contrast to the previous assumption that a public persona was more opaque because the 'credit' of individuals was constantly judged by public means.[65] The rise of 'interest-based' association meant that interpersonal trust could became calculated when membership of voluntary associations was considered, based on the rational probabilistic calculus of the potential results of personal action.[66]

The key to this was the success of self-discipline which allowed the 'self' itself to become a unified 'architectural' construction crucial to the construction of the modern sense of identity.[67] As a result, 'interested' 'individuals' could come together to form voluntary associations of large numbers, and then subsequently to create rule-based bureaucracies to enable 'individuals' to follow the rules set by structures to reduce risk and prevent conflict.[68] Of course negotiation continued to take place and still takes place, but with the rise of a public sphere of political criticism and scepticism, much of pre-modern negotiation increasingly came to be seen as a form of corruption. Also, as Michael Mascuch has pointed out, modern individualist selves are 'hypnotised by the illusion of individual personal authority' and 'autonomous self-creation' to the extent that they have constantly to deny that their self-identities are still always the product of interpersonal negotiation.[69] Rules and laws are administered as public measures which can be understood by the millions of citizens in modern polities, and supposedly applied with equanimity. This stands in contrast with the early modern legal system, which was shot through with discretion and negotiation. Discretion and negotiation still play an important role in the modern legal process, but the ideology of modern law is penal rather than the concilial. Now the maxims of equality before the law and in punishment, and the notion that ignorance of the law is no excuse of guilt, mask such negotiation, and are more important to the way the law is supposed to be understood by those subject to it than discretion or reconciliation.[70]

As a result individuals are necessarily judged in public by such rules, and this has created an intolerance of private deviance which social libertarians like Foucault and many other critics of institutionalised psychiatry and other total institutions have so forcefully argued against. Such architectural social structures have also been highly gendered because the reason needed for self-control was originally conceived of as a specifically masculine possession, just as early modern public authority had been the preserve of masculine physical strength, and as a result new organisations were generally created by men for men.[71] Women were excluded, and then subsequently criticised by men for not having in their terms the 'rational' rule-bound personalities which such institutions defined and brought into being.[72]

Thus co-operation has become highly abstract and bureaucratised as the profit motive has moved out of the household and into the corporation or business, which provides highly structured authority in the workplace in order to make supply and demand, and thus profits, more predictable and more stable. This has also been achieved by an internalisation of discipline into the self which is meant to control conflictual emotions in order to permit a degree of co-operation which can be rationally calculated.[73] This has provided an even further expansion of geographical mobility, which is now moving to a global level, as the minimisation of conflict allows strangers with very little in common to co-operate within multinational corporations, the European Union and other pan-national bodies. The ethics of contract and trust based on the household have gradually come to be replaced by the ideology of utilitarianism in which community has become *calculated* through accounting practices, marketing surveys, censuses and elections, and in many other ways. The social bonds which constitute economic communities are no longer interpreted by economists and administrators in terms of interpersonal relations, or in terms of neighbourhoods bound by common aspirations, or of competing households bound by trust or contract, but in terms of mutual security obtained through the calculation of resources, or the formation of *capital*. The calculated community is one where large pools of financial institutional credit in the form of capital organised through accounting exist to supply material needs and wants. This capital can take many forms, including bank accounts, mortgages, insurance policies, corporate value, wage payments, or tax revenue used to provide social services and to pay for infrastructure and defence.

We now trust in the efficacy of such institutions to make the economy work rather than in the ethics of interpersonal relations. The emotional content of such utility is radically minimised to process the interaction of millions of geographically unlocated agents whose happiness is judged *collectively* as in a community, but it is one which does not need to be *located* anywhere. Location as a notion in calculated community has been taken over by the nation state, while the welfare- and police-state has taken over the vertical functions of older urban, parochial and manorial paternalist communities of the medieval and early modern periods. Modern individualism, defined as freedom of choice and belief, has come to flourish because such utility of scale has freed individuals from the tangled bonds of local economic and social obligation. That in turn has reduced the potential for interpersonal social conflict, although it has probably increased the degree of conflict over the security of the nation state as a repository of communal ideologies, such as ethnic identity and political beliefs, and 'technologies' such as legal and political institutions, which provide the resources for self-understanding. But, just as importantly, it has also affected how those who believe in a liberal notion of the individual self 'see' the concepts of community or society, and the perspective would look very different if we were an early modern person 'thinking' community rather than 'seeing' it as something outside ourselves.

NOTES

1 Max Weber, *Economy and society: an outline of interpretative sociology*, ed. Gunther Roth and Claus Wittich (Berkeley CA, University of California Press, 1978), I, pp. 40–2; Ferdinand Tönnies, *Gemeinschaft und Gesellschaft* (Darmstadt, Wissenschaftliche Buchgesellschaft, 1979), chapters 21–3, 27.

2 These debates are discussed critically in Richard M. Smith, '"Modernisation" and the corporate medieval village community in England: some sceptical reflections', in Alan R. H. Baker and Derek Gregory (eds), *Explorations in historical geography* (Cambridge University Press, Cambridge, 1984), pp. 140 ff.; and by Susan Reynolds in *Kingdoms and communities in Western Europe, 900–1300* (Oxford, Clarendon Press, 1997), pp. xi–

lxxv. See also Zvi Razi, 'Family, land and the village community in later medieval England', *Past and Present* 93 (1981), 4–36.

3 Alan Macfarlane, *The origins of English individualism* (Oxford, Blackwell, 1978), p. 163.

4 John Bossy, *Christianity in the West* (Oxford, Oxford University Press, 1985), pp. 3–13, 57–75.

5 Reynolds, *Kingdoms and communities*, pp. 333–9.

6 Miri Rubin, 'Small groups: identity and solidarity in the late Middle Ages', in Jennifer Kermode (ed.), *Enterprise and individuals in fifteenth-century England* (Stroud, Sutton, 1991), pp. 135, 147–8.

7 Gervase Rosser, 'Crafts, guilds and the negotiation of work in the medieval town', *Past and Present* 154 (1997), 3–31, pp. 9, 30–1; *id.*, 'Going to the fraternity feast: commensality and social relations in late medieval England', *Journal of British Studies* 33 (1994), 430–46.

8 Christopher Dyer, 'The English medieval village community and its decline', *Journal of British Studies* 33 (1994), 407–29, pp. 421, 428–9.

9 E.g. Keith Wrightson has shown how neighbourliness and paternalism could continue in the seventeenth century while the more customary inclusive village festivities such as church ales and parish feasts were attacked by wealthy godly villagers as disorderly. Keith Wrightson, *English society, 1580–1680* (New Brunswick NJ, Rutgers University Press, 1982), pp. 51–65.

10 Anthony Giddens, *Modernity and self-identity: self and society in the late modern age* (Cambridge, Polity Press, 1991).

11 Charles Taylor, *Hegel* (Cambridge, Cambridge University Press, 1975), pp. 76–124, 148–96, 389–427.

12 John Stuart Mill, *On liberty*, in Mary Warnock (ed.), *Utilitarianism* (London, Fontana, 1962), *passim*, but especially pp. 126–40.

13 Norbert Elias, *The civilizing process: the history of manners and state formation and civilization* (Oxford, Blackwell, 1994), p. 213.

14 Recent work on the concept of 'social capital' has stressed the economic advantage of co-operation in business organisations. See Robert D. Putnam, *Making democracy work: civic traditions in modern Italy* (Princeton NJ, Princeton University Press, 1993), pp. 163–85; Francis Fukuyama, *Trust: the social virtues and the creation of prosperity* (London, Hamish Hamilton, 1995), pp. 149–70, 272–306.

15 Michael Ignatieff, 'State, civil society and total institutions: a critique of recent social histories of punishment', in Stanley Cohen and Andrew Scull (eds), *Social control and the state* (Oxford, Blackwell, 1983).

16 Michel Foucault, *Ethics, subjectivity and truth*, ed. Paul Rabinow (New York, New York Press, 1997), pp. 163–73, 223–301.

17 Charles Taylor, *Sources of the self: the making of the modern identity* (Cambridge MA, Harvard University Press, 1989), pp. 185–233.

18 Weber, *Economy and society* I, pp. 339–51; Wolfgang J. Momsen, '"Toward the iron cage of future serfdom"? On the methodological status of Max Weber's ideal-typical concept of bureaucratization', *Transactions of the Royal Historical Society*, fifth series, 30 (1980), 157–81; Craig Muldrew, 'Interpreting the market: the ethics of credit and community relations in early modern England', *Social History* 18 (1993), 163–83.

19 Sidney Pollard, *The genesis of modern management* (London, Arnold, 1965).

20 Max Weber, *The Protestant ethic and the spirit of capitalism* (London, Routledge, 1992), p. 181.

21 *Ibid.*, pp. 156–9, 163, 167–8, 173–5. The link between puritanism and work discipline had in fact already been made by Matthew Arnold. Matthew Arnold, *Culture and anarchy* (Cambridge, Cambridge University Press edition, 1966), pp. 132, 140–4.

22 For the puritan work ethic see Weber, *Protestant ethic*, p. 172; R. H. Tawney, *Religion and the rise of capitalism* (Harmondsworth, Penguin, 1926), pp. 240–2. Charles Taylor has also offered a critique of what he sees as the spiritually alienating 'search for pure subjective expressive fulfilment' in modern society; Taylor, *Sources of the self*, pp. 495–521.

23 Craig Muldrew, *The economy of obligation* (Basingstoke, Macmillan, 1998), pp. 40–5; C. W. Brooks, 'Interpersonal conflict and social tension: civil litigation in England, 1640–1830', in A. L. Beier, David Cannadine and J. M. Rosenheim (eds), *The first modern society* (Cambridge, Cambridge University Press, 1989), pp. 393–4.

24 Craig Muldrew, 'The culture of reconciliation: community and the settlement of economic disputes in early modern England', *Historical Journal* 39 (1996), 915–42, pp. 920–2, 927–35.

25 Keith Thomas, 'Cases of conscience in seventeenth-century England', in John Morrill, Paul Slack and Daniel Woolf (eds), *Public duty and private conscience in seventeenth-century England: essays presented to G. E. Aylmer* (Oxford, Clarendon Press, 1993).

26 Renes Descartes, *Discourse on the method of properly conducting one's reason and of seeing the truth in the sciences*, trans. F. E. Sutcliffe (Harmondsworth, Penguin Books, 1968), pp. 36–7.

27 *Ibid.*, pp. 27–52; Descartes, *Meditations*, in *ibid.*, pp. 95–101; Roger Smith, 'Self-reflection and the self', in Roy Porter (ed.), *Rewriting the self: histories from the Renaissance to the present* (London, Routledge, 1997), pp. 49–57.

28 Descartes, *Discourse on method*, pp. 35–51.

29 Ernest Gellner, *Reason and culture: the historic role of rationality and rationalism* (Oxford, Blackwell, 1993), pp. 5–6; Weber, *Economy and society* II, pp. 956–8, 968, 983–9.

30 George Unwin, *Industrial organization in the sixteenth and seventeenth centuries* (Oxford, Clerendon Press, 1904); Joseph P. Ward, *Metropolitan communities: trade guilds, identity, and change in early modern London* (Stanford CA, Stanford University Press, 1997).

31 For a summary of the main criticisms see Anthony Giddens's introduction to *The Protestant ethic*, pp. xxiii–xxvi.

32 Muldrew, *Economy of obligation*, pp. 15–36; J. R. Wordie, 'Deflationary factors in the Tudor price rise', *Past and Present* 154 (1997), 32–70.

33 Henry Roseveare, *The financial revolution, 1660–1760* (Harlow, Longman, 1991), pp. 21–8, 54–60.

34 Muldrew, *Economy of obligation*, chapters 7–9.

35 *Ibid.*, pp. 329–31. For a contemporary discussion of the meaning of pleasure see Montaigne's essay 'On some lines of Vergil' in Michel de Montaigne, *The complete essays*, ed. and trans. M. A. Screech (Harmondsworth, Penguin Books, 1993).

36 Maryanne Kowaleski, 'The commercial dominance of a medieval provincial oligarchy: Exeter in the late fourteenth century', *Mediaeval Studies* 46 (1984), 355–64, p. 369; Elaine Clark, 'Debt litigation in a late medieval vill', in J. A. Raftis (ed.), *Pathways to medieval peasants* (Toronto, Pontifical Institute of Medieval Studies, 1981); Richard Britnell, *Growth and decline in Colchester, 1300–1525* (Cambridge, Cambridge University Press, 1986), pp. 95, 98–114, 206–21, 281.

37 For changes in criminal and regulatory prosecutions see Keith Wrightson, 'Two concepts of order: justices, constables and jurymen in seventeenth-century England', in John Brewer and John Styles (eds), *An ungovernable people: the English and their law in the seventeenth and eighteenth centuries* (New Brunswick NJ, Rutgers University Press, 1980); J. A. Sharpe, *Crime in early modern England, 1550–1750* (Harlow, Longman, 1984), chapters 2–4; Craig Muldrew, 'Rural credit, market areas and legal institutions in the countryside in England, 1550–1700', in C. W. Brooks and Michael Lobban (eds), *Communities and courts: proceedings of the twelfth Legal History Conference, held in Durham* (London, Hambledon Press, 1997).

38 Martin Ingram, 'Juridical folklore in England illustrated by rough music', in Brooks and Lobban, *Communities and courts*; E. P. Thompson, *Customs in common* (New York, New Press, 1991), chapter 3; Andy Wood, 'The place of custom in plebeian political culture: England, 1550–1800', *Social History* 22 (1997), 46–60; Tim Stretton, 'Women, custom and equity in the Court of Requests', in Jenny Kermode and Garthine Walker (eds), *Women, crime and the courts in early modern England* (London, UCL Press, 1994).

39 Wrightson, 'Two concepts of order'. For a discussion of long-term changes in the means and practice of public social discipline see Marjorie K. McIntosh, *Controlling misbehaviour in England, 1370–1600* (Cambridge, Cambridge University Press, 1998). See also Steve Hindle, 'The keeping of the public peace', in Adam Fox, Paul Griffiths and Steve Hindle (eds), *The experience of authority in early modern England* (Basingstoke, Macmillan, 1996).

40 Tim Hitchcock, *English sexualities, 1700–1800* (Basingstoke, Macmillan, 1997), pp. 11–12; Laura Gowing, *Domestic dangers: women, words and sex in early modern London* (Oxford, Oxford University Press, 1996), pp. 30–8, 50, 111–38.

41 Tim Stretton, *Women waging law in Elizabethan England* (Cambridge, Cambridge University Press, 1998), chapters 4–7; Adam Fox, 'Ballads, libels and popular ridicule in Jacobean England', *Past and Present* 145 (1995), 47–83.

42 Jonathan Barry, 'Bourgeois collectivism? Urban association and the middling sort', in Jonathan Barry and Christopher Brooks (eds), *The middling sort of people: culture, society and politics in England, 1550–1800* (Basingstoke, Macmillan, 1994).

43 Conrad Russell, *The crisis of parliaments: English history, 1509–1660* (Oxford, Oxford University Press, 1971), pp. 77–80; Craig Muldrew, '"Amputations of the body politic": episodes in the public life of Oliver St John, 1629–41' (unpublished M.A. dissertation, University of Alberta, 1986), pp. 102–37, 268–71.

44 Robert Latham and William Mathews (eds), *The diary of Samuel Pepys*, 11 vols (London, Bell & Hyman, 1970–83), IV, pp. 398, 404; V, p. 36.

45 *Ibid.*, IV, pp. 16, 34, 153, 171–2, 394, 396, 411, 421. Brooks, 'Interpersonal conflict', pp. 391–2; Thomas A. Green, *Verdict according to conscience* (Chicago IL, University of Chicago Press, 1985), chapter 4.

46 W. J. Jones, 'The Exchequer of Chester in the last years of Elizabeth I', in A. J. Slavin

(ed.), *Tudor men and institutions* (Baton Rouge LA, Louisiana State University Press, 1972), pp. 143–6; Morton J. Horwitz, *The transformation of American law, 1780–1860* (Cambridge MA, Harvard University Press, 1977), pp. 160–73. J. H. Baker has also argued that this was not radically different from the application of jury discretion in standard common law trials in 'From sanctity of contract to reasonable expectation?', *Current Legal Problems* 32 (1979), 17–39.

47 Stretton, *Women waging law*, chapter 7.

48 *Ibid.*, pp. 106, 187–94, 201–2, 211–15; William Hutton, *The Court of Requests* (Edinburgh, 1840), pp. 22, 35, 44, 45, 61–2.

49 The most comprehensive philosophical treatment is Taylor, *Sources of the self*. For the social impact of such ideas see Michael Mascuch, *Origins of the individualist self, autobiography and self-identity in England, 1591–1791* (Cambridge, Polity Press, 1997).

50 Elias, *The civilizing process*, pp. xv, 48–57, 214–15, 275–98, 340–1, 445, 453, 465 ff.

51 *Ibid.*, pp. 27, 32, 39, 57, 63–5, 112–13, 156, 350, 391–5.

52 *Ibid.*, pp. 42–7, 105–31, 209, 445, 476, 533.

53 Anna Bryson, *From courtesy to civility: changing codes of conduct in early modern England* (Oxford, Clarendon Press, 1998), chapter 4. The presentation of self-control was also important in the construction of pleading strategies in the Court of Requests. Stretton, *Women waging law*, pp. 199–201.

54 For a modern explanation of reason see Richard Rorty, *Truth and moral progress: philosophical papers* III (Cambridge, Cambridge University Press, 1998), pp. 186–7.

55 Susan James, *Passion and action: the emotions in seventeenth-century philosophy* (Oxford, Clarendon Press, 1997), p. 3; Geoffrey Baldwin, 'The self and the state in England, 1580–1651' (unpublished Ph.D. dissertation, University of Cambridge, 1998), pp. ii–v, 12, 20–4, 41–6, 74–90, 163–85.

56 Alexandra Shepard, 'Meanings of manhood in early modern England, with special reference to Cambridge, c. 1560–1640' (unpublished Ph.D. dissertation, University of Cambridge, 1998), pp. 27–56; Susan Dwyer Amussen, *An ordered society: gender and class in early modern England* (Oxford, Blackwell, 1988), pp. 34–66.

57 Susan James, 'Reasons, the passions, and the good life', in Daniel Garber, Michael Ayers and Roger Ariew (eds), *The Cambridge History of Seventeenth-century Philosophy*, 2 vols (Cambridge, Cambridge University Press, 1998), II, pp. 13, 77–81; C. W. Brooks, 'The place of Magna Carta and the ancient constitution in sixteenth-century English legal thought', in Ellis Sandoz (ed.), *The roots of liberty: Magna Carta, ancient constitution, and the Anglo-American tradition of rule of law* (Columbia MO, University of Missouri Press, 1992), pp. 65–6.

58 Thomas, 'Cases of conscience', pp. 30–1.

59 On the importance of reason in intellectual discussions of the common law, especially by Sir Edward Coke, see Alan Cromartie, *Sir Matthew Hale, 1609–76: law, religion and natural philosophy* (Cambridge, Cambridge University Press, 1995), pp. 11–29. Ian W. Archer, *The pursuit of stability: social relations in Elizabethan London* (Cambridge, Cambridge University Press, 1991), pp. 215–56.

60 W. A. Champion, 'Recourse to the law and the meaning of the great litigation decline, 1650–1750: some clues from the Shrewsbury local courts', in Brooks and Lobban (eds), *Communities and courts*, pp. 195–8; Barry, 'Bourgeois collectivism?', pp. 109–12.

61 Lawrence E. Klein, *Shaftesbury and the culture of politeness: moral discourse and cultural politeness in early eighteenth-century England* (Cambridge, Cambridge University Press, 1994), pp. 8, 11–12, 54–5, 71–109.

62 John Brewer, 'Commercialization and politics', in Neil McKendrick, John Brewer and J. H. Plumb, *The birth of a consumer society* (London, Hutchinson, 1983).

63 John Money, 'Teaching in the market place, or, "Caesar adsum jam forte: Pompey aderat": the retailing of knowledge in provincial England during the eighteenth century', in Roy Porter and John Brewer (eds), *Consumption and the world of goods* (London, Routledge, 1993).

64 On the rise of 'interest' as a moral motivation of conduct, and as a concept, see Albert O. Hirschman, *The passions and the interests: political arguments for capitalism before its triumph* (Princeton NJ, Princeton University Press, 1977).

65 E. G. Hundert, *The Enlightenment's fable: Bernard Mandeville and the discovery of society* (Cambridge, Cambridge University Press, 1994), pp. 116–74.

66 On the increasing influence of probabilistic reasoning see Barbara Shapiro, *Probability and certainty in seventeenth-century England: a study of the relationships between natural science, religion, history, law, and literature* (Princeton NJ, Princeton University Press, 1983), pp. 3–44. On its relation to risk see Lorraine J Daston, 'The domestication of risk', in Lorenz Krüger, Lorraine J. Daston and Michael Heidelberger (eds), *The probabilistic revolution* (Cambridge MA, MIT Press, 1987), pp. 244–60; Geoffrey Clark, 'Life insurance in the society and culture of London, 1700–75', *Urban History* 24 (1997), 17–36.

67 The current prevalence of the metaphors of social and linguistic construction and deconstruction in contemporary discourse is also evidence of the influence which sociology has had in interpreting societies in a structural way in that society is now understood in an architectural rather than a negotiated sense.

68 Giddens, *Modernity and self-identity*, chapters 1–2, 4.

69 Mascuch, *Individualist self*, p. 52; Linda Levy Peck, *Court patronage and corruption in early Stuart England* (Cambridge MA, Unwin Hyman, 1990), pp. 1–29.

70 On the importance of discretion in early modern law see John Beattie, *Crime and the courts in England, 1660–1800* (Oxford, Clarendon Press, 1986), pp. 269–72, 406, 420–2, 440–7, 662; David Lieberman, *The province of legislation determined: legal theory in eighteenth-century Britain* (Cambridge, Cambridge University Press, 1989), pp. 219 ff.

71 James, *Passion and action*, pp. 17–20; Genevieve Lloyd, *The man of reason: 'male' and 'female' in Western philosophy* (London, Methuen, 1984), pp. 38–56.

72 Mike Savage and Anne Witz (eds), *Gender and bureaucracy* (Oxford, Blackwell, 1992), pp. 3–62, 253–76.

73 Keith Hoskin and Richard Macve, 'Writing, examining, disciplining: the genesis of accounting's modern power', and Peter Miller and Ted O' Leary, 'Governing the calculable person', both in Anthony G. Hopwood and Peter Miller (eds), *Accounting as social and institutional practice* (Cambridge, Cambridge University Press, 1994).

Part III

Rhetoric

Chapter 10

Rhetorical constructions of a national community: the role of the King's English in mid‹Tudor writing

Cathy Shrank

This chapter explores the use of language in attempts to construct and enforce a national identity in mid-Tudor England through a programme of linguistic standardisation promoted by a group of authors, active between 1540 and 1570, who centred on Sir John Cheke, the charismatic Cambridge humanist and tutor to Edward VI. It included Roger Ascham, Sir Thomas Hoby, Sir Thomas Smith, Thomas Wilson and the lesser known John Hart, the Chester Herald, author of *An orthographie conteyning the due order and reason howe to write or paint thimage of a mannes voice* (1569) and *A methode or comfortable beginning for all vnlearned, whereby they may bee taught to read English* (1570). Also tangentially connected with Cheke (through their employment in Edward VI's household), but not part of this scholarly clique, was William Thomas, an early exponent of education in the English tongue. The views these writers held on language are neither uniform in all ways, nor part of a coherently engineered project, and vary in focus from Smith's orthographically based interests to Wilson's concentration on vocabulary, or Hart's combination of the two. Nevertheless, there is sufficient consistency in their aims and methods, and enough interaction between them, for them to be treated as a collective body. They supplied each other with dedicatory letters, referred supportively to each other's linguistic works and talents, and shared a commitment to the regulation and standardisation of their native tongue: a process which united them as a community of scholars; proved the means by which they hoped to unite a nation of speakers and readers; and which has implications for a chronology of nationhood, the nature of English humanism and the intellectual significance of the mid-Tudor period.[1]

In 1565, planning the subjugation of Ireland, Smith singled out 'our tongue, our laws, and our religion' as the 'three ... true bands of commonwealth',[2] terms he would apply to his definition of the 'nacyon' in the *De Republica*

Anglorum (also written *c.* 1564–65).[3] The impact of language on nation formation was nothing new. In the early 1420s, when the term 'nation' was
beginning to evolve from its technical, medieval function (describing groupings at church councils or universities) into its modern meaning of a people or
race,[4] it was 'peculiarities of language', rather than 'blood-relationship and
habit of unity', that Henry V's ambassadors pronounced the 'most sure and
positive sign and essence of a nation in divine and human law'.[5] Language, in
other words, was not solely a means of defining a nation: it was a means of
creating one, overriding issues of blood or long-standing alliances by its ability,
on a practical as well as a rhetorical level, to gather potentially disparate groups
into one cohesive national community, using and understanding one tongue.

Henrician governments were aware of the need for linguistic uniformity
when imposing an English identity on the Celtic fringes. Legislation for
Ireland in 1537 consequently forbade diversity of language, dress and manners
(albeit unsuccessfully);[6] the Acts of Union for Wales in 1534 and 1543 were
accompanied by regulations enforcing the use of English in the law courts.[7]
Access to the law depended on access to the English language, and arguably
one of the major reasons for the acquiescence of most Welsh elites to the
union was the advantage of the English legal system.[8] For Welshmen such as
William Salesbury, a member of one of the leading Denbighshire families,
English was a language of opportunity. His English–Welsh dictionary, 'moche
necessarye to all suche Welshmen as wil spedly learne the englyshe tongue',
was published in 1547.[9] Dedicated to Henry VIII as a means of consolidating
the union and of drawing 'euery parte and membre' into one 'Dominion', it
clothed opportunism in rhetoric that subscribed to the unifying properties of
language.[10] 'The communion of one tonge' offered 'a bonde and knotte of loue
and frendshyppe' and a remedy for the 'great hatred debate and stryffe'
resulting from the current 'dyuersitie of language'.[11] Political unity, the
'dominion of one most gracious Hedde and kynge', necessitated the use of
'one language', 'that euen as theyr hertes agree in loue and obedience to your
grace so may also theyr tongues agree in one kynde of speche & language'.[12]
Salesbury's prospective readers were both individual, biological bodies with
tongues and hearts, and metaphorical limbs [membres] of a larger national
corpus. It was by using their actual tongues to express their hearts that they
would become one figurative body, with the monarch at its head. The drive
towards unity worked on an oral as well as a semantic level, and with a
practical as well as rhetorical function. The dictionary was also 'prefixed [by] a
litle treatyse of the englyshe pronunciation of the letters'.[13] The Welsh were not
only to be taught how to speak English, but to speak English like the English,
knitting them into one seamless community of undifferentiated speakers.

The use of one language, and one pronunciation, as a means of unifying
England's outlying territories was thus established by the late 1540s, when

Smith drafted a small treatise on the reformation of English spelling, published in 1568 as *De recta et emendata linguae Anglicae scriptione, dialogus*.[14] What was not established was a concern either to address the linguistic diversity of dialect and accent within England itself, or to counteract the disparaging opinion with which the capabilities of the English vernacular were regarded. Although English had been the language of government since the reign of Richard II, even by the mid-Tudor period it was still not regarded as a natural medium for scholarship. Where used, the native tongue was a functional language of instruction, not a manifestation of elegance and style, defined by the physician Andrew Borde in the 1540s as 'a base speche to other noble speches, such as Italyon, Castylion and French'.[15] For writers such as Borde and Sir Thomas Elyot, enhancing the English language meant making it more like Latin, and the medium through which scholars such as John Leland sought fame for English learning was neo-Latin poetry. Smith and his fellow reformers consequently intended to benefit the nation in two ways. They would both raise the status of English as a ruled, and therefore civilised, language, and unify a nation of language speakers, standardising the dialects of northern and western England; pulling the Welsh and Irish into one linguistic, and thus politically united, English family; and distinguishing England from continental Europe, binding it in by language as it was by the sea.[16]

By echoing the phrasing of Erasmus's 1528 treatise *De recta Latini Graecique sermonis pronuntiatione* the title of Smith's *Dialogus* proclaimed the intellectual origins which it both emulated and, like all true emulators, sought to overthrow. Erasmus had tried to establish greater oral homogeneity among an international, Latin-speaking community by reforming neo-classical orthography (the bulk of the book was concerned with Latin, not Greek). His work was pitched against the rise of diverse European vernaculars. Smith redirected Erasmus's techniques of linguistic analysis to promote the use of, and pride in, a vernacular language. The ramifications of language use were more than aesthetic. In fighting to 'retain' Latin 'as a written and spoken method',[17] Erasmus aimed to foster fluid communication, and thus understanding, among the peoples of Europe by providing them with a common tongue. In contrast, preference for the vernacular followed a separatist, anti-continental agenda of defining and drawing together a nation of English speakers: what the poet Edmund Spenser would later dub 'the kingdome of oure owne Language'.[18]

Using the word *recta*, the literal meaning of which is 'ruled' or 'regulated', Smith's choice of title, moreover, announced the 'rectitude' that English apparently already displayed. It claimed English as a potentially logical language, a status habitually attributed only to the classical languages – although Smith's choice of Latin in which to write his treatise and its subsequent contents, bemoaning the ragged state of the vulgar tongue, reveal the vulnerability of this professed confidence. Although striving to assert the worth of the vernacular, the standards of judgement, demanding rational regularity, were nevertheless set by classical tongues. In struggling to establish English as a ruled language, Smith and his fellow reformers were thus characteristic of linguistic patriotism in an age where Greek and Latin provided the models. The French poet Joachim Du Bellay felt the same pressure to establish the systematic nature of his mother tongue in *La deffence et illustration de la langue Françoyse* (1545). 'Is [French] not so curiously regular?' he asked, producing evidence of the language's declensions, tenses, moods and persons, the French word *curiousement* [curiously] playing on and emphasising the artificial, man-made nature of that methodicalness.

When mid-sixteenth-century humanists did turn to the vernacular, then, they did not so much reject their classical roots as reinterpret them. The vernacular was not (as for Erasmus) in direct competition with Latin, but drew inspiration from it. For Du Bellay and the English reformers, Latin held no intrinsic worth, but was instead inspirational precisely because it was a once rude vernacular which (like Italian) had grown elegant through the 'skill and industry of men'.[19] Authorities such as Quintilian and Cicero were cited no longer as exempla of a classical literary style, but in order to support investment in the vulgar tongues.[20] Knowledge of the classics was harnessed to promote the vernaculars that scholars had previously neglected. Hart commended his own 'maner of teaching' as being 'after the councell of the excellent Latine rhetorician Quintilian';[21] Smith revealed in the preamble to his *Dialogus* that his interest in English linguistics dated from his involvement with reforming Greek pronunciation in Cambridge during the early 1540s. It was whilst Smith was 'busy with a book, with the object … of correcting our pronunciation of Greek' that Quintus (a character in the *Dialogus*) remembered finding 'some observations on the writing of our own language, in your hand'.[22] The book, *De recta et emendata linguae Graecae pronuntiatione*, was published with the *Dialogus* in Paris in 1568.

Humanist knowledge of the classics, therefore, paradoxically advanced the English vernacular, just as in the second half of the sixteenth century it was university education in England, and the rise of the vulgar tongue there, that inspired Welsh humanists to invest in their own language.[23] As a response to classical models and in line with contemporary Continental trends, the linguistic changes recommended by these English reformers are thus marked by a desire to regularise the vernacular. At its most extreme (in Hart's works) this process of standardisation entailed overhauling the entire orthographic system, employing symbols to represent compound sounds such as *sh* and recasting spelling along phonetic lines.[24] Misguided as this scheme might seem in retrospect, it should not be dismissed as marginal. Its principles, if not their rigorous application, were shared by his fellow reformers, a group comprising the most significant thinkers of the day and distinguished by its proximity to the circles of power: Cheke as tutor to Edward VI, Smith as secretary to Protector Somerset, political channels that were reactivated in the 1560s by the close association of Ascham, Wilson, Smith and Hart with the Cambridge-educated William Cecil, later Lord Burghley, one of Elizabeth I's most influential ministers. Intellectually, Wilson's *Arte of Rhetorique* (1553) and its strictures against 'inkhorne termes' continued to be an authority into the seventeenth century. The works of Smith and Hart were acknowledged by future generations of English linguists, William Bullokar and Alexander Gill, Milton's mentor, just two among them.[25] Gabriel Harvey (to whom Spenser addressed his comments about 'the kingdome of our own language') owned a copy of Smith's *Dialogus*, originally dedicated by Harvey to Sir Walter Mildmay,[26] Chancellor of the Exchequer under Elizabeth, and one of William Thomas's associates during the Edwardian era.[27] Even Hart's system produced dedicated adherents such as Thomas Whythorne, who wrote an autobiography in the new orthography, and the Elizabethan ambassador Sir William Waad.[28]

'Our own tung shold be written cleane and pure, unmixt and unmangeled with borowing of other tunges,' Cheke wrote to Hoby in 1557 in a letter later appended to Hoby's translation of Castiglione's *Il Cortegiano*, a project Hoby began in 1550.[29] Cheke's words epitomise the ethos of purification through which this reforming coterie hoped to unify, refine and linguistically enfranchise their fellow Englishmen. As these English humanists began to promote their mother tongue they reacted not only to the 'rawness' of which their language stood accused, but to their forebears who had, in their view, inundated it with foreign terms. For these writers, language should be comprehensible, 'plain for all men to perceiue',[30] and one major gripe about the use of loan words was the confusion they caused, particularly among the less educated. For Hart 'straunge termes ... beautifieth an Orators tale, which knoweth what he speaketh, and to whom: but it hindereth the vnlerned from vnderstanding of the matter, and causeth many of the Countrie men to speake chalke for cheese', so that (like proto-Mrs Malaprops) they mistook 'temporall' for 'temperate'; 'for stature, statute'; 'for abiect, obiect'.[31]

When Hoby wished in his *Book of the Courtier* 'that we alone of the worlde maye not bee styll counted barbarous in oure tongue, as in time out of minde we have bene in our maners',[32] he highlighted the belief that a country's language and manners were inextricably linked, a theory encapsulated in the humanist doctrine that 'at least ideally, good societies produce good speakers, as good speakers produce good societies', or their converse.[33] In Smith's *Communication of the Quenes highnes mariage* (1561), Germanic habits of drunkenness extended as far as the limits of their language. 'The Dutchman and the Dane and all suche countries as draweth in language and condition towards them [share] *the* great loue *w*hich they haue to drinke,' Smith declared.[34] Language was seen to delineate habits of thought and behaviour, and besides practical objections to baffling the unlearned, ideologically, the linguistic pollution caused by non-English words also threatened to undermine national identity. Englishmen returning from abroad risked contaminating their native tongue and 'like as thei loue to go in forei[n] apparell, so thei wil pouder their talke with ouersea language'.[35] These French-talking Englishmen and 'Angleschi Italiani' displayed a tongue as unEnglish and effeminate ('pouder[ed]' like women's faces) as their exotic garb. In Wilson's words, their language was physically 'outlandish', not of England's shores. This combination of estrangement and emasculation was latent in Hart's recurrent references to Circe, as he aligned the alienation of orthography from 'our' English speech with 'a maner of Metamorphosis, or a worke of Circes', and deemed those adherents to 'mangeled' convention 'bewitched by Circes inchauntments',[36] wandering in to enervating licentiousness akin to that facing Ascham's traveller at the 'Circes Court' of Italy in his *Scholemaster* (1570).[37]

The solution Wilson called for was linguistic exportation, that 'we must of necessitee, *banishe* al such affected Rhetorique'.[38] Hart provided a list of French derivatives he would expunge: 'surgian' replaced with 'flesh clenser', for example; 'barber' with 'bearder'.[39] The language to which these writers sought to return was, in Cheke's phraseology, 'the mould of our own tung',[40] by which he meant one of Anglo-Saxon derivation, since the Anglo-Saxons, for Smith, 'looked much more closely into the nature of letters, and wrote more correctly than we do to-day'.[41] Cheke's compound words of Anglo-Saxon origin ('welspeakinges', 'overstraight') strove to evade Continental-style eloquence, whilst Hart's rejection of even the order of the Roman alphabet exorcised a past of imperial and papal suppression, when 'the Romaines, gouerning in maner the whole worlde, constreyned such of euery nation of their subiection ... to learne, vse and exercise the Romaine or Latine tongue and writing'.[42] As each nation 'ha[d] and use[d] certain sounds',[43] so these 'characteristic and special sounds' required distinct letters to express them.[44] Both Hart and Smith compiled alphabets peculiar to English, to be used for writing English alone, distinguishing it visually from other European and classical tongues. Within the *Orthographie*, for example, whilst English is given in Hart's 'English' script, French (a romance language) remains in Roman type, 'Dutche' in Gothic black letter. 'Notwithstanding that I have devised this new manner of writing for our English, I mean not that Latin should be written in these letters, no more then the Greek or Hebrew ... but when as I would write English,' Hart explained.[45]

Despite frequent misreadings, however, neither Cheke nor any of his supporters advocated blanket avoidance of borrowings. Cheke acknowledged the need to fill lexical lacunae in the language 'as being imperfight she must';[46] Wilson approved the use of borrowings where necessary 'to set furthe our meanyng'.[47] Such words, though, should be supplied from 'old denisoned words' familiar, and rendered English, through long use.[48] Even the trenchant Hart, as can be seen from his use of derivatives like 'signification', made no attempt to extradite established Latinate vocabulary.[49] Indeed, it was a strong language that was able to appropriate, or 'denizen', foreign terms. As was argued in a contemporary Italian treatise, *Il discorso interno alla nostra lingua*, attributed to Machiavelli, 'a national language is one which converts the vocabulary that it has acquired from others into its own use, and is so powerful that those words do not disrupt it, but that it disrupts them'.[50] Or, in Hart's words, 'so ought the strange worde (of what language soeuer) haue the generall and perfite marke of the Idiomate'.[51] His objection to francophone spelling stemmed primarily from the affectation of those compatriots who refused to anglicise French words, as if 'we would not haue any straunger to be conuersant, nor dwell amongst vs, though he be a free Denison, and is fully bent to liue and die with vs to thend of his life'. His system colonised these verbal settlers, in contrast to those who preferred 'he should weare continually some mark, to be knowen whence he is, to thend we shuld be able to know thereby how to refuse him when some of vs listed'.[52]

Twentieth-century linguists have repeatedly linked language standardisation to the administrative needs of emergent empires and the growth of central government.[53] In the Tudor age, and as a tool of centralisation, the pursuit of comprehensibility consequently required more than removing foreign words. For Tudor writers, sixteenth-century England was a nation riven by differing dialects. The expected beneficiaries of Hart's *Orthographie* extended beyond 'the Welsh and Irish' to include 'vnlearned naturall English people'.[54] Such was the need to purge contaminating dialect words from 'accustomed' speech, and anxiety as to their incursion, that the pictures Hart used to demonstrate pronunciation of the letters in his *Methode* (*a* is for 'apple', *b* is for 'ball') could not stand alone as sufficient indication of the desired sound: they had to be accompanied by labels giving the 'right' English word for each icon.[55]

The desire of these English humanists to eliminate dialect is illuminated by comparison with Castiglione's *Il Cortegiano*. The significance of language to Italian communal identity is evident from the length and preoccupations of the discussion on vernacular style, which dominates the second half of Book I. Straying from the right use of language, for instance, is described in terms of geographical dislocation reminiscent of Wilson's 'outlandish' meanderings, 'as he that walketh in the darke without lyght, and therefore many times strayeth from the right way'.[56] The use of the vernacular, moreover, proved a similar matter of communal pride. 'I say that I have written it in mine owne [tongue], and as I speak, and unto such as speake as I speake,' pronounced Castiglione in his prefatory epistle.[57] Yet it is also the manifestation of this pride that highlights the different intentions and remit of Castiglione's text from those of the English humanists. Castiglione championed the place of his Lombard dialect within the Italian vernacular, defending his right 'in writing [to take] the wholl and pure woord of [his] owne Countrye, then the corrupt and mangled of an other'.[58] 'Purists know the enemy very well,' comments Brian Weinstein.[59] For Castiglione, the 'enemy' was the Florentine dialect (then the dominant literary tongue) and those Italians who spoke nothing but 'Petrarca and Boccaccio'.[60] Through the Count, his most authoritative protagonist, Castiglione argued for an Italian speech that would 'choose gorgeous and fine woordes out of every parte of Italye'.[61] His pleas mirror the composite nature of Italian identity. In contrast, the model suggested by the English reformers reflects their pursuit of national uniformity, advocating one dialect, and one pronunciation, for one nation: that they might 'vse altogether one maner of language'.[62]

Speech, like government, was to be centralised. The uniformity sought, to 'bring our whole nation to one certain, perfect and general speaking', was that of 'the Court, and London'.[63] For Wilson, just as 'to bee an Englishe manne borne, is muche more honour, then to be a Scotte', so 'London', where 'the people [are] more ciuill, and ... for the moste parte more wise', was preferred over 'Lincolne', Wilson's home town.[64] In the 1390s, at the beginning of the ascendancy of south-eastern dialect over other dialect forms, and its emergence as the precursor of modern English, Chaucer dubbed his king the 'lord of this langage'.[65] Towards the end of that process of linguistic standardisation, Wilson also placed language under royal authority as the 'kynges English'[66] – a term for which the first citation given by the *OED* is over forty years after Wilson's *Arte*, in Shakespeare's *Merry Wives of Windsor*, a play in which characters tellingly seek to exclude foreigners (here including Welshmen who make 'fritters of English') from, and by, use of what they judge 'good English'.[67]

Where Falstaff and friends utilise their perceptions of standard language to humiliate outsiders, however, Wilson (in an era of only nascent concepts of 'good English') attacked internal division and the unnaturalness of jargon, which held the potential to drive communities and even families apart. 'I dare swere this, if some of their mothers were aliue, thei were not able to tell, what thei say,' he complained of his linguistically corrupted Englishmen.[68] Social sub-sets, incomprehensible to others, remain locked in their own linguistic systems, providing a Babel tower of non-communication. The lawyer 'store[s] his stomack with the pratyng of Pedlers'; the auditor 'makyng his accompt and rekenyng, cometh in fife fould, and cater denere, for vi.s. iiii.d'; courtiers gabble 'nothyng but Chaucer', while 'Poeticall Clerkes' talk 'nothyng but quaint prouerbes', each 'delityng muche in their awne darkenesse, especially, when none can tell what thei dooe saie'.[69] Loyalty to linguistic factions overrides greater social impulses towards comprehensibility, and counteracts the humanistic belief in eloquence (literally meaning fluent *speaking*) as the factor by which savage men were persuaded into forming civilised communities, a myth which Wilson retold in the preface to his *Arte*.[70]

Unlike Shakespeare's *Merry Wives*, the tone of these works is far from comic. In the 1590s, and in city comedies throughout the late Elizabethan and Jacobean periods, stage accents were consistently used a source of fun,[71] or, as in *Henry V* (in which dialect distinguishes Englishmen not from Englishmen but from Scots, Irish and Welsh), as a demonstration of the union possible between British territories, with Gower, Jamy, Macmorris and Fluellen join in brave and loyal service to the English crown. For mid-Tudor writers, provincial identities, and the lack of conformity, were no laughing matter, however. 1549 had seen a spate of nation-wide riots, and two serious rebellions, the Western Rising and Kett's Norfolk Rebellion (to which Wilson repeatedly referred in his *Arte*), which prompted a flurry of obedience tracts, including Cheke's *Hurte of sedicion* (1549).[72] The divisiveness of regionalism haunted these works. The staple butt of jest books, the yokel whose garbled pronunciation won him a bare head rather than a boar's head, was transformed into an icon of geographical fragmentation, accompanied by disharmonious sounds of scornful laughter.[73] As Hart lamented in the earliest draft of his *Orthographie* in 1551, 'yf they heare their neyghbour borne of their next Citie, or d[w]elling not past one or two dais Iorney from theim, speaking some other word then is emongest theim used, yt so litell contenteth their eare, that (more then folishli) they seem the stranger were therfore worthie to be derided'. Hart, seeking to draw disparate regions into one nation, here compressed geographical distance, transforming inhabitants of different towns into 'neyghbours'.[74]

Linguistic order reflected social order, for 'who is so folyshe as to saye the counsayle and the kynge, but rather the Kinge and his counsayle, the father and the sonne, and not contrary?' Wilson queried.[75] Metaphorical links between law and language ran deeper than Smith's tripartite bands of commonwealth suggest. Language served as a social contract, and it was those who operated outside, and against, society and its laws that sought to subvert it. 'We find that among cunning higglers, and pedlars, and that mob of rascals, prostitutes and thieves, whom they call *Gypsies*, a different and distinct language is current, unknown to others and serving only themselves and their cheating,' Smith related,[76] pre-empting William Harrison, who had 'the first deviser thereof ... hanged by the neck, as just reward ... for his deserts',[77] and Elizabethan coney-catching pamphlets.[78]

The structural rhetoric of ideas designed to further a cohesive community of users was thus strengthened by recurrent recourse to three interrelated vocabularies of social belonging: those of citizenship, the family and social *mores*. We have already seen the term 'denizen' used to describe the anglicisation of loan words, which should become, in Hart's words, 'imployed' (like all good humanists) in 'seruice' of the 'Prince'.[79] In a carefully constructed extended allegory, individual letters of the alphabet were themselves similarly converted into citizens in a commonwealth of language, placed by Smith, for example, in a 'senate of letters'.[80] Letters, as good citizens, should furthermore avoid the two evils of Italian political thought: the idleness and ambition found for Hart when letters were 'ydle' (i.e. extraneous) or 'vsurpe others powers' (by representing more than one sound, like the letter *c*).[81]

Hart made the political nature of his vocabulary explicit. 'Iustly' such malpractice should 'be refused, and the vicious parts therof cut away, as are the ydle or offensiue members, in a politike common welth,' he posited.[82] His explanation adds resonance to the corporeal and naval imagery – both of which were commonplace metaphors for the common weal – used to portray the proper functioning of language. Like a statesman anatomising the body politic in terms of the human frame (think of Menenius in Shakespeare's *Coriolanus*),[83] Hart demanded a 'Doctor' who 'may proceede without daunger to minister purgations of the vicious humours' displayed by his 'mangeled' English tongue.[84] Bringing a people to the right use of language, meanwhile, was like steering a ship by 'the right course ... to the desired hauen ... assured from all offences of rockes or sandes, in reading, whatsoeuer variable blastes of contrary windes rooted in abuse, may rise agaynst them'.[85]

Familial metaphors, on the other hand, were easily conjured through the almost commonplace term 'the mother tongue'. To abandon your native tongue was, for Wilson, equivalent to the unnatural wresting of the maternal bond, or symbolic of a perverted order in which mothers fail to recognise their own sons, and the female-gendered 'mother tongue' is displaced by ambiguously gendered 'poudered' talkers and the perverse mother 'custome ... the sucke geuer vnto all error'.[86] In contrast, the proper use of language displayed propriety. To ridicule Obstinatus's resistance to linguistic reform, Smith's Quintus threatened to make his son a coat, patched together absurdly, like the illogical nature of the English tongue that his father would conserve.[87] As Cheke argued, any borrowings should, as befitted a woman's attire, be done with 'bashfulnes' (again reminding us of the link between language and manners).[88]

Eliminating dialect words and jargon was consequently not only conducted for comprehensibility and national harmony. It also represented a move towards uniform refinement: that all may speak the 'flower' of English. To be 'plain' was to be 'perfite', as in the doubling 'plaine and perfite'.[89] In contrast, those resisting change were, in Hart's words, like bestial swine 'bewitched by Circes inchauntments' or uncivilised people, who

> meane to be content with Acornes as their predecessours were, contenting
> themselues with Hides and Felles for their clothing ... and dwell in their dens,
> rather than to fell the wood, and make them houses therewith ... and make the
> grounde arable, to plowe the grounde and sowe and reape good corne.[90]

Linguistic and socio-economic advancement went hand in hand, as in Wilson's anecdote about a poor man denied help with his rent because he asked for 'contrary Bishoppes' and 'reuiues', not 'contribution' and 'relief'.[91] As Paula Blank points out, the man's language and poverty were directly related.[92]

The value of linguistic reform was underlined by recurrent financial vocabulary, as Cheke's unreformed language threatened to turn 'bankrupt' with the 'counterfeitness' of other tongues.[93] This linguistic economy also operated on a more mundane level. Cheke, Smith and Hart all intended to produce a more streamlined language, of which one salient feature was the removal of extraneous letters;[94] recommended by Hart for potential savings in 'at least the one quarter, of the paper, ynke, and time which we now spend superfluously'.[95] Smith's system, which recurrently attacked that same excess of redundant letters, introduced five new signs, commended for the 'ease of their devising' and used to symbolise, with fewer characters, complex sounds such as *th* as in 'then'; *th* in 'thick'; *sh*; the *j* of 'judge'; and *v* in 'five'.[96] Hart promoted his new symbols, necessary to avoid '*penurie*' of language,[97] as 'easie and swift for the hande and eye', particularly insisting that his script was 'fit for print'.[98] Such was the efficacy of this 'profitable' system that, in the original version of his *Orthographie*, Hart proposed that Edward VI should 'use his princeli liberalite' to bear the cost of making the 'new punchons' necessary for printing his reformed script: a king's alphabet to match a king's English.[99]

When Erasmus fought for the preservation of Latin, it was to benefit a diplomatic and scholarly elite, political and intellectual exchange.[100] Promotion of English, on the other hand, was intended to permeate all social layers. By purging the language of 'ynkehorne termes' and encouraging comprehensibility, these reformers would enfranchise a nation of language users, providing a language that was accessible to all both in vocabulary and, thanks to spelling standardised along phonetic lines, once represented in writing. Hart pursued this to its logical conclusion in his *Methode*, which endeavoured to promote national literacy through a 'newe maner of teaching, whereby who so can read English onely, may alone learne the order folowing, and so bee able to teach the same to others that knowe no letter'.[101] The book was designed as a self-help manual, evangelising literacy via the book. His works drew their readers into his method. As he switched increasingly from 'old' orthography to his new phonetic system, the act of reading became one of forcible conversion. His books were, moreover, directed not at the leisured aristocracy, but at working households, where 'some one such in a house, as now can read our present maner, may be able to teach it to all the rest of the house, euen the whiles their handes may be otherwyse well occupied, in woorking for their liuing ... without any further let or cost.'[102] Letters were to become part of the living environment. The moral emblems that decorated the ideal home in Erasmus's 'Godly Feast' in order to inspire their beholders to virtuous living were here replaced by Hart's alphabet, so that 'if the figures with their letters wer drawen on the walles, pillers, and postes of churches, tounes and houses, they mought muche helpe and further the ignorant of al letters, to atteine to reade'.[103]

The letters 'drawen' on Hart's 'walles, pillers, and postes' did not only represent an Erasmian path to virtue. They also reflected the impact of English Protestantism on religious wall paintings.[104] Through the course of the sixteenth century, such pictures, discredited by association with Catholic idolatry, sported growing amounts of text, allowing them to feature as narratives, not icons. A programme of increased general literacy was of obvious need with the introduction of text-based Protestant worship, and the link between reformed language and a reformed national church held strong for these writers. Pertinently, none of Hart's or Smith's printed linguistic works was addressed to a noble dedicatee. Smith supplied no prefatory matter at all; Hart's prefaces were directed at general readers, and as such, reflect the ethos which he announced in his *Methode*: that 'in this haue I trauayled for the behoofe of the multitude'.[105] This preference for addresses to general readers over dedicatory epistles to elite patrons was characteristic of controversial Protestant literature during the 1530s, 1540s and 1550s, radical writing which hoped both to win a wider public to its cause and (central to that cause) win the right for that greater majority to have access to a vernacular scripture, and thus an understanding of religion. The choice of an open, prefatory address, embracing the general reader, was central to that ethos, and that of the linguistic reformers.

These writers consequently imbued their linguistic theorising with a pronounced religious idiom. Whilst for Castiglione 'custome' [*consuetudine*] was the fitting 'maistresse' [*maestra*] of speech,[106] and for Louis Meigret (an acknowledged inspiration for Hart's *Orthographie*), 'l'uzage' provided the authority for his suggested changes in French orthography,[107] these English linguists repeatedly turned against custom, which was made to hold distinctly 'papist' connotations. As Wilson argued,

> where we are taught by nature, to knowe the euer liuyng God, and to worship him in spirite, we turnyng natures light, into *blynde custome*, without Goddes will, haue vsed at lengthe to beleue, that he was really with vs here in yearthe, and worshipped hym not in spirite, but in Copes, in Candlestickes, in Belles, in Tapers.[108]

Religious and linguistic abuse was specifically aligned. When Wilson attacked Borde in his *Arte*, Borde was castigated as much for the pretensions of his prose (ridiculed for his signature mark, 'of Phisike Doctour', which inverted the familiar order of the phrase) as for his suspected Catholicism.[109] Borde's unnatural syntax, rejecting the standard pattern, proved as deviant as his doctrine.

For Smith, whilst advocates of reform were 'true, *pious*, wise and learned men', whoever 'defends errors and abuses' did so 'whether in religion, and rituals, or in forms of teaching, dressing and living', offending religious, social and intellectual standards alike.'[10] Spurious letters, meanwhile, were denoted as 'mendicant',[11] a word replete with connotations of corrupt Catholic friars living off the fat of society (as seen in the works of Chaucer and Langland, both of whom were appropriated as proto-Protestants by their sixteenth-century editors, a religious link that lends further piquancy to Chaucer's habitual celebration as the 'father' of the English language).[12] The association recurred in Ascham's correspondence with the humanist Hubert Leodius in the early 1550s, where the Englishman's attack on 'Usage' as justification for Greek pronunciation found added sting in his aside 'that Usage alone produces and fosters errors even in the true religion of Christ himself, just as a stinking sow suckles its little pig, and bites to protect it'.[13]

Ascham's vilification of custom during a discussion on reforming Greek pronunciation acts as a reminder of the connection between religious and linguistic enquiry in Cambridge during the 1540s, processes with which Cheke, Smith and Ascham were all involved. An attempt to restore 'authentic' Greek pronunciation through close attention to Greek literature accompanied their interrogation of contemporary religious practice by examining original texts, with 'the scriptural canons as [their] guide'.[14] Both projects earned the censure of the authorities (Stephen Gardiner as chancellor of the university in the first instance; Archbishop Cranmer in the second).[15] For these scholars, the word of God was a written word, and the desire for linguistic 'reformation' for which they called with evangelical 'zeale' (the words are Hart's) had logical religious implications. Both the actual and metaphorical end of Hart's *Methode* was that his new readers might read the scriptures for themselves, as its closing pages climax in phonetic versions of 'the Christian beliefe, the ten Commaundmentes of God, and Lordes prayer'.

The staunchly Protestant tone of these authors was suited to the tenor of their times. Their periods of linguistic enquiry show identifiable peaks during the reign of Edward and the late 1560s. The bent of their reforms was, in part, to enable their compatriots' participation in Protestant, book-based worship, but also in the form of worship sanctioned by the governments of the day. There was nothing radical about Hart's replication of the Creed, command-ments and Lord's prayer, the reading of which, in English, on all days when there was no sermon, was prescribed by Edwardian and Elizabethan injunc-tions.[16] The linguistic uniformity at which these writers aimed was congruent with the verbal uniformity of worship promoted by the Book of Common Prayer, introduced in 1549. The production of the prayer book was a carefully master-minded project of striking conformity. Different printers were mobilised to publish identical texts, all carrying the same preface arguing the need for standardised religion as a 'remedy' for current abuses, disorder and different provincial protocol. 'Where hertofore, there hath been great diuersitie

... within this realme: some folowing Salsburye vse, some Herford vse, some the vse of Bangor, some of Yorke, & some of Lincolne ... from hencefurth, al the whole realm shall haue but one vse', it proclaimed.[117]

The religion these reformers preached was that of the royal supremacy, whereby 'they may the better with bookes (which are dumbe maisters) ... comfort themselues, meditate and record prayers meete for Christians, and learne the better to obay their Princes and Magistrates'.[118] Inherent in the linguistic uniformity at which they aimed was a vocabulary of regulation. In Wilson's paradigm, a man should be as liable to be 'charge[d] for counter-feityng' the 'kynges Englishe' as for forging the King's coin, a comparison that aligned control of language with control of the coinage, one of the marks of sovereignty.[119] Despite the inescapably regulatory tone of these writers, the form taken by their efforts to further a government-led Reformation does offer a modified view of the revisionist model of the Reformation proposed by historians such as Christopher Haigh and Eamon Duffy, in which the Reform-ation was a process imposed on an unwilling nation from above.[120] The impetus still came from above, but through education, not legislation. The English were to be drawn to love, not compelled to accept, the new religion.

However, as Blank points out, these 'language reformers practised a kind of sleight of hand: although they claimed to be the bearers of the royal seal ... the changes they envisioned were also implicitly designed to enhance their own claims to cultural authority'.[121] In order to be rehabilitated, 'custom' required the redefinition that it received at end of Hart's *Orthographie*. It was no longer 'that the most do ... a most dangerous precept'.[122] Rather, 'custom of speech [was] the consent of the learned, as of living the consent of good men', a tenet that once again linked speech and manners, language and morality, and endowed them (the learned) with linguistic precedence. The metaphor that Smith used was, after all, 'a senate of letters', a conciliar, not democratic, version of government that mapped the paradigm of wise advisers con-sistently advocated by his *De Republica Anglorum*.[123] When George Puttenham proposed a similarly oligarchic system for judging linguistic standards two decades later in *The arte of English poesie*, the differences were that his mediators of taste were not scholars, but courtiers ('men ciuill and graciously behauoured and bred'),[124] and that the end was the furtherment of poetry and fine speaking, not the regulation of common speech, aimed at national and religious uniformity and conformity.

NOTES

I am grateful to Colin Burrow and the participants in the 'Archipelagic Identities' conference in Oxford for their helpful comments on earlier versions of this chapter.

1 'English' (although used to encompass Ireland and Wales) is not used prescriptively. In the anglocentric vision of these Tudor writers a national identity was an English identity, to be achieved in part by the use of one uniform language which they themselves advocated.

2 Cited in Mary Dewar, *Sir Thomas Smith: a Tudor intellectual in office* (London, Athlone Press, 1964), p. 157.

3 Thomas Smith, *De Republica Anglorum*, ed. Mary Dewar (Cambridge, Cambridge University Press, 1982), p. 61. Law is replaced by 'progenie'.

4 *OED*, senses 1c, 1a.

5 Cited by C. H. Lawrence, *The English church and the papacy in the Middle Ages* (London, Burns & Oates, 1965), p. 211.

6 PRO SP 27 Henry VIII, cap. 63.

7 Cited by R. Brinley Jones, *The old British tongue: the vernacular in Wales, 1540–1640* (Cardiff, Avalon, 1970), p. 33.

8 See Glanmor Williams, *Welsh Reformation essays* (Cardiff, University of Wales Press, 1967).

9 William Salesbury, *A dictionary in Englyshe and Welshe* (London, 1547), sig. A.i^r.

10 *Ibid.*, sig. A.i^v.

11 *Ibid.*, sig. A.ii^r.

12 *Ibid.*, sig. A.ii^r.

13 *Ibid.*, sig. A.i^r.

14 Dates from reference to draft 'twenty years ago' and revisions made 'a year and nine months after the treaty with the king of France at Troyes', Thomas Smith, *De recta et emendata linguae Anglicae scriptione, dialogus*, facsimile edition with parallel translation, ed. Bror Danielsson, *Literary and linguistic works* III (Stockholm, Almquist & Wiksell, 1983), pp. 23, 25.

15 Andrew Borde, *First boke of the introduction of knowledge* (London, 1547), sig. B.ii^r. See Richard Foster Jones, *The triumph of the English language: a survey of opinions concerning the vernacular from the introduction of printing to the Restoration* (Stanford CA, Stanford University Press, 1953).

16 For the political nature of language standardisation see Robert L. Cooper, *Language planning and social change* (Cambridge, Cambridge University Press, 1989). For three functions of standard language as unifying, separatist and prestige-giving see Paul L. Garvin and Madelaine Mathiot, cited by Amy J. Devitt, *Standardizing written English: diffusion in the case of Scotland, 1520–1659* (Cambridge, Cambridge University Press, 1989), p. 12.

17 Desiderius Erasmus, *De recta Latini Graecique sermonis pronuntiatione, dialogus*, trans. Maurice Pope (Toronto, Toronto University Press, 1985), introduction, p. 350.

18 Edmund Spenser and Gabriel Harvey, *Three proper and wittie, familiar letters* (London, 1580), p. 6.

19 Joachim Du Bellay, *La deffence et illustration de la langue Françoyse* (Paris, 1545), sig. a.iv^v.

20 John Hart, *A methode or comfortable beginning for all vnlearned, whereby they may bee taught to read English* (London, 1570), sig. A.i^v.

21 *Ibid.*, sig. A.i^v.

22 *Dialogus*, p. 23.

23 Brinley Jones, *Old British tongue*, p. 34.

24 Throughout, quotations from phonetic passages of Hart's works are transcribed into modern English; quotations from sections in the 'old' orthography appear in the original spelling.

25 Alexander Gill, *Logonomia Anglica* (London, 1619), sig. B.3^r; William Bullokar, *The amendment of orthographie for English speech* (London, 1580), sig. A.ii^r and *passim*.

26 Frontispiece reproduced in Danielsson's edition of *Smith's works*, Part III, p. 9.

27 *DNB*.

28 See Bror Danielsson, *Hart's works* II (Stockholm, Almquist & Wiksell, 1963), pp. 35–7.

29 Thomas Hoby, *The book of the courtier*, ed. Virginia Cox (London, Everyman, 1994), p. 10; Cox's introduction, p. viii.

30 Thomas Wilson, *Arte of rhetorique* (London, 1553), fol. 88^r.

31 *Methode*, sig. A.iii^r.

32 *Courtier*, p. 7.

33 Martin Elsky, *Authorizing words: speech, writing, and print in the English Renaissance* (Ithaca NY, Cornell University Press, 1989), p. 84.

34 BL. Additional MS 48,047, fol. 123^r.

35 *Arte*, fol. 86^r.

36 *Methode*, sig. A.iv^r, *.i^r.

37 Roger Ascham, *The scholemaster* (London, 1570), fol. 26^r.

38 *Arte*, fol. 87^r (emphasis added).

39 *Methode*, sig. A.iii^r.

40 *Courtier*, p. 10.

41 *Dialogus*, p. 141.

42 John Hart, *An orthographie conteyning the due order and reason howe to write or paint thimage of a mannes voice, most like to life or nature* (London, 1569), fol. 7^r.

43 *Ibid.*, fol. 66^v.

44 Smith, *Dialogus*, p. 47.

45 *Orthographie*, fol. 44^r.

46 *Courtier*, p. 10.

47 *Arte*, fol. 87^v.

48 Cheke, in *Courtier*, p. 10.

49 *Methode*, sig. A.iii^r.

50 Niccolò Machiavelli, *Il discorso intorno alla nostra lingua*, ed. Franco Gaeta (Milan, Felltrinelli, 1965), p. 193.

51 *Orthographie*, fol. 17ʳ.

52 *Ibid.*, fol. 15ᵛ.

53 See Dieter Stein, 'Sorting out the variants: standardization and social factors in the English language, 1600–1800', in Dieter Stein and Ingrid Tieken-Boon von Ostade (eds), *Towards a standard English, 1600–1800* (Berlin, Mouton de Gruyter, 1994), pp. 1–17.

54 *Orthographie*, fol. 4ʳ.

55 *Methode*, sig. B.iᵛ–B.iiʳ.

56 Baldassare Castiglione, *Il libro del cortegiano*, ed. Ettore Bonora (Milan, Ugo Mursia, 1972), p. 68; *Courtier*, p. 60.

57 *Cortegiano*, p. 28; *Courtier*, p. 17.

58 *Cortegiano*, p. 27; *Courtier*, p. 16.

59 Brian Weinstein, 'Francophonie: purism at the international level', in Björn H. Jernudd and Michael J. Shapiro (eds), *The politics of language purism* (Berlin, Mouton de Gruyter, 1989), p. 54.

60 *Cortegiano*, p. 68; *Courtier*, p. 60.

61 *Cortegiano*, p. 73; *Courtier*, p. 66.

62 Wilson, *Arte*, fol. 87ʳ.

63 Hart, *Orthographie*, fol. 43ᵛ.

64 *Arte*, fol. 7ᵛ.

65 Geoffrey Chaucer, *A treatise on the astrolabe*, ed. Larry D. Benson, *The riverside Chaucer*, third edition (Oxford, Oxford University Press, 1988), p. 662.

66 *Arte*, fol. 86ʳ.

67 William Shakespeare, *Merry Wives of Windsor*, ed. Peter Alexander, *Complete works* (London, Harper Collins, 1951), V.v.139, 130.

68 *Arte*, fol. 86ʳ.

69 *Ibid.*, fols 86ʳ⁻ᵛ.

70 *Ibid.*, sig. A.iiiʳ⁻ᵛ.

71 See, for example, Thomas Dekker, *The shoemakers holiday* (London, 1600); William Haughton, *Englishmen for my money* (London, 1616).

72 John Guy, *Tudor England* (Oxford, Oxford University Press, 1988), p. 208.

73 See, for example, A. B., *Merie tales of the mad men of Gotam*, ed. Stanley J. Kahrl (Evanston IL, Renaissance English Texts, 1965), pp. 16–17.

74 John Hart, *The opening of the unreasonable writing of our Inglish toung* (c. 1551), MS. Royal 17.C.vii, pp. 14–15.

75 *Arte*, fol. 89ʳ.

76 *Dialogus*, fol. 6ʳ, p. 33.

77 William Harrison, *A description of England*, ed. Georges Edelen (New York, Dover Publications, 1968), p. 184.

78 E.g. Robert Greene, *A notable discouery of cosenage* (London, 1591).

79 *Orthographie*, fol. 17ʳ.

80 *Dialogus*, p. 109.

81 *Orthographie*, fol. 12ʳ and *passim*.

82 *Ibid.*, fol. 12ʳ.

83 William Shakespeare, *Coriolanus*, ed. Alexander, I.i.43 ff.

84 *Orthographie*, fol. 10ʳ.

85 *Ibid.*, fol. 10ʳ.

86 *Arte*, fol. 86ʳ; Thomas Wilson, *Rule of reason* (London, 1551), sig. T.vʳ.

87 *Dialogus*, p. 23.

88 *Courtier*, p. 10.

89 *Ibid.*, p. 10.

90 *Methode*, sig. *.iʳ; *Orthographie*, fols 42ᵛ–43ʳ.

91 *Arte*, fol. 87ᵛ.

92 Paula Blank, *Broken English: dialects and the politics of language in Renaissance writings* (London, Routledge, 1996), p. 42.

93 *Courtier*, p. 10.

94 For a comprehensive description of Cheke's system see John Strype, *The life of the lerned Sir John Cheke* (London, 1705), pp. 211–15.

95 *Orthographie*, fol. 5ʳ.

96 *Dialogus*, fol. 38ʳ.

97 *Orthographie*, sig. π.4ᵛ (emphasis added).

98 *Ibid.*, fol. 35ᵛ.

99 *Opening*, pp. 170, 169.

100 *De Recta ... Pronuntiatione*, trans. Pope, especially pp. 390, 472–3.

101 *Methode*, sig. A.iʳ.

102 *Ibid.*, sig. *.iiʳ.

103 Desiderius Erasmus, 'Convivium religiosum', trans. Craig R. Thompson (Toronto, Toronto University Press, 1997), pp. 177–81; *Methode*, sig. *.iiʳ.

104 See Tessa Watt, *Cheap print and popular piety, 1550–1640* (Cambridge, Cambridge University Press, 1991), pp. 217–53.

105 *Methode*, sig. A.ivᵛ.

106 *Cortegiano*, p. 74.

107 Louis Meigret, *Le tretté de la grammere Françoeze* (Paris, 1550). See Hart, *Orthographie*, fol. 53ʳ.

108 *Arte*, fol. 18ᵛ (emphasis added).

109 *Ibid.*, fol. 89ᵛ.

110 *Dialogus*, fol. 1ᵛ (emphasis added).

111 *Ibid.*, fol. 33ᵛ.

112 See, for example, Robert Crowley's preface to *The vision of Pierce Plowman* (London, 1550), and John Leland, *Commentarii de scriptoribus Britannicis*, ed. Anthony Hall, 2 vols (Oxford, 1709), II, p. 422.

113 *The whole works of Roger Ascham*, ed. J. A. Giles, 3 vols (London, 1864–65), I, 346; trans. Maurice Hatch and Alvin Vos, *Letters of Roger Ascham* (New York, Peter Lang, 1989), p. 149.

114 *Letters of Roger Ascham*, p. 106.

115 *Ibid.*, pp. 6, 106.

116 *Iniunccions* (1547), fol. a.iiiᵛ; Gerald Bray (ed.), 'The Elizabethan Injunctions, 1559', *Documents of the English Reformation* (Cambridge, Clarke, 1994), p. 336.

117 *The boke of the common praier and administracion of the sacrementes and other rites and ceremonies of the churche*, Edward Whitchurch's edition (London, 4 May, 1549), sig. π.iiʳ.

118 Hart, *Methode*, sig. A.ivᵛ.

119 *Arte*, fol. 86ʳ.

120 Christopher Haigh, *English reformations: religion, politics, and society under the Tudors* (Oxford, Clarendon Press, 1993); Eamon Duffy, *The stripping of the altars: traditional religion in England, c. 1400–1580* (New Haven CT, Yale University Press, 1992).

121 *Broken English*, p. 29.

122 *Orthographie*, fol. 51ʳ.

123 *Dialogus*, fol. 25ʳ.

124 George George Puttenham, *The arte of English poesie*, ed. Gladys Doidge Willcock and Alice Walker (Cambridge, Cambridge University Press, 1970), p. 114.

Chapter 11

———◆———

The 'public' as a rhetorical community in early modern England

Geoff Baldwin

Communities exist on two levels: first, that of the relations between the members of the community and the hierarchies that obtain within in it; and second, that of the perceptions and imaginations of those involved. Intellectual history has shown that the use of imagined or rhetorical communities was a very powerful tool when employed by early modern political writers. Playing upon communities of the imagination, on people's ideas of communities they regarded themselves as belonging to, could provide a very powerful motivation for action.[1] It would not be cogent to attempt to link too directly the history of such uses of ideas with the history of changes in the nature of social relations and hierarchies, but the juxtaposition of these different sorts of enquiry is instructive. The creation of a community of the imagination is a very powerful political tool, and one where the definition of such a community does not necessarily have to be relevant to the situation in which it is deployed. Often imagined communities have strong connections with the phenomenological world, and can become a more permanent and integrated part of modern political understanding.

Individuals may well regard themselves as simultaneously members of several different communities in the spheres of economics, religion or politics. I would like to concentrate upon what would be for many one of the largest communities they would regard themselves as belonging to: the public. To describe a group so large as a 'community' could be regarded as stretching the definition somewhat, but it is an imaginative development – the textual emergence of a nominal and national public – which is the subject of this chapter. The emergence of a national public was part of widespread upheaval and realignment in both the political and the confessional communities in the seventeenth century.

The development of the idea of an active public was one of the most significant of the seventeenth century. Since Habermas's *The structural transformation of the public sphere* of 1962, historians have been interested in the idea that the seventeenth century saw the development of a new and more inclusive political space. Even those that have not shared Habermas's Marxist assumptions have become fascinated by such a possibility. Historians of political culture, especially of the eighteenth century, have regarded as one of their major themes the contested membership of a politically active public, a successful appeal to which could secure legitimacy.[2] It is possible to trace the emergence of the idea of such a public in the seventeenth century alongside the fact of a public sphere, and so gain insight into how contemporaries saw, and attempted to manipulate, the developments in which they were involved.

One analogue of the emergence of one or more public spheres is a linguistic and philosophical shift that I would like to trace in this chapter: the emergence of the notion of 'the public' as an active body of people. This development, which has affected political ideas down to the late twentieth century, occurred during a period when the structure of the state was contested, and the idea of the public was important in making certain types of claim about the utilisation of state power. Indeed, the idea of the 'state' emerged at the same time as that of the 'public', being something which acted on behalf of a community. One way of describing such a community would be as a 'nation', and this was used extensively, but there was a necessity to have recourse to a community which was not imagined in such abstract terms, and could less easily be thought of as represented in very abstract terms, say by a monarchy. It is for this reason that the 'public' gained favour.

Although there are other words which were used to denote an imagined community for rhetorical purposes, I would like to concentrate on 'public', as this term underwent the most significant changes. In the sixteenth century, it came to be used to describe a particular set of common concerns, or a particular set of administrative, political and judicial offices, and their concomitant duties. By extension, those who held such offices could be described as public people. During the crisis in the middle of the seventeenth century there was a gradual shift to a conception of the public as an aggregate of people who made up a particular community: that of the whole nation. This had the effect of making the abstract or imagined communities employed for political purposes both more effective and more closely linked with society as a whole, whose representatives could claim a right to act in their name.

The concept of the public differed in significant respects from previous ways of describing the nation as a whole. The way in which the idea of the 'public' was used rendered it more of a community than older terminology, and enabled more extensive claims to be made on its behalf. During the late fifteenth century, several terms came into use which had similar sorts of meanings. 'Commonweal', which in the sixteenth century became synonymous with a nation or a state, originally had a meaning closer to the felicity or welfare common to the whole of the people, and never entirely lost such overtones. It became the standard translation of the classical term *res publica*. This literally meant the public thing, and conveyed a similar idea. *Res publica* was an identification of the political with that which pertained to the common life of the citizens: thus *a* republic denoted the sort of state which stressed common involvement with decision making. In classical usage the term *publica* was used descriptively, and that was how it entered the political language of northern Europe in the sixteenth century.

In the early modern period such ways of thinking about a society had great political significance. Monarchic government did not preclude the development of a mode of political thinking which posited the public or common good as the highest possible aim: most theories of kingship would include such a provision and argue that a unified monarchy was the best way of achieving such an aim. What early modern republics and monarchies had in common was the notion of there being certain public people who acted to procure the public good, whether they be rotated, elected or appointed. The adaptation of the humanist tradition of the *vir virtutis* to the seigniorial politics of fifteenth-century Italy is well documented; what is less obvious is that this tradition, which in Britain could draw on both humanist and medieval sources, became vital to how politics could be understood.[3] Cicero's *De officiis* was a key and oft reprinted text which describes the duties of the holder of public office. Other classical texts revived and popularised during the Renaissance gave similar accounts, and their popularity attests to the importance that a description of the ethics of public office had for political discussion. Contemporary texts used these as the basis for a moral discussion of politics. Christian ethics and medieval ideas of chivalry combined with this classical, pagan vision when contemporaries came to describe what being public entailed.[4] Politics concerned a public realm, what was common; and it was the job of public people, the monarch being the most significant of them, to act with honour and skill to administrate and govern this sphere.

The danger to the idea of monarchy posed by the idea of the *res publica* was tempered by those who introduced such thinking from the Italian Renaissance into northern Europe. If politics is about the public thing, then this could make a monarchy, by contrast, into something private and indeed irrelevant. One of the most sensitive to the problems of introducing a new vocabulary was Sir Thomas Elyot, whose *Boke of the Gouernour* was published in 1531.[5] He opposed the use of the fifteenth-century term 'commonweal' which had become current by the time he was writing. He argues etymologically, 'Publike (as Varro saith) is diriuied of people, whiche in latin is called *Populus*, wherfore hit semeth that men haue ben longe abused in calling *Rempublicam* a commune weale.'[6] He takes 'common' in this context not as an adjective, but to refer to commoners, as a translation of *plebis*. His point is that 'commonweal' would be an appropriate translation of *res plebia*, rather than *res publica*, which means that the term now in use has a set of connotations that Elyot, following Cicero, finds dangerous. Politics should not be about the supposedly irrational and volatile desires of the multitude of the people as a whole, but only as considered as part of a natural order. For Elyot, divinely ordained order, in the realm and in the minds of those who govern it, saves the world from the chaos from which 'ensuethe uniuersall dissolution'.[7] He therefore wishes to use 'public weal' instead of the 'commonweal', as the public for him implies the people arraigned in their natural order. As he puts it, it is only 'a publike weale, where, like as god hath disposed the saide influence of understandyng, is also appoynted degrees and places accordynge to the excellencie thereof'.[8] Putting the people in such order tempers the notion of politics being a common concern, by restricting the number of those who could be thought qualified to deal with public affairs.

Elyot thus establishes a tradition of recasting the vocabulary and thrust of humanist political thinking to fit in with the political assumptions and institutions of a monarchic Britain. He is concerned about the implication of assumptions of substantive equality in humanist thought, and so neutralises it by redefining the public. This somewhat exceptional strategy stems from the depth of his concern with the political and social vocabulary employed by political writers. He felt the need to re-establish a notional order within a political culture he was at the same time attempting to redescribe along classical humanist lines. It illustrates very well the tension inherent in the term 'public', which itself reflects the tension inherent in the translation of classical and republican traditions of thought into a political culture which was not based upon small cities, and moreover had at its centre the court of a powerful monarch.

In the second half of the sixteenth century it became standard to use the word 'public' to describe an area of common concern, which should be governed by a relatively small group, who themselves could be described as public men. The notion of the public that was employed in the late sixteenth and early seventeenth century was a descriptive one: 'public' could describe a set of concerns, or a type of person who was employed to deal with them. It may well be regarded as delineating the political or the contestable from the private. There were public concerns or public things, and public people whose job it was to deal with them. A sphere of activity was regarded as public, which could be broadly defined as that which had relevance to everybody, but that did not mean that everybody should have some part in decision making or even debate. Indeed, this was regarded as having disastrous consequences, since only those with particular virtues and education were considered capable of acting responsibly in such a position.

One good illustration of this is the work of Pierre de la Place, whose *Politique Discourses* was translated into English in 1578.[9] He concerned himself with different 'vocations' which individuals could follow. He divided them into two groups: the public and the private. The public vocation was divided into the political and religious, and was incompatible with the private, being a higher calling. Those of a public calling attended to that which was of common concern, to which the activities of those engaged in private vocations were only contributory: 'All their drifts ending, and resting in this scope of vocation publique, whiche Philosophers say to be an action, and operation by vertue, wherevnto all Priuate vocations tend, neither more nor lesse, then all springes and Riuers doe to the sea.'[10] Those of the public vocation had not only to be virtuous, but must also come to their public office by legitimate means, and not purchase their place. 'Public' was thus a description of a sphere of action, and the people who performed the actions.

Such use of the term was ubiquitous. The writer and translator of Osorio, William Blandy, argued that magistrates and soldiers fulfilled the public role as agents of the monarch.[11] George Whetstone was a poet, adventurer and soldier who made a living composing eulogies and translating stories from Italian. He likened magistrates, especially the senior officers of the London government, to 'Goddes' when arguing for reform. He later emphasised the distinction between public and private people by arguing that princes may take ruthless action denied to private individuals, because of their care for 'our English peace'. He echoes de la Place in talking of the 'calling' of the nobility, magistracy and clergy.[12] For Richard Beacon, the situation in Ireland required a distinction between a magistrate's and a citizen's scope for action, putting his words in the mouth of Solon, 'that in a publike magistrate, the same is rightlie tearmed pollicie, but in private persons, the same is not vniustly condemned by the name of deceite'.[13]

Shakespeare portrayed the new king Henry VI as brought to sit at the 'chiefest stern of public weal', and has Coriolanus attacked as 'a fo' to th' public weal'.[14] In *Anthony and Cleopatra* Anthony's suicide is contrasted with a legitimate death at the hands of 'a public minister of justice'.[15] 'Public', then, was a current and significant term, but it did not yet refer to an imagined community. It was a significant development when, later in the seventeenth century, 'public' moved from being merely descriptive to standing for the whole nation imagined as one community: there was *a* public. There were radical political implications of such a shift: thinking of a community as an aggregate of all the individuals involved, rather than what could be said to be common between a group of individuals, empowers those individuals. Merely by using the language in such a way, it implies they have a legitimate interest in any decision-making process and cannot be thought of as the passive beneficiaries of the virtue of a public person such as a monarch or counsellor.

The crisis of the English civil war provided the impetus for this shift in meaning. The idea of the 'public' was one important means among a nexus of rhetorical strategies by which the seizure of the apparatus of the state could be justified. In order to justify its actions, one of the things that Parliament had to do was to describe itself as a public rather than private power in a fairly traditional way. The public, and therefore legitimate, advice of Parliament was often contrasted with the private advice of courtiers, and the private nature of the court. This rhetoric came into its own during the initial confrontation between King and Parliament in 1642.[16] The descriptive power of the idea of the public could be expanded and its meaning broadened. In May, Parliament denounced anyone who would harass those who supported the Parliament at York as 'publike enemies of the State'.[17] Portraying one's opponents as private men who had no right to take charge of public affairs and were thus fundamentally unsuited to do so was a powerful rhetorical strategy. It was employed by both sides in the propaganda war of 1642.

This was, however, only part of the claim that had to be made for either side to win the propaganda battle. In such a fraught situation, in part deliberately inflamed by those writing in support of parliamentary claims, the issue became a question of who had the right to act for the whole nation in a time of emergency when there was a palpable threat to it. The claim was made that Parliament rather than the King had the executive power to defend the nation. Such a radical change in the locus of such power demanded a concomitant change in how the nation could be thought of as acting, or indeed existing. Parliament had to claim to act for and represent the whole society, and so it became necessary to imagine the whole nation as one community. Something more was required than a deployment of the idea of the commonwealth to give Parliament legitimacy: the institution would have to be linked with an imagined community – the public – in order to do so. This was such an important part of Civil War argument that a novel terminology was employed in order to link Parliament and the imagined community of the whole nation.

The language of interest, both public and private, came into being in the early seventeenth century, and was first widely employed in the Civil War. In 1640 Henri duc de Rohan's *L'interesse des princes* of 1634 was translated, and from this point onward the idea of an individual or group having a specific interest or group of interests came to be regularly employed in political debate.[18] Rohan invoked an idea of a true interest, which could be contrasted with the flawed perceptions of those involved: 'The Prince may deceiue himselfe, his *Counsell* may be corrupted, but the interest alone can neuer faile.'[19] Any country or group had an interest independent of the perceptions of those involved in making decisions, so that the claim being made is one of an infallible political guide. The power of this form of analysis was that it gave clarity through being abstracted from moral concerns. The public interest attained a precision of definition, in terms of what qualifications were necessary in order to be accounted its arbiter, that had previously eluded any previous conception of the public good.

The idea of interest could be used when attempting to discuss the concept of representation and the ability or right of Parliament to act to defend the nation. Interests, rather than people, could also be thought of as being represented, and thus, in discussions of representation, interest could either have neutral or pejorative connotations. Private interests were a legitimate component of the nation, and should be represented, but could also be something which could lead individuals to betray the public. In this context, the phrase 'the public interest' became important in contrast to a private interest which could be corrupting if it determined public action. This indicated a notion of the public as something which itself could have a specific interest, rather than being an area where virtuous or corrupt political action took place. Through having an interest the public could become real. The word 'public' could stand for the aggregated members of the whole society through their having a common interest. Interest could distract or mislead an individual, or it could be represented fully and so help to define a necessarily rational decision-making body.

It became important for both sides in these debates to attempt to create an identity of interest between themselves and the public, as an imagined community of everyone in the nation. In this endeavour, the idea of interest became indispensable to any attempt to describe any individual or institution as having true public power in the conventional sense of having a right and duty to deal with public affairs. The concept of interest made it possible to reify the society politically. Henry Parker made these points especially important in two pamphlets, both confusingly with the word 'observations' in the title.[20] In the first, published on 19 May 1642, he argued that Parliament should be trusted because it was 'more knowing than any other privadoes' such as the King's advisers, and, more importantly, 'in regard of their publique interest, they are more responsible than any other ... thirdly, they have no private interest to deprave them'.[21] These were the qualifications that Parker felt were requisite to judge necessity and provide a new basis for the state.

He was forced to expand his arguments after the publication of *His Majesties answer to the XIX propositions*. This was a response to Parliament's last peace offer, which had demanded concessions that it was very unlikely the King would make. It outlined a constitutional case to demonstrate that Parliament could not play the role it was attempting to take in the defence of the community. To respond to this, in the later *Observations* Parker elaborated his ideas. It was public interest that made the community real: it was important for Parker to speak of the 'interest of the people' as a whole.[22] The idea of common interest helped him to bring the public into being and, through the idea of identity of interest, show that Parliament could be regarded as virtually that community. In response to royalist arguments about the potential for parliamentary tyranny and the dubious intentions of those leading the House, Parker reinforced the representative credentials of his institution. It had to be the whole nation, for 'a community can have no private ends to mislead it, and make it injurious to it selfe'. The Parliament is 'freely elected' and therefore will not infringe either the rights of the community or indeed of the monarch.[23] To resist Charles, a community of the whole nation had to be called into being, not in an abstract sense of a common or public weal, but as a composite of real people. This had permanent political significance.

Support was enlisted for Parliament by identifying the individual interest with the public as promoted by Parliament. On 17 August a pamphlet appeared, the *Considerations for the Commons in this age of distractions*, that used the language of interest to attempt to enlist support for the Parliament. All should contribute to the cause because 'its no more than our owne interest requires, that wee apply our selves to the common good'.[24] Here interests were appealed to in a positive way to demonstrate that the rational course of action would be to support the Parliament, because its interests were identified with those of individuals. This marks a new sophistication with which the concept of interest was employed. Parliament should be trusted to defend the interests of the individuals who support it because of its ability to judge the circumstances when necessity applies and when armed action is justifiable. The *Observator defended* of 26 August, a robust defence of Parker, argued that 'publike interest of State' must be determined in Parliament, because of the public nature of that institution: this public interest had extraordinary power because 'a particular propriety may be destroyed by a Community to preserve it self'.[25] The anonymous J.M. argued that Parliament was able to judge in such an instance, and would not be moved by selfish affection or passion, as Spelman had alleged in a pamphlet of January 1643, it being strange that 'severall constitutions and inclinations should all combine to labour for themselves, not the publique'.[26] The mixture in Parliament would necessarily work for the public as a whole.

Opponents of the Parliament attempted either to employ a similar rhetoric, or systematically to deny the legitimacy of the notion of the public. The royalist Dudley Digges argued for a similar identity of interest with the public which did not rely on a theory of representation. The mythical legislators had acted to 'grant to them the greatest power of Government, to whom the preservation of the Present state would be most beneficiall: because their private Interests were the same with the Publique'.[27] The unity and power of the monarchy for Digges create the same desired identity of interest with the public as Parliament claimed. To give it added power, and to emphasise its stabilising qualities, he associated this idea of interest with the ancient constitution.

Thomas Hobbes's theory of association as described in *Leviathan* and *De cive* takes an alternative line, as it excludes the possibility of the existence of a public prior to the sovereign, such that it could have an interest, or act, and so determine the location of political power.[28] The act of contract which creates the association is not that of an existing community to choose a ruler, but that of a disparate group of individuals who create a community only in the act of agreeing to a common umpire or legislator. He thus closes the space available for a juxtaposition of the public, its interest and the sovereign; the only way to determine the public interest would be through the judgement of the sovereign.

The less well known John Hall of Richmond was less systematic but more specific. His *Of government and obedience* of 1654 was somewhat more conventional than Hobbes's *Leviathan* but advanced similar arguments against parliamentary positions, while at the same time approving of the Cromwellian church settlement. Hall declared a 'falacy lies under the notion of Community', so that it could not be politically important.[29] He further stated that both the commonwealth and the public were 'bare political notions, not living creatures capable of addres or interest: and that they are not otherwise manageable, or to be represented or collected into a sum or total, then as in relation to the persons therein intrusted'.[30] In denying legitimacy to the parliamentary cause, and at the same time the regime that emerged from its victory, Hall found it necessary to specifically deny the existence of the public, and its ability to have an interest that could be identified or represented. The emergence of the public as a rhetorical community was not then uncontested, but the vehemence of the denials point to its significance and potential.

After the Civil War 'the public' entered the British political vocabulary for good, even if many of the public themselves were slow to be admitted to consideration in political affairs. It was apparent during the debates of the 1650s, when the remnants of Parliament, the army, Scots, Irish, Cromwell, republicans and more radical groups fought with the sword and the pen for the political fortunes of Britain, and the shape of its future constitution. Republicans tended to be most keen to employ this new vocabulary, especially as they attempted retrospectively to define the aims of the original conflict, and so establish a continuity between their programme and the debates that had led to the deployment of the idea of the public on such a wide scale. James Harrington and John Milton both used 'public' frequently, but most usually in a purely adjectival sense, perhaps reflecting Harrington's preoccupation with systems and Milton's mistrust of popular prejudices. Marchmont Nedham, on the other hand, put 'the public' at the centre of his political programme.

Nedham was a highly productive propagandist, who worked mostly on the side of the Commonwealth administration, demonstrating in weekly editorials in the *Mercurius Politicus* the superiority of the republican arrangements now in force.[31] In 1653 Cromwell had dissolved the Rump and taken more direct control, and in 1656 there was a great danger that this administration would be formalised with the *Instrument of government*. As an attack upon Cromwell's attempt, in republican eyes, to return the nation to a virtual monarchy under his own rule, Nedham published a collection of his editorials as *The excellencie of a free state*.

Nedham sets out to show the natural superiority of a republican system of government by showing how the political system relates to the public as a whole. He makes the by now standard contrast between a republic and a monarchy, 'it being usual in Free-States to be more tender of the Publick in all their Decrees, than of particular Interests: whereas the case is otherwise in a Monarchy'.[32] The advantage of a republic is that its political system can take account of, and care for, every member of the public; a monarchy, as a closed, private system, cannot. Monarchy structurally excludes the public, and so can never, for Nedham, adequately act for the common good. This aspect of a republic is not only good in itself, but it changes the character of those who live under such a regime.

This inclusiveness creates a certain spirit within the nation, conscious of its own freedom and therefore courageous and powerful. This is possible because the private and the public are linked: the political system links each particular member of the public with the whole. The spirit consists in 'that apprehension which every particular Man hath of his own immediate share in the publick Interest, as well as of that security which he possesses in the enjoyment of his private Fortune, free from the reach of any Arbitrary power.'[33] Such immediate public involvement would help Britain emulate the achievements of Rome and Carthage. Government by those who had been elected was the only method of creating an identity of interest between those in power and the public. Others would 'care not to serve the Publick any further, than the publike serves them'.[34] A mercenary attitude to government, and a disenchanted populace, would be the inevitable result of a detachment between the public and the government. A system in which the public were able to act as a political force, and be imagined to have an interest that could be represented, would, for Nedham, change the character of that public for the better, and so enable Britain to gain her due glory.

The Restoration curtailed the opportunity for the expression of straight-forwardly republican political opinions, but by that stage the idea of the public had become quite common and widely used. It was not confined to a specifically republican theory of politics. The 'public' gained an existence that went beyond the political, and could be used in a wide variety of contexts. Robert Boyle, for instance, referred in his *Occasional reflections* to the public as an audience for his work, citing 'the favourable Reception that the publick has vouchsafed to what hath been presented it, of mine'.[35] Its existence was assumed. One good indication of ubiquity is the definition of the word in contemporary dictionaries. The word 'public' had not appeared in any of the 'hard word' dictionaries or vocabularies composed before the Civil War, but the 1696 edition of Edward Phillips's *The new world of words* contained a dual definition, as an adjective and a collective noun:

> *Publick, (a relative and collective Word.)* The Generality of Fellow-Citizens or People. Love of the *Publick*, is the Love which we owe to the Country we were born and live in. To appear, to speak in Publick, that is, in the Face of all Men.[36]

In his 1708 *Dictionarium Anglo-Britannicum*, John Kersey made the distinction between the two meanings clearer by having two separate entries, one being what was 'common, belonging to the Poeple [sic]', and the other the 'generality of People'.[37] Nathaniel Bailey followed this definition in his *Universal etymological English dictionary* of 1727. The new collective meaning of the word 'public' was well established after the Commonwealth.

The exclusion crisis of 1679–83 provided the occasion for the composition of two of the most significant political texts of the seventeenth century. The occasion was again the conflict of a king and a parliament, and again the spectre of an autocratic and tyrannous regime was raised. Algernon Sidney and John Locke defended opposition to the Stuart regime, and presented a vision of politics in which armed opposition was justified toward any regime which did not take into account the interests of the people as a whole. Both texts were popular with writers on politics in the eighteenth century, not just in Britain, but in France and America, and provided some of the intellectual ammunition for both revolutions. The idea of a community of the whole nation was still a contested one, the most obvious alternative vision of politics being Filmer's *Patriarcha*, which espoused a natural and fatherly authority as the main determinant of political action. Its posthumous publication in 1681, and the popularity of its ideas, prompted both Algernon Sidney and John Locke to compose discussions of politics as replies to this text. The doctrine of *Patriarcha* excluded any active role for the public, and indeed denied that the public had any existence as a collective body beyond that conferred on it by the sovereign.

In his *Discourses concerning government* Algernon Sidney puts forward a similar argument to that of Marchmont Nedham during the Interregnum to justify a republic. Although not published until 1698, it was written between 1682 and 1683, when Sidney was executed for treason on the evidence of its contents. Free states, or republics, he argued, would be greater because of the relationship of the part to the whole, thus as 'every man finding his own good comprehended in the Publick, as those that sail in the same Ship, employs the Talent he has in endeavouring to preserve it, knowing that he must perish if that miscarry.'[38] Individuals would thus not spare their property, their friends or themselves, so long as 'publick Powers are employ'd for the publick

Benefit'.[39] The identification of each individual with the public as a whole is, for Sidney, possible only in a republic. A republic is the only form of government which can therefore qualify as truly public, and so have any legitimacy. A government has to enter into a particular relationship with the public in order to qualify for the adjective 'public', and so gain legitimacy.

John Locke's *Two treatises on government* were probably begun in 1680 but were not published until 1689, in the aftermath of the Glorious Revolution. He expands the scope of action of society by positing two distinct stages by which disparate individuals are brought into government. People first of all congregate together and form a society, and so agree to the idea of government. This creative act of cohesion precedes the agreement by a majority to set up any particular government: 'For when any number of Men have, by the consent of every individual, made a *Community*, they have thereby made that *Community* one Body, with a Power to Act as one Body, which is only by the will and determination of the *majority*.'[40]

It is important for Locke that the community of the whole nation exists first. What this theory of association does is to open up the space, which Thomas Hobbes had attempted to close down in *Leviathan*, for the public to exist prior to the political, and prior to the imposition of any authority. This is one of the strategies by which Locke ameliorates the possibly absolutist implications of a theory of natural rights.[41] A political society is said to exist when 'the Community comes to be Umpire, by settled standing Rules, indifferent, and the same to all Parties'.[42] The foundation of his vision of politics is the imagining of a community which has the power to act. While this community is abstract, its active principle is represented by the idea of the public. Locke uses the ideas of the public good and the public weal in judging laws and the actions of those who have public power, and in that way provides part of the justification for revolution. He goes further by imagining the public as a community. In describing the structure of government, Locke argues that the executive power acts to ensure the '*security and interest of the publick*', the power they have coming from the 'Force of the Publick', which must act only through those channels designated by the public.[43] The individuals that make up a society when aggregated act by constituting a public: as a public that can both act and be acted upon.

This becomes clear when Locke moves from the directly political to economic matters. After the Glorious Revolution of 1688, when he had revised the *Two treatises* for publication, Locke became involved in the economic debates about interest rates and the problem of clipped money. To restore faith in the currency, and avoid inflation, he advocated melting down and recoining. He opposed devaluation, either by acceptance of clipped coinage or by issuing lighter coins:

But which way soever this falls, 'tis certain, the Publick (which most Men think, ought to be the only reason of changing a settled Law, and disturbing the common current course of things) receives not the least Profit by it: Nay, as we shall see by and by, it will be a great Charge and Loss to the Kingdom.[44]

The effect on the public is for Locke the only measure of proposed legislation. The public has an economic existence as well as a political existence. It was only by calling up the public as an economic community that Locke could effectively argue against those measures which he felt would be harmful. It is the cumulative effect of the devaluation of each individual who makes up the public that interests Locke, rather than some vague and general idea of the common good. The use of the public relates these precise impacts of a particular policy to the community imagined as a whole, and so gives them an immediacy and a direct relevance they would otherwise be denied.

The use of the public in economic affairs could be taken to a more utopian level by those who believed that the public constituted a more close knit community than did Locke. The Quaker William Penn was a great campaigner on religious toleration and other issues in the later seventeenth century. He used the idea of interest to argue for toleration. In *One project for the good of England*, of 1679, he argues that the identity of interest between Nonconformists and Anglicans should be the basis of a civil union that would transcend their religious differences. In terms of the political relations of the nation, and the economic good of the nation, both groups have one interest and therefore form one community, making the persecution of one part of it senseless. It was not 'the *Interest* of *England* to let a great Part of her Sober and Useful Inhabitants be destroy'd about Things that concern another World'.[45] The interest of the community here is regarded as determining the correct policy toward all the inhabitants of the nation. The interest of individuals, bound up with that of the community, should drive them to support for such a policy.

Penn imagined the public as a very close-knit community, his model for the relationships between the community of the whole nation being that of neighbours rather than a colder, more distant, contractarian relationship. In his earlier polemic he is economically orthodox in the sense of advocating honest dealing with others as the main moral imperative, but later, in 1693, he brings the community even closer together. In *Some fruits of solitude* Penn advocates a Christian attitude to property. 'Hardly any Thing is given us for our selves, but the Publick may claim a Share with us. But of all we call ours, we are most accountable to God and the Publick for our Estates.'[46] He goes on to envisage a straightforward communism in the name of the public: 'If all Men were so far Tenants to the Publick, that the Superfluities of Gain and Expence were applied to the Exigencies thereof, it would put an End to Taxes, leave never a Beggar, and make the greatest Bank for National Trade in Europe.'[47]

Penn moves from a standard statement of Christian responsibility to a notion of public ownership and common endeavour. Such a radical view was relatively rare, but what is significant is 'the public' become the measure of economic policy-making, rather than any more abstract measure of the common good. The use of the idea of the public makes concrete the nature of the responsibility of policy makers, and makes that responsibility more pressing.

While many terms were used in the seventeenth century to describe rhetorical communities for a variety of purposes, I would like to argue that the increase in the range of meanings that the word 'public' could have has great significance. It shifted from being used as an adjective to acquiring a meaning as a noun. This change demonstrates that, with increasing frequency after the Civil War, a community that encompassed the whole nation was invoked for political purposes. It became necessary, in political argument, not merely to refer to the good of the community in the abstract, but to ask of what in particular did that good consist. To substantiate any claim to act on behalf of the community, on the grounds that it had the capacity to organise itself and defend itself, the community had to be called into existence as a potentially active, rather than passive, agent. The public, or the people, could act, but it would be practically very difficult; the public could have an interest, however, which would make it clear who was acting on their behalf.

Ever since the medieval period an imagined general community was often invoked. It was important in a variety of spheres to use the idea of the community for a variety of different ends. The intellectual resources for this came from native communitarian traditions, the Roman law of corporations, as well as republican and conciliarist language. This was not necessarily inconsistent with a partly hierarchical view of society. The 'commonweal' could contain a great chain of being. The 'public' was not the only term that could be used for an imagined or rhetorical community, but the shift in meaning makes it a good illustration of the importance of a community of the imagination. Furthermore, the persistent ambiguity with which it was used demonstrates the complexity of the relationship between the public as an entity, as a group of individuals and as an area or a space.

The idea of a public space seems to require a public to occupy it. That public, as a national imagined community, came into existence during the seventeenth century. The 'public' claimed to bring together the people and the political space that they inhabited.

NOTES

1 Benedict Anderson applied this idea to the genesis of nationalism; Benedict Anderson, *Imagined communities: reflections on the origin and spread of nationalism* (London, Verso, 1983).

2 See, for instance, K. M. Baker, *Inventing the French revolution: essays on French political culture in the eighteenth century* (Cambridge, Cambridge University Press, 1990); C. J. Calhoun (ed.), *Habermas and the public sphere* (Cambridge MA, MIT Press, 1992); François Furet, *Interpreting the French revolution*, trans. Elborg Forster (Cambridge, Cambridge University Press, 1981); Tim Harris, *London crowds in the reign of Charles II* (Cambridge, Cambridge University Press, 1987); id., *Politics under the later Stuarts* (London, Longman, 1993); Mark Knights, *Politics and opinion in crisis, 1678–81* (Cambridge, Cambridge University Press, 1994); Steven Pincus, *Protestantism and patriotism: ideologies and the making of English foreign policy, 1650–88* (Cambridge, Cambridge University Press, 1996). The issue of public and private has been especially important to feminist historians. See J. B. Elshtain, *Public man, private woman: women in social and political thought* (Princeton NJ, Princeton University Press, 1981), and Amanda Vickery, 'Golden age to separate spheres? A review of the categories and chronologies of English women's history', *Historical Journal* 36 (1993), 383–414.

3 F. Gilbert, 'The humanist concept of the prince and *The Prince* of Machiavelli', *Journal of Modern History* 2 (1939), 449–83; Nicolai Rubinstein, *The government of Florence under the Medici, 1434–94* (Oxford, Clarendon Press, 1966); Quentin Skinner, *The foundations of modern political thought*, 2 vols (Cambridge, Cambridge University Press, 1978), I, pp. 94–138; Gary Ianziti, *Humanistic historiography under the Sforzas: politics and propaganda in fifteenth-century Milan* (Oxford, Clarendon Press, 1988).

4 On Renaissance ethics in general see M. P. Gilmore, *The world of humanism, 1453–1517* (New York, Harper, 1952); Jill Kraye, 'Moral philosophy', in Eckhard Kessler, Charles B. Schmitt and Quentin Skinner (eds), *The Cambridge history of Renaissance philosophy* (Cambridge, Cambridge University Press, 1988); Richard Tuck, 'Humanism and political thought', in Anthony Goodman and Angus MacKay (eds), *The impact of humanism on western Europe* (London, Longman, 1990); Brendan Bradshaw, 'Transalpine humanism', in J. H. Burns and Mark Goldie (eds), *The Cambridge History of Political Thought, 1450–1700* (Cambridge, Cambridge University Press, 1991); Marrku Peltonen, *Classical humanism and republicanism in English political thought, 1570–1640* (Cambridge, Cambridge University Press, 1995).

5 On Elyot see J. M. Major, *Sir Thomas Elyot and Renaissance humanism* (Lincoln NE, University of Nebraska Press, 1964); J. K. McConica, *English humanists and reformation politics* (Oxford, Clarendon Press, 1965).

6 Sir Thomas Elyot, *The boke of the gouernour*, ed. H. H. S. Croft, 2 vols (London, Kegan Paul, 1880), I, p. 2.

7 *Ibid.* I, p. 4.

8 *Ibid.* I, p. 7.

9 De la Place (1520–72) was an *advocat du roi* at the Cour des Aides before converting to Protestantism in 1560. He retired to Poitiers and wrote several Calvinist tracts before being restored to his post by Charles IX.

10 Pierre de la Place, *Politique discourses, treating of the differences and inequalities of vocations* (London, 1578), fols 55^r, 56^r. The philosophers here are either Plato or Cicero, who

quotes this Platonic definition in *De officiis*.

11 William Blandy, *The castl, or, picture of pollicy* (London, 1581), pp. 15–26.

12 For a biography of Whetstone (1545–87) see Thomas C. Izard, *George Whetstone, mid-Elizabethan man of letters* (New York, Columbia University Press, 1942). His play *Promos and Cassandra* has been identified as one of the sources of *Measure for Measure*, Charles T. Prouty, 'Whetstone and the sources for *Measure for Measure*', *Shakespeare Quarterly* 15 (1964), 131–45; George Whetstone, *A mirour for magestrates of cyties* (London, 1584), sig. A, 3ᵛ; id., *The English myrror* (London, 1586), prelims., sig., G, 5ʳ; p. 214.

13 On this text see Sidney Anglo, 'A Machiavellian solution to the Irish problem: Richard Beacon's *Solon his follie* (1594)', in Edward Chaney and Pete Mack (eds), *England and the Continental Renaissance: essays in honour of J. B. Trapp* (Woodbridge, Boydell, 1990), pp. 153–64; Richard Beacon, *Solon his follie, or, A politique discourse touching the reformation of commonweals* (London, 1594), p. 12.

14 William Shakespeare, *I Henry VI*, I.i; id., *Coriolanus*, III.i [William Shakespeare, *Complete Works*, ed. Stanley Wells and Gary Taylor (Oxford, Clarendon Press, 1988)].

15 William Shakespeare, *Anthony and Cleopatra*, V.i.

16 There are many accounts of these political events, including J. H. Hexter, *The reign of King Pym* (Cambridge MA, Harvard University Press, 1941); G. E. Aylmer, *The struggle for the constitution: England in the seventeenth century* (London, Blandford Press, 1963), pp. 103–39; Ivan Roots, *The Great Rebellion* (London, Batsford, 1966), pp. 32–66; Robert Ashton, *The English civil war* (London, Weidenfeld & Nicolson, 1978), pp. 129–88; Anthony Fletcher, *The outbreak of the English civil war* (London, Arnold, 1981). The best general accounts of the political thought of this crisis remain J. W. Allen, *English political thought, 1603–60 I, 1603–44* (London, Methuen, 1938), and Margaret Judson, *The crisis of the constitution* (New Brunswick NJ, Rutgers University Press, 1949).

17 *The declarations of both Houses of Parliament*, [42 May 12; 669f5(23)].

18 Henri duc de Rohan (1579–1638) was a soldier who became leader of the Huguenots in 1610 and remained so until 1629, when he joined the service of the Venetians, before returning to France in 1633. See M. H. de la Garde, *Le duc de Rohan et les Protestants sous Louis XIII* (Paris, 1885); Auguste Langel, *Henri de Rohan: son rôle politique et militaire sous Louis XIII, 1579–1638* (Paris, 1889).

19 Henri duc de Rohan, *A treatise of the interest of the princes and states of Christendome*, trans. H. Hunt (Paris, 1640), p. 1.

20 On Parker's career as a parliamentary propagandist see Michael Mendle, *Henry Parker and the English Civil War* (Cambridge, Cambridge University Press, 1995).

21 Henry Parker, *Some few observations upon His Maiesties late answer to the declaration or remonstrance of the Lords and Commons*, 19 May 1642, [42 May 21; E151(23)], p. 3.

22 Henry Parker, *Observations upon some of His Majesties late answers and expresses* [42 July 2; E144(20)], p. 5.

23 *Ibid.*, p. 22.

24 *Considerations for the Commons in this age of distractions*, [42 August 17; E112(17)], sig. A. 1ᵛ.

25 *The observator defended* [42 August 26; E114(19)], pp. 2, 6.

26 J. M., *A reply to the answer (printed by His Majesty's command at Oxford) to a printed booke intituled Observations* [43 February 3; E245(35)], p. 26.

27 On Digges and his views see Richard Tuck, *Natural rights theories* (Cambridge, Cambridge University Press, 1979), chapter 5; David L. Smith, *Constitutional royalism and the search for a settlement, c. 1640–49* (Cambridge, Cambridge University Press, 1994); Dudley Digges, *An answer to a printed book, intitled Observations upon some of His Majesties late answers* [42 November 20; E242(16)], p. 53.

28 See Michael Oakeshott, *Hobbes on civil association* (Oxford, Blackwell, 1975).

29 John Hall of Richmond, *Of government and obedience* (London, 1654), p. 87. Very little is known about the biography of John Hall.

30 *Ibid.*, p. 93.

31 On Nedham see the inaccurately titled *Cromwell's press agent: a critical biography of Marchmont Nedham, 1620–78* (Lanham MD, University Press of America, 1980) by Joseph Frank; Joad Raymond, *The invention of the newspaper: English newsbooks, 1641–49* (Oxford, Clarendon Press, 1996).

32 Marchmont Nedham, *The excellencie of a free state* (London, 1656), pp. 19–20.

33 *Ibid.*, p. 54.

34 *Ibid.*, p. 192.

35 Robert Boyle, *Occasional reflections upon several subjects* (London, 1665), sig. A8^r.

36 Edward Phillips, *The new world of words, or, a universal English dictionary* (London, 1696).

37 John Kersey, *Dictionarium Anglo-Britannicum* (London, 1708).

38 Algernon Sidney, *Discourses concerning government* (New York, Arno Press, 1979), p. 215.

39 *Ibid.*, p. 217.

40 John Locke, *Two treatises of government* (Cambridge, Cambridge University Press, 1960), II §96.

41 See Tuck, *Natural rights theories*; Annabel Brett, *Liberty, right and nature: individual rights in later scholastic thought* (Cambridge, Cambridge University Press, 1997).

42 Locke, *Two treatises of government*, II §87.

43 *Ibid.*, II §147, II §148.

44 John Locke, *Some considerations of the consequences of the lowering of interest, and raising the value of money*, in Patrick Hyde Kelly (ed.), *Locke on money*, 2 vols (Oxford, Clarendon Press, 1991), I, pp. 309–10.

45 William Penn, *Works*, 2 vols (London, 1726), II, p. 686.

46 *Ibid.*, I, p. 854.

47 *Ibid.*, I, p. 854.

Chapter 12

Contesting communities?
'Town' and 'gown' in Cambridge,
c. 1560₎1640

Alexandra Shepard

The history of town–gown relations in early modern Cambridge depicts a place uniquely riven by and renowned for conflict – unrivalled in its extremes except perhaps by Oxford. Although such an impression is not restricted to the early modern period of Cambridge's history, the late sixteenth and early seventeenth centuries have been feted as a time of particularly acute antagonism within an enduring pattern of tension. The established consensus is that '[f]rom the year 1231 ... the story of the relations of town and gown was one of endemic border warfare, with recurrent crises, the longest and fiercest being that under Elizabeth I'.[1]

Such an account is not entirely unwarranted, but nor is it entirely justified. It stems primarily from the sharp contemporary rhetoric and mythology of division rather than from the more complex reality of relations between the town and the university. This is not to argue that conflict did not exist in early modern Cambridge; to pursue such an extreme revisionist line would be as blinkered as seeing town–gown relations solely in terms of discord.[2] However, the portrayal of 'town' and 'gown' at war with each other, literally and metaphorically engaged in violent conflict, does vast disservice to the complexity of community relations and to the politics of identity and association in early modern Cambridge. Conflict was by no means exclusive to Cambridge, yet town–gown antagonism tends to be viewed in isolation as a somewhat comical peculiarity, precluding analysis of its more general relevance. There is a danger of perceiving 'town' and 'gown' as rigid categories defined solely in oppositional terms, predicated on the assumption that each formed separate and straightforwardly distinct communities of interest and affinity. While the juxtaposition of 'town' and 'gown', both in an abstract and in a literal sense, could evoke powerful alliances and hostilities, the template of town and gown was not neatly pasted on to the Cambridge landscape and automatically or unproblematically adopted by its inhabitants.

This chapter questions the image of Cambridge as systematically severed into two warring communities, in order to illustrate the complexity of the conception and experience of community in this particular early modern urban setting. 'Community' will be approached here as a collective identity articulated in terms of loyalty based on mutual interest and affinity. As such, community was both structurally and symbolically defined in early modern Cambridge. A distinction can be made between the ways in which notions of community were *narrated* in ideological and symbolic terms, and *experienced* in structural terms, as collective life and loyalties were shaped and mediated by the institutions of the town and the university. Analysis of community in an exclusively socio-structural sense has recently been rejected in preference for a definition of community as ideology constructed through symbolic boundaries.[3] What is perhaps most interesting about Cambridge is the ways in which the structures and symbolism of community were *interrelated*, since the symbolic construction of community drew its conceptual strength from the structural framework within which it was conceived, without necessarily being fully determined by it. In early modern Cambridge the symbolism or *narratives* of community in terms of collective identities and loyalties were heavily determined by, yet also at times in stark contrast to, the structural complexities of relations between the town and university. Although the staunch rhetoric of town–gown rivalry had very definite roots in the existence of two distinct institutions of urban government, there is a risk of allowing stereotypes of 'town' and 'gown' to obscure the numerous axes along which town and university interlocked as well as divided. Furthermore, the degree of structural overlap often produced other, possibly fleeting, yet nonetheless potent, symbolic boundaries, which, as this chapter will argue, were sometimes viewed by the authorities as potentially more threatening to social stability than the town–gown divide.

Neither the structural peculiarities of early modern Cambridge nor the powerful narratives of town and university identities were sufficiently pervasive to preclude notions of an overarching urban community encompassing both town and gown. Nor did they rule out multiple points of overlap between, or acute political division within, each corporation of town and university. The town corporation was not without its fair share of factional dispute during this period, and the interests of the 'public' body of the university – officially comprising its chancellor, fellows, and scholars – did not always easily coincide with the concerns of its 'private' subsidiaries, the colleges.[4] These points are illustrated below in two sections. The first briefly outlines the sources of jurisdictional conflict between the governing bodies of town and university and the rhetoric surrounding it, before situating it within the broader context of institutional co-operation, shared interests and interdependence. The conflict in Cambridge neither signalled the absence of any larger concept of urban community (in rhetorical terms at least) nor functioned as a measure of its decline, but was instead a product of mutual interdependence in changing social and political circumstances. The second section looks beyond the formal relations of the two governing bodies to explore how identities of 'town' and 'gown' were experienced and manipulated across a broader social spectrum, and it suggests some of the other axes of alliance and tension which existed alongside those of town and gown and which produced contrary sets of loyalty and identity. Such evidence demonstrates that multiple communities of interest and affinity were formed and reformed along numerous lines of division and cohesion cutting across the town–gown divide. The town and university were not neatly defined 'separate spheres'. Nor were the categories of 'town' and 'gown' such rigid sources of identity and loyalty as has been maintained; they were embedded in a much more complex and fluid network of shifting alliances and interests. Through contextualising the often mythical narratives of town–gown discord within the practical relations between the town and university, this chapter demonstrates the intricate complexity of articulations and experiences of community in early modern Cambridge.

Cambridge was not alone in experiencing factional disputes over liberties, privileges and jurisdiction in the late sixteenth and early seventeenth centuries.[5] It differed from many other early modern towns in having two separate arms of urban government which provided an additional dimension of division and conflict. Yet in many ways even this feature was not dissimilar to the state of affairs in cathedral towns, where the dean and chapter were also incorporated.[6] The primary sources of tension between the two corporations of borough and university were the latter's jurisdiction in Cambridge and the privileges enjoyed by university members and servants. Disputes over these issues produced and drew upon a range of florid myths portraying town and gown locked in venomous conflict as each side attempted to bolster its case. Although undoubtedly stemming from real tensions, such rhetorical flourishes constructed politically motivated symbolic boundaries between town and gown which can easily obscure the extent of routine town–gown co-operation and interdependence.

Royal favour engendered both the consolidation and expansion of the university's considerable jurisdiction and privileges during this period. The university was entitled to determine a significant range of legal business involving its members and servants according to its own customs, and its several courts rivalled the mayor's borough court and the Bishop of Ely's consistory in Cambridge.[7] The university also held extensive regulative powers within the town over a broad range of offences. It had dominated the economic administration of the town since 1382 by a grant of the assizes of bread and ale in response to the town's insurrection during the Peasants' Revolt. Disciplinary matters also occupied the university courts, which were empowered to punish various forms of disorder either involving or tending to the corruption of scholars, and the university enjoyed the right to search out and banish all vagrants, prostitutes and suspicious persons within a one-mile radius of the town. Depending on the offence, a variety of sanctions were employed against suspected and guilty parties, ranging from fines, imprisonment and penance to 'discommuning' – by which university custom was denied to particular traders in the town. Added to this extensive jurisdiction, the university and its servants (who, as we shall see, were numerous) enjoyed many other privileges. They were exempt from the routine charges and duties of the borough, from military service and from financial contribution to it. Their horses were safe from being requisitioned by royal commission and their markets were excused from provisioning the royal household. Finally, they were exempt from all subsidies, minus the token £10 paid annually to the Exchequer for the assizes of bread and ale.

That such privileges were a source of resentment is hardly surprising. The university jealously guarded its rights against any hint of infringement by the town authorities, and the years between 1560 and 1640 saw a series of grievances and petitions submitted by both bodies to the Privy Council for arbitration and redress. The university stood poised to defend any perceived encroachment by the town. Royal directives to Justices of the Peace concerning the regulation of victuallers during periods of Lenten fasting or high grain prices intermittently provoked flashes of tension whenever the town authorities attempted their implementation – a move which the university interpreted as an assault on its jurisdiction over victuallers, and against which its authorities sought and won royal protection in 1564, 1586, 1590 and 1597.[8] The university's right to license victuallers and set prices was similarly asserted and defended in two lengthy cases: one in the 1580s, when the intervention of a Queen's official in licensing a Cambridge vintner aroused considerable town support, and another in 1629 when several chandlers and their associates were discommuned for selling overpriced goods.[9] The limits of the university's jurisdiction were regularly tested in Chesterton, a village in the suburbs of Cambridge, where several incidents in which local officials refused to concede the university's regulatory authority over entertainments (such as plays and bear-baitings) generated more university complaints.[10] Attempts to assess university members and their servants for musters incurred another flurry of petitions in 1569, 1588 and 1591, and a rejection of their right to common land for grazing hogs in 1587 unleashed further lengthy rehearsals of university privileges and town grievances by both bodies.[11]

Just as the university sought external intervention and arbitration when it perceived its privileges to be under threat, so the town mounted similar appeals to the Privy Council when it believed those privileges were being abused. In 1596 thirty-two articles of complaint were drawn up by the corporation, ranging from several grievances against the university night watch for aggressive and unlawful searches to charges of bribery and corruption in the university's regulation of the market and Sturbridge fair. The town subsequently issued a further set of similar complaints, also protesting that the university's jurisdiction undermined the work of the justices at the quarter sessions. This was especially resented because the university justices neglected to attend either the sessions or gaol delivery and claimed exclusive jurisdiction over their own members. Privileged status was a particular point of contention, with town complaints that the university abused its powers of patronage in appointing too many 'scholars' servants', thereby exempting many of the town's wealthiest inhabitants from borough charges and subsidies.[12]

Privileged status was extended by the university beyond its graduates in the town to the many Cambridge inhabitants (both male and female) who supplied it with provisions and services as well as many of their servants and dependants.[13] Members of the town corporation objected that the number of 'scholars servants' in the town compounded the severe financial burden of subsidies, complaining in 1596 that privileged persons (exempt from such assessments) outnumbered 'the Subsedye men of the towne'.[14] Unsurprisingly, town grievances such as these coincided with periods of considerable economic hardship. The corporation's petitions of the 1590s were undoubtedly related to the high grain prices and increased demands for relief consequent upon harvest failure, just as recurrent objections to the number of privileged persons in the 1630s were a response to further heavy demographic pressure on resources exacerbated by the considerable burden of ship money. Privileged status increased the economic burden of the town, and the university's jurisdiction restricted the autonomy of both the corporation and the county justices to compensate through regulative measures.

Conflicts of interest between the two corporations were therefore inevitable (particularly in years of economic strain), given the expansive jurisdictional status of the university and the marked structural impact of the university's presence in Cambridge. Both bodies jealously guarded their rights and precedence through the cultivation of patrons at court and appeals for external arbitration and redress. The university was particularly well placed to benefit from such political manoeuvrings, since the Crown retained a vested interest in it as an arm of government with responsibility for moulding future generations of statesmen and clergy. Styled as 'nurseries ... of good learnynge and vertuous educacion', the universities were regarded as instruments of state, and their privileges were preserved intact during this period with the aid of heavy royal backing.[15]

The jurisdictional disputes followed formulaic patterns and entailed reams of colourful rhetoric and myth-making. Conflict between the two corporations was played out like an injury suit writ large, with exaggerated appeals addressed to external arbitrators. The town typically accused the university of violent and unlawful abuses, which the university countered with charges of malice and envy, and both sought to emphasise their victimisation in the face of the other side's aggression. The town detailed violent affronts and fraudulent exactions by university officials, and cast the university courts as the 'Townesmen['s] scourge', claiming that the university was deliberately biased in suits against townspeople and unlawfully protective of its own interests.[16] The university was particularly deft at marshalling precedents of conflict and elaborating a tradition of discord and antagonism. Its petitions sought to delineate an often implausible history of helplessness and to emphasise the custom of royal protection. University grievances repeatedly referred to 'the auncient practise of our old malicious neighbours of the towne' which was part of a history of 'querrelous disposition[s] and insolent behavior'. Violent images were invoked, such as the reference to the mayor and justices' designs to 'geve our charters a deadly stroke', and patrons were acknowledged for (and thereby reminded of) their role as 'a stronge bucklar and a speciall defence'.[17] The university's commemorative techniques could recall as far back as the Peasants' Revolt, with implicit and explicit references to the town's insurrection and subsequent subordination. The dramatic events of 1381, including the myth of townsmen burning university charters (belied by surviving muniments), were frequently recalled.[18] Such appeals to the past were punctuated by characterisations of particular individuals who were deemed to epitomise this long-running trend of malice. Hence the mayor of 1587 was condemned by the vice-chancellor for his 'singular inhumanity', his 'savage cruelty' and his 'terrible envy', verging on 'madness'.[19]

However, despite the rhetorical power of such images, and beyond the evidence of instances of conflict between the two Cambridge corporations (particularly in the 1590s and 1630s), we should be wary against colluding too far with the myth-making indulged in by both town and gown to further their political interests. For all the charges of malice, envy and corruption, the rhetoric of petitions also indirectly invoked an ideal of co-operation – which was furthermore a significant feature of the reality of relations between the town and university in early modern Cambridge. Although motivated by considerable exasperation with the town–gown disunity of 1596, the university's chancellor, Lord Burghley, chastisingly appealed to an ideal of co-operation: 'you and the Towne are by Corporacion two severall Bodies, so yet consideringe yowe as both derived under one Head, which is the Queens Majestie, yow may also unite yourselves under that Heade'.[20] Such co-operation was regularly achieved in Cambridge, although inevitably it did not receive the degree of attention or elaboration surrounding the tradition of conflict, devoid of much political mileage, and a far less eye-catching strand in the overall fabric of town–gown relations. There is also a danger of over-drawing the urban conflict of this period – particularly of the 1590s. As has been observed of late Elizabethan London, 'the polemics into which men are drawn in the heat of a particular conflict are not necessarily typical of their normal positions'.[21] Furthermore, conflict and community were not mutually exclusive: more often the former is suggestive of the latter.[22] Indeed, many of the Cambridge petitions were suggestive of an ideal – possibly even a norm – of neighbourly association and collaboration between the two bodies. Imputations of malice and envy were the typical constituents of disputes between neighbours, and were a regular feature of litigation during this period (particularly in the church courts) which ideally sought the restoration of Christian harmony.[23] The conflict in Cambridge was articulated in compar-able terms, similarly exploiting and appealing to norms of concord, and – as in other early modern towns – reconciliation was regularly sought through the mediation and arbitration of the Privy Council.[24]

Invoking the language of concord and good fellowship, the town and university consistently referred to each other as 'neighbours' who ideally combined to protect 'the commonwealth of this University and Town of Cambridge', as it was put in a composition between them in 1575. This ideal was mirrored in Privy Council orders, such as those which urged the vice-chancellor and mayor to 'consulte, accord, and agree, in one good minde' – in this case for the implementation of measures against unlawful games.[25] There is plentiful evidence that such alliance was regularly achieved between the two corporations, which raises the possibility that conflict was the exception rather than the rule. Although permanent sources of tension between the two bodies undoubtedly did exist, they were generally subordinated to the need for co-operation, and outright conflict was comparatively rare. At best, collaboration may be viewed as more typical than conflict in town–gown relations; at the very least, it is possible to demonstrate that co-operation and overlap between the town and university were as much a feature in Cambridge as strife and division.

The administrative bodies of town and gown routinely combined to implement a wide range of measures for the health and safety of Cambridge inhabitants, and to provide employment and relief for the increasing numbers of the town's destitute. Of enduring concern to both governing bodies was the joint provision of clean and safe streets in Cambridge – in terms of their basic fabric and their human traffic. In 1575 a composition between the university and the town was drawn up to ensure that the town's streets were well paved, sufficiently lit at night, without risk of fire, and dung-free. Stemming from the Paving Act of 1544, and renewed again in 1616 and 1628, this composition involved considerable administrative co-operation by the mayor and vice-chancellor. They jointly appointed carters, overseers and assessors from each parish, and combined twice yearly for sessions of the Paving Leet for the punishment of offenders. It also involved a joint annual perambulation of the town by the mayor and vice-chancellor, ritually symbolic of the coalescence of town and gown authorities.[26]

This was not the only occasion on which the mayor and vice-chancellor combined in civic ritual. They joined forces regularly in commissions and at the quarter sessions and assizes, and attended meetings and weekly services at Great St Mary's, which was both the university and the corporation church. Positioned equidistant from the Guildhall and the university's Schools, Great St Mary's thus functioned as a shared and overlapping public space for each body. More informal civic ritual also ensured the social association of town and gown officials. The vice-chancellor was customarily invited by the mayor and bailiffs to their annual feast on Michaelmas Day, and it caused great offence when the invitation was not extended in 1586.[27] Somewhat less formal hospitality between the two bodies was also frequent, as in 1589 – not long after an episode of town–gown division over grazing rights – when the town accounts recorded £4 3s spent on 'a supper at Mr. Maiors bestowed upon certeyne of the Universitie and certeyne of the heads of the towne'.[28]

Such interaction was not merely the product of a shared environment, but stemmed from the acute administrative and regulative concerns of both the town and the university in response to a steadily increasing influx of migrants from the 1580s. This was particularly evident in combined measures to combat deterioration in Cambridge housing. The quality of tenements was of considerable mutual concern to the governors of both town and university, as well as to central authorities, leading to extensive co-operation in regulative measures, particularly in the 1620s. From the 1580s the Privy Council issued a steady flow of directives to the vice-chancellor and mayor to reduce the risk of overcrowding in Cambridge. These involved commissioning regular surveys – jointly administered – of the number of inmates lodging in Cambridge, of the subdivision of tenements and of the extent of thatched roofing, and by the late 1610s the mayor and vice-chancellor were holding weekly sessions for the presentment of offenders and the publication of joint orders.[29]

One of the major anxieties behind such co-operation was the fear of disease and disorder associated with poverty and overcrowding. Such fears were not misplaced, as Cambridge suffered several bouts of plague in this period, with major outbreaks in 1625 and 1630–31. Unlike the crisis years of the 1590s, when town and gown relations ruptured in the face of administrative pressure, in times of plague the official regulative bodies of the university and the corporation pulled together in attempts to contain the spread of disease and to distribute relief to the infected and the indigent, many of whom were impoverished by the mass exodus of scholars from Cambridge at the first sign of contagion. The mayor and vice-chancellor convened emergency sessions (sometimes daily) to enforce orders for the control of infection and for the distribution of relief.[30] Churchwardens, overseers, sergeants and constables were marshalled alongside university officials to direct and discipline the ranks of Cambridge householders (including scholars' servants), acting as agents of the joint authority of town and university. Although colleges fortified themselves against the threat of diseased 'outsiders' from the town,[31] town–gown distinctions were superseded at the level of government at least by the shared responsibility of the mayor and vice-chancellor to act as 'publick men' – as it was put in a letter drafted by them both in 1631. This letter endorsed its plea for help against crippling trading restrictions in Cambridge with the 'hands and seals of two corporations now united not only in place but in care and providence'.[32]

Yet, as we have seen, such unity was not only a product of the very extreme straits of plague such as in 1630–31 when weekly poor relief could exceed £200 and a national brief was deemed necessary by the Crown for the collection of sufficient aid for the town.[33] In times of such acute need the spectre of riot began to loom, as was threatened in a letter penned by the mayor and vice-chancellor to a neighbouring Justice of the Peace, claiming 'it is impossible for us any longer to restraine our poore, & keepe them in that awe, & obedience which we have hitherto done'.[34] Concern for order was a perennial feature of urban government in the late sixteenth and early seventeenth centuries, even without the threat of plague, and Cambridge was no exception. Its population had trebled between 1560 and 1620, and the numerous Privy Council orders regarding overcrowding in Cambridge were a measure of the perceived seriousness of the problem. It was blatantly in the interests of the governing bodies of both town and university to join together in regulating the town's poor. This mutual interest far outweighed any division over jurisdiction and privileges in the late sixteenth and early seventeenth centuries. Co-operation over poor relief continued even at the height of town–gown division in the late 1590s, with the mayor and vice-chancellor implementing measures to establish a house of correction in 1597 and to reassess the systems of relief in Cambridge's most overburdened parishes in 1598.[35]

Such collaboration, provoked by a shared interest in maintaining order, is not the stuff of the myth-making or the collective memory which informs group identity, and so it is largely absent from the commemorative narratives either of the town or the university in early modern Cambridge and beyond.[36] Yet it was a prevailing feature of town–gown relations which demonstrates that jurisdictional conflict between the two corporations by no means out-balanced or undermined the mutual interests of their governing bodies in an ordered and stable urban environment. Hostility between the two governing bodies was the product of specific and largely contained jurisdictional grievances, the rhetoric of which should not be allowed to mask the reality of formal town–gown relations, which were routinely based on strategic co-operation born out of mutual interest.

Beyond the formal relationship of the two corporations, town–gown conflict and interdependence were both more broadly experienced and exploited in Cambridge. Furthermore, town–gown connections were superseded by many other axes of alliance and interest – as well as division and conflict – which both overlapped with and diverged from the concerns and loyalties of the governing elites. Although the symbolic categories, as well as the structural foundations, of 'town' and 'gown' variously informed the identities, interests and loyalties of Cambridge inhabitants, they were also undercut by other complex networks of alliance and affinity. To varying degrees, the inhabitants of Cambridge occupied multiple communities of interest and identity which run the risk of being obscured by the dominant rhetoric of town–gown conflict. Despite holding powerful sway over many Cambridge residents, the symbolic narratives of 'town' and 'gown' coexisted with and were muddied and contradicted by structural ambiguities and competing bonds of interest and concern.

The degree to which town–gown hostilities were conveniently exploited, if not deeply felt, is evident in the many outbreaks of violence between townspeople and university members in sixteenth and seventeenth-century Cambridge, although there is a risk of reading too much into such incidents if they are viewed without reference to the broader context of routine violent exchange in this period. Men on both sides were quickly mobilised when group pride or boundaries of status or territory were threatened. This was particularly true of the youthful populations of both town and university, whose willingness to enlist their support could be exploited by their office-holding counterparts to add weight to jurisdictional grievances. In 1591, for example, Richard Parish, a constable of Chesterton, escaped arrest by university officers with the help of the apprentices at Sturbridge fair, having appealed to them that he had once been an apprentice and needed their support against the scholars who had wronged him.[37] Such violence was not merely the product of youthful high spirits, as young men willingly engaged in any excuse to demonstrate their manly prowess. More established inhabitants of the town were motivated to provide an intimidating presence on occasion. The numerous clashes involving university officers and householders of the town are evidence that many of Cambridge's inhabitants felt implicated in the jurisdictional differences between town and gown, as university officials impinged on their lives in the shape of aggressive night searches and present-ments which aroused deep-felt resentment and violent retaliation. Such violence was not simply the product of random outbursts of uncontrolled anger, but ritually staged and self-consciously stylised by its actors in symbolic contests for authority and precedence.[38]

Yet, however characteristic of late sixteenth and early seventeenth-century Cambridge, the rituals of town–gown violence appear somewhat less sensational or extraordinary when placed beside the many other violent expressions of group rivalries, and when they are understood as part of a wider context of disputed authority routinely confronted by officials from both corporations. Of all the assault cases brought before the university courts between 1591 and 1640 for which depositions survive, those involving a clash of university members with townspeople were in a minority (20·5 per cent). The vast majority of cases (68·5 per cent) were between townspeople alone, while the remaining 11 per cent exclusively involved university members. It should be noted that by far the most serious incidents of group violence in this period were those mounted by university members against others of their own body. Violence on a grand scale was a regular feature at college plays, at which college rivalries were acted out alongside the drama, often along the lines of a geographical divide between north and south.[39] The most serious incident of university violence in this period stemmed from constitutional division between junior and senior members. In 1594 newly and controversially elected university officials were barred from the Regent House, and the ensuing tumult so alarmed the vice-chancellor and heads of the colleges that they appealed to Lord Burghley for immediate intervention, claiming that:

> Such a notorious ryotte and disorder lately happening amongst us, and yet also in some degree continueing as in case it be not forthwith severely mette with, it is very likely to shake the groundeworke of all peace and government both privately in our Colledges and publicquely in the Universitye[40]

This breach of order was deemed by both university and central authorities to be as serious as any comparable friction between town and gown.

Violence on a smaller scale also revealed fissures within the broader bodies of both town and gown besides the tensions between them. University officials were vulnerable to assault and retaliative ridicule by students as well as townspeople, and town constables seem to have encountered episodes of resistance to their authority in Cambridge parishes similar to those weathered by university proctors. Objections to official intervention by agents of both bodies were often couched in the same terms of disputed authority and jurisdiction, with resistance to the university proctors matched by resentment against constables, as Cambridge inhabitants sought to question or avoid the regulative arm of the law.[41] Such contests often – although not always – coincided with an agenda of town–gown antagonism, and were consequently articulated in terms of town–gown division, although this was by no means the only basis for friction. Alongside rapid social polarisation, university government was becoming decreasingly democratic, and the town authorities increasingly oligarchic, all of which put strains on vertical ties of allegiance. At a time when popular disaffection was a major concern for authorities through-out England, the template of town–gown division therefore may well have served the mutual interests of both governing bodies in Cambridge, since it encouraged at least the impression of vertical ties of affinity and loyalty within the town, and deflected popular discontent on to the rival institution of the university. Somewhat paradoxically, it is possible that town–gown disharmony – particularly in the 1590s – actually functioned indirectly as a source of political and social stability. Emphasis on the fissure between 'town' and 'gown' contrived to reiterate notions of community and social harmony, since it was a means of privileging vertical over horizontal solidarities. In this way, Cambridge inhabitants played their own particular variation of the 'common-weal tune', ironically founded upon discordant relations between the two corporations, in a precarious bid to preserve the social order.[42]

Yet town–gown loyalties, however partial or contrived, did not always supersede other more horizontal ties. A series of examinations in 1633 affords a glimpse of violent protest against the enclosure of an area of common ground known as Parker's Piece – which involved combined forces of scholars and townspeople in defiance of the university proctors. Scholars from several colleges were presented for pulling up rails and creating a disturbance along-side servants from the town and several women. John Parker of Emmanuel confessed that he had overheard three women behind the college garden wall saying that 'there would be some thing to doe at Parkers Peece', and another witness said that he had heard the women in conversation with students urge that they 'did hope that the schollers would take theere parts'.[43] It is impossible to know how lasting such alliances may have been, but their existence is nonetheless significant. Other numerous examples of fleeting ties are those which were formed between students and young men in the town when they embarked on joint ventures of illicit hunting, carousing and excess, forming elaborate drinking and gambling networks.[44] The potential for disruption in such ties was not lost on the university, and was regretfully summed up in a marginal note to examinations taken concerning an affray of 1592 between scholars and the villagers of Coton, which observed, 'thus townsmen and ther sons keep misrule in the felds as well as schollers but all goeth in the name and slander of schollers and the universitie'.[45] This rueful statement alone demonstrates that even when violence was ostensibly pitched along town–gown lines, it could nonetheless involve more complex and contradictory alliances. This incident also provides indirect evidence of a phenomenon which was a perpetual source of anxiety for both university and town authorities: young men from a broad social spectrum and different affiliations had a common interest in pursuing counter-codes of disorderly conduct in collective bids for manly stature among their peers which often overcame town–gown allegiances. Increasingly, in the early seventeenth century, the university took particular pains to keep its charges separate and contained from the corrupting influence of the town youth, in recognition of the threat to order posed by such links.[46]

Not all points of contact and alliance between town and gown were quite so fleeting or illicit, however. More lasting and comparatively 'respectable' bonds of friendship (in its full range of early modern meanings) and of business linked and cut across the two communities of town and gown. Having been found in the Rose tavern supping and listening to musicians in the company of students, Margaret Litchfield objected to the officious intervention of the university proctor and protested that 'she did not know but she might have gone to the Taverne to supper with her frendes'.[47] Such innocuous ties of friendship claimed by this examinant did indeed exist, and can occasionally be glimpsed in the incidental details of depositional evidence. Students of Corpus Christi College involved in an injury suit between two townswomen had witnessed the incident while playing tennis at the defendant's house, which suggests at the very least a friendship of convenience serving the scholars' recreational interests. Cultivation of more traditional networks of hospitality is evident in witnesses' accounts of university members regularly dining with inhabitants of the town.[48] Links were often fostered along regional lines, with expressions of county loyalty providing the basis for friendship, as in the case of Paul Glisson of Trinity Hall, who deposed that he had often kept company with Giles Sandford of Cambridge as a result of being his 'Cuntryman' from Dorset.[49] Religious affinity could also form the basis of connections between town and gown. The doctrinal disputes waged during this period by Cambridge scholars were by no means confined to college chapels and the university Schools. University radicals often received backing from the town, such as the puritan divine, John Preston of Emmanuel College, who was offered the lectureship of Trinity Church in 1624 at the behest of its parishioners, who, despite royal intervention, were prepared to double the stipend and to spurn the more moderate candidate put forward by the heads of colleges.[50]

Many town–gown connections had economic foundations. The commercial interests of the two bodies were deeply enmeshed, with the university heavily dependent on the town for its provisions and the town likewise reliant on the university for a significant portion of its livelihood. At an individual level, university members were variously bound to people in the town, and not simply through running up debts with local traders. College fellows entered into numerous bonds, often jointly with men from the town, as they engaged in a variety of business dealings. For example, John Betts of Trinity Hall dealt in Saffron, John Johnson of St John's College undertook an extensive building project at Barnwell, and many fellows were active in money-lending ventures.[51] Nor did credit networks flow solely in one direction, as fellows borrowed money from townspeople as well as lending it to creditors. Hence a witness in a testamentary suit of 1611 declared that Mr Sleepe of Trinity College had borrowed £10 worth of plate from Mistress Warren before her death. Lower-scale loans were also raised by students through pawning goods (particularly clothing) in exchange for small sums of cash.[52] Town and gown were similarly linked through land-holding patterns, with leases and land being exchanged between both the institutions of town and university and the individuals belonging to them.[53]

Elaborate networks of lasting economic interdependence grew out of such transactions, which were often founded on equally significant ties of patronage. The university wielded weighty powers of patronage in Cambridge, which were both sought after and manipulated by the town's inhabitants. The sizeable population of privileged persons functioned as a kind of ambiguous buffer zone between town and gown, alternately claimed or rejected by either body according to the circumstances. So, for example, when the vice-chancellor and heads published orders regarding the impending visit of their chancellor in 1629, townspeople (banned from the proceedings in Trinity College) were defined as 'privileged persons, burgesses or foreynors', yet when the university barred its members from trading with certain individuals in the town, privileged persons were classed as being of the university.[54] Cambridge inhabitants also manipulated the ambiguities surrounding privileged status. Thomas Barker sought to evade the charges brought against him before a university court by Agnes Bradley, claiming that he was not subject to its jurisdiction because at the time of the alleged injury he was 'not hiered by eny scholler', although at the time of his warning to appear he 'was in a schollers worcke'.[55] It is doubtful he would have been willing to draw such a distinction had *he* been making the allegations.

In other instances privileged status was claimed more positively, as by William Waggett, the porter of Trinity Hall, who confidently expected the university to champion his cause when in conflict with town constables, crying out as he was dragged to the stocks that 'they had done moore then they could answer, & that he waggett had freinds or his masters of trinity hall that should right him'.[56] Privileged status was highly sought after, not merely as a defence against enraged constables but as a lucrative form of patronage which in turn seems to have generated a secondary trade in selling on university offices.[57] It conferred the benefits of exemption from subsidies and borough duties; it assigned eligibility to university jurisdiction, which (for all the complaints against the university courts' criminal jurisdiction) provided swift and comparatively cheap justice in civil actions for debt and injury, and it entailed perquisites such as privileged access to college leases. Perhaps most importantly, the existence of privileged status is a reminder that, even in jurisdictional terms, the population of Cambridge could not be neatly categorised in terms of 'town' and 'gown' – a situation which was further complicated by the ever-increasing number of 'foreigners' and immigrants with no firm roots or jurisdictional status.

Yet the category of 'scholars' servant' also involved more than jurisdictional boundaries. Lasting contracts of service engendered deep-rooted loyalties, which found expression in the wills left both by university masters and their servants. In 1588, for example, Roger Harrison, who was both the innkeeper of the Ram in Cambridge and the college barber of St John's, left his swan mark and its proceeds to the college. Thomas Taylor, butler of the same college, also left a bequest of 100s to be spent on a feast in his memory for the entire college.[58] University men could be generous to their employees, sometimes leaving them sizeable bequests, and demonstrating their considerable trust by appointing their retainers from the town as executors and witnesses of their wills.[59] Such instances were related to more abstract feelings of mutual obligation which are evident in charitable bequests by university members to the town. Some of these were substantial, such as the £1,000 left to the town corporation to foster the careers of young tradesmen by the will of Stephen Perse, a Doctor of Medicine and fellow of Gonville and Caius College.[60] Certain wills are indicative of the deep roots and alliances felt by university men who made their home in the town, such as that of Thomas Lorkin, another Doctor of Medicine, who left elaborate arrangements for four annual feasts to be held for the twelve jurors of Chesterton, alongside money for the poor and for church repairs.[61] His ties with Chesterton were obviously as strong as those he felt towards any of the three Cambridge colleges of which he had been a member. Charitable impulses could also flow from town to gown, as recorded in the town accounts, which itemised 5s given by the mayor in 1633 to 'two schollers in want'.[62]

Such evidence is indicative of just a few of the many points of overlap and alliance which served to entwine various levels of 'town' and 'gown', and which ranged from fleeting associations of interest to enduring links of loyalty and affinity. Cutting across such 'overlapping circles'[63] of interest and alliance were other lines of division and tension, of which town–gown antagonism was only one dimension. The template of 'town' and 'gown' was a powerful set of identities which intersected with and overlaid many of the other axes of division, manipulated by both governing bodies to gain political mileage, and appropriated by many Cambridge inhabitants to serve their varied needs and interests. But the myth-making and resultant narratives of town–gown antagonism also served to mask and offset other sources of tension, by providing an alternative focus for popular discontent in times of economic pressure such as the 1590s, or by acting as a counterbalance to the threat of disruption associated with the large population of male youth. In this and other ways the images of town and gown pitted against each other could, albeit at times precariously, be used to override the deep divisions *within* both the town and the university, and could therefore function indirectly as a source of stability.

The symbolic boundaries of community created and exploited in Cambridge belied the complexity of mutual interlocking and overlap. In practice, town–gown jurisdictional hostilities were routinely overcome and superseded by the mutual interest of both governing bodies in disciplining and regulating the burgeoning population. Although the corporations of town and gown at times presented themselves as warring counterparts, they nonetheless were heavily dependent on each other economically – an interdependence which was daily acted out via face-to-face credit networks of exchange and mutual obligation. The jarring rhetoric of petitions by the mayor and burgesses or the vice-chancellor and heads to their respective patrons or to the Privy Council is significantly muted when placed beside the mundane dealings and co-operation that sustained the two bodies throughout this period. Conflict in early modern Cambridge did not preclude communities of interest and affinity between town and gown, but instead grew out of them. 'Community' in early modern Cambridge was therefore neither as absent (in terms of an overarching urban community) or as present (in terms of separate communities of town and gown) as either contemporaries or their historians would have us believe. Its rhetoric also served to mask other axes of tension which were played out along lines of class, age and gender. The existence of town–gown tensions did not exclude the possibility of town–gown alliance, and the existence of 'town' and 'gown' as rigid and unbending categories of identity into which the inhabitants of Cambridge neatly fell was as much a myth as the so-called 'endemic warfare' between them.

NOTES

I am grateful to Patrick Collinson, Konstantin Dierks, David Jarvis, Elisabeth Leedham-Green, Keith Wrightson and the participants in seminars at the Centre for Urban History at the University of Leicester and the Centre for Local History at the University of East Anglia for their comments on earlier versions of this chapter.

1 J. P. C. Roach (ed.), *A history of Cambridgeshire and the Isle of Ely*, 9 vols (London, Oxford University Press, 1938–89), III, p. 76. See also Roland Parker, *Town and gown: the 700 years' war in Cambridge* (Cambridge, Stephens, 1983); Nick Mansfield, 'Grads and snobs: John Brown, town and gown in early nineteenth-century Cambridge', *History Workshop Journal* 35 (1993), 184–98.

2 For a revisionist account of 'symbiosis' between town and gown in Oxford see Carl I. Hammer, Jr, 'Oxford town and Oxford university', in *The history of the University of*

Oxford, 8 vols (1984–), III, ed. James McConica (Oxford, Oxford University Press, 1986).

3 Anthony P. Cohen, *The symbolic construction of community* (London, Routledge, 1989). See also Benedict Anderson, *Imagined communities: reflections on the origin and spread of nationalism*, revised edition (London, Verso, 1991).

4 For a contemporary usage of this 'public/private' analogy see below, p. 226.

5 See Peter Clark, '"The Ramoth-Gilead of the good": urban change and political radicalism at Gloucester, 1540–1640'; Roger Howell, Jr, 'Newcastle and the nation: the seventeenth-century experience'; David Harris Sacks, 'The corporate town and the English state: Bristol's 'little businesses', 1625–41', all in Jonathan Barry (ed.), *The Tudor and Stuart town: a reader in English urban history, 1530–1688* (Harlow, Longman, 1990). See also C. G. Curston, '"Wild as colts untamed": radicalism in the Newbury area in the early modern period', in Barry Stapleton (ed.), *Conflict and community in southern England* (Stroud, Sutton, 1992).

6 See, e.g., P. J. Withington, 'Urban political culture in later seventeenth-century England: York, 1649–88' (unpublished Ph.D. dissertation, University of Cambridge, 1998).

7 Alexandra Shepard, 'Legal learning and the Cambridge university courts, *c.* 1560–1640', *Journal of Legal History* 19 (1998), 62–74, pp. 63–6.

8 C. H. Cooper, *Annals of Cambridge*, 5 vols, vol. V, ed. J. W. Cooper (Cambridge, Warwick & Co., 1842–1908), II, pp. 180–1, 416–17, 481–3, 565.

9 *Ibid.* II, pp. 399–400, 405–6, 418, 431; III, pp. 214–17. See also C[ambridge] U[niversity] A[rchive], CUR 37.1.

10 See, e.g., Cooper, *Annals* II, pp. 383–5, 514–18.

11 *Ibid.* II, pp. 240–1, 249, 455, 490–1, 437–49.

12 *Ibid.* II, pp. 548–56, 559–61.

13 *Ibid.* II, pp. 473–5.

14 *Ibid.* II, p. 561. See also CUA, CUR 36.1 for similar complaints in the 1630s.

15 Privy Council to University of Cambridge, 29 July 1593, transcribed in Alan H. Nelson (ed.), *Records of early English drama: Cambridge*, 2 vols (Toronto, University of Toronto Press, 1989), I, p. 348. The price paid by the university for royal patronage was extensive royal intervention in its internal affairs. See Victor Morgan, 'Country, court and Cambridge University, 1558–1640: a study in the evolution of a political culture' (unpublished Ph.D. dissertation, University of East Anglia, 1984), chapters 7–12; Alexandra Walsham, '"Vox Piscis, or, The book-fish": providence and the uses of the Reformation past in Caroline Cambridge', *English Historical Review* 114 (1999), 574–606.

16 Cooper, *Annals* II, p. 559.

17 Cooper, *Annals* II, pp. 506, 575, 418. See also III, p. 216.

18 See, e.g., Cooper, *Annals* II, p. 577; Bodleian Library, Oxford, MS Gough Camb. 46, fol. 79ᵛ. See also Elisabeth Leedham-Green, *A concise history of the University of Cambridge* (Cambridge, Cambridge University Press, 1996), pp. 8–11.

19 Cooper, *Annals* V, p. 325.

20 *Ibid.* II, pp. 561–2.

21 Ian W. Archer, *The pursuit of stability: social relations in Elizabethan London* (Cambridge, Cambridge University Press, 1991), p. 102.

22 For a discussion of the ways in which conflict could be 'a measure of the strength of community life' see Colin Bell and Howard Newby, *Community studies: an introduction to the sociology of the local community* (London, Allen & Unwin, 1971). See also Jeanette Neeson, *Commoners: common right, enclosure and social change in England, 1700–1820* (Cambridge, Cambridge University Press, 1993), pp. 153–4; and Chapter 9 above.

23 Martin Ingram, 'Communities and courts: law and disorder in early seventeenth-century Wiltshire', in J. S. Cockburn (ed.), *Crime in England, 1550–1800* (London, Methuen, 1977); J. A. Sharpe, '"Such disagreement betwyx neighbours": litigation and human relations in early modern England', in John Bossy (ed.), *Disputes and settlements: law and human relations in the West* (Cambridge, Cambridge University Press, 1983); Craig Muldrew, 'The culture of reconciliation: community and settlement of economic disputes in early modern England', *Historical Journal* 39 (1996), 915–42; Keith Wrightson, 'The politics of the parish in early modern England', and Steve Hindle, 'The keeping of the public peace', both in Paul Griffiths, Adam Fox and Steve Hindle (eds), *The experience of authority in early modern England* (London, Macmillan, 1996).

24 See, e.g., the case of Bristol in Harris Sacks, 'The corporate town'.

25 Cooper, *Annals* II, pp. 332, 340.

26 For an account of this event see Cooper, *Annals* II, p. 305.

27 *Ibid.* II, p. 426.

28 *Ibid.* II, p. 476.

29 See CUA, V.C.Ct I.47. See also Nigel Goose, 'Household size and structure in early Stuart Cambridge', *Social History* 5 (1980), 347–85.

30 See CUA, TX 19 and CUR 54.

31 See, e.g., Joseph Mead's description of the measures taken by Christ's College in 1630, Cooper, *Annals* III, p. 222. I am grateful to Patrick Collinson for reminding me of this.

32 CUA, CUR 54, no. 116.

33 For accounts of weekly disbursements, see CUA, CUR 54, nos. 92, 94, 95, and for accounts of money collected nationally see nos. 133–95.

34 CUA, CUR 54, no. 105.

35 Cooper, *Annals* II, pp. 579, 594.

36 For the processes of commemoration in constructing narratives of identity see Yael Zerubavel, *Recovered roots: collective memory and the making of Israeli national tradition* (Chicago IL, University of Chicago Press, 1995), chapter 1.

37 Cooper, *Annals* II, pp. 494–7.

38 See Alexandra Shepard, 'Meanings of manhood in early modern England, with special reference to Cambridge, c. 1560–1640' (unpublished Ph.D. dissertation, University of Cambridge, 1998), chapter 4.

39 See, e.g., the Great Gate riot of 1610/11, transcribed in Nelson (ed.), *Records of early English drama* I, pp. 424–86.

40 Cooper, *Annals* II, p. 526.

41 See, e.g., CUA, TX 19, fol. 19^v; CUR 54, nos. 20, 38; and Comm.Ct II.2, fol. 62.

42 Paul Slack, *Poverty and policy in Tudor and Stuart England* (Harlow, Longman, 1988), p. 145. See also John Walter, 'The social economy of dearth in early modern England', in John Walter and Roger Schofield (eds), *Famine, disease and the social order in early modern society* (Cambridge, Cambridge University Press, 1989), pp. 123–8; John Walter and Keith Wrightson, 'Dearth and the social order in early modern England', *Past and Present* 71 (1976), 22–42; Paul Griffiths, *Youth and authority: formative experiences in England 1560–1640* (Oxford, Clarendon Press, 1996), pp. 374–82.

43 CUA, Comm.Ct I.18, fols 89 and 88^v.

44 See Shepard, 'Meanings of manhood', chapter 5.

45 CUA, V.C.Ct III.2, no. 233.

46 Special court sessions were established in 1626 specifically to enforce student discipline by restricting their associations in the town. See CUA, V.C.Ct I.49, the sessions of which were a response to a royal admonition to improve university discipline, reprinted in Cooper, *Annals* III, pp. 182–3. See also CUA, Comm.Ct I.18. The often disruptive fraternal bonds which often overrode distinctions between young men of the town and of the university are more fully discussed in Shepard, 'Meanings of manhood', chapter 5.

47 CUA, Comm.Ct I.18, fol. 43.

48 See, e.g., CUA, V.C.Ct II.32, fol. 103; V.C.Ct II.30, fol. 64^v; Comm.Ct II.2, fol. 5^v.

49 CUA, V.C.Ct II.30, fol. 71. See also fol. 64^v.

50 Cooper, *Annals* III, p. 168.

51 See, e.g., CUA, Comm.Ct II.3, fol. 14^v–15; Comm.Ct II.3, fol. 60^v; Comm.Ct II.17, fol. 37; V.C.Ct I.5, fol. 68^v.

52 See, e.g., CUA, Comm.Ct II.17, fol. 71; Comm.Ct I.6, fol. 167.

53 For land deals between the Corporation and Trinity College see Cooper, *Annals* II, p. 366; III, pp. 57–8. For leases from the corporation to various colleges and university members see the town Treasurer's Accounts, Downing College, Cambridge, Bowtell MSS, nos 2–5. For cases involving the exchange of leases between individuals of the town and university see, e.g., CUA, Comm.Ct II.16, fol. 171; Comm.Ct II.17, fol. 129.

54 CUA, V.C.Ct III.30, no. 149.

55 CUA, Comm.Ct II.2, fol. 95.

56 CUA, V.C.Ct II.30, fol. 48.

57 See, e.g., Cooper, *Annals* II, p. 427.

58 CUA, Wills II, fols 107, 109^v.

59 See, e.g., CUA Wills III, fol. 191^v. See also CUA, V.C.Ct II.29, fol. 7; Comm.Ct II.17, fol. 88^v.

60 Cooper, *Annals* III, pp. 94–5. See also p. 389 and CUA, Wills II, fol. 37.

61 CUA, Wills II, fols 127^v–130.

62 Cooper, *Annals* III, p. 262. See also CUA, Wills II, fol. 39.

63 See above, Chapter 7.

Chapter 13

Readers, correspondents and communities: John Houghton's *A Collection for Improvement of Husbandry and Trade* (1692–1703)

Natasha Glaisyer

Developing from the Royal Society's Baconian project to write the histories of trades, the apothecary, John Houghton (d. 1705), charted a programme of 'improvement' based on a vision of the mutual dependence of husbandry, trade and the new financial world in his long-running periodical, *A Collection for Improvement of Husbandry and Trade* (1692–1703). Houghton's publication, a weekly periodical of at most two folio sheets, combined essays concerned with trade and husbandry with a medley of current information – the price of shares, grain prices from various market towns, the London bills of mortality, job and property advertisements – gleaned from correspondence, and extracted from other newspapers and publications.

In his introduction to the periodical Houghton hoped that 'there are few People in the Nation, who first or last may not be advantag'd by them.'[1] Although at times he did distinguish between his readers on the basis of the different uses they might make of the material in his papers, he claimed 'the Generality' for his community of readers. Unlike a number of other long-running papers of the period which were the outcome of joint editorships, Houghton's papers appeared to have been undertaken by him alone. At the helm of his project, Houghton, appealing to the rhetoric of friendship, fashioned himself as a mediator between his readers and the material he selected, digested, organised and published. He acted as a broker of various goods and services as well as allowing readers to witness his 'useful' endeavours.

More powerful for the creation of a community, however, were the opportunities he provided for his readers to participate directly in the production of the text. Like other periodicals in this period Houghton invited contributions from his readers to create what Kathryn Shevelow has called the 'community of the text'.[2] The survival of important manuscript material including Houghton's initial proposal, contributors' letters, and evidence of reader reception, however, allows a fuller picture of this newspaper to be constructed than is usually possible in newspaper histories. In particular, it allows the dimensions of the various communities associated with the text to be charted. Indeed, this evidence reveals that Houghton drew upon an extensive network of correspondents, many of whom were members of the existing correspondence network of the Royal Society, to produce his *Collection*, and in doing so he was employing and developing well established practices of scholarly exchange. Yet this network of correspondents was also a rhetorical community; by making continual reference to the exchange of knowledge and services in the printed pages of his periodical, Houghton created a sense of his periodical being a collective project. All his readers could imagine themselves as participants in this community of exchange.

First printed in March 1692, Houghton's *A Collection for Improvement of Husbandry and Trade* was published in 583 issues over a period of more than a decade. Each issue contained a leading essay, signed by Houghton, in which he presented accounts of topics as diverse as soap making, the uses of hazel wood and methods of trading stocks. Published in every copy was a table of prices of agricultural products from over thirty provincial centres, and a listing of various stock prices. Many issues also detailed exchange rates, Exchequer transactions and the prices in London of other goods, and every issue included advertisements, not only for the goods Houghton sold – mainly tea, coffee, chocolate and spa water – but also for jobs, books, property, lotteries and advowsons. Like issues of John Dunton's *Athenian Mercury*, each issue of the *Collection* was published as part of a volume, and like the *Philosophical Transactions* each volume was indexed. As Houghton wrote of his periodical in issue 52, the first issue expanded to accommodate two extra folio pages of advertisements: 'It's also lasting, to be put into Volumes with Indexes; and particularly there shall be an Index of all the Advertisements, whereby, for Ages to come, they may be useful.'[3] He had undertaken his project with a methodical posterity in mind.

In an initial manuscript proposal Houghton invited readers to become subscribers to the newspaper and to pay quarterly instalments, but by the time the first issue went to press in March 1692 the paper was available for the flat cost per issue of 2d.[4] Within a month Houghton was not only listing five London booksellers who stocked his twice-weekly papers, but also advertising that 'any body in England may have them by the Post. But where that is thought too much, it may be eased by ten or twelve obliging themselves constantly to take them from a Bookseller, Coffee Man, or some other, who may afford to pay a Carrier, and sell them there for 2d. or at most 3d. or Carriers themselves may gain well, if they'll serve the Country Gentlemen.'[5] So keen was he to distribute the periodical that in the following issue he offered his papers on a sale or return basis, and by the tenth number George Rose of Norwich was listed alongside the London booksellers.[6] Some first volume issues carried advertisements that the paper was sold by hawkers, and although later issues contained details of the indictment and whipping of hawkers, by the turn of the century Houghton was defending hawking as a trading practice in his leading essays.[7]

'By reason of the extraordinary Charge' Houghton had undertaken, the first issue of the second volume was published six months after the last issue of the first volume, and by then he had revised his scheme a second time. The *Collection* became a weekly publication, produced every Friday, which was a foreign-post day. It cost 1d an issue, and was supported by 'a Contribution of a Guinea a Year from some Gentlemen', and continued to be available for delivery by the post and carriers.[8]

By the middle of 1693, over a year since the first issue, Houghton was claiming that the *Collection* was the 'first Hand maid' to the *London Gazette* 'because it goes (tho' not so thick, yet) to most parts'.[9] According to Houghton, it was sold by most of the booksellers in England, and the first two bound folio volumes 'may be had from most Booksellers of England, Scotland, or Ireland'.[10] Contrary to Larry Neal's claim, that '[n]o mention of foreign readers is made', by the third volume, issues were supposedly going weekly to Amsterdam, and by the fourth, to 'Scotland, Ireland, [and] the Plantations'. As Houghton emphasised, the papers were 'made not only for the Curious about Town'.[11] Whether or not Houghton's paper did have such a geographically broad circulation, through these references he framed his project as an ambitious and widely supported venture allowing his readers to identify with other readers in an extensive community.

Houghton more explicitly claimed an audience for his papers in the very first issue when he announced that his project was designed 'for the Advantage of Tenant, Landlord, Corn-Merchant, Meal-man, Baker, Brewer, Feeder of Cattel, Farmer, Maulster, Grazier, Seller and Buyer of Coals, Hop-Merchant, Soap-Boyler, Tallow Chandler, Wool-Merchant, their Customers'.[12] Indeed, he contended that most of the material in the *Collection* was relevant, albeit in different ways, to the whole population. He argued, for example, that the collations of the published bills of entry – lists of quantities of various goods brought into and exported from London – were published in the first volume of the periodical not only so 'that the Country may be expert in the London-Trade, to make amends for what the City learns from it' but because the bills offered advantage to all.[13] The court could use the figures to calculate whether customs had been paid on the totals of various goods imported, and whether a greater consumption ought to be encouraged. 'The Parliament, by knowing what goes out, may lay on or take off a Duty, and so increase or decrease the Trade.' For the 'Political-Arithmetician' the figures could be used to calculate the 'Wealth and Strength of the Nation', and the 'Philosopher or

Naturalist' could enquire after each of the things traded and 'learn the Explanation of each particular'. The quantity of goods usually consumed would help 'the Merchant and other inquisitive Trader' to know 'whither 'tis best to bring in more, or there's too much already for their Advantage'. The value of these lists to the country shopkeeper, the farmer, the tenant and the housewife, who 'will know when to lay in their Store of Sugar, Plums, Rice, and other Necessaries, and the best time of buying Oranges and Limons', was also discussed.[14] So here Houghton claimed an audience which encompassed men and women from a wide range of social groups.

Anne Goldgar's work on the republic of letters, and that of John Sommerville on the seventeenth-century periodical press, provide valuable comparisons. Goldgar argues that 'to read a journal was in some ways to belong to a club, the club initiated with information provided by that journal'.[15] Sommerville charts the use of the club motif by periodical writers at this time as 'a way of making readers welcome' and 'to generate the brand loyalty that periodicals depend on'.[16] Rather than this club motif, or indeed the anachronistic notion of 'brand loyalty', the *Collection* appealed to the notion of a 'correspondency' – the periodical was reliant upon the continuous contributions from a network of 'ingenious Men' – to achieve these aims and create a sense of the community involved in the text.[17] To understand this dimension of the periodical it must be situated in the contexts of existing practices of information exchange, particularly those developed by natural philosophers, and the history of the Royal Society, its fellows, and their scholarship, as well as its programmes for agriculture, and the history of trades. Although the inception of Houghton's periodical rests within these contexts, its development extended beyond the Royal Society's programme and networks of members to encompass a more wide-ranging agenda and a far larger range of correspondents.

Houghton had been elected a fellow of the Royal Society on 29 January 1680, following his nomination by Robert Hooke. One of the 'active enthusiasts' of the society, Houghton served on the committee for agriculture and contributed to the *Philosophical Transactions*, and also enthusiastically, but not always successfully, nominated candidates, some with trading credentials, to fellowships.[18] From its inception, connections between Houghton's 1690s improvement project and the society were prominent. The issue that launched the *Collection* in the 1690s carried a testimonial, to the 'approv'd Abilities and Industry of Mr. John Houghton, Citizen of London, and Fellow of the Royal Society there, in the Discovery and Collection of Matters worthy [of] Observation, and more particularly such as relate to the Improvement of Husbandry and Trade', signed by twenty-four fellows of the Royal Society, including John Evelyn, Robert Southwell, Edmund Halley and John Hoskins.[19]

Moreover, members of the Royal Society, like John Beaumont, were involved in promoting the periodical. Beaumont wrote to Houghton in 1693,

'I have shown y[ou]r papers to several Gentlemen who tell me they will subscribe for setts of them, w[i]th my selfe to the Bookseller at Wells.'[20] Such was the significance of the contributions from members of the Royal Society to Houghton's project that he warmly acknowledged their assistance in the final issue of his paper: 'I must particularly say, for a great many of the Royal Society, that they have been genteel, kind, and ready to communicate most Knowledges I have asked them, in their Power, without which, I own, I could not have carried on a great deal of what I have written.'[21]

Houghton's project, which was endorsed and supported by members of the Royal Society, can be placed among the society's intellectual agendas. The programme for compiling natural histories of mechanical trades advanced, and partially realised, by Francis Bacon in the early sixteenth century, was taken up by Samuel Hartlib and his associates in the Interregnum, and by members of the Royal Society in the Restoration period. In this context, the term 'history' meant a comprehensive account, since, as Houghton recommended, to 'make a perfect History every thing must be taken in'.[22] The history of trades programme entailed, in Michael Hunter's words, the collection of '[i]nformation about technical processes ... for its value in its own right and as a potential source of data for scientific hypotheses, while, through collation and comparison, it was also hoped that improvements noted in one area could be introduced in others'.[23] The programme ended prematurely after only a handful of full accounts had been produced on such subjects as wine selling and glass manufacture; many partial accounts were published in the *Philosophical Transactions* in the period up to 1688. The agricultural counterpart of the history of trades programme, the Georgical Committee, had undergone an earlier decline.

Despite the demise of these programmes, individual members of the society continued to pursue, often independently, studies in agriculture and trade. Houghton's 1690s periodical was a project that attempted to realise, and develop, some of the goals of the society's Baconian programmes. Although some of the material that Houghton digested in the leading essays of his periodical was new, much was based upon findings of Royal Society members in the previous decades, and among the authors he drew upon were John Aubrey, John Evelyn, Edmund Halley, Martin Lister, John Ray, William Petty and Robert Plot. From the first issue Houghton took this 'useful Matter already divulg'd' and set out to explain it to 'the Generality', couching himself as an epitomiser of others' accounts for the 'Plain Man'.[24] Through his undertaking Houghton systematically consolidated in a single publication much of the scholarship relating to trades and agriculture that had been undertaken in Bacon's shadow since the Restoration.

Central to Houghton's project, and indeed to many of the studies of agriculture and trade undertaken by other Royal Society members, was the concept of improvement. Although derived from the term for profit and employed principally in relation to agrarian concerns, by the seventeenth century 'improvement' was not associated exclusively with these contexts, and had developed broader connotations, which, by the eighteenth century, included social and aesthetic considerations. In describing his aims, Houghton emphasised the path from useful knowledge to improvement: 'And the more we know of these Islands, the better, I presume, may they be manag'd ... I shall greatly (although not altogether) avoid speculation, and chiefly mind those things that tend to useful Practice.'[25] 'I shall think,' wrote Houghton a few weeks later, following his plea for a better understanding of soil types, vegetation, and the use of dung, 'that Husbandry may be brought towards an Art, and the Practice may prove as pleasant and profitable, as a great many others in Cities are. And that it may flourish and trade too, is my hearty desire.'[26] For Houghton, trade and husbandry were closely connected in this project, and the emerging world of the joint-stock company could, in Houghton's vision, build upon this connection and bring about further improvement. Houghton imagined that stock prices would be useful to those who could not go to Garraway's coffee house each day, and that:

> satisfi'd once a Week how it is ... the whole Kingdom may reap Advantage by those Trades: Also they may learn hence some of the Cunning of Merchandizing, and have this Advantage, by laying their Monies there, in one or two days time they may sell, and have their Money to supply their wants at any time. Without doubt, if those Trades were better known, 'twould be a great Advantage to the Kingdom.[27]

Indeed the *Collection* was rich in other materials relating to the financial and commercial revolutions. Houghton, who operated his business from the heart of the City, in Bartholomew Lane behind the Royal Exchange, and later in Grace Church Street, advertised his own investment brokering services in the periodical.[28] Moreover, beginning in July 1694, he listed funds deposited in, and advanced by, the Exchequer, and from January 1695 onwards he included rates of exchange at a dozen foreign cities. The *Collection* also carried advertisements for meetings of the East India Company, for the services of John Castaing, who 'at Jonathan's Coffee-house, or Exchange, buys and sells all Blank and Benefit Tickets; and all other Stocks and Shares', and proposals and developments of numerous lotteries.[29]

Although Houghton, through his projects, redefined the scope of the concept of improvement, many of the practices of gathering and distributing knowledge that he employed were well established by the end of the seventeenth century. Samuel Hartlib, for example, had made attempts to formalise the role of the intelligencer – one who gathered and channelled intelligence – in his proposals for an office of address for communications. Later in the century the Royal Society operated as an 'intellectual clearing-house';

correspondence was central to this undertaking.[30] Indeed, Rob Iliffe has gone as far as to claim that to 'an overwhelming extent, the Society *was* its correspondence'.[31]

It is in this context that Houghton's fashioning of the *Collection*, in both its preliminary and later stages, as a collective project must be considered. Houghton outlined his intentions in a manuscript proposal:

> The matters thus intended to be insisted upon, being very various, and not the worke of one or few hands, will oblige me to lay out for as wide a correspondence as may be procured, and it is hoped I may obtain, Every weeke one Letter at least out of each County of the Kingdome, to w[hi]ch purpose, all lovers of this worke, are invited.[32]

At the beginning of the second volume Houghton was more ambitious: 'I intend to settle a large Correspondence, not only in all Counties of England, but in many other places of the World, in order to gain all the Knowledg that is worth getting.'[33] At various points Houghton requested his correspondents not only to send market prices, for which 'I'll return them in lieu one of my Collections', but also daily observations of 'the height of the Quicksilver in the Weather-Glass, in places about 200 miles from London', and less current information, such as 'the History of Nature and Art of any Town', 'curious Receipts of Liquors made from Grain, Fruits, Honey, Sugar, or any thing else produc'd in England', accounts of libraries, weights and measures around the kingdom, 'In short, all things that are worth Knowing.'[34] On occasion he had to encourage his correspondents to send him 'frequently and exactly the Prices of every thing ... assuring all that I chearfully pay the Charge of their Letters to me, and that if at any time the prices be wrong, 'tis not my Fault; I am as punctual as I can.'[35] Although Houghton desired to be 'as exact as possible', the prices quoted contain unusual uniformities, suggesting his failure to maintain the steady correspondence he desired.[36]

The periodical's reliance on information provided by correspondents was developed into a framing device for much that was presented in the papers. For example, in previewing the following week's leading article in March 1693 on methods of curing sheep diseases, in which he would 'relate Matter of Fact, as I have learnt from my Correspondents', Houghton emphasised the authenticity and usefulness of his source of information.[37] Writing at the end of a series of essays on Derbyshire based on a correspondent's accounts, he explicitly situated the periodical more generally within these exchanges of letters:

> [the correspondent] has since left the Country, and I want there, and in most other Places such other Correspondent [*sic*], to give me faithfully an account of such like things as are remarkable: And I believe some will do so, for I have received several Letters tending this way, all which shall be considered in due time; but particular

from one Mr. F. R. who is so kind as to say that he thinks himself and others who have oportunity are bound to encourage and assist me; therefore he has sent me an Account of the River Sour in Leicestershire[38]

Such was the value of the material provided by correspondents that Houghton declared that the first 100 issues of the papers had 'not been altogether collected from Books, but in a great measure from the Knowledge and Practice of Men of this Age'.[39]

Some accounts, like those concerning wheat by the apothecary and botanist Samuel Dale, were presented in the leading essays in the form of letters to Houghton.[40] A manuscript letter from Dale to Houghton, written before the first issue was published, and probably in response to the initial proposals, reveals that this was a long-standing correspondence. In it Dale listed the prices of wheat, malt and other goods at Braintree market, promised to send them every week, gave an account of the medicinal springs in his county, and suggested that an account of county contributions to the quarterly poll be published in the papers.[41] Other manuscript letters survive which suggest the texture of this culture of contribution from the angle of the letter writers. Richard Saunders, who produced almanacs, sent Houghton the prices of various grains and beans in Melton Mowbray, described the previous week's weather and planned to send 'ere long ... further account of things here'.[42] Arthur Charlett, Master of University College, Oxford, wrote to Houghton in 1694 with the prices of wheat, malt and barley, and, like Dale, made suggestions concerning content with his desire that 'your advice to Foreigners goes on'.[43]

Throughout the periodical Houghton appealed to the notion that his paper was supported by a community of correspondents. As the project developed, Houghton included increasing numbers of advertisements for jobs, people available for positions, lotteries, medicines, books, property and advowsons. Some of these expansions were couched in terms of his taking advantage of the network of correspondents: 'By reason of my great Correspondency, I may help Masters to Apprentices, and Apprentices to Masters.' Later he promised that:

> Seeing the Buying and Selling Estates and Advowsons do often fall in my way, I will endeavour to help those that would either buy or sell in any County of England: In order to the entring of which fairly in a Book, I desire all my Correspondents to send me word what Estates they hear are to be sold, whereabout the Value, who sells them, and how they may be sent to[44]

Reinforcing this construction of a community of correspondents were Houghton's invitations for readers to contribute to other projects. He encouraged his correspondents to send in, for example, corrections to William Camden's *Britannia*, to be inserted as marginal notes in Abel Swall and

Awnsham Churchil's reprinting of the volume; he requested memoranda for inclusion in the chronology of the *Historian's Guide*; and he asked for lists of privately owned manuscripts for insertion in a general catalogue compiled by Edward Bernard.[45] Such was Houghton's reputation for having an extensive network of letter writers that over twenty years after his death Richard Bradley, in a preface to the volumes in which the leading essays from the periodical were republished, dared to claim that 'It is certain, that gentleman had the largest correspondence of any writer of this kind in his time'.[46]

Houghton was not the only late seventeenth-century editor of a periodical to encourage contributions from readers. The *Athenian Mercury*, first published in 1691, a year before the *Collection* began, was established to publish answers to readers' various queries. Furthermore, Peter Motteux conceived, and from January 1692 edited, *The Gentleman's Journal*, which in the following May announced that the 'Ingenious are desired to continue to send what ever may be properly inserted in this Journal, either in Verse or Prose'.[47] Such was the significance of this climate of contribution that it was parodied in *The post-boy rob'd of his mail*, printed in 1692 for Dunton, which contained satirical letters both to the Athenian Society and to the editor of the *Gentleman's Journal*.[48]

Houghton's periodicals alone represent a massive exercise in information exchange. However, there are hints that there were numerous other exchanges being carried out beyond the text. In his initial manuscript proposal of the periodical Houghton described how only part of the information he intended to gather would appear in the pages of the periodical, and other materials would appear in 'Books, under their proper Head where every thing may be seen in as short a Compass as the nature of it will bear, by such whose Interest or curiosityes shall encourage to come unto me att my house ... where they shall find as much diligence and faithfulness as they can reasonably desire.'[49] Near the beginning of the periodical Houghton offered to show to 'any that are curious to see it' a lengthy account of 'an extraordinary Chirurgical Case', and he later invited his benefactors to peruse the knowledge he was accumulating.[50]

Indeed, Houghton was involved in a much wider network of exchange than that presented in the periodical. From the time that he became a member of the Royal Society in 1680 until his death twenty-five years later he contributed regularly to the meetings of the society. He exhibited numerous curious artefacts, among them a model of the Grand Duke of Tuscany's diamond, bread made from turnips, East Indian cockroaches, a live tortoise and a parcel of early ripening barley.[51] Also, he presented the findings of his own experiments concerning the absence of saltpetre in snow, a chemical analysis of fresh herrings and the germination of coffee beans.[52] More frequently, however, and especially in the 1690s, he read letters written by his numerous correspondents on such subjects as cider making, fossil trees, and the weather in various parts of the country.[53] Some of this material appeared in the pages of the *Collection*, sometimes days and sometimes years after its initial presentation to the Royal Society.[54]

The nature of the exchanges Houghton had with his various correspondents can be explored further by considering his relationship with one of his Royal Society colleagues, the collector and Leeds merchant, Ralph Thoresby. Connections between Houghton and Thoresby can be traced through a number of sources and suggest that Houghton's business, scholarly and publishing interests overlapped (as they did in his periodical). Houghton sent Thoresby ten volumes of the *Collection* for his museum, probably some time in 1700.[55] As Houghton wrote to Thoresby in February 1701, he would have sent him copies of the paper each week 'but I am afraid of the Charge of Postage'.[56] Later that year Thoresby visited 'the obliging Mr Jo[hn] Houghton' in London, and on Thoresby's return to Leeds their correspondence continued, with Houghton sending the prices of coffee and tea in anticipation of doing some business.[57] By January 1702 Houghton was soliciting the participation of Thoresby in his periodical project: 'if without too much trouble I could often hear how Corn goes I would put Leeds in my paper'.[58] Corn prices in Leeds, however, never appeared in the table of grain prices. A couple of months later, at a meeting of the Royal Society, Houghton read aloud a letter from Thoresby concerning a silk tail, a German bird, lately found in England.[59] In 1715, a decade after Houghton's death, Thoresby acknowledged in print a gift from Houghton of a number of autograph letters.[60] Houghton's relationship with Thoresby was probably initiated by mutual friends at the Royal Society and was maintained by gifts, letters and visits. It encompassed business, their interest in natural knowledge and Houghton's periodical. This is not to say that the periodical was produced exclusively upon the foundation of Houghton's existing correspondence and was largely connected with the Royal Society. Indeed, through the periodical Houghton not only exploited opportunities to draw in correspondents, but he also developed the existing practices of scholarly exchange through the medium of the print-published periodical.

Concentrating on the correspondency that was constructed within the *Collection* provides only a partial understanding of the reader for whom Houghton wrote. This is especially so after the periodical was reduced to a single sheet; in the shorter form of the *Collection* correspondents were mentioned less frequently and there were fewer references to engaging them in any sort of schemes. Houghton employed a number of different strategies throughout the periodical to create, at least rhetorically, a community of readers. Much of the material in the paper was taken from other newspapers: Houghton presented an abstract of the bills of mortality, presumed to 'be very useful for al that are concern'd in Physick' in most issues published in the first five years, and he regularly drew on material from the *Philosophical Trans-*

actions. This newspaper was in part a medley of other newspapers, and in this respect it anticipated the *Gentleman's Magazine* of the 1730s. In selecting the newspapers to digest and reproduce for his paper Houghton claimed to be responding to readers' requests. Before the end of the first volume of issues, for example, he proposed, with the support of political arithmetic, to publish summaries from the *Gazette*:

> I find the Generality are desirous of News; I hear about 7 or 8000 Gazettes at a time are printed, which is but small for 10000 Parishes, or 8 Millions of People; 'twould be much for the Improvement of Trade to have them spread, and its probable, Not-Seers having a tast of the principal things contained therein (which I shall strive to shew in my following Papers) may long for more particulars.[61]

This practice runs counter to the claim of E. S. De Beer that, because of the *Gazette*'s near monopoly of news of the activities of the English government, 'it would detract' from other newspapers' 'selling power to repeat it'.[62] The synopses usually comprised about half a dozen lines, although later they were longer, of foreign news that Houghton considered 'useful to Posterity', and on occasion included advertisements for books, innovations in japanning techniques and patents in gun casting.[63] In issue 60 Houghton gave his first listing of a ship's cargo, and discontinued the digests of the *Gazettes*, giving the reason 'Several think that Cargoes, and other things may be more useful than the Gazette.'[64] Just over two years later, Houghton resumed his summaries: 'I Find by the Wishing for it again that an Abstract of the Material things in the Gazette will be useful for History.'[65] At other times as well Houghton claimed to be in touch with his readers, as in 1695 when he prefaced a brief discussion of books with 'I find by several of my Correspondents that more Books would be bought if well recommended'.[66]

The sense of community constructed in this periodical was strengthened by references within issues to previous numbers, and regular anticipation of the content of the following week's publication. Houghton ended the leading essay of issue 500 on cypress trees, for example, by promising 'a Secret, as well to confute popular Error, as for the Instruction of our Gardiners, which Expect next Friday'.[67] As Sommerville has argued more generally about periodicals published in this period, 'by their self-referencing character – citing previous issues and alluding to future ones – a periodical eventually became a world in itself'.[68]

Throughout the periodical Houghton adopted the rhetoric of friendship to describe his correspondents and some of the authorities upon whose findings he based his accounts, as well as himself. In her work on Samuel Richardson's *Pamela*, Naomi Tadmor suggests the centrality of three interpretations of the word 'friend': 'an individually chosen companion to whom one is attached by ties of affection', 'the opposite of an enemy' and 'a general and heterogeneous category of guardians, protectors and supporters'.[69] In most instances Houghton's employment of the rhetoric operates to reinforce this last usage – the well established rhetoric of patronage associated with friendship – rather than to introduce a more affective dimension. Perhaps in an attempt to confer credit on his publication and the material it contained, Houghton employed this rhetoric to define his relations with prominent contemporaries, as can be seen in his references to 'my very good Friend, the great Naturalist, Dr. Robert Plot', 'my constant Friend Mr. Edmund Hally' and 'my very good Friend' Samuel Pepys.[70] Following a proposal to publish by subscription William Leybourn's *Pleasure with profit*, Houghton remarked, 'I am told by some of my Friends of the first Rank for knowledge in these affairs, that they believe Mr Leybourn will perform what he promised.'[71] Similarly, he described his correspondents 'My Derbyshire Friend', 'my ingenious Friend, Mr. Everard of Southampton' and 'a Lancashire Friend'.[72] This is not to deny that Houghton may also have had ties of affection with these men. Indeed, he wrote to Pepys at least once and received a ring at his funeral in 1703, which may signal an affective relationship.[73]

Houghton presented himself as a broker of jobs, advowsons, property and investments, as well as a range of other goods and, for a short period of time, marriage partners. Few advertisements linked the prospective buyer with the seller, as most were mediated through Houghton.[74] In some, the proprieties of patronage were explicitly invoked through the use of the term 'friend', as in the advertisement: 'A French Gentleman, a Protestant, would willingly wait upon some Person of Quality, to teach him, or any of his Family French, and if desired, to be in the quality of a Gentleman-Usher, or any other place reputable. From a valuable Divine, my good Friend, I hear a very good Character of him.'[75] However, most employed a variant on the phrase 'I can help', as in 'If any that very well can draw Japan Figures, wants an Employment; or any Boy whose Genius lies that way will be an Apprentice, if they will come to me, I believe I can help them.'[76] In mediating between buyer and seller Houghton fashioned himself as his readers' friend. He ended his offer to act as an estate broker, for example, with the statement that 'there shall be neither Shams nor Tricks used by me; and I'll strive to make it as Reputable to put any such thing in here at the first, as it shall be to speak to any particular Friend'.[77] Similarly, Houghton invited his readers to trust him in his capacity as matchmaker: 'These Proposals for Matches are real; and I do promise to manage them and such like with so much Secresie and Prudence, that none shall discourse with their best Friends with more Confidence of Fidelity than with me, let them be of what Rank soever.'[78] Through this rhetoric of instrumental friendship the reader was constructed as a client, or sometimes a patron, in a relationship of patronage. Houghton had institutionalised and commercialised existing patterns of patronage and exchange through his periodical.

Speculative conclusions about the identity of some of the periodical's readers can be reached through surveying the numerous advertisements. For example, the *Collection* carried an advertisement requesting an apprentice who 'makes fine Works in Brass and Silver for Cabinets and East-India Goods', and another for a 'Game-keeper, that understands all sorts of Fowling' to work for a 'Gentleman in Berk shire'. Houghton claimed that he could help 'any Merchant' who wanted 'a Lodging at a Packer's House, and a little distance from the Exchange, with or without Diet, having all other Conveniences', and that he could help 'any Lady that is going to the East-Indies' to secure 'one to wait on her ... that is well bred, can do all manner of Work fit for such, and have sufficient recommendation and security.'[79] It cannot be inferred from these advertisements, however, that the wide range of readers they addressed necessarily read other parts of the periodical.

Some historians suggest that Houghton's agrarian advice and information 'was influential among Londoners and also among visitors to London', and that the *Collection* generally 'did a good deal to break down old prejudices and remove barriers to the flow of ideas between one region and another'.[80] Although a handful of readers can be identified with confidence, such as those discussed above who contributed market prices to the periodical, the question of the 'influence' of this periodical remains problematic. A little fragmentary evidence survives that suggests varied responses to the periodical from readers with different occupations and interests. The naturalist John Ray noted his reservations about the *Collection* in a letter to John Aubrey: 'I have seen one of Mr. Houghton's papers, and doe think they may be of use to some men, though not of much to me.'[81] James Petiver, a botanist and entomologist, was more interested. In his commonplace book, between jottings on Boyle's natural philosophy and prescriptions for various diseases, are notes he took from the leading essays of the first volume of the *Collection* on earth, water, air and fire.[82] A steward, William Gilpin, writing from an estate in Whitehaven to his employer in January 1698, gives the most detailed evidence of having used the papers: 'Some of Haughton's weekly papers have of late given us such an account of the prices of coals at Falmouth and other places in that chanel that (if they be to be depended on) seem to give good encouragement to us to send coals thither.'[83]

Goldgar suggests a parallel between the development of literary journals that stemmed 'from an institutionalization of previous contacts' and 'manuscript *nouvelles à la main*, news-sheets, and eventually newspapers [that] grew out of an increasingly voracious market for information, not to mention an increasingly organized business designed to supply it'.[84] Houghton's turn-of-the-century periodical, in drawing on the support of an existing Royal Society network of members to establish a wider correspondence, and by regularly supplying its audience with many different types of information, brings these two traditions together. The periodical was one dimension of a larger correspondence project being conducted by Houghton, and although this project drew upon existing practices of information exchange among correspondents he made many of the exchanges before a reading 'public'. Moreover, by soliciting for further correspondents in a periodical that was widely available he introduced an element of serendipity into a culture of scholarly exchange that conventionally relied upon at least weak ties between individuals. He employed rhetorical strategies to create a sense of a community of readers, not all of whom he imagined were correspondents. John Houghton was the hub of this community and as such he mediated between readers, advertisers and the authors of the works and letters upon which he drew. His project 'to make these the most useful Papers that ever in this kind were published' was for the 'Benefit of my Country'.[85] He imagined in this periodical, if not created, a community of readers and correspondents who were interested in husbandry, trade and the developing financial world of the 1690s, in an attempt to realise his ideal: 'the whole Kingdom made as one trading City'.[86]

NOTES

My thanks to Mark Goldie and Helen Berry for their helpful comments on earlier versions of this chapter. I would also like to thank the British Library, the Royal Society and the Yorkshire Archaeological Society for permission to quote from material in their archives. All dates are old-style except that the year is taken to begin on 1 January.

1 John Houghton, *A Collection for Improvement of Husbandry and Trade*, no. 3 (hereafter *Collection*, followed by its number).

2 Kathryn Shevelow, *Women and print culture* (London, Routledge, 1989), pp. 43–9.

3 *Collection*, 52.

4 BL, Sloane MS 2903, J. Houghton, 'A Proposall for Improvement of Husbandry and Trade', fols 167–8; *Collection*, 1.

5 *Collection*, 6.

6 *Ibid.*, 7, 10.

7 *Ibid.*, 9, 45, 50, 399, 400, 435.

8 *Ibid.*, 25, 27, 40.

9 *Ibid.*, 52.

10 *Ibid.*, 52, 48.

11 Larry Neal, 'The rise of a financial press: London and Amsterdam, 1681–1810', *Business History* 30 (1988), 163–78, p. 166; *Collection*, 54, 93.

12 *Collection*, 1.

13 *Ibid.*, 4; John J. McCusker, 'The business press in England before 1775', *The Library*, sixth series, 8 (1986), 205–31, p. 212.

14 *Collection*, 7.

15 Anne Goldgar, *Impolite learning: conduct and community in the republic of letters* (New Haven CT, Yale University Press, 1995), p. 63.

16 C. John Sommerville, *The news revolution in England: cultural dynamics of daily information* (Oxford, Oxford University Press, 1996), p. 149.

17 The phrase 'ingenious Men' appears in Houghton's recurring request to establish a correspondency 'In order to encourage a Political Arithmetick all the World over' which prefaced the summarised Bills of Mortality, *Collection*, 140.

18 Michael Hunter, *The Royal Society and its fellows, 1660–1700: the morphology of an early scientific institution*, second edition (London, British Society for the History of Science, 1994), pp. 29, 41, 43, 59–60, 62–3, 130–1; id., *Establishing the new science: the experience of the early Royal Society* (Woodbridge, Boydell Press, 1989), pp. 344–5.

19 *Collection*, 1.

20 BL, Stowe MS 747, J. Beaumont to J. Houghton, 2 July 1693, fol. 18ʳ.

21 *Collection*, 583.

22 *Ibid.*, 94.

23 Michael Hunter, *Science and society in Restoration England* (Cambridge, Cambridge University Press, 1981), p. 91.

24 *Collection*, 1, 485, 52.

25 *Ibid.*, 3.

26 *Ibid.*, 9.

27 *Ibid.*, 2.

28 *Ibid.*, 33, 379, 393.

29 *Ibid.*, 76, 127.

30 Marie Boas Hall, 'The Royal Society's role in the diffusion of information in the seventeenth century', *Notes and Records of the Royal Society of London* 29 (1975), 173–92, p. 177.

31 Robert Iliffe, 'Author-mongering: the "editor" between producer and consumer', in Ann Bermingham and John Brewer (eds), *The consumption of culture, 1600–1800* (London, Routledge, 1995), p. 173, his emphasis.

32 BL, Sloane MS 2903, Houghton, 'Proposall', fol. 167ᵛ.

33 *Collection*, 25.

34 *Ibid.*, 2, 33, 50, 116.

35 *Ibid.*, 172.

36 *Ibid.*, 64; J. A. Chartres, 'The marketing of agricultural produce', in Joan Thirsk (ed.), *The agrarian history of England and Wales* (Cambridge, Cambridge University Press, 1967–), V, *1640–1750*, II, *Agrarian change* (Cambridge, Cambridge University Press, 1985), p. 457. Similarly, the price Houghton quoted for bank stock remained the same for the first fourteen weeks of 1701, suggesting a 'lapse of attention on the part of the editor of the *Collections*', William Robert Scott, *The constitution and finance of English, Scottish and Irish joint-stock companies to 1720*, 3 vols (Cambridge, Cambridge University Press, 1910–12), III, p. 217.

37 *Collection*, 33.

38 *Ibid.*, 45.

39 *Ibid.*, 104.

40 *Ibid.*, 86, 95. Dale wrote other letters to Houghton that were published in the *Collection*. See, e.g., his account of herbs that coagulate milk which was included in Houghton's account of milk products, *Collection*, 165.

41 BL, Stowe MS 747, S. Dale to J. Houghton, 8 March 1692, fol. 13^r.

42 BL, Stowe MS 747, R. Saunders to J. Houghton, 20 March 1692/3, fol. 14^r.

43 BL, Additional MS 4275, A. Ch[arlet]t to J. Houghton, 28 March 1694, fol. 101^r.

44 *Collection*, 27, 146.

45 *Ibid.*, 47, 90, 105.

46 R. Bradley, 'An introductory discourse to Mr Houghton's husbandry', in J. Houghton, *Husbandry and trade improved*, ed. R. Bradley, 4 vols (London, 1727–28), I, p. iv.

47 [P. Motteux], *The Gentleman's Journal* (May 1692).

48 [C. Gildon], *The post-boy rob'd of his mail* (London, 1692), pp. 32–42, 275–6.

49 BL, Sloane MS 2903, Houghton, 'Proposall', fol. 167^r.

50 *Collection*, 12, 25.

51 Thomas Birch, *The history of the Royal Society*, 4 vols (London, 1756–67), IV, p. 80; R[oyal] S[ociety] A[rchives] (London), JBC VIII, p. 206; JBC IX, pp. 165, 218; JBC X, p. 29.

52 RSA, JBC VIII, pp. 101, 205; JBC IX, p. 155.

53 RSA, JBC VIII, p. 291; JBC IX, pp. 36, 59.

54 Houghton's experiment with snow, e.g., appeared in *Collection*, 12, two months after it had been presented before the Royal Society.

55 Y[orkshire] A[rchaeological] S[ociety] (Leeds), MS 27, p. 61.

56 YAS, MS 15, J. Houghton to R. Thoresby, 15 February 1701, item 55.

57 'MSS written or possessed by Ralph Thoresby, FRS', *Publications of the Thoresby Society* 28 (1928), 431–63, p. 453; YAS, MS 15, J. Houghton to R. Thoresby, 4 November 1701, item 94.

58 YAS, MS 15, J. Houghton to R. Thoresby, 8 January 1702, item 110.

59 RSA, JBC X, p. 21.

60 R. Thoresby, *Ducatus Leodiensis* (London, 1715), p. 551. See also YAS, MS 27, p. 61.

61 *Collection*, 16.

62 E. S. de Beer, 'The English newspapers from 1695–1702', in Ragnhild Hatton and J. S. Bromley (eds), *William III and Louis XIV* (Liverpool, Liverpool University Press, 1968), p. 119.

63 *Collection*, 30.

64 *Ibid.*, 60.

65 *Ibid.*, 140.

66 *Ibid.*, 142.

67 *Ibid.*, 500.

68 Sommerville, *News revolution*, p. 151.

69 Naomi Tadmor, '"Family" and "Friend" in *Pamela*: a case study in the history of the family in eighteenth-century England', *Social History* 14 (1989), 289–306, pp. 298–9.

70 *Collection*, 3, 40, 486.

71 *Ibid.*, 46.

72 *Ibid.*, 43, 84, 113.

73 J. Houghton to S. Pepys, 13 July 1702; 'A List of all the Persons to whom rings and mourning were presented upon the occasion of Mr Pepys's Death and Funeral [1703]', in J. R. Tanner (ed.), *Private correspondence and miscellaneous papers of Samuel Pepys, 1679–1703*, 2 vols (London, Bell, 1926), II, pp. 263–5, 317. Alan Cook suggests that 'Halley evidently kept Houghton informed on various matters', *Edmond Halley* (Oxford, Clarendon Press, 1998), p. 240.

74 As H. R. Fox Bourne phrased it, 'the editor constitut[ed] himself in a curious way an intermediary between his advertisers and his readers', *English newspapers*, 2 vols (London, Chatto & Windus, 1887), I, n. 1, p. 51.

75 *Collection*, 105.

76 *Ibid.*, 93.

77 *Ibid.*, 143.

78 *Ibid.*, 158.

79 *Ibid.*, 84, 272, 115, 527.

80 Joan Thirsk, 'Agricultural policy: public debate and legislation', in *id.*, *Agrarian change*, p. 338; Charles Wilson, *England's apprenticeship, 1603–1763*, second edition (Harlow, Longman, 1984).

81 J. Ray to J. Aubrey, before 15 December 1692, in R. T. Gunther (ed.), *Further correspondence of John Ray* (London, Ray Society, 1928), p. 177.

82 BL, Sloane MS 2347, J. Petiver, 'Collectanea Botanica', fols 3^{r-v}.

83 D. R. Hainsworth (ed.), *The correspondence of Sir John Lowther of Whitehaven, 1693–98* (Oxford, Oxford University Press, 1983), p. 471.

84 Goldgar, *Impolite learning*, p. 56.

85 *Collection*, 19, 583.

86 *Ibid.*, 6.

Select Bibliography

Aers, David (ed.), *Community, gender and individual identity: English writing, 1360–1430* (London, Routledge, 1988)

Agnew, John A., *Politics and place: the geographical mediation of state and society* (London, Allen & Unwin, 1987)

Alexander, Jeffrey C., and Steve Seidman (eds), *Culture and society: contemporary debates* (Cambridge, Cambridge University Press, 1990)

Allen, J. W., *English political thought, 1603–60* I, 1603–44 (London, Methuen, 1938)

Allen, Robert C., *Enclosure and the yeoman: the agricultural development of the south Midlands, 1450–1850* (Oxford, Oxford University Press, 1992)

Amussen, Susan Dwyer, *An ordered society: gender and class in early modern England* (Oxford, Blackwell, 1988)

Anderson, Benedict, *Imagined communities: reflections on the origin and spread of nationalism*, revised edition (London, Verso, 1991)

Appleby, Joyce Oldham, *Economic thought and ideology in seventeenth-century England* (Princeton NJ, Princeton University Press, 1978)

Archer, Ian W., *The pursuit of stability: social relations in Elizabethan London* (Cambridge, Cambridge University Press, 1991)

Arnold, Matthew, *Culture and anarchy* (Cambridge, Cambridge University Press, 1966)

Aston, T. H., P. R. Coss, C. Dyer and J. Thirsk (eds), *Social relations and ideas: essays in honour of R. H. Hilton* (Cambridge, Cambridge University Press, 1984)

Aveling, J. C. H., *Northern Catholics: the Catholic recusants of the North Riding, 1558–1790* (London, Chapman, 1966)

Baker, K. M., *Inventing the French revolution: essays on French political culture in the eighteenth century* (Cambridge, Cambridge University Press, 1990)

Barnes, J. A., 'Class and committees in a Norwegian parish', *Human Relations* 7 (1954), 39–58

Barry, Jonathan (ed.), *The Tudor and Stuart town: a reader in English urban history, 1530–1688* (Harlow, Longman, 1990)

Barry, Jonathan, and Christopher Brooks (eds), *The middling sort of people: culture, society and politics in England, 1500–1800* (Basingstoke, Macmillan, 1994)

Beattie, John, *Crime and the courts in England, 1660–1800* (Oxford, Clarendon Press, 1986)

Beaver, Daniel C., *Parish communities and religious conflict in the Vale of Gloucester, 1590–1690* (Cambridge MA, Harvard University Press, 1998)

Beier, A. L., '"Utter strangers to industry, morality and religion": John Locke on the poor', *Eighteenth-century Life* 12 (1988), 28–41

Bibliography

Beier, A. L., and Roger Finlay (eds), *London, 1500–1700: the making of the metropolis* (Harlow, Longman, 1986)

Beier, A. L., David Cannadine and James M. Rosenheim (eds), *The first modern society* (Cambridge, Cambridge University Press, 1989)

Bell, Colin, and Howard Newby, *Community studies: an introduction to the sociology of the local community* (London, Allen & Unwin, 1971)

Bell, Ian A., *Literature and crime in Augustan England* (London, Routledge, 1991)

Bermingham, Ann, and John Brewer (eds), *The consumption of culture, 1600–1800* (London, Routledge, 1995)

Biagini, Eugenio F. (ed.), *Citizenship and community: liberals, radicals and collective identities in the British Isles, 1865–1931* (Cambridge, Cambridge University Press, 1996)

Blank, Paula, *Broken English: dialects and the politics of language in Renaissance writings* (London, Routledge, 1996)

Boas Hall, Marie, 'The Royal Society's role in the diffusion of information in the seventeenth century', *Notes and Records of the Royal Society of London* 29 (1975), 173–92

Borsay, Peter, *The English urban renaissance: culture and society in the provincial town, 1660–1770* (Oxford, Clarendon Press, 1989)

Borsay, Peter (ed.), *The eighteenth-century town: a reader in English urban history, 1688–1820* (Harlow, Longman, 1990)

Bossy, John, 'The character of Elizabethan Catholicism', *Past and Present* 21 (1962), 39–59

— 'Blood and baptism: kinship, community and Christianity in western Europe from the fourteenth to the seventeenth centuries', in Derek Baker (ed.), *Sanctity and secularity: the Church and the world* (London, Oxford University Press, 1973)

— 'The English Catholic community, 1603–25', in Alan G. R. Smith (ed.), *The reign of James VI and I* (London, Macmillan, 1973)

— *The English Catholic community, 1570–1850* (London, Longman, 1975)

— *Christianity in the West* (Oxford, Oxford University Press, 1985)

— 'Unrethinking the Wars of Religion', in Thomas A. Kselman (ed.), *Belief in history: innovative approaches to European and American religion* (Notre Dame IN, University of Notre Dame Press, 1991)

Bossy, John (ed.), *Disputes and settlements: law and human relations in the West* (Cambridge, Cambridge University Press, 1983)

Boulton, Jeremy, *Neighbourhood and society: a London suburb in the seventeenth century* (Cambridge, Cambridge University Press, 1987)

Braddick, Michael J., 'State formation and social change in early modern England: a problem stated and approaches suggested', *Social History* 16 (1991), 1–17

Brett, Annabel, *Liberty, right and nature: individual rights in later scholastic thought* (Cambridge, Cambridge University Press, 1997)

Brinley Jones, R., *The old British tongue: the vernacular in Wales, 1540–1640* (Cardiff, Avalon, 1970)

Bristol, Michael D., *Carnival and theatre: plebeian culture and the structure of authority in Renaissance England* (London, Routledge, 1985)

Britnell, Richard, *Growth and decline in Colchester, 1300–1525* (Cambridge, Cambridge University Press, 1986)

Brooks, C. W., and Michael Lobban (eds), *Communities and courts: proceedings of the twelfth Legal History Conference, held in Durham* (London, Hambledon Press, 1997).

Bruster, Douglas, *Drama and the market in the age of Shakespeare* (Cambridge, Cambridge University Press, 1992)

Bryson, Anna, *From courtesy to civility: changing codes of conduct in early modern England* (Oxford, Clarendon Press, 1998)

Burke, Peter, *Popular culture in early modern Europe* (London, Temple Smith, 1978)

— *The historical anthropology of early modern Italy* (Cambridge, Cambridge University Press, 1987)

Burke, Peter, and Roy Porter (eds), *Languages and jargons: contributions to a social history of language* (Cambridge, Polity Press, 1995)

Burns, J. H., and Mark Goldie (eds), *The Cambridge History of Political Thought, 1450–1700* (Cambridge, Cambridge University Press, 1991)

Calhoun, C. J., 'Community: toward a variable conceptualization for comparative research', *Social History* 5 (1980), 105–29

Calhoun, C. J. (ed.), *Habermas and the public sphere* (Cambridge MA, MIT Press, 1992)

Carpenter, Christine, 'Gentry and community in medieval England', *Journal of British Studies* 33 (1994), 340–80

Clark, Peter, *English provincial society from the Reformation to the Revolution* (Hassocks, Harvester Press, 1977)

Clark, Peter (ed.), *The transformation of English provincial towns, 1600–1800* (London, Hutchinson, 1984)

Clark, Peter, and Paul Slack (eds), *Crisis and order in English towns, 1500–1700: essays in urban history* (London, Routledge, 1972)

Clark, Peter, and David Souden (eds), *Migration and society in early modern England* (London, Hutchinson, 1987)

Cohen, Anthony P., 'Of symbols and boundaries, or, Does Ertie's greatcoat hold the key?', in id. (ed.), *Symbolising boundaries* (Manchester, Manchester University Press, 1986)

— *The symbolic construction of community* (London, Routledge, 1989)

Cohen, Stanley, and Andrew Scull (eds), *Social control and the state* (Oxford, Blackwell, 1983)

Coleman, D. C., and A. H. John (eds), *Trade, government and economy in pre-industrial England* (London, Weidenfeld & Nicolson, 1976)

Collinson, Patrick, 'The monarchical republic of Queen Elizabeth I', *Bulletin of the John Rylands University Library* 69 (1987), 394–424

— *The birthpangs of Protestant England: religious and cultural change in the sixteenth and seventeenth centuries* (Basingstoke, Macmillan, 1988)

— *De Republica Anglorum, or, History with the politics put back* (Cambridge, Cambridge University Press, 1990)

Condren, Conal, *The language of politics in seventeenth-century England* (Basingstoke, Macmillan, 1994)

Cooper, Robert L., *Language planning and social change* (Cambridge, Cambridge University Press, 1989)

Corbin, Alain, *The foul and the fragrant: odour and the social imagination* (Leamington Spa, Picador, 1994)

Corfield, Penelope (ed.), *Work in towns, 850–1850* (Leicester, Leicester University Press, 1990)

Crane, Mary Thomas, *Framing authority: sayings, self and society in sixteenth-century England* (Princeton NJ, Princeton University Press, 1993)

Cressy, David, 'Kinship and kin interaction in early modern England', *Past and Present* 113 (1986), 38–69

Damousi, Joy, *Depraved and disorderly: female convicts, sexuality, and gender in colonial Australia* (Cambridge, Cambridge University Press, 1997)

Devitt, Amy J., *Standardizing written English: diffusion in the case of Scotland, 1520–1659* (Cambridge, Cambridge University Press, 1989)

Douglas, Mary, *Purity and danger: an analysis of the concepts of pollution and taboo* (London, Routledge, 1966)

Duffy, Eamon, *The stripping of the altars: traditional religion in England, 1400–1580* (New Haven CT, Yale University Press, 1992)

Dyer, Christopher, 'The English medieval village community and its decline', *Journal of British Studies* 33 (1994), 407–29

Eales, Jacqueline, *Puritans and roundheads: the Harleys of Brampton Bryan and the outbreak of the English civil war* (Cambridge, Cambridge University Press, 1990)

Earle, Peter, *A city full of people: men and women in London, 1650–1750* (London, Methuen, 1994)

Egmond, Florike, *Underworlds: organized crime in the Netherlands, 1650–1800* (Cambridge, Polity Press, 1993)

Elias, Norbert, *The civilizing process: the history of manners and state formation and civilization* (Oxford, Blackwell, 1994)

Elshtain, J. B., *Public man, private woman: women in social and political thought* (Princeton NJ, Princeton University Press, 1981)

Elsky, Martin, *Authorizing words: speech, writing, and print in the English Renaissance* (Ithaca NY, Cornell University Press, 1989)

Estabrook, Carl B., *Urbane and rustic England: cultural ties and social spheres in the provinces, 1660–1780* (Manchester, Manchester University Press, 1998)

Evans, Richard J. (ed.), *The German underworld: deviants and outcasts in German history* (London, Routledge, 1988)

Everitt, Alan, *Landscape and community in England* (London, Hambledon Press, 1985)

Ezell, Margaret, *The patriarch's wife: literary evidence and the history of the family* (Chapel Hill NC, University of North Carolina Press, 1987)

Farge, Arlette, *Subversive words: public opinion in eighteenth-century France*, trans. Rosemary Morris (Cambridge, Polity Press, 1994)

Fincham, Kenneth, and Peter Lake, 'Popularity, prelacy and puritanism in the 1630s: Joseph Hall explains himself', *English Historical Review* 111 (1996), 856–81

Foucault, Michel, *Discipline and punish: the birth of the prison* (London, Allen Lane, 1977)

— 'What is an author?' in Josué V. Harari (ed.), *Textual strategies: perspectives in post-structuralist criticism* (Ithaca NY, Cornell University Press, 1979)

— *Ethics, subjectivity and truth*, ed. Paul Rabinow (New York, New York Press, 1997)

Fox, Adam, 'Ballads, libels and popular ridicule in Jacobean England', *Past and Present* 145 (1995), 47–83

Freist, Dagmar, *Governed by opinion: politics, religion, and the dynamics of communication in Stuart London, 1637–45* (London, Tauris, 1997)

Fukuyama, Francis, *Trust: the social virtues and the creation of prosperity* (London, Hamish Hamilton, 1995)

Furet, François, *Interpreting the French Revolution*, trans. Elborg Forster (Cambridge, Cambridge University Press, 1981)

Garber, Daniel, Michael Ayers and Roger Ariew (eds), *The Cambridge history of seventeenth-century philosophy*, 2 vols (Cambridge, Cambridge University Press, 1998)

Gellner, Ernest, *Reason and culture: the historic role of rationality and rationalism* (Oxford, Blackwell, 1993)

Geremek, Bronislaw, *The margins of society in late medieval Paris*, trans. Jean Birrell (Cambridge, Past and Present, 1987)

Giddens, Anthony, *Modernity and self-identity: self and society in the late modern age* (Cambridge, Polity Press, 1991)

Gilmore, M. P., *The world of humanism, 1453–1517* (New York, Harper, 1952)

Goldgar, Anne, *Impolite learning: conduct and community in the republic of letters* (New Haven CT, Yale University Press, 1995)

Goodman, Anthony, and Angus MacKay (eds), *The impact of humanism on western Europe* (London, Longman, 1990)

Gowing, Laura, *Domestic dangers: women, words, and sex in early modern London* (Oxford, Oxford University Press, 1996)

Greenblatt, Stephen, *Shakespearean negotiations* (Oxford, Clarendon Press, 1988)

Gregory, Annabel, 'Witchcraft, politics and "good neighbourhood" in early seventeenth-century Rye', *Past and Present* 133 (1991), 31–66

Griffiths, Paul, *Youth and authority: formative experiences in England 1560–1640* (Oxford, Clarendon Press, 1996)

Griffiths, Paul, Adam Fox and Steve Hindle (eds), *The experience of authority in early modern England* (Basingstoke, Macmillan, 1996)

Guy, John, *Tudor England* (Oxford, Oxford University Press, 1988)

Guy, John (ed.), *The reign of Elizabeth I: court and culture in the last decade* (Cambridge, Cambridge University Press, 1995)

Haigh, Christopher, *Reformation and resistance in Tudor Lancashire* (Cambridge, Cambridge University Press, 1975)

— 'The fall of a church or the rise of a sect? Post-Reformation Catholicism in England', *Historical Journal* 21 (1978), 181–6

Bibliography

— 'From monopoly to minority: post-Reformation Catholicism in England', *Transactions of the Royal Historical Society*, fifth series, 31 (1981), 129–47

— 'The continuity of Catholicism in the English Reformation', *Past and Present* 93 (1981) 37–69

— 'Revisionism, the Reformation and the history of English Catholicism', *Journal of Ecclesiastical History* 36 (1985), 394–406

— *English reformations: religion, politics, and society under the Tudors* (Clarendon Press, Oxford, 1993)

Halliday, Paul D., *Dismembering the body politic: partisan politics in England's towns, 1650–1730* (Cambridge, Cambridge University Press, 1998)

Harris, Tim, *London crowds in the reign of Charles II: propaganda and politics from the Restoration until the exclusion crisis* (Cambridge, Cambridge University Press, 1990)

— *Politics under the later Stuarts: party conflict in a divided society, 1660–1715* (Harlow, Longman, 1993)

Hay, Douglas, *et al.*, *Albion's fatal tree: crime and society in eighteenth-century England* (London, Allen Lane, 1975)

Hearn, Karen (ed.), *Dynasties: painting in Tudor and Stuart England, 1530–1630* (London, Tate Gallery, 1995)

Heidensohn, Frances, *Crime and society* (Basingstoke, Macmillan, 1989)

Hibbard, Caroline, 'The contribution of 1639: court and country Catholicism', *Recusant History* 16 (1980), 42–56

— *Charles I and the Popish Plot* (Chapel Hill NC, University of North Carolina Press, 1983)

Hindle, Steve, 'Exclusion crises: poverty, migration and parochial responsibility in English rural communities, c. 1560–1660', *Rural History* 7 (1996), 125–49

— 'Persuasion and protest in the Caddington Common enclosure dispute, 1635–39', *Past and Present* 158 (1998), 37–78

— 'Hierarchy and community in the Elizabethan parish: the Swallowfield articles of 1596', *Historical Journal* 42 (1999), 835–51

Hirschman, Albert O., *The passions and the interests: political arguments for capitalism before its triumph* (Princeton NJ, Princeton University Press, 1977)

Hitchcock, Tim, *English sexualities, 1700–1800* (Basingstoke, Macmillan, 1997)

Holmes, Clive, 'The county community in Stuart historiography', in Richard Cust and Ann Hughes (eds), *The English civil war* (London, Arnold, 1997)

Hopwood, Anthony G., and Peter Miller (eds), *Accounting as social and institutional practice* (Cambridge, Cambridge University Press, 1994)

Houlbrooke, Ralph, *The English family, 1450–1700* (Harlow, Longman, 1984)

Hughes, Ann, 'Warwickshire on the eve of civil war: a county community?' *Midland History* 7 (1982), 47–72

— 'Thomas Dugard and his circle in the 1630s: a 'parliamentary–puritan' connexion?' *Historical Journal* 29 (1986), 771–93

— *Politics, society and civil war in Warwickshire, 1620–1660* (Cambridge, Cambridge University Press, 1987)

Hundert, E. G., *The Enlightenment's fable: Bernard Mandeville and the discovery of society* (Cambridge, Cambridge University Press, 1994)

Hunt, William, *The puritan moment: the coming of revolution in an English county* (Cambridge MA, Harvard University Press, 1983)

Hunter, Lynette, and Sarah Hutton (eds), *Women, science and medicine, 1500–1700* (Stroud, Sutton, 1997)

Hunter, Michael, *Science and society in Restoration England* (Cambridge, Cambridge University Press, 1981)

— *Establishing the new science: the experience of the early Royal Society* (Woodbridge, Boydell Press, 1989)

— *The Royal Society and its fellows, 1660–1700: the morphology of an early scientific institution*, second edition (London, British Society for the History of Science, 1994)

Hurwich, Judith J., '"A fanatick town": the political influence of dissenters in Coventry, 1660–1720', *Midland History* 4 (1977), 15–57

Ianziti, Gary, *Humanistic historiography under the Sforzas: politics and propaganda in fifteenth-century Milan* (Oxford, Clarendon Press, 1988)

Ingram, Martin, 'Communities and courts: law and disorder in early seventeenth-century Wiltshire', in J. S. Cockburn (ed.), *Crime in England, 1550–1800* (London, Methuen, 1977)

Ives, E. W., R. J. Knecht and J. J. Scarisbrick (eds), *Wealth and power in Tudor England: essays presented to S. T. Bindoff* (London, Athlone Press, 1978)

James, Susan, *Passion and action: the emotions in seventeenth-century philosophy* (Oxford, Clarendon Press, 1997)

Jernudd, Björn H., and Michael J. Shapiro (eds), *The politics of language purism* (Berlin, Mouton de Gruyter, 1989)

Jones, Gareth Stedman, *Outcast London: a study in the relationship between classes in Victorian Society* (Oxford, Clarendon Press, 1971)

Jones, Richard Foster, *The triumph of the English language: a survey of opinions concerning the vernacular from the introduction of printing to the Restoration* (Stanford CA, Stanford University Press, 1953)

Jones, W. J., *The Elizabethan Court of Chancery* (Oxford, Clarendon Press, 1967)

Judson, Margaret, *The crisis of the constitution* (New Brunswick NJ, Rutgers University Press, 1949)

Karras, Ruth Mazo, *Common women: prostitution and sexuality in medieval England* (New York, Oxford University Press, 1996)

Kaushik, Sandeep, 'Resistance, loyalty, and recusant politics: Sir Thomas Tresham and the Elizabethan state', *Midland History* 21 (1996), 37–72

Keene, Derek, *Cheapside before the Great Fire* (London, Economic and Social Research Council, 1985)

Kelley, Donald R., and David Harris Sacks (eds.), *The historical imagination in early modern Britain: history, rhetoric, and fiction, 1500–1800* (Cambridge, Cambridge University Press, 1997)

Bibliography

Kent, D. V., and F. W. Kent, *Neighbours and neighbourhood in Renaissance Florence* (New York, Augustin, 1982)

Kermode, Jenny, *Medieval merchants: York, Beverley and Hull in the later Middle Ages* (Cambridge, Cambridge University Press, 1998)

Kermode, Jenny, and Garthine Walker (eds), *Women, crime and the courts in early modern England* (London, UCL Press, 1994)

Kessler, Eckhard, Charles B. Schmitt and Quentin Skinner (eds), *The Cambridge history of Renaissance philosophy* (Cambridge, Cambridge University Press, 1988)

Klein, Lawrence E., *Shaftesbury and the culture of politeness: moral discourse and cultural politeness in early eighteenth-century England* (Cambridge, Cambridge University Press, 1994)

Knights, Mark, *Politics and opinion in crisis, 1679–81* (Cambridge, Cambridge University Press, 1994)

Kümin, Beat, *The shaping of a community: the rise and reformation of the English parish, c. 1400–1560* (Aldershot, Scolar Press, 1996)

Lake, Peter, and Michael Questier, 'Agency, appropriation, and rhetoric under the gallows: puritans, Romanists and the state in early modern England', *Past and Present* 153 (1996), 64–107

Levine, David, and Keith Wrightson, *The making of an industrial society: Whickham, 1560–1765* (Oxford, Oxford University Press, 1991)

Lieberman, David, *The province of legislation determined: legal theory in eighteenth-century Britain* (Cambridge, Cambridge University Press, 1989)

Lloyd, Genevieve, *The man of reason: 'male' and 'female' in Western philosophy* (London, Methuen, 1984)

Love, Harold, *Scribal publication in seventeenth-century England* (Oxford, Clarendon Press, 1993)

McConica, J. K., *English humanists and Reformation politics* (Oxford, Clarendon Press, 1965)

McCusker, John J., 'The business press in England before 1775', *The Library*, sixth series, 8 (1986), 205–31

MacDonald, Michael, *Mystical Bedlam: madness, anxiety and healing in seventeenth-century England* (Cambridge, Cambridge University Press, 1981)

Macfarlane, Alan, *The family life of Ralph Josselin, a seventeenth-century clergyman: an essay in historical anthropology* (Cambridge, Cambridge University Press, 1970)

— 'History, anthropology and the study of communities', *Social History* 5 (1977), 631–52

— *The origins of English individualism* (Oxford, Blackwell, 1978)

Macfarlane, Alan, Sarah Harrison and Charles Jardine, *Reconstructing historical communities* (Cambridge, Cambridge University Press, 1977)

McGrath, P., and J. Rowe, 'The imprisonment of Catholics for religion under Elizabeth I', *Recusant History* 20 (1991), 415–35

McIntosh, Marjorie K., *Controlling misbehaviour in England, 1370–1600* (Cambridge, Cambridge University Press, 1998)

McKendrick, Neil, John Brewer and J. H. Plumb, *The birth of a consumer society* (London, Hutchinson, 1983)

McMullan, John L., 'Criminal organization in sixteenth and seventeenth-century London', *Social Problems* 29 (1981), 311–23

— *The canting crew: London's criminal underworld, 1550–1750* (New Brunswick NJ, Rutgers University Press, 1984)

— 'Crime, law and order in early modern England', *British Journal of Criminology* 27 (1987), 252–74

Major, J. M., *Sir Thomas Elyot and Renaissance humanism* (Lincoln NE, University of Nebraska Press, 1964)

Malcolmson, Robert, and John Rule (eds), *Protest and survival: the historical experience: essays for E. P. Thompson* (London, Merlin, 1993)

Manley, Lawrence, *Literature and culture in early modern London* (Cambridge, Cambridge University Press, 1995)

Manning, Roger B., *Village revolts: social protest and popular disturbances in England, 1509–1640* (Oxford, Oxford University Press, 1988)

Markus, Thomas A., *Buildings and power: freedom and control in the origin of modern building types* (London, Routledge, 1993)

Marland, Hilary (ed.), *The art of midwifery: early modern midwives in Europe* (London and New York, Routledge, 1993)

Marland, Hilary, and Margaret Pelling (eds), *The task of healing: medicine, religion and gender in England and the Netherlands, 1450–1800* (Rotterdam, Erasmus, 1996)

Marotti, Arthur F., *Manuscript, print, and the English Renaissance lyric* (Ithaca NY, Cornell University Press, 1995)

Mascuch, Michael, *Origins of the individualist self: autobiography and self-identity in England, 1591–1791* (Cambridge, Polity Press, 1997)

May, Steven W., 'Manuscript circulation at the Elizabethan court', in *New ways of looking at old texts: papers of the Renaissance English Text Society, 1985–1991* (Binghamton NY, Medieval and Renaissance Texts and Studies, 1993)

Mendelson, Sara, and Patricia Crawford, *Women in early modern England, 1550–1720* (Oxford, Oxford University Press, 1998)

Milton, Anthony, *Catholic and reformed: the Roman and Protestant churches in English Protestant thought, 1600–40* (Cambridge, Cambridge University Press, 1995)

Momsen, Wolfgang J., '"Toward the iron cage of future serfdom"? On the methodological status of Max Weber's ideal-typical concept of bureaucratization', *Transactions of the Royal Historical Society*, fifth series, 30 (1980), 157–81

Morrill, John (ed.), *Reactions to the English civil war, 1642–49* (Basingstoke, Macmillan, 1982)

Morrill, John, Paul Slack and Daniel Woolf (eds), *Public duty and private conscience in seventeenth-century England: essays presented to G. E. Aylmer* (Oxford, Clarendon Press, 1993)

Morris, Lydia, *Dangerous classes: the underclass and social citizenship* (London, Routledge, 1994)

Moss, Anne, *Printed commonplace books and the structuring of Renaissance thought* (Oxford, Clarendon Press, 1996)

Bibliography

Muldrew, Craig, 'Interpreting the market: the ethics of credit and community relations in early modern England', *Social History* 18 (1993), 163–83

— 'The culture of reconciliation: community and the settlement of economic disputes in early modern England', *Historical Journal* 39 (1996), 915–42

— *The economy of obligation* (Basingstoke, Macmillan, 1998)

Mullaney, Steven, *The place of the stage: license, play, and power in Renaissance England* (Chicago, University of Chicago Press, 1988)

Munkhoff, Richelle, 'Searchers of the dead: authority, marginality, and the interpretation of plague in England, 1574–1665', *Gender and History* 11 (1999), 1–29

Neal, Larry, 'The rise of a financial press: London and Amsterdam, 1681–1810', *Business History* 30 (1988), 163–78

Neeson, Jeanette, *Commoners: common right, enclosure and social change in England, 1700–1820* (Cambridge, Cambridge University Press, 1993)

Peck, Linda Levy, *Court patronage and corruption in early Stuart England* (Cambridge MA, Unwin Hyman, 1990)

Pelling, Margaret, *The common lot: sickness, medical occupations and the urban poor in early modern England* (London and New York, Longman, 1998)

Peltonen, Markku, *Classical humanism and republicanism in English political thought, 1570–1640* (Cambridge, Cambridge University Press, 1995)

Perry, Mary Elizabeth, *Crime and society in early modern Seville* (Hanover NH, University Press of New England, 1980)

Phythian-Adams, Charles (ed.), *Societies, cultures and kinship, 1580–1850: cultural provinces and English local history* (Leicester, Leicester University Press, 1996)

Pincus, Steven C. A., *Protestantism and patriotism: ideologies and the making of English foreign policy, 1650–68* (Cambridge, Cambridge University Press, 1996)

Pocock, J. G. A., *The Machiavellian moment: Florentine political thought and the Atlantic republican tradition* (Princeton NJ, Princeton University Press, 1975)

Pollard, Sidney, *The genesis of modern management* (London, Arnold, 1965)

Pollock, Linda, *With faith and physic: the life of a Tudor gentlewoman* (London, Collins & Brown, 1993)

Porter, Roy (ed.), *Rewriting the self: histories from the Renaissance to the present* (London, Routledge, 1997)

Porter, Roy, and John Brewer (eds), *Consumption and the world of goods* (London, Routledge, 1993).

Purkiss, Diane, 'Women's stories of witchcraft in early modern England: the house, the body, the child', *Gender and History* 7 (1995), 408–32

Putnam, Robert D., *Making democracy work: civic traditions in modern Italy* (Princeton NJ, Princeton University Press, 1993)

Questier, Michael, *Conversion, politics, and religion, 1580–1625* (Cambridge, Cambridge University Press, 1996)

— 'The politics of religious conformity and the accession of James I', *Historical Research* 71 (1998), 14–30

Rappaport, Steve, *Worlds within worlds: structures of life in sixteenth-century London* (Cambridge, Cambridge University Press, 1989)

Raymond, Joad, *The invention of the newspaper: English newsbooks, 1641–49* (Oxford, Clarendon Press, 1996)

Razi, Zvi, 'Family, land and the village community in later medieval England', *Past and Present* 93 (1981), 4–36

Reynolds, Susan, *Kingdoms and communities in western Europe, 900–1300* (Oxford, Clarendon Press, 1997)

Richardson, R. C., *Puritanism in north-west England: a regional study of the diocese of Chester to 1642* (Manchester, Manchester University Press, 1972)

Richardson, R. C. (ed.), *Town and countryside in the English revolution* (Manchester, Manchester University Press, 1992)

— *The English civil wars: local aspects* (Manchester, Manchester University Press, 1998)

Roper, Lyndal, '"The common man", "the common good", "common women": gender and meaning in the German Reformation commune' *Social History* 12 (1987), 1–22

Roseveare, Henry, *The financial revolution, 1660–1760* (Harlow, Longman, 1991)

Rosser, Gervase, 'Going to the fraternity feast: commensality and social relations in late medieval England', *Journal of British Studies* 33 (1994), 430–46

— 'Crafts, guilds and the negotiation of work in the medieval town', *Past and Present* 154 (1997), 3–31

Rubin, Miri, 'Small groups: identity and solidarity in the late Middle Ages', in Jennifer Kermode (ed.), *Enterprise and individuals in fifteenth-century England* (Stroud, Sutton, 1991)

Rubinstein, Nicolai, *The government of Florence under the Medici, 1434–94* (Oxford, Clarendon Press, 1966)

Rublack, Ulinka, *The crimes of women in early modern Germany* (Oxford, Oxford University Press, 1999)

Rushton, Peter, 'The poor law, the parish and the community in north-east England, 1600–1800', *Northern History* 25 (1989), 132–52

Sabean, David, *Power in the blood: popular culture and village discourse in early modern Germany* (Cambridge, Cambridge University Press, 1984)

Salgado, Gamini, *The Elizabethan underworld* (London, Dent, 1977)

Savage, Mike, and Anne Witz (eds), *Gender and bureaucracy* (Oxford, Blackwell, 1992)

Scott, Jonathan, *Algernon Sidney and the restoration crisis, 1677–83* (Cambridge, Cambridge University Press, 1991).

Scribner, Robert, 'Is a history of popular culture possible?' *History of European Ideas* 10 (1989), 175–91

— 'Communities and the nature of power' in *id.* (ed.), *Germany: a new social and economic history, 1450–1630* (London, Arnold, 1996)

Shapiro, Barbara, *Probability and certainty in seventeenth-century England: a study of the relationships between natural science, religion, history, law, and literature* (Princeton NJ, Princeton University Press, 1983)

Bibliography

Sharpe, J. A., *Crime in early modern England, 1550–1750* (Harlow, Longman, 1984)

— 'Witchcraft and women in seventeenth-century England: some northern evidence', *Continuity and Change* 6 (1991), 179–99

— *Early modern England: a social history, 1550–1760,* second edition (London, Arnold, 1997)

Shevelow, Kathryn, *Women and print culture* (London, Routledge, 1989)

Shoemaker, Robert B., *Gender in English society, 1650–1850: the emergence of separate spheres?* (Harlow, Longman, 1998)

Short, Brian (ed.), *The English rural community: image and analysis* (Cambridge, Cambridge University Press, 1992)

Sibley, David, *Geographies of exclusion: society and difference in the West* (London, Routledge, 1995)

Simpson, Claude Mitchell, *The British broadside ballad and its music* (New Brunswick NJ, Rutgers University Press, 1966)

Skinner, Quentin, *The foundations of modern political thought,* 2 vols (Cambridge, Cambridge University Press, 1978)

— *Liberty before liberalism* (Cambridge, Cambridge University Press, 1998)

Slack, Paul, *Poverty and policy in Tudor and Stuart England* (Harlow, Longman, 1988)

Smith, David L., *Constitutional royalism and the search for a settlement, c. 1640–49* (Cambridge, Cambridge University Press, 1994)

Smith, David L., Richard Strier and David Broughton (eds), *The theatrical city: culture, theatre and politics in London, 1576–1649* (Cambridge, Cambridge University Press, 1995)

Smith, Richard M., '"Modernisation" and the corporate medieval village community in England: some sceptical reflections', in Alan R. H. Baker and Derek Gregory (eds), *Explorations in historical geography* (Cambridge, Cambridge University Press, 1984)

Smith, Richard M. (ed.), *Land, kinship and life cycle* (Cambridge, Cambridge University Press, 1984)

Smuts, R. Malcolm, 'The court and its neighbourhood: royal policy and urban growth in the early Stuart West End', *Journal of British Studies* 30 (1991), 117–49

Sommerville, C. John, *The news revolution in England: cultural dynamics of daily information* (Oxford, Oxford University Press, 1996)

Spufford, Margaret (ed.), *The world of rural dissenters* (Cambridge, Cambridge University Press, 1995)

Staden, Heinrich von, 'Women and dirt', *Helios* 19 (1992), 7–30

Stapleton, Barry (ed.), *Conflict and community in southern England: essays in the history of rural and urban labour from medieval to modern times* (Stroud, Sutton, 1992)

Stein, Dieter, and Ingrid Tieken-Boon von Ostade (eds), *Towards a standard English, 1600–1800* (Berlin, Mouton de Gruyter, 1994)

Stoyle, Mark, *Loyalty and locality: popular allegiance in Devon during the English civil war* (Exeter, University of Exeter Press, 1994)

Stretton, Tim, *Women waging law in Elizabethan England* (Cambridge, Cambridge University Press, 1998)

Sumner, Colin, *The sociology of deviance: an obituary* (Buckingham, Open University Press, 1994)

Sweet, Rosemary, *The writing of urban histories in eighteenth-century England* (Oxford, Clarendon Press, 1998)

Tadmor, Naomi, '"Family" and "Friend" in *Pamela*: a case study in the history of the family in eighteenth-century England', *Social History* 14 (1989), 289–306

Tawney, R. H., *Religion and the rise of capitalism: a historical study* (Harmondsworth, Penguin, 1990)

Taylor, Charles, *Sources of the self: the making of the modern identity* (Cambridge MA, Harvard University Press, 1989)

Thomas, Keith, *Religion and the decline of magic: studies in popular beliefs in sixteenth and seventeenth-century England* (London, Weidenfeld & Nicolson, 1971)

Thompson, E. P., *Customs in common* (London, Merlin, 1991)

Tittler, Robert, *Architecture and power: the town hall and the English urban community, c. 1500–1640* (Oxford, Clarendon Press, 1991)

— *The Reformation and the towns in England: politics and political culture, c. 1540–1640* (Oxford, Clarendon Press, 1998)

Tönnies, Ferdinand, *Gemeinschaft und Gesellschaft* (Darmstadt, Wissenschaftliche Buchgesellschaft, 1979)

Trimble, William Raleigh, *The Catholic laity in Elizabethan England, 1558–1603* (Cambridge MA, Belknap Press, 1964)

Tuck, Richard, *Natural rights theories* (Cambridge, Cambridge University Press, 1979)

Twycross, Meg (ed.), *Festive drama* (Woodbridge, Boydell & Brewer, 1996)

Twyning, John, *London dispossessed: literature and social space in the early modern city* (Basingstoke, Macmillan, 1998)

Tyacke, Nicholas (ed.), *England's long Reformation, 1500–1800* (London, UCL Press, 1998)

Underdown, David, 'Community and class: theories of local politics in the English revolution', in Barbara C. Malament (ed.), *After the Reformation: essays in honour of J. H. Hexter* (Manchester, Manchester University Press, 1980)

— 'The problem of popular allegiance in the English civil war', *Transactions of the Royal Historical Society*, fifth series, 31 (1981), 69–94

— *Revel, riot and rebellion: popular politics and culture in England, 1603–60* (Oxford, Oxford University Press, 1987)

Unwin, George, *Industrial organization in the sixteenth and seventeenth centuries* (Oxford, Clarendon Press, 1904)

Venuti, Lawrence, *Our halcyon dayes: English pre-revolutionary texts and post-modern culture* (Madison WI, University of Wisconsin Press, 1989)

Vickery, Amanda, 'Golden age to separate spheres? A review of the categories and chronologies of English women's history', *Historical Journal* 36 (1993), 383–414

— *The gentleman's daughter: women's lives in Georgian England* (London, Yale University Press, 1998)

Vigarello, Georges, *Concepts of cleanliness: changing attitudes in France since the Middle Ages*, trans. Jean Birrell (Cambridge, Cambridge University Press, 1988)

Walker, Julia M. (ed.), *Dissing Elizabeth: negative representations of Gloriana* (Durham NC, Duke University Press, 1998)

Walsham, Alexandra, '"The fatall vesper": providentialism and anti-popery in late Jacobean London', *Past and Present* 144 (1994), 36–87

Walter, John, 'The social economy of dearth in early modern England', in John Walter and Roger Schofield (eds), *Famine, disease and the social order in early modern society* (Cambridge, Cambridge University Press, 1989)

Walter, John, and Keith Wrightson, 'Dearth and the social order in early modern England', *Past and Present*, 71 (1976), 22–42

Ward, Joseph P., *Metropolitan communities: trade guilds, identity and change in early modern London* (Stanford CA, Stanford University Press, 1997)

Watt, Tessa, *Cheap print and popular piety, 1550–1640* (Cambridge, Cambridge University Press, 1991)

Weber, Max, *Economy and society: an outline of interpretive sociology*, ed. Gunther Roth and Claus Wittich (Berkeley CA, University of California Press, 1978)

— *The Protestant ethic and the spirit of capitalism* (London, Routledge, 1992)

Webster, Tom, 'Writing to redundancy: approaches to spiritual journals and early modern spirituality', *Historical Journal* 39 (1996), 33–56

Williams, Glanmor, *Welsh Reformation essays* (Cardiff, University of Wales Press, 1967)

Williams, Raymond, *Keywords: a vocabulary of culture and society* (London, Fontana, 1976)

Wilson, Adrian, *The making of man-midwifery: childbirth in England, 1660–1770* (London, UCL Press, 1995)

Wilson, Adrian (ed.), *Rethinking social history: English society, 1570–1920, and its interpretation* (Manchester, Manchester University Press, 1993)

Wilson, Kathleen, *The sense of the people: politics, culture and imperialism in England, 1715–85* (Cambridge, Past and Present, 1995)

Wood, Andy, 'The place of custom in plebeian political culture: England, 1550–1800', *Social History* 22 (1997), 46–60

Woudhuysen, H. R., *Sir Philip Sidney and the circulation of manuscripts, 1558–1640* (Oxford, Clarendon Press, 1996)

Wright, S. J. (ed.), *Parish, church and people* (London, Hutchinson, 1988)

Wrightson, Keith, 'Two concepts of order: justices, constables and jurymen in seventeenth-century England', in John Brewer and John Styles (eds), *An ungovernable people: the English and their law in the seventeenth and eighteenth centuries* (New Brunswick NJ, Rutgers University press, 1980)

— *English society, 1580–1680* (London, Hutchinson, 1982)

— 'Northern identities: the *longue durée*', *Northern Review* 2 (1995), 25–35

Wrightson, Keith, and David Levine, *Poverty and piety in an English village: Terling, 1525–1700*, second edition (Oxford, Clarendon Press, 1995)

Wurzbach, Natascha, *The rise of the English street ballad, 1550–1650*, trans. Gayna Walls (Cambridge, Cambridge University Press, 1990)

Young, Iris Marion, *Justice and the politics of difference* (Princeton NJ, Princeton University Press, 1990)

Zerubavel, Yael, *Recovered roots: collective memory and the making of Israeli national tradition* (Chicago, University of Chicago Press, 1995)

Index

Index